BETWEEN CULTURAL DIVERSITY AND COMMON HERITAGE

Cultural Diversity and Law

Series Editor:

Prakash Shah, School of Law, Queen Mary, University of London, UK

Around the world, most states are faced with difficult issues arising out of cultural diversity in their territories. Within the legal field, such issues span across matters of private law through to public and constitutional law. At international level too there is now considerable jurisprudence regarding ethnic, religious and cultural diversity. In addition, there are several layers of legal control – from communal and religious regulation to state and international regulation. This multiplicity of norm setting has been variously termed legal pluralism, inter-legality or internormativity and provides a fascinating lens for academic analysis that links up to cultural diversity in new and interesting ways. The umbrella of cultural diversity encompasses various population groups throughout the world ranging from national, ethnic, religious or indigenous groupings. This series particularly welcomes work that is of comparative interest, concerning various state jurisdictions as well as different population groups.

Also in the series

Legal Reform and Business Contracts in Developing Economies
Trust, Culture, and Law in Dakar
Julie Paquin

Socio-Legal Integration
Polish Post-2004 EU Enlargement Migrants in the United Kingdom
Agnieszka Kubal

Law, Religious Freedoms and Education in Europe
Edited by Myriam Hunter-Henin

Islamic Law in Europe?
Legal Pluralism and its Limits in European Family Laws
Andrea Büchler

The Challenges of Justice in Diverse Societies
Constitutionalism and Pluralism
Meena K. Bhamra

Between Cultural Diversity and Common Heritage

Legal and Religious Perspectivcs on thc Sacred Places of the Mediterranean

This volume is an initiative of the Sovereign Order of Malta

COORDINATED BY

SILVIO FERRARI
University of Milan, Italy

AND

ANDREA BENZO
Italian Ministry for Foreign Affairs, Italy

ROUTLEDGE
Routledge
Taylor & Francis Group
LONDON AND NEW YORK

First published by Ashgate Publishing

2 Park Square, Milton Park, Abingdon, Oxfordshire OX14 4RN
52 Vanderbilt Avenue, New York, NY 10017

Routledge is an imprint of the Taylor & Francis Group, an informa business

First issued in paperback 2020

British Library Cataloguing in Publication Data
A catalogue record for this book is available from the British Library

The Library of Congress has cataloged the printed edition as follows:
Library of Congress Cataloging-in-Publication Data

Between cultural diversity and common heritage : legal and religious perspectives on the sacred places of the Mediterranean / by Silvio Ferrari and Andrea Benzo.
pages cm. – (Cultural diversity and law)
Includes bibliographical references and index.
ISBN 978-1-4724-2601-7 (hardback)
1. Sacred space–Law and legislation–Mediterranean Region. 2. Cultural property–Protection (International law) I. Ferrari, Silvio, editor of compilation. II. Benzo, Andrea, editor of compilation.
K3791.B48 2014
344'.1822094–dc23

2013031202

ISBN 978-1-4724-2601-7 (hbk)
ISBN 978-0-367-60055-6 (pbk)

Contents

List of Figures

Notes on Contributors

Jack Bemporad currently serves as Professor of Interreligious Studies at the Vatican's Angelicum University in Rome and is the author of numerous books and articles, including 'Our Age: The Historic New Era of Christian-Jewish Understanding' (New City Press, 1996). As director of the non-profit Center for Interreligious Understanding (CIU), he has been at the centre of many of the negotiations improving the relationship between Christians and Jews.

Andrea Benzo is Head of the Economic and Commercial Affairs Section of the Italian Embassy in Riyadh. He holds a Doctorate in Canon and Ecclesiastical Law from the University of Macerata, Italy. His main fields of interest are law and religion in the Middle East and the role of religion in international relations.

Marshall J. Breger is Professor of Law at the Columbus School of Law, The Catholic University of America. He has written or edited numerous books on holy places issues. During 1987–89 he served as Alternate Delegate of the US to the UN Human Rights Commission in Geneva and from 1982–84 as Special Assistant to President Reagan and his liaison with the Jewish Community.

Alessandro Chechi is a researcher at the Art-Law Centre of the University of Geneva. He is a lecturer in public international law at the Université Catholique of Lille and a reporter for Italy of the International Law in Domestic Courts – Oxford University Press project. His fields of research include international cultural heritage law, international dispute settlement and international organizations.

Silvio Ferrari is Professor of Law and Religion at the University of Milan. He has been Visiting Professor at the University of California (Berkeley, 1994 and 2001), the Institute for Advanced Legal Studies (London, 1998–99) and the École pratique des hautes études (Paris, Sorbonne, 2004). His main fields of interest are law and religion in Europe, comparative law of religions (particularly Jewish law, Canon law and Islamic law) and the Vatican policy in the Middle East. He has published widely on these and related areas and is coordinator of the Holy Places Project of the Sovereign Order of Malta

Pier *Francesco* Fumagalli is Vice Prefect of the *Biblioteca Ambrosiana* (Ambrosian Library) in Milan. He was secretary of the Commission of the Holy See for Religious Relations with the Jews (*1986–93). He authored a number of books on ecumenism and Judaism, Hebrew and Arab manuscripts, oriental religions and Chinese culture.*

Umberto Leanza is former Professor of International Law in the University of Rome 'Tor Vergata' and former head of the Legal Service of the Italian Ministry for Foreign Affairs (1994–2003). He is Vice President of the Italian Society for the International Organization (SIOI) and legal consultant at the Italian Ministry for Foreign Affairs and the Ministry for the Defense. He is author of 15 books, about 100 articles, essays and comments on International Public Law and European Union Law and editor of about 10 volumes on the same subject areas.

Yahya Pallavicini is Imam of the Al-Wahid Mosque in Milan and Vice President of CO.RE.IS (Comunità Religiosa Islamica Italiana). He is President of the Supreme Council for Muslims in the West within ISESCO (Islamic Organization for Education, Science and Culture). He is long-time advisor on Islam to the Italian Ministries for Interior, Foreign Affairs, Culture and Integration. He is the author of *Islam in Europe* (Il Saggiatore 2004), *Inside the Mosque* (Rizzoli 2007), The Merciful (Messaggero 2009) and Mary's Soura (Morcelliana 2010).

Rafael Palomino is Professor of Law at Universidad Complutense de Madrid and Member of the Consultative Board, International Association for the Defense of Religious Liberty (IADRL). His research fields include religious freedom, comparative law, civil rights, religious conscientious objection, church-state legal affairs in the Middle East, educational rights and legal research methodology.

Charalambos K. Papastathis (*1940 †2012) was Professor of Ecclesiastical Law at Aristotle University. He was also a practising lawyer at the Bar of Thessaloniki for more than 20 years. In the field of ecclesiastical law, his main areas of research were church-state relations, religious freedom and the status of Mount Athos on which he was a renowned expert.

Simon Page has studied sociology, political science and international relations in Rome and Bologna. His main research interests are in the field of political sociology, sociology of religion, Islamic and Middle East studies, intercultural and interfaith dialogue and the Perennialist tradition in philosophy. He is the author of several articles on Islam and intercultural dialogue.

Peter Petkoff has studied law and theology in Sofia, Leeds, Oxford and Rome and his research interests are in the area of law and religion, European Company Law, Intellectual Property and Comparative and International Law. He has taught EU Law, International Law and Intellectual Property, Canon law and Islamic Law.

Dušan Rakitić is assistant lecturer in Serbian Legal History at the Legal History Department of the Belgrade University School of Law. He holds Master of Laws degrees from both Harvard Law School and the Belgrade University School of Law. His research has so far encompassed legal historical aspects of religious freedom in Serbia, as well as of capital markets regulation. In addition, he has written extensively on restitution issues from a policy perspective.

Moussa Abou Ramadan is visiting Professor of Islamic Law at the University of Strasbourg. He is a member of the Israeli Bar, Chair of the Jaffa Association for Human Rights and a member of the board of Adalah (The Legal Center for Arab Minority Rights in Israel). He has written extensively on the status of Arab minorities in Israel, Islamic Law and Shari'a courts in Israel.

Yuri Stoyanov is based at the Department of the Languages and Cultures of the Near and Middle East, at the School of Oriental and African Studies, University of London, and is currently a Senior Fellow at the Albright Institute of Archaeological Research and at the Kenyon Institute, both in Jerusalem. He has worked on a number of research projects focusing on the status of religious sites as well as the history and current situation of religious minorities in the Eastern Mediterranean, the Middle East and Central Asia.

Baki Svirca is currently working at the Institute for War Crime Research of the Ministry of Justice of Kosova. He served within the United Nations Mission in Kosovo (UNMIK/PISG), the Kosova negotiating team for status settlement, the Office of the Prime Minister of Kosova, the Kosova Institute for Monuments Protection and the Council for Defense of Human Rights and Freedoms. His research fields include history and cultural heritage management, transitional justice and intercultural dialogue.

Preface

The Mediterranean is considered 'the cradle of civilization'. At present, along its shores, one can find 20 countries and territories, more than 20 languages and all three monotheistic religions. If there is a place in the world where universal religious heritage matters enormously, it is the Mediterranean. This region has an historical and cultural richness unparalleled in the world.

The Sovereign Order of Malta believes in the necessity of safeguarding religious monuments and sacred places and preserving their outstanding cultural, historical and spiritual value, both for the communities with which they are associated and for all humankind. It believes that freedom of religion is essential to strengthen the inter-cultural dialogue.

However, in recent years, anti-religious violence has been on the rise. Shrines, sacred places and monuments of worship have come under attack, been damaged or destroyed. Thus, safeguarding religious heritage of outstanding universal value of the Mediterranean region, today and for future generations, requires new forms of action, among them continuity in educational, cultural and scientific advances. Governments and political authorities together with international organizations and civil society all have a political responsibility and the obligation to safeguard cultural heritage and contribute to the peaceful development of the whole region.

Considering the strong historical links with the Mediterranean region, the Sovereign Military Hospitaller Order of St John of Jerusalem of Rhodes and of Malta (also known as Sovereign Order of Malta) has endeavoured to help to protect such universal heritage with a view to maintaining the multi-cultural and multi-religious character of the Mediterranean while promoting peace and stability in the region.

In 2007, the Sovereign Order of Malta launched a project concerning 'the protection of sacred places in the Mediterranean area', inviting a group of experts under the direction of Professor Ferrari of the University of Milan with a view to establishing common principles and guidelines for access to and protection of sacred sites of the Mediterranean region with a universal cultural and social significance. In the following year, it approached the European Commission and proposed its project. Since then, the experts involved have studied indepth the historical and legal characteristics and have prepared papers on universal sacred places of the Mediterranean, which are collected in this publication.

In March 2012, the European Commission and the Sovereign Order of Malta jointly organized a seminar on 'Protecting the Sacred Places of the Mediterranean – a Contribution to the Intercultural Dialogue', which took place at the Berlaymont building in Brussels, under the chairmanship of President Barroso.

In November 2012, the Republic of Cyprus, during its term of the presidency of the Council of the European Union, and willing to contribute to a European Union that stands as a force of progress, peace, stability and social cohesion for its citizens, its neighbouring countries and the world, has kindly offered to host an international meeting on the 'Protection and Conservation of Cultural Heritage in the Mediterranean: A Common Responsibility' in Limassol, Cyprus, in collaboration with UNESCO and the European Commission.

I believe that this long-term project on the preservation of the cultural and religious heritage is relevant and timely for the future of the Mediterranean region which requires a renewed form of diplomacy, and I am confident that the exchange of thoughts and knowledge initiated with this project will be able to produce important outcomes for the Mediterranean communities and States that should adopt common principles and rules for protection and conservation of their cultural heritage.

Let me conclude by thanking Professor Silvio Ferrari of the University of Milan for the coordination of this ambitious project, all the experts who have contributed to the research, the European Commission and UNESCO for their valuable cooperation, as well as the French Foundation of the Order of Malta and the Foundation Baldi of the Order of Malta for their financial contribution.

H.E. Jean-Pierre Mazery,
Grand Chancellor
Sovereign Military Hospitaller Order
of St John of Jerusalem of Rhodes and of Malta

Chapter 1

Introduction: The Legal Protection of the Sacred Places of the Mediterranean

Silvio Ferrari

The Meaning of 'sacred place'

First of all, what do we mean here? The expression 'sacred place'[1] by no means has a clear-cut and univocal significance. In Chapter 3, Yuri Stoyanov shows how complex the notion of sacred place is. It is at the crossroads of theological, anthropological, historical, sociological and legal research, each of these tending to define the object of its analysis in different terms. After describing the state of the art of the studies on sacred places, Stoyanov concludes that 'the multiple religious, spiritual, social and political functions ascribed to' sacred places in human societies and cultures are reflected in the 'interpretative and methodological ambiguities' that affect these studies, so that it remains uncertain how much helpful input they can provide to legal and political initiatives focused on the safeguarding of sacred places. Even leaving aside any ambitious attempt to formulate a theoretical definition and concentrating on the more modest task of elaborating a notion of sacred place through the examination of the places that are commonly qualified as sacred does not help. In Chapter 5, Peter Petkoff continually notes that 'because of the inherent uniqueness of sacred places, developing a taxonomy of sacred places is virtually impossible [...]. Sacred places range from those with very clearly defined borders and physical specifications, to geographical areas, national parks, processions, pilgrimages, sacramental places and places where the faithful congregate and their spiritual leaders teach'.

These remarks are enough to deter any reasonable person from attempting to provide a definition of a sacred place. However, it is necessary to clarify the meaning given to these words in this book.

The expression 'sacred places' is used here because it is currently employed to indicate places like the Wailing Wall, Mecca, the Basilica of the Holy Sepulchre and so on. However, the book is devoted to 'religious places' – that is, sacred

1 On the meaning of 'sacred places' and 'holy places' see Chapter 2 by Andrea Benzo, 'Towards a definition of sacred places. Introductory remarks'. However, in this book the two expressions are frequently used as synonyms.

places that have an explicit religious significance. Therefore the book does not deal with places that may have a spiritual significance but which are disconnected from clearly identifiable religious traditions and communities, nor does it deal with places whose (sometimes exclusively 'secular') sacredness depends on the historical or political events that took place there, like the birthplace of the father of a nation, or a battleground, for example.[2]

Even within this limited 'religious' sphere the expression 'sacred places' – as employed in this book – needs to be further circumscribed. Paraphrasing Orwell and without any intention of disrespect, it is possible to say that all places are sacred but some places are more sacred than others. The point is made by Yahya Pallavicini in Chapter 8: 'Although it is possible for the believer to participate in the presence and the communication with the Lord of the Worlds in all the mosques and in every corner of the earth where God has made a carpet upon which to worship Him, the Muslim knows that the very same Creator has chosen certain places above others to manifest some of His signs, like in Mecca, Jerusalem and Medina'. This remark applies equally well to the sacred places of Judaism and Christianity that share with Islam the faith in a God creator who manifested himself to human beings in specific times and places.[3]

Again, once it is accepted that some sacred places are deemed to be more important than others it is impossible to define precisely what elements differentiate the first from the second group. Sacred places are living entities and as such are in constant evolution. Politicians, diplomats and lawyers know very well how difficult it is to define them and for this reason they have frequently avoided any definition and have drawn up lists of sacred places, as happened with the sacred places of the Holy Land.[4] However, while it is useless to strive for a definition, it may be helpful to look for some signs that show the particular importance of a sacred place. This search has been performed in Chapter 2 by Andrea Benzo. After establishing that 'no universally accepted definition of *sacred place* exists' in international and domestic legal instruments, Benzo proposes a 'definition by induction' based on four features that recur in the sacred places considered in this book (the link to a manifestation of the sacred; the role played by a place as a historical landmark; the veneration of believers coming from different parts of the world; the consensus developed through history on its sacred character). It is interesting to note that similar features are recalled in the decision of the International Criminal Tribunal

2 On the distinction between religious and sacred with specific reference to sacred places see the intervention of Catherine Colonna in Andrea Benzo (ed.), *Proceedings of the Seminar 'Protecting the Sacred places of the Mediterranean'* (Brussels, 6 March 2012, Order of Malta 2012) 74–6.

3 For these two features of sacred places – their religious nature and their outstanding importance – see Article 2 of the *Declaration on the Protection and Enhancement of Sacred Places in the Mediterranean Area* published as appendix to this book.

4 See H. Eugen Bovis, *The Jerusalem Question, 1917–1968* (Hoover Institution Press 1971).

for the Former Yugoslavia in the Kordic and Cerkez case.[5] The Appeal Chamber, reversing a judgment given three years before by the Trial Chamber, made a distinction between the general protection provided in international instruments for places of worship and the special protection granted to places of worship that 'constitute the cultural or spiritual heritage of peoples', specifying that 'cultural or spiritual heritage covers objects whose value transcends geographical boundaries, and which are unique in character and are intimately associated with the history and culture of a people'.[6] Not always does a single sacred place possess all these features, but they all point in the same direction and give us some helpful indications for appraising the particular sacredness attributed to a specific place.

Starting with the four indicators identified by Benzo, a group of sacred places can be set apart that have a special significance in the religious traditions of the Mediterranean. They are the subject of the contributions collected in this book. The fact that there is no neat line separating these sacred places from other places of worship and veneration reflects the continuity between these two groups of places, and the wide grey zone between them should be regarded as the buffer area that unites instead of separating places that have different importance but the same quality, because in the end the sacredness of places 'derives from the uses to which they are put'.[7]

There is also a geographical limitation that should be taken into account before concluding these introductory remarks: this book deals with the sacred places of the Mediterranean area.

It is a fact, recently reaffirmed by the Council of the European Union, that 'Europe and the Mediterranean region share a common history and cultural heritage'[8] which also includes its religious and sacred legacy. Many sacred places of the Mediterranean are associated with three religions – Judaism, Christianity and Islam – which share a monotheistic creed and believe in a God who manifested himself to humans in specific times and *places*. These two elements – monotheism and revelation – constitute the foundation upon which these religions developed

5 *Prosecutor v. Kordic & Cerkez*, ICTY Case No. IT-95-14/2-T (ICTY Judgment, Trial Chamber, 26 February 2001); *Prosecutor v. Kordic & Cerkez*, ICTY Case No. IT-95-14/2-T (ICTY Judgment, Appeals Chamber, 17 December 2004).

6 *Prosecutor v. Kordic & Cerkez*, ICTY Case No. IT-95-14/2-T (ICTY Judgment, Appeals Chamber, 17 December 2004), paras 90 and 91. The general and special protection mentioned by the Court is the protection granted by Articles 52 and 53 of the Protocol Additional to the Geneva Convention of 12 August 1949, and relating to the Protection of Victims of International Armed Conflicts (Protocol 1), 8 June 1977. For a discussion of these decisions see Marco Ventura, 'Global Laws on Holy Places after Bamiyan and the Twin Towers', forthcoming in the *Oxford Journal of Law and Religion*.

7 The quotation is taken from Chapter 6 by Jack Bemporad in this book. The continuity between sacred places and places of worship is underlined in Chapter 5 by Peter Petkoff.

8 Council Conclusions on Developments in the Southern Neighbourhood, Brussels, 21 February 2011, available at <www.consilium.europa.eu/uedocs/cms_Data/docs/pressdata/EN/foraff/119420.pdf> accessed 7 April 2013.

their respective conceptions of sacred place. History of divine revelation offers a chain of events – all geographically located – that make a particular place sacred: the most important sacred places of Judaism, Christianity and Islam are connected to a divine manifestation or command, directly (when it is God himself who gets in touch with human beings) or indirectly (when the divine message is manifested by men and women of God, like saints, prophets, sages). Monotheism paves the way (better: should pave, as this point is too frequently forgotten) for respecting the 'other', as God is the same for all human beings,[9] and consequently for recognizing the universal openness of each sacred place. This historical and theological background – marked by the dialectics between the particular and universal dimension of sacred places – opens up the possibility of identifying a protection framework that takes into account the elements of commonality shared by the sacred places of the Mediterranean area and distinguishes them from the sacred sites revered in other parts of the world.

From a political point of view, the development of such a protection framework is required by another fact that marks the sacred places of the Mediterranean: they are so many and so close to each other that they are constantly in danger of becoming elements of conflict. The proximity of the sacred places is such that sometimes they physically overlap and the same place is sacred to two or more religions. This frequently gives rise to tensions that need to be prevented, or at least reduced, through an effective system of safeguards.

After many years of neglect, the European Union seems to have understood that peace and stability in the Mediterranean region cannot be attained without dealing with the issue of sacred places. In 2010 the EU President Manuel Barroso called upon all the interested parties to cooperate in the effort 'de faire des grand sites religieux des espaces de paix et de culture',[10] and two years later the EU Commissioner for Education affirmed that 'the sacred places of the Mediterranean are an important part of our [European] identity' and can give a relevant 'contribution to intercultural dialogue'.[11] These statements show that there is a growing awareness that the European Union, together with the States of the Southern shore of the Mediterranean and other stakeholders, has a precise interest in taking the initiative to promote the recognition of some guidelines providing effective protection to sacred places and contributing to the peaceful development of the whole region.

This book intends to be a step in this direction. After a few contributions that provide a general overview of the notion of sacred places in anthropological, sociological and legal studies (Part I), three chapters then examine this notion

9 The link between monotheism and respect of the 'other' is highlighted in Chapter 6.

10 Addressed at the meeting with the Grand Master of the Order of Malta, Rome 22 May 2010.

11 Androulla Vassiliou, 'Opening Remarks', in Andrea Benzo (ed.), *Proceedings of the Seminar 'Protecting the Sacred places of the Mediterranean'* (Brussels, 6 March 2012, Order of Malta 2012) 8, 10.

in the light of Jewish, Christian and Islamic theological and legal thought (Part II). Understanding the meaning of sacred places in these three religious traditions is the starting point for discussing how sacred places can be protected: Part III offers a detailed analysis of the legal status of the most important sacred places of the Mediterranean. This examination aims at identifying a set of legal principles (contained in the Declaration published at the end of the book) that can be applied to all of them and that can provide a general framework within which more specific legal measures (if needed) can find their place. However, before starting this long journey, it is necessary to address two other preliminary topics, discussing why and how sacred places should be protected.

The Importance of Sacred Places

The importance of sacred places is widely recognized all over the world. They have valuable religious, cultural, political and economic significance: sacred places are a living testimony of the religious faith of a community, provide people with a sense of identity, play a vital role in safeguarding cultural diversity, help in fostering the social cohesion of a population and attract millions of pilgrims and visitors. To give an idea of the importance of the sacred places issue, suffice it to say that 20 per cent to 30 per cent of the properties inscribed on the UNESCO World Heritage List have been included specifically for their religious or spiritual association.[12]

On the other hand, sacred places are a catalyst for conflict, as clearly demonstrated by the wars in the Balkans after the collapse of Yugoslavia. Precisely because sacred places are important for building and maintaining the identity of a community, destroying them is a blow that weakens the strength of the people whose history, culture and religion are symbolized by these places.[13] Demolishing or desecrating the defeated enemy's sacred place or, worse, converting it into the conqueror's sacred place – the mosque into a church and vice versa – is one of the most common and age-old tactics aimed at demoralizing the enemy population and breaking its will to resist.

For these reasons, there is wide agreement about the need for adequate protection of sacred places. Recently UNESCO has underlined that religious and sacred sites require specific policies for protection and management that take into

12 See the *Conclusions, Recommendations and Statement* of the 'International Seminar on The Role of Religious Communities in the Management of the World Heritage Properties', Kyiv, 2–5 November 2010, para III, 2, available at <www.kplavra.kiev.ua/seminar/rap_en.pdf> accessed on 19 April 2013.

13 In the sentence of the International Criminal Tribunal for the Former Yugoslavia quoted at the footnote 2 (Trial Chamber) it is explicitly stated that the destruction of religious buildings 'when perpetrated with the requisite discriminatory intent, amounts to an attack on the very religious identity of a people' (para 207).

account their distinct spiritual nature as a key factor in their conservation and that such policies cannot be sustainable without in-depth consultation with the appropriate stakeholders.[14] It has also been recognized that as the existing standard-setting instruments may not adequately address the matter, 'it is particularly timely to define an integrated strategy for the development of a World Heritage Thematic Programme for Religious Heritage in collaboration and close coordination between all stakeholders, and that this Programme should create an action plan for the protection of religious heritage worldwide aimed at enhancing the role of communities and the avoidance of misunderstandings, tensions, or stereotypes'.[15]

While this recent evolution is welcome, approaching the question of sacred places exclusively from the angle of their protection may be reductive as it limits the contribution they can provide to developing the traditions of the three monotheistic religions of the Mediterranean and, as a result, to encouraging the growth of a healthy civil society. Protecting sacred places is the precondition for enabling them to perform their religious and civil role and so the emphasis should not be placed on protection as preservation but on protection as enhancement of sacred places.[16]

The need to shift from the first to the second paradigm (from protection-preservation to protection-enhancement) can be better explained by looking at the Mediterranean area as a whole as well as at the three monotheistic religions that developed in this part of the world.

The concept of sacred space in the Jewish, Christian and Islamic tradition is based on the tension between two principles. These religions teach that the presence of God cannot be confined to a specific place, as God inhabits the whole universe.[17] This teaching, however, is not in contradiction with the belief that God manifested himself in specific places that are termed sacred because they are directly connected to divine revelation. As already said, the belief that God

---

14 See *Initiative on Heritage of Religious Interest*, available at <www.whc.unesco.org/en/religious-sacred-heritage> accessed 7 April 2013.

15 *Kyiv Statement on the Protection of Religious Properties within the Framework of the World Heritage Convention*, n. 9 (November 5, 2010), available at the website listed in footnote 12.

16 In this perspective, when defining what should be preserved, the starting point is a correct understanding of 'the social-functional integrity of the place' and of 'the functions and elements that together form the heritage' (Jukka Jokilehto, 'Conservation of Living Religious Heritage', available at <www.kplavra.kiev.ua/seminar/repo/7.pdf> accessed 19 April 2013.

17 In this book Yahya Pallavicini quotes the Koran verse, saying that 'God has made the earth like a carpet' to underline that every place on earth is a possible sacred space for the ritual worship of God. The same point (the divine presence cannot be limited to a specific place) is made by Pier Francesco Fumagalli who mentions a verse from a Jewish liturgical poem ('God is the Place of the Temple / and the Temple without a place') and the Gospel passage where Jesus tells the Samaritan woman that 'true worshipers will worship the Father in spirit and truth'.

revealed himself to human beings in specific places is central to the development of the notion of the sacred place in these religions. Sacred places, according to John Paul II in 1980, are the 'geographical point of tangency between God and man, between the eternal and history'.[18] They enshrine God's revelation, but the forms through which revelation is expressed are constantly reshaped, so that they remain able to reflect the growing understanding of the divine message on the part of the faithful and to answer the changing needs of the religious community. This is the meaning of the encounter between the eternal (representing God's absoluteness and permanence) and history (symbolizing the relative and changeable elements that are part of human nature) evoked by John Paul II. The same idea can be expressed in the words of Martin Heidegger to define the nature of works of art: 'creative custodianship of truth'. The truth of divine revelation is entrusted to the faithful community, which has the responsibility to guard it as a *living* heritage through a constant process of formulation and reformulation of the doctrines, practices and rituals that keep revelation alive in the believers' life. In other words, the identity of the Jewish, Christian and Islamic communities is rooted in traditions that go back to God's revelation: keeping these traditions alive means that their content is appropriated time and again by the community, through a continuous learning and adaptation process.[19] All these remarks point in the same direction: sacred places are a living heritage and should be protected and promoted as such.[20] Protecting sacred places then means enabling them to perform the function of communication between heaven and earth that is vital for the life of a religious community (as Stoyanov reminds us, sacred places are frequently defined as the meeting points between heaven and earth).

Protecting sacred places as the living heritage of a particular religious community, however, is not enough. They need to be protected also as centres of interreligious dialogue. It is surprising how little is the role played by sacred places in this field. Sometimes one has the impression that the more a place is central for the life of a religious community, the less a community is ready to regard that place as a meeting point with the followers of other religions, in some cases going as far as to deny them access to it. In Chapter 7 Pier Francesco Fumagalli notes

---

18 John Paul II, 'Gerusalemme, quante immagini, quanta passione e quale grande mistero!', in *L'Osservatore Romano* (19 September 1980) 1.

19 I am indebted for these remarks (including the reference to Heidegger) to Jukka Jokilehto's text quoted at footnote 16.

20 Synthesizing the papers collected in Herb Stovel, Nicholas Stanley-Price and Robert Killick (eds), 'Conservation of Living Religious Heritage'. In *Papers from the ICCROM 2003 Forum on Living Religious Heritage: conserving the Sacred*, Rome, ICCROM, 2005, available at <www.iccrom.org/pdf/ICCROM_ICS03_ReligiousHeritage_en.pdf> accessed 15 April 2013, Stovel underlines that 'what distinguishes religious heritage from secular heritage is its inherent "livingness"'. In this perspective 'the primary goal of conservation becomes continuity itself, based on processes of renewal that continually "revive the cultural meaning, significance [...] and symbolism attached to heritage', Herb Stovel, *Introduction*, 1.

that 'contemporary experience and the historical experience of the past testifies that it is not easy to bestow holiness upon a place in an inclusive way. Indeed the most common trend is the opposite one, whereby a sacred place – or parts of it – is declared as one group's exclusive possession instead of something that can be enjoyed together'. In this way the particular significance of a sacred place for the faith and identity of a specific religious community – something that surely deserves to be protected – does not become the starting point for reaching out to other communities – something that surely deserves to be promoted. Although this last step, which implies delicate theological questions, can be taken only by the involved religious communities and should not be forced upon them, a non-sectarian approach to the issue of sacred places should be based on the awareness that identity and dialogue are not mutually excluding. For this reason, as better explained in the following pages, the protection and enhancement of sacred places has to reflect a careful balance between their particular and universal significance: only if both dimensions are taken into account can the political and legal measures aimed at securing the status of sacred places enhance their role as centres of identity of a religious community and, at the same time, as centres of dialogue between different religious communities.[21]

Besides their religious significance (more exactly: because of their religious significance), sacred places can provide significant contributions to the development of a vital civil society. From this point of view, sacred places are not only a source of tension and conflict that endanger peaceful coexistence, they can also be an asset for fostering social plurality and diversity, two features that are frequently regarded as necessary conditions for democracy itself. Exactly because sacred places are a central component of the history, tradition and belief of a particular community, under certain conditions they can become a bridge towards other communities. Sacred places represent identity and diversity at the same time. Each is strictly associated with the history and culture of a community and, together, they manifest the variety of cultural traditions and belief systems of the populations living in the Mediterranean area. Like many works of art, this mosaic of diversities – where each tessera reflects the features of a particular community – is extremely delicate: both its single components and the overall pattern are constantly in danger of being lost, with the consequence that intercultural dialogue would become much poorer and would have a scant chance of rebuilding the Mediterranean as a space of peace and security. This explains why safeguarding sacred places is a matter of general interest, not the concern of the believers only. While religious communities have the primary responsibility to maintain the character of *living* religious heritage of sacred places, the potential role they can play in fostering intercultural dialogue goes beyond their strictly religious significance and is of interest for the building of a plural and democratic society.

21 In Chapter 8 of this book, Yahya Pallavicini underlines that '*the holy places and cities display universal meanings that transcend local and religious specificities and therefore they cannot become vehicles for forms of exclusivity*'.

In this perspective a protection system of the sacred places should develop their capacity to function as centres of intercultural dialogue. Fortunately there is no insurmountable contradiction between the cultural and the religious dimension of sacred places: safeguarding the specificity and diversity of each is the best way to enable them to become elements of both interreligious and intercultural dialogue.

In any case, if sacred places have to play a role in the rapprochement of the two shores of the Mediterranean, conceiving their protection in terms of preserving their physical existence is not enough. Protection of the sacred places needs to be re-conceptualized in a much more positive and proactive form, stressing all the elements that enable them to become centres of reconciliation between different religious and cultural communities. This task involves responsibilities that by far exceed those of States and international organizations and requires the active participation of religious communities and, more generally, civil society actors.

These remarks help to understand part of the meaning to be given to 'protection of sacred places'. However, there is a second side to this expression that still has to be discussed.

While sacred places are reasonably well protected as part of cultural heritage, their religious significance is still underestimated. For this reason a sound political and legal framework for the protection and enhancement of sacred places has not been fully developed. In order to fill this gap, two questions need to be answered.

First, are the sacred places to be protected because of their cultural or their religious significance? As already said, in many cases the two go together, but it is easy to imagine a different scenario. Preserving a sacred place as a museum can save most of its cultural value but it can be utterly useless for safeguarding its religious significance. The sacred places we are speaking of are living entities and as such both their religious and cultural meaning is largely lost if they are disconnected from the life of their community of faithful, the pilgrimages, festivals, religious ceremonies and devotional activities that are the living expressions of their sacredness. In other words, protecting the Karnak temples is not exactly the same thing as protecting the Holy Sepulchre or the Wailing Wall: in the first case, the cultural dimension is prevailing, while in the second the centre stage is taken by the religious dimension. Consequently, also the protection system may be partially different and give more importance both to the human component of the religious heritage and to its link with the needs of religious practice. From the first point of view, attention should be paid not only to the conservation of buildings, but also to the protection of spatial structures, environmental areas, human activities and settlements that surround the sacred places and constitute their habitat, in compliance with the 1976 UNESCO Recommendations Concerning the Safeguarding and Contemporary Role of Historic Areas. From the second point of view, the interest by religious communities for the continuing use and renewal of their sacred places should be taken into account. Such an approach would foster, on the one hand, the search for and development of conservation strategies and instruments that respect the religious character of the place and, on the other, the involvement of the concerned religious communities in the conservation of their own sacred places. As stated in the conclusion of the ICCROM 2003 Forum 'Conserving the Sacred', sometimes the risks to living religious heritage 'may reflect well-meant efforts to preserve physical testimonies of faith within broad conservation policies which do not, however, recognize the specificity of religious values'.[22] Strengthening the dialogue between conservation professionals and religious communities is the best way to overcome this danger.

Second, is freedom of religion to be taken into account when envisaging a protection system of sacred places? Freedom of religion is not only a matter that concerns conscience and beliefs: it also regards visible and external manifestations of religion. For this reason the right to establish and maintain a place for worship and assembly – including the right to visit it and to perform ritual and ceremonial acts in it – is generally considered to be part of the right to religious freedom, as stated in Article 6 of the UN Declaration on the Elimination of All Forms of Intolerance and Discrimination Based on Religion or Belief and in n. 4 of the UN Human Rights Committee General Comment No. 22 (48).[23] However, freedom of religion is conspicuously absent from the debate on sacred places, which is dominated by an approach that has magnified their cultural significance and downplayed their religious meaning. Historically, offences to sacred places have been understood as a sub-section of the offences to the cultural heritage of a people or of the whole of humankind, while their character of offences to the religious freedom of these subjects has remained in the shadows. This approach has led to building the protection system of sacred places into the framework of the rules concerning cultural heritage. As freedom of religion has little significance in this area, no use was found for the whole set of legal provisions safeguarding it at the national and international level. As a consequence, the level of protection granted to sacred places was weakened and, more importantly, their meaning in the religious traditions of the Mediterranean was obscured. In the legal systems of the three main Mediterranean religions, sacred places mean something more than places of worship: praying in the place where God manifested himself, directly or through men and women who acted in his name, is deemed by millions of people to be a religious obligation or at least a recommended practice. Although Judaism, Christianity and Islam teach that God can be worshipped in every place, the practice of pilgrimages to sacred places goes

22 Herb Stovel, *Introduction*, in Herb Stovel, Nicholas Stanley-Price and Robert Killick (eds), 'Conservation of Living Religious Heritage', 9.

23 See Cornelius D. de Jong, *The Freedom of Thought, Conscience and Religion or Belief in the United Nations (1946–1992)* (Intersentia-Hart 2000) 359–422; Noel G. Villaroman, 'The Right to Establish and Maintain Places of Worship: The Development of its Normative Content under International Human Rights Law', in Silvio Ferrari and Sabrina Pastorelli (eds), *Religion in Public Spaces. A European Perspective* (Ashgate 2012) 295–322. The link between protection of religious freedom and security of sacred places is also underlined by some religious communities. See Protecting religious freedom and holy sites, a Declaration of the International Catholic-Jewish Liaison Committee, New York, 4 May 2001, available at <www.vatican.va/roman_curia/pontifical_councils/chrstuni/relations-jews-docs/rc_pc_chrstuni_doc_20010504_new-york-meeting_en.html> accessed 15 April 2013.

back to the origins of these religions and continues to be widespread in our times. This uninterrupted stream of pilgrims is the best proof that sacred places have much to do with religious freedom, which would be hampered if a place is destroyed or made inaccessible to people who want to visit it not (only) as a cultural attraction, but as a religious practice. An effective legal system cannot avoid recognizing the link between manifestations of religious faith and sacred places and looking at their protection through the lenses provided by the provisions that safeguard the individual and collective rights of religious freedom.

When the legal status of sacred places is discussed, these two characteristics – their religious significance and their connection with religious freedom – are frequently ignored, downplayed or misunderstood. As a consequence, the protection of sacred places has not yet attained a level that is adequate for the new importance that religion has acquired in international and domestic politics. After 1989 the process of de-privatization of religion and its forceful re-establishment in the public sphere has added a new dimension to the conflicts around sacred places. The destruction of the Buddhas of Bamiyan in 2001 and of the shrines of Timbuktu in 2012 signals that they have become the target of efforts to cleanse whole regions from the presence of symbols that challenge the dominant religion. Sacred places are not destroyed to weaken the military or political strength of the enemy, as was the case in the Balkan Wars of the 1990s: no Buddhists lived in Afghanistan in 2001. Sacred places are destroyed because a place must be purified from any impious sign.[24] This transformation challenges old legal patterns of protection and requires a fresh approach to the whole issue of sacred places. First of all, it requires a better understanding of what are the features and functions of the sacred places that need to be protected in this new scenario, where the religious significance of the sacred places has gained an unexpected and sometimes threatening importance.

The Protection of Sacred Places

A recently published UNESCO document underlines that 'collectively, the religious and sacred properties capture a range of cultural and natural diversity, and each can singularly demonstrate the spirit of a particular place'.[25] This statement correctly identifies the two dimensions – particular and universal – which should be kept in mind when approaching the issue of sacred places.[26]

24 This new profile of the sacred places issue is underlined by Marco Ventura, 'Global Laws on Holy Places'.

25 UNESCO Executive Board, Report by the Director General on the Follow-Up to Decisions and Resolutions Adopted by the Executive Board and the General Conference at Their Previous Sessions, Paris, 18 April 2011, available at <http://unesdoc.unesco.org/images/0019/001920/192094e.pdf> accessed on 8 April 2013.

26 Bemporad writes that a 'key issue in recognizing the sacred is the relationship between the particular and the universal', so that 'on the one hand, we must give proper

Sacred places (and this is particularly true for the sacred places of the Mediterranean, as it has already been noted) are frequently connected to a particular manifestation of the 'sacred' (God, a prophet, a supernatural event and so on) which took place at a specific place and time: the sacredness of the place is a consequence of this manifestation. The fact that God manifested himself in that place makes the sacred place irreplaceable: therefore each sacred place (giving this expression the meaning that has already been discussed) possesses a unique dimension which makes that place an essential component of the constitutive narrative of a specific religious group.

At the same time, sacred places have a significance that cannot be confined within the borders of a single community, as they are the manifestation of a transcendent dimension which is constitutive of the human experience. Every religion has its own sacred places and this fact indicates that the connection of the 'sacred' to a particular place is something that is shared by all religions. But also people who are not members of any religion have their own sacred places: war memorials, national historical landmarks, outstanding works of art, mausoleums and cemeteries are visited and revered by men and women who – independently of the fact that they believe or not in religion – sense that in those places there is something that goes beyond their individual lives and has to do with the fundamental meaning of human existence. This helps to understand that each sacred place is the particular manifestation of an experience of the 'sacred' that is shared in different forms by all human beings, because all of them (including those who are inappropriately called 'non-believers') need a 'sacred' centre that gives sense and direction to their lives. In other words, each particular sacred place has a universal significance which is relevant also for people who are not members of the specific religion connected to the events which made that place sacred or even for people who are not members of a religion at all.[27]

This interplay between the particular and the universal dimensions of sacred places – more precisely, the fact that the universal can be apprehended only through the experience of the particular[28] – must be taken into account when reflecting on the best way to protect them. The specific character of each sacred place – its unique way to manifest the 'sacred' through the faith, creed and ritual of a community of believers – should be protected because it is irreplaceable: its loss would affect not only the particular religious community that is connected to it but the whole of humankind, because the experience of the sacred – which is a central

due to and strengthen the universal, while on the other, we must not minimize the radical particularity of a religious tradition' (*Sharing Sacred Spaces*, in this book).

27 This point is underlined in Herb Stovel, *Introduction*, where it is written that 'efforts to conserve tangible and intangible living religious heritage deserve particular support for their role in supporting and testifying to the nature of our search for the fundamental meaning of human existence', 9.

28 In Chapter 6 Jack Bemporad underlines that the particular 'often contains the universal element'.

element of the human experience – would be impoverished. In this perspective, the destruction of the Wailing Wall, or of the Basilica of the Holy Sepulchre or of the Dome of the Rock would make every human being poorer because one of the paths that connect man to the transcendent dimension of life would be forever lost.

In the last decades, the balance between the particular and the universal dimension of sacred places has shifted dramatically. All over the world sacred places are increasingly perceived as the symbol of religious identity of a specific group. This is part of a broader transformation affecting religions in many parts of the world and stressing their character of identity providers (sometimes in connection with other identity markers such as nationality or ethnicity). As a consequence, the particular dimension of a sacred place – its connection to a specific culture, religion, community – has been brought to the forefront and the universal profile which is inherent to the sacred places has been largely forgotten, with the risk that an excessive 'assertion of identity, fed by fundamentalism, may lead to the destruction of religious symbols'.[29]

This change of role played by religion on the national and international stage is a challenge that – as far as sacred places are concerned – should be dealt with primarily on the grounds of international law. The sacred places of the majority religion are usually given some protection by national laws and the increasing significance of religion as identity provider is likely to increase the level of this protection; on the other hand, national legislation is unlikely to protect the places sacred to minority religions or, at least, to protect them to the same degree. In this last case the best chance for safeguarding the sacred places of minority religions is provided by international law that, in the present situation, is better placed to provide adequate guarantees for the universal dimension of sacred places.

This universal-particular interplay can also be helpful in reflecting on the legal status of sacred places. The framework aimed at granting their protection and enhancement ought to be based on the balance between these two dimensions, respecting and reflecting both the particular and the universal profiles presented by the sacred places.

On the one hand there are the particular rights of a specific community in respect of its sacred places: the right to own, control and manage them, the right to gather for religious purposes in that place, the right to perform religious ceremonies and so on. These rights are manifestations of individual and collective religious freedom and should be considered in the light of the provisions devoted to the protection of religious liberty in international and domestic law. At the same time they reflect the responsibility of religious communities, upon which rests the burden to maintain the character of *living* heritage of a sacred place, and provide them with the tools required to effectively manage these places.

However, as already underlined, sacred places are not significant for the members of a religious community only: they have a value that goes beyond the limits of a specific community. Therefore they should be respected and protected

29 Jean-Louis Luxen, quoted by Herb Stovel, *Introduction*, 2.

as a 'common good', a heritage of general interest, and not only as the property of a particular group. That could mean, for example, granting them some kind of public support (even in cases where they are the sacred places of a minority religion), giving them enhanced protection in the case of conflict or making them accessible to all people who wish to visit them (respecting, of course, their nature of the sacred place of a specific religion).

These two sets of rights need to be harmonized through a careful process aimed at minimizing the potential clashes between the rights of the particular community on the one hand and the expectations of the universal community on the other. The reconciliation of these potentially conflicting interests could be particularly challenging because each sacred place is part of a specific historical, cultural and political context. It is therefore necessary to approach the sacred places issue through a process that recognizes the different roles of the parties concerned and offers each of them the possibility to contribute to the definition of a satisfactory strategy for the protection and enhancement of sacred places. This is the contribution that the authors of this book hope to offer to the debate on the sacred places of the Mediterranean.

PART I
What is a Sacred Place?

Chapter 2
Towards a Definition of Sacred Places: Introductory Remarks

Andrea Benzo

Whereas the expression 'holy places' is used to refer in particular to the most notable Israeli and Palestinian religious sites, the term 'sacred places' seems more apt in embracing all the sites covered by this research, which are different in origins, history and geographical location. At the same time, the religious sites this research will focus on enjoy a more prominent status than other common 'places of worship', such as churches, synagogues and mosques.

Nevertheless, international law does not provide any definition for 'sacred places'. Against this backdrop, one may argue that no definition is needed in order to protect sacred places. Whereas this assumption might hold true for conventions or laws dealing with specific sites, it becomes less sustainable if the objective is the drafting of a legal tool with a broader scope and focusing on the protection of sacred places in general which, in turn, stems from freedom of religion as a human right. In this case, providing a clear, though flexible definition of the subject of such protection can help make legal provisions more effective and focused, as a clear link is established between these provisions and those features that make a place sacred and therefore deserving of special protection.

Sacred Places in International Materials

Devotion to the protection of sacred places by international law and intergovernmental organizations is not a recent phenomenon. For instance, since the Congress of Berlin in 1878 the question of the sacred places in the Holy Land has ceased to be settled by the Sultan's unilateral decisions and has become the object of international agreements between the main European Powers.

Among recent international documents concerning sacred places in general, we could mention the 'Projet de régime juridique pour les Lieux Saints en Terre Sainte – Patrimoine Commun de l'Humanité' (2006) by the 'Groupe de La Laguna', the 'Principles and Guidelines for the Management of Sacred Natural Sites Located in Legally Recognised Protected Areas' (2008) by UNESCO (United Nations Educational, Scientific and Cultural Organization) and IUCN (International Union

For Conservation of Nature and Natural Resources)[1] and the 'Universal Code on Holy Sites' by the 'Holy Sites Conference' (Oslo 2009).[2]

The first instrument was drawn up and adopted by a group of experts headed by Federico Mayor, Former Director-General of UNESCO, and it has not obtained any binding legal status yet. In light of the universal value of sacred sites, this document draws an interesting parallel between the concept of a holy place and that of common heritage of mankind outlined in the well-known UNESCO Convention of 1972. The notion of common heritage of mankind made its first appearance in a legal document in the 1966 'Declaration on the principles of international cultural cooperation' by the UNESCO General Assembly, but a similar rationale lies at the root of the 1959 Antarctic Treaty. By the same token, sovereignty claims on the Holy Land should be 'frozen' – according to the Laguna project – and protecting holy places should become a common concern of humankind, given their universal value. To attain this objective, the drafters have proposed a new legal regime. Although it does not aim at replacing the UNESCO World Heritage Convention system, this has clearly been taken into account as a relevant model. In order to define a specific site as a sacred place, this draft makes reference to the fact that it is considered as such by history, or tradition or by the religious community (or communities) concerned. Whereas these communities can propose the inclusion of a certain site in the 'Register of common heritage of mankind' to the committee thereby established, a list of the most notable holy places in the Holy Land was to be added to the final version of the project, in order for them to enjoy the status granted by this regime once it entered into force, with no need for a proposal of inclusion. It was added that, '... Le régime du patrimoine commun de l'humanité pourra également être appliqué aux Lieux Saints qui ne sont pas situés sur les territoires d'Israël et de Palestine, à condition que l'accord y relatif soit donné par l'État sur le territoire duquel les dits Lieux Saints sont situés'. The final decision on the inclusion of additional sites is to be taken by the 'International Authority of the common heritage of mankind' thereby established. This committee is appointed by the United Nations Security Council and consists of no more than seven members, including representatives of the State of Israel and Palestine and nationals of those states having historical ties with the Holy Land. Representatives of religious communities enjoy observer status. The members of the Authority can also propose a site for inclusion but the consent of the religious communities is required. These are responsible for the administration of holy places whereas the Authority is primarily charged with applying the whole regime. As for protection, basic principles include non-expropriation, peaceful use, conservation in the interest of future generations and freedom of access. Territorial states are responsible for the maintenance of public order and security within holy places. Disputes between

1 This document is available at <http://data.iucn.org/dbtw-wpd/edocs/PAG-016.pdf> accessed 24 May 2013.

2 This document is available at <www.sfcg.org/programmes/jerusalem/Universal%20Code%20on%20Holy%20Sites.pdf> accessed 24 May 2013.

states parties and religious communities shall be settled by the Authority. No legal status is explicitly foreseen for the document; although, as the drafters argue in their explanatory note, a bilateral treaty between Israel and Palestine under the aegis of the Security Council would be the most suitable solution.

The UNESCO/IUCN guidelines are aimed at helping protected area managers in guaranteeing an adequate degree of protection to areas of land or water which are the object of worship by local and indigenous communities – and also by mainstream faiths – given their peculiarities. Here, a *sacred site* is defined as 'an area of special spiritual significance to peoples and communities'; they are deemed as deserving urgent support since they 'remain outstanding assets of the whole of humanity'. The need for continuous cooperation with the religious communities concerned is also stressed. The primacy of traditional custodians is recognized with a view to promoting cooperation between them and protected area managers as a prerequisite for the enhanced conservation of these special places. Mount Athos is mentioned as an example of a sacred natural site according to the IUCN categories.

A 'Code on Holy Sites' was drawn up in 2009 by the 'Holy Sites conference', assembling religious leaders and academics and organized by 'One World in Dialogue' and the 'Oslo Center for Peace and Human Rights'. The Code has been endorsed by interfaith networks, religious communities and leaders such as the 'Religions for Peace World Council', the 'World Sikh Leadership', the President of the 'All India Imam Organization', the 'World Council of Churches' and the Russian Orthodox Church – Moscow Patriarchate. As a first implementation of this Code, a two-year pilot project has been launched in Bosnia Herzegovina, in partnership with the Inter-religious Council (IRC) of Bosnia and Herzegovina, an independent NGO.[3]

In the preamble, the drafters acknowledge the great value attached to holy sites by people all over the world, irrespective of their religious affiliations. They also recall international conventions on freedom of religion and belief, cultural heritage and protection of civilians in armed conflicts. Holy sites are broadly defined as 'places of religious significance to particular religious communities', such as places of worship, cemeteries and shrines, incorporating their immediate surroundings when these form an integral part of the site. They are designated as such by each religious community according to its customs. Communities enjoy the right to establish and maintain their holy sites and shall be consulted regarding the public promotion of such places for tourist, scientific, educational and other purposes. Regarding protection, the document calls for the preservation of holy sites, freedom of access, reconstruction and 'memorialization' of destroyed sacred places as well as protection from desecration. Expropriation and nationalization of parts of a holy site are permitted, provided that the religious communities concerned are equally represented and consulted on all aspects of the process. Their agreement is required in the case of archaeological excavations. As far as

3 See <www.sfcg.org/programmes/jerusalem/holysites.html> accessed 24 May 2013.

the duties of territorial states are concerned, public authorities shall not arbitrarily prohibit the residence of foreign personnel connected with the sites. When sacred sites are shared among different communities, national authorities shall provide for arrangements whereby all members are granted equal access. Education and public speech shall be oriented towards the acknowledgement and promotion of the significance of holy sites.

The draft foresees the creation of monitoring bodies endowed with an advisory role for its implementation at the local, regional and national level. Such committees shall consist of representatives of religious communities, public authorities and other relevant institutions. They shall draw up a list of holy sites to fall under the provisions of the code, advise national authorities and settle, through their good offices, any dispute over the status of a sacred place. Besides monitoring bodies, an international committee is provided for which is charged, *inter alia*, with monitoring the implementation of the guidelines, promoting the adoption of the code in all relevant fora and reporting on violations of its provisions. Nothing is foreseen about its membership. The Code follows the soft-law model and it seems to have been conceived particularly for war-torn regions and occupied territories, since there are various references to the duties of an occupying power, damaged sites and the need for stressing the spiritual value rather than any strategic, territorial or military significance of sacred places.

Among the international legal instruments dealing with some particular sacred places, Resolution 181/1947 of the United Nations General Assembly on the Palestinian Question and some resolutions of the European Parliament on Mount Athos deserve special attention. In the first document, even though no official definition is given, 'the unique spiritual and religious interests located in the city of the three great monotheistic faiths throughout the world, Christian, Jewish and Moslem' is stressed.

Whereas in the 1972 UNESCO Convention Concerning the Protection of the World Cultural and Natural Heritage we can only find a reference to 'sites which are of outstanding universal value from the ... ethnological or anthropological point of view', the 2005 Operational Guidelines on the selection of World Heritage sites explicitly refer to a direct and tangible association 'with events or living traditions, with ideas, or with beliefs, with artistic and literary works of outstanding universal significance' although 'the Committee considers that this criterion should preferably be used in conjunction with other criteria'.

On the 7th of May 1981 the European Parliament passed a resolution[4] calling for initiatives in support of Mount Athos, taking into consideration '... la tradition culturelle, religieuse et historique du Mont Athos, ensemble unique dans le monde chrétien d'une Communauté vivante et active, dont l'histoire et la vie couvrent près de 11 siècles', and the fact that 'le problème de la conservation et du développement indispensable de cette Communauté monastique relève non seulement de la Grèce, mais aussi de toute la Communauté et du monde civil

4 J.O./C.E., C-144/15-06-1981.

en général, comme il relève autant de tout les chrétiens que des orthodoxes'. Likewise, another resolution,[5] following the fires which broke out on Mount Athos, was approved by the European Parliament after considering that 'le Mont Athos constitue un monument religieux et archéologique unique et sans équivalent dans toute l'Europe, ainsi qu'un symbole représentatif de la spiritualité et des valeurs incarnant les idéaux européens'.

Sacred Places in Literature and Religious Traditions

Even though most of the existing works on sacred places have been written with special attention to the Christian sites in the Holy Land, the definitions they provide also aim at embracing sacred places of different religions located in diverse areas. According to Bernardin Collin,[6] 'sacred places' are 'monuments or sites specially and perpetually worshipped by faithfuls for an event linked to them, in general the memory of the founder or an event in his life' [my translation]. In Jean-Dominique Montoisy's[7] definition a 'sacred place' is '… a well defined sanctuary, the spiritual interest of which has been historically entrenched by the members of one or more religions and which commemorates an event linked to these religions' [my translation]. In the same fashion, according to Reiter/Eordegian/Abu Khalaf, a holy site is 'a place, whether or not it is enclosed within a building, which is venerated by most of the followers of a religion because of its association with a founding figure of that religion'.[8] Paolo Pieraccini,[9] while providing no particular definition, mentions the frequent relations with European history and the central role played in international politics as main features of some Christian sacred places in the Holy Land. These definitions show how crucial is the role played by religious communities, through the centuries, in providing a place with a sacred character: this sacredness 'is the inherited value that makes religious heritage different from other types of heritage'.[10] Such spiritual meaning pre-exists secular law on the protection of sacred places and has to be taken into account when

5 *Procès Verbaux 28 II* (pe 144.654) 13-09-1990.

6 Bernardin Collin, *Pour une solution au problème des Lieux Saints* (G.P. Maisonneuve et Larose 1974) 43.

7 Jean-Dominique Montoisy, *Le Vatican et le problème des Lieux Saints* (Franciscan Printing Press 1984) 8.

8 Y Reiter, M Eordegian and M Abu Khalaf, 'Between Divine and Human: The Complexity of Holy Places in Jerusalem', in Moshe Ma'oz and Sari Nusseibeh (eds), *Jerusalem: Points of Friction, and Beyond* (Kluwer Law International 2000) 109–10.

9 Paolo Pieraccini, *Gerusalemme, Luoghi Santi e comunità religiose nella politica internazionale* (Edizioni Dehoniane 1996) 3–6.

10 Gamini Wijesuriya, 'The past is in the present. Perspectives in caring for buddhist heritage sites in Sri Lanka', in Herb Stovel, Nicholas Stanley-Price and Robert Killic (eds), 'Conservation of Living Religious Heritage', *Papers from the ICCROM 2003 Forum on Living Religious Heritage: conserving the sacred* (ICCROM 2005) 31.

drafting international or municipal norms on this matter since 'a holy place is distinguished from any other, its significance based on a unique character that no human action can confer'.[11]

In the Jewish view, the concept of holiness is connected more with land than with specific sites, as highlighted in the *Encyclopedia Judaica*.[12] According to the *Mishnah*, it is the land of Israel that enjoys the highest degree of holiness. However, history provides strong evidence showing that Jews, as well as Christians and Muslims with their holy cities and places, have always seen some particular sites as deserving special worship because of their crucial role in religious history. In addition to this, according to Jewish scholars a 'sacred place' is a well-defined physical space, having a particular identity which renders it distinguishable from the surrounding environment. By the same token, Islam also acknowledges that some places have been chosen by God to manifest himself to mankind and therefore enjoy a higher degree of sanctity.

A Definition by Induction

Since no universally accepted definition of 'sacred place' exists, the only solution to overcome any problem of terminology could be found by shaping a 'definition by induction'. From the abovementioned examples it is possible to draw up a list of particular features characterizing a 'sacred place'. The presence of one or more of them allows us to speak of a 'sacred place', instead of a more common place of worship:

1. a link to a manifestation of the 'sacred' (God, a prophet, a supernatural event and so on) which took place there: that is the case of some sacred places in the Holy Land and Mecca;
2. an important role played in the history of a religion as a permanent landmark and which makes it unique: that is the case, among others, of Mount Athos;
3. the fact that it is the object of veneration and interest not only for local communities but also for believers from different parts of the world and even for members of different religions. Such a status gives it a universal dimension: that is the case, for instance, of the Orthodox Sanctuaries in Kosovo;
4. the fact that a general consensus within the religious community (or communities) concerned, or throughout history and tradition has developed to consider it as such.

Such a definition, focused on history and religious tradition, is meant to be comprehensive enough to cover all those sites that deserve special protection, even

11 See supra, footnote 8.

12 *Encyclopedia Judaica* (Keter Publishing House 1971) vol. 8, 921.

if each of them has some features that make it unique.[13] Given that the protection of sacred places stems from freedom of religion, religious law and tradition play a fundamental role that cannot be neglected when defining the nature of a sacred place. At the same time, a 'secular' definition is needed to establish what the object of such special international protection should be and to ensure that such a regime is tailored to the specific characteristics of these places, on the basic assumption that one cannot effectively protect something which is not clearly identified in its main features.

13 Nonetheless, it is not meant to be exclusive and the reader will find other definitions of a sacred place throughout this book itself.

Chapter 3

The Sacred Spaces and Sites of the Mediterranean in Contemporary Theological, Anthropological and Sociological Approaches and Debates

Yuri Stoyanov

In the last two decades or so a range of topics related to secular and religious attitudes to sacred space and sites have been receiving increasing attention and varied, sometimes contradictory, treatment in legal, theological, anthropological and sociological analyses and debates. With a predominant focus on the historical and contemporary religio-political role and diverse usages of sacred space and places, these expanding multi- and inter-disciplinary debates have evolved against the background of various recent significant developments on the international scene such as the growing politicization and radicalization of certain currents in world religions, the process of the deprivatization of religion and its forceful reinstatement in the political and public space. The consequences of this process include multiplying outbreaks of religiously motivated and religiously justified state-sponsored group and individual political violence, triggered on occasion by interreligious strife in and around sacred sites and places of worship. The emergence (and re-emergence) of such inter-confessional fault-lines and flashpoints at sacred sites sometimes signal the violent termination of religious coexistence and/or sharing at the respective sites or the appearance of new religious authorities and actors seeking to 'purge' the sacred space (which they claim to legitimately own and manage) from 'alien' religious presence and practices.

These conflicts over sacred space in general have caught international political, diplomatic and military decision-makers, security analysts, opinion-formers and academic political science think-tanks by surprise and unprepared. At least until the end of the Cold War these figures have largely subscribed to the (until very recently) prevalent thesis of an irreversibly advancing global secularization, as the anticipated universalization of the values and institutions of secular humanism and Western modernity were supposed to bring about the progressive decline of religious influence on the socio-political and socio-cultural spheres. There is an increasing awareness that the encounters and interaction between the globalizing and secularizing outcomes of Western-driven modernity and the religio-political forces of counter- and de-secularization have been reactivated and developed in new directions since the late 1980s. This further interaction was given an extra dimension by the debates on the current role of religion in world politics and inter-civilizational confrontation and/or dialogue in the wake of the articulation and popularization of Samuel Huntington's and Francis Fukuyama's respective theses of the 'Clash of Civilizations'[1] and 'The End of History'.[2]

Notwithstanding the intense and far-reaching debates in the public sphere, the bulk of scholarly discussion provoked by the theories of Huntington and Fukuyama took place in the field of political science. With the publication of Jonathan Sacks' *The Dignity of Difference: How to Avoid the Clash of Civilizations* in 2002,[3] the debate on the 'clash' or 'dialogue' of civilizations was brought into the sphere of theology (more specifically, historical and moral theology), with a strong focus on the relevance of Jewish religious, social and political history in wider socio-confessional frameworks. Sacks appealed for updated and subtler paradigms in the manner in which the three Abrahamic monotheistic religions view and approach each other and interpret and treat the non-Abrahamic religious world. Such paradigms are expected to make it possible for religious authorities and leaders, as well as for lay people, to acknowledge the religious and spiritual integrity of those who do not profess their respective faith,[4] rather than to feel threatened by the encounter with other religiosities. In this way they should be able to achieve more confidence in their own religiosity[5] and thus conceptualize a shared and cognitive space for the religious differences, acknowledging them as sources of values and human creativity.[6]

Both the influential 'Clash of Civilizations' and 'Dignity of Difference' models and discourses have been utilized in the ongoing disputes on and approaches to the phenomenon of the resurgence of politicized and prophetic religion and the crisis of the universal secularization theory, including the increasingly topical problems of inter-cultural and interreligious conflicts or bridge-building and sharing related to sacred space and holy places. The topicality of the various issues related to the multiplicity of old and new threats to sacred sites arise from the diverse nature of these threats, as sacred places have increasingly suffered destruction and damage not only in conflict and post-conflict situations, but as a result of aggressive commercial development, mass tourism and even incautious archaeological excavations. Consequently, in addition to the various guidelines of the relevant international conventions, recent new international legal, heritage and

1 Samuel P. Huntington, 'The clash of civilizations' [1993], *Foreign Affairs* 22; Id., *The Clash of Civilizations and the Remaking of World Order* (Simon & Schuster 1996).

2 Francis Fukuyama, 'The End of History?' [1989], *The National Interest* 3; Id., *The End of History and the Last Man* (Free Press 1992).

3 Jonathan Sacks, *The Dignity of Difference: How to Avoid the Clash of Civilizations* (Continuum International Publishing Group, 2002).

4 Sacks, *The Dignity of Difference*, 4–5.

5 Sacks, *The Dignity of Difference*, 65–6.

6 Sacks, *The Dignity of Difference*, 13–15, 53–5.

inter-disciplinary initiatives (such as the *Groupe de La Laguna* project for a legal regime for the holy places in Israel and the Palestinian Territories of 2006[7] and the Universal Code on Holy Sites of 2009-2011)[8] have addressed the need to find new instruments, strategies and policies to secure the protection of sacred places.

The subject-matter of sacred space and places has lately been subjected not only to theological, but also to anthropological and sociological analyses and it is certainly worth exploring whether the contributions of these three disciplines to the study of this problematic can be usefully integrated into similar future inter-disciplinary initiatives focused on the safeguarding of sacral heritage. Approaches, perspectives and conclusions in the treatment of sacred places in these disciplines have varied more than somewhat and the following exposition intends to summarize the main trends and state of research on the problematic.

Significantly, within the field of anthropology a characteristic application of versions of a 'clash of civilizations' conflict-focused approach to the balance of power in intercommunal relations around sacred sites and its dormant, occurring and contingent tensions and shifts, with their potential for expulsive violence, is discernible in the much-discussed recent thesis of 'antagonistic tolerance' (underlying the sharing of religious sites in South Asia and the Balkans), advanced in the anthropological studies of Robert Hayden[9] and Ron E. Hassner's subsequent arguments for the essential 'undivisibility' and 'unshareability' of sacred places.[10] On the other hand, alternative evolving anthropological approaches to the patterns of negotiating and bridging differences and intercommunality at mixed holy places have shown that conflict-prioritizing models are not sufficient to analyse and do justice to the multi-layered socio-religious fields of interaction at such shared sites.[11]

Brought thus into the forefront of the intense discussion and debates on the ongoing re-religiofication of politics and religiously motivated political violence within the modern state and in inter-state relations, the issue of sacred space and sites have attracted the renewed interest of contemporary theological, legal,

7 Document available at<www.fund-culturadepaz.org/spa/03/DOCUMENTOS/SANTOS_LUGARES_2006.pdf> accessed 30 April 2013.

8 Document available at: <http://http://www.rfp-europe.eu/index.cfm?id=353568 accessed 7 February 2014.

9 Robert Hayden, 'Antagonistic Tolerance: Competitive Sharing of Religious Sites in South Asia and the Balkans' [2002], *Current Anthropology* 205; Id., 'Religious Structures and Political Dominance in Belgrade' [2005], *Ethnologia Balcanica*, 214.

10 Ron E. Hassner, 'To Halve and to Hold: The Politics of Sacred Space and the Problem of Indivisibility' [2003], *Security Studies* 1; Id., *War on Sacred Grounds* (Cornell University Press, 2009).

11 See, for example, the contributions in Dionigi Albera and Maria Couroucli (eds), *Sharing Sacred Spaces in the Mediterranean: Christians, Muslims, and Jews at Shrines and Sanctuaries* (Indiana University Press 2012); Glenn Bowman (ed.), *Sharing the Sacra: the Politics and Pragmatics of Inter-Communal Relations around Holy Places* (Berghahn Books 2012).

anthropological and sociological critical enquiry. As the Mediterranean area (and the adjacent Arabian peninsula) comprise the locations of the paradigmatic holy sites of Judaism, Christianity and Islam, studies on the sacred geographics[12] and pilgrimage circuits of the Mediterranean have focused predominantly on the attitude to and concept and structuring of sacred space in the Abrahamic religions. The exploration of the notion of sacred space in religious worldviews has already become one of the main topics of religious studies, especially in the disciplines of history of religion and phenomenology of religion. The exploration of sacred space in religious studies has been much indebted to Rudolf Otto's[13] and Mircea Eliade's[14] seminal treatments of the religious mind and the phenomenon of sacrality and holiness. In Otto's influential understanding of the sacred/holy/numinous it represents a universal transcendent reality which is the essence and 'innermost core' of all religions and religious experience and while it can be acknowledged and approached, it eludes strict definitions.[15] One of the concerns of such reappraisals is whether a differentiation can be established between two different types of sacrality: the 'awesome holy' (which could be seen as characteristic of earlier or more 'primitive' forms of religion) and the 'ethical holy' (understood as a supremely elevated moral purity arousing a sense of moral reverence) and what the nature of their relationship and its chronology is.[16]

A fully developed theory proposing a reconstruction of the mechanisms through which religious cultures translate such views and experiences of the sacred into their organization and orientation of sacralized space has been consistently formulated and elaborated in the well-known studies of Mircea Eliade. By applying the sacred-profane dichotomy (central to his study of religion) to sacralized space, Eliade emphasizes its heterogeneity, as some of its spatial points are seen to have been the loci of divine manifestations through theophanies, hierophanies, miraculous occurrences and so on. Epitomizing the differentiation between cosmos and chaos, such sacred places serve also as variously conceptualized and represented *axis mundi* – passages and communication channels between different strata of reality, indeed 'meeting points between heaven and earth', 'a point of junction between earth, heaven and hell', 'the navel of the earth, a meeting place

12 On the methodology and terminology of the study of 'geographics' of religion, see Jamie Scott and Paul Simpson-Housley (eds), *Sacred Places and Profane Spaces. Essays in the Geographics of Judaism, Christianity and Islam* (Greenwood Press 1991); Robert H. Stoddard and Alan Morinis (eds), *Sacred Places, Sacred Spaces. The Geography of Pilgrimages* (Lousiana State University 1997).

13 Rudolf Otto, *The Idea of the Holy* (Humphrey Milford 1925 [1917]).

14 Mircea Eliade, *Traité d'histoire des religions* (Payot, 1953); Id., *The Sacred and the Profane. The Nature of Religion* (Willard Ropes Trask tr, Harcourt, Brace & World, 1959); Id., *Le mythe de l'éternel retour. Archétypes et repetition* (Gallimard, 1969 [1949]).

15 Otto, *The Idea of the Holy*, 4–5, 7.

16 John W. Oman, 'The Sphere of Religion' in Joseph Needham (ed.), *Science, Religion and Reality* (The Macmillan Company, 1925) 285–95.

for the three cosmic regions',[17] providing the religious mind with the sacred centre around which it can proceed with the creation of the ordered cosmos. The qualities, symbolism and imagery attributed to such sacralized spaces and sacred centres/axes are accordingly transferred to and reflected in the architecture, iconography and status of the man-made religious buildings (sanctuaries, shrines, temples and so on), palaces and cities associated with the respective sacred places.[18]

The Eliade perspective on sacred space and places has been applied with differing degrees of perceived success or failure to a variety of religious cultures and currents which in the case of the Abrahamic faiths have ranged from normative Islam[19] to Jewish mysticism[20] and Constantinian period-Christianity vis-à-vis contemporaneous non-Christian Neo-Platonism and Graeco-Roman religiosity.[21] The Eliade theory of holy space (as related to the dichotomies of sacred-profane and cosmos-order) have generated some extensive debates within religious studies and attracted critical reassessments on methodological grounds and/or on the basis of analysis of empirical cosmological and cosmographic material of various religious traditions not taken into account by Eliade.[22] Such reassessments have also offered alternative approaches to the problem and definition of sacred space as in the case of Jonathan Z. Smith's dichotomy of 'locative' and 'utopian' vision of space[23] (Smith defines sacred site as 'a place of clarification (a focusing lens) where men and gods are held to be transparent to one another')[24] and Christoph Auffarth's distinction between a locally fixed shrine and a site which acquires a sacred character through

17 Mircea Eliade, *Patterns in Comparative Religion* (Sheed and Ward, 1958) 358.

18 Mircea Eliade, *Traité d'histoire*, 315–332; Id., *The Sacred and the Profane*, 20–65, 116–160; Id., *Le mythe de l'éternel retour*, 17–35.

19 Clinton Bennett, 'Islam', in Jean Holm and John Bowker (eds), *Sacred Place* (Pinter Publishers – distributed in the US and Canada by St Martin's Press, 1994) 88–114.

20 Haviva Pedaya, 'The Divinity as Place and Time and the Holy Place in Jewish Mysticism', in Benjamin Z. Kedar and R.J. Zwi Werblowsky (eds), *Sacred Space: Shrine, City, Land: Proceedings of the International Conference in Memory of Joshua Prawer* (Macmillan – Israel Academy of Sciences and Humanities, 1998) 84–110.

21 Ilinca Tanaseanu-Döbler, 'Mircea Eliade and Concepts of Holy Places in Late Antiquity' [2009], *Archaeus. Studies in the History of Religions*, 281.

22 See, for example, Jonathan Z. Smith, 'The Wobbling Pivot' [1972], *The Journal of Religion*, 134 – reprinted in Jonathan Z. Smith, *Map is not Territory: Studies in the History of Religions* (Brill, 1978) 88–103; Christoph Auffarth, 'Sind heilige Stätten transportabel? *Axis mundi* und soziales Gedächtnis', in A. Michaels (ed.), *Noch eine Chance für die Religionsphänomenologie?* (Peter Lang AG, 2001) 235–57; David Cave, 'Eliade's Interpretation of Sacred Space and its Role Towards the Cultivation of Virtue', in Bryan Rennie (ed.), *Changing Religious Worlds: The Meaning and End of Mircea Eliade* (State University of New York Press, 2001) 235–48; Tanaseanu-Döbler, 'Mircea Eliade and Concepts of Holy Places'.

23 Smith, 'The Wobbling Pivot'.

24 Jonathan Z. Smith, 'The Bare Facts of Ritual' [1980], *History of Religions* 112 (reprinted in Jonathan Z. Smith, *Imagining Religion: From Babylon to Jonestown* (University of Chicago Press, 1982) 54.

cultic observances.[25] While clearly demonstrating that the Eliadean perspective lacks universal applicability (being based on select evidence, sometimes stripped of its immediate religious and historical context), these reappraisals also suggest that it remains a useful general heuristic tool in the study of religion, and new approaches and theories of sacred space can be formulated in criticism, revision or refinement of its theoretical and ideological premises.[26]

Whether drawing on, elaborating or polemicizing against such coexisting scholarly approaches to the phenomenon of holy space, theologians and religious historians have lately been contributing significant new material and observations to the exploration of this problematic in Jewish, Christian and Islamic contexts. This growing study of the spatial dimension of the early, medieval and modern Abrahamic faiths' discourses on sacrality and holiness and their *geographia sacra*, especially in the Mediterranean, are essential to understanding the religio-political background of the current inter-Abrahamic tensions and reconciliation efforts over shared or currently (but not historically) mono-confessional sacred places in the region. This can be clearly demonstrated, for example, by a brief discussion of the novel theological and ecclesiastical approaches to and appropriations of sacred space and religiously significant sites in Palestine (marking God's acts and epiphanies in history), formulated and implemented in the course of the evolving Christianization of the Roman Empire during the 4th century.

While a number of facets of Jewish, Christian and Muslim attitudes to sacred space and their interaction still await more systematic investigation, it is now evident that they do not represent essentially static and unchangeable stances but have undergone a series of transmutations. One of these crucial transmutations in the Christian case occurred during the Constantinian and post-Constantinian periods in the 4th century, in the wake of Constantine the Great's (306–37) and his co-Emperor Licinius' (308–24) issue of the Edict of Milan in 313 and the ensuing legitimization and institutionalization of the Christian Church in the Roman Empire. This led to the revalorization of the sites of epiphanies and hierophanies in Palestine (as recounted in the New and Old Testament) as places of special and in some cases paradigmatic religious significance for Christendom.[27] These sustained Christian Roman endeavors, initiated originally by Constantine the Great and his mother St Helena (c.255–c.330), to Christianize Palestine promoted devotional pilgrimage and actively erected churches and monasteries, marking the expanding system of sacred and pilgrimage centres in the Holy Land. The Christian 're-discovery' and infatuation with the physical Holy Land and Jerusalem, underlain by the Church's supersessionist theology recognizing itself as the 'True Israel' or

25 Auffarth, 'Sind heilige Stätten transportabel?', 254.

26 For suggestions for such a constructive use of Eliade's theory of holy space and places, see Tanaseanu-Döbler, 'Mircea Eliade and Concepts of Holy Places', 297–301.

27 See, for example, Peter W.L. Walker, *Holy City, Holy Places? Christian Attitudes to Jerusalem and the Holy Land in the Fourth Century* (Clarendon Press 1990); Joan E. Taylor, *Christians and the Holy Places: The Myth of Jewish-Christian Origins* (Clarendon Press 1993).

the 'New Israel' triumphant over the rejected 'Old Israel', led to the flourishing of Palestinian monasticism in the 5th century and the elevation of the Jerusalem See to a Patriarchate in 451.

The transformation of Christian secular and ecclesiastical elites' attitudes to the Holy Land and its sacred sites find patent and forceful expression in Constantine the Great's stance and statements on Jerusalem and Mamre (the site of God's appearance to Abraham in Genesis 18:1–8 and where the patriarch had built an altar to the Lord according to Genesis 13:8), as reported by his imperial apologist, Eusebius of Caesarea (c.260–c.340). Both Jerusalem and Mamre are described in his letters to bishops in Palestine as primordially holy places (by divine decree), whose sacredness had been concealed and then revealed again.[28] In the case of Mamre, as it was the place where 'the cultic observance of the holy law' was originally initiated, it needed to be purified from all impure forms of worship practiced subsequently at it and restored to its 'ancient holiness'.[29] Significantly, despite the efforts of the political and clerical elites of the newly Christianized Roman Empire to make Mamre an exclusive sacred space, at the level of popular pilgrimage and veneration its status and appeal was actually internationally enhanced and it continued to be a shared Abrahamic site and magnet for a variety of religious groups.[30]

In the emerging and crystallizing notions and conceptualizations of sacred space in the early Christian Roman Empire the principal holy sites of Palestine thus played a much augmented role in its new political theology and were elevated as inherently and in some cases primaevally sacred places in the 'imperial-normative' space of its ecumene. These concepts of the ontologically sacred nature of the singled-out foremost holy sites of Palestine clearly contrasted with contemporaneous non-Christian attitudes to sacred sites, precincts and temples in the Graeco-Roman world, as exemplified and implemented by the last Roman pagan emperor, Julian the Apostate (361–63), during his campaigns to restore the prestige and vitality of paganism and reverse the tide of the Christianization of the empire. In Julian's functionalist approach to the sacrality of temples and cultic sites they are not intrinsically sacred but acquire a temporary sanctification through the presence of the respective gods, correct cultic observances and human religious attitudes.[31] Indicative of the dynamics of ritual space in Late Antiquity, including the question

---

28 See the analysis of Constantine the Great's articulation of the newly evolving Christian attitudes to sites such as Jerusalem and Mamre as the primal and divinely instituted holy places and the dialectic of the concealment and revelation of their holiness, in Tanaseanu-Döbler, '*Mircea Eliade and Concepts of Holy Places*', *285–90.*

29 Eusebius, *Life of Constantine*, 3: 52–3.

30 See, for example, Aryeh Kofsky, 'Mamre: A Case for a Regional Cult?' in Aryeh Kofsky and Guy Gedalyah Stroumsa (eds), *Sharing the Sacred. Religious Contacts and Conflicts in the Holy Land, 1st–15th Century* (Ben Zvi Institute 1989) 19–30.

31 On Julian's functional and flexible attitudes to temples as sites of temporary hierophanies and meeting-points between the gods and their human worshippers, representing the gods but not divine as such, see Tanaseanu-Döbler, '*Mircea Eliade and Concepts of Holy Places*', *290–296.*

of the extension of sacrality from the temples/sanctuaries to the cities serving as their locations,[32] these views of the last Roman pagan emperor show various points of continuity with Hellenism and Platonism as well as some innovative ideas which deserve further exploration, especially against the background of contemporaneous Christian theories and practices of sacralization of cultic sites.

This summary of research on the formative period of the creation of the new and enduring models of Christian sacred space and places (against the background of contemporaneous non-Christian Graeco-Roman models and Jewish-Christian relations in Palestine in Late Antiquity) was intended to show the main approaches to the theological developments and religious history underlying these seminal changes in Christian discourses on spatiality and *geographia sacra* in which certain places began to play a more literal role of being physical sites of God's acts and intervention in history. These altered spatial constructs and spiritual geography of Christianity become thus inextricably linked to its concepts of historicity which it shares with Judaism and Islam and is central to the self-conceptualization and perception of the three Abrahamic faiths. An awareness and further study of the continuities, interrelations and mutual dependencies between the Abrahamic religions' theologies of historicity and sacred space is thus indispensable to understanding of the inter-Abrahamic tensions and competing spatial claims, especially in early and high medieval Palestine and Jerusalem.

The culmination of these inter-Abrahamic rivalries over sacred space and sites during the period of the Crusades and Counter-Crusades has been the subject of intense study and debate. The Crusading era conflicts were preceded, however, by some less explored but significant episodes such as the reported Jewish attempt to reclaim and resacralize the lost holy locus of Judaism, the Temple Mount, in the wake of the Persian Sasanian conquest of Jerusalem in 614 and the possible endeavour of Emperor Heraclius (610–41) to repossess the Temple Mount for Christianity upon its return to East Roman/Byzantine control in 628.[33] These insufficiently clarified episodes were followed by the better explored process of the Umayyad Islamic re-sanctification and transformation of the Temple Mount (following the Umayyad annexation of Jerusalem in 638) into the sacral enclosure of Haram al-Sharif, the high point of which was the building of the Dome of the Rock, with its manifest supersessionist and missionary ramifications.[34]

32 J. Bouffartigue, 'Les villes saintes dans la vision religieuse de l'empereur Julien' in Béatrice Caseau, Jean-Claude Cheynet and Vincent Déroche (eds), *Pèlerinages et lieux saints dans l'Antiquité et le Moyen Âge. Mélanges offerts à Pierre Maraval* (Association des Amis du Centre d'Histoire et Civilisation de Byzance 2006) 90–96; Tanaseanu-Döbler, '*Mircea Eliade and Concepts of Holy Places*', 295–6.

33 See the analysis of the state of evidence and research on these two episodes in Yuri Stoyanov, *Defenders and Enemies of the True Cross* (Austrian Academy of Sciences Press 2011) 52–3, 68–9.

34 See the analysis in Robert G. Hoyland, *Seeing Islam as Others Saw It: a Survey and Evaluation of Christian, Jewish, and Zoroastrian Writings on Early Islam* (Darwin

In addition to the progressing exploration of this spatial dimension of the interaction between inter-Abrahamic faiths, a growing number of theological and religio-historical studies have also focused on the provenance and chronology of the internal development of the coexisting (and sometimes competing) models of sacred spaces and places within each of the Abrahamic religions. Apart from identifying a series of predictable analogies between these models in Judaism, Christianity and Islam, these studies have highlighted some interrelated themes, patterns and largely new areas of inquiry of considerable relevance to anthropological, sociological and legal approaches to holy sites, including the contemporary and topical dimension of this problematic. Regarding Judaism, for example, such subjects and areas include the historical interaction between ideological (Biblical and rabbinic) functional sacred space in Judaism, the dichotomy between single and multiple sacred spaces (also related to the process of the hierarchical organization of Jewish *geographia sacra* and the centralization/ unification of holy space in Jerusalem and the Temple). Other such spheres of study with respect to Judaism include the messianic understanding of the ideological strata of sacred space and its significance for the transition to functional holy space as well as the development of contrasting spatial discourses and practices approaches in the Jewish diaspora such as the democratization of sacred space among the Orthodox communities vis-à-vis the re-emphasis of its exclusivity among the Progressive and Hasidic groups.[35] The study of the fundamentally important Biblical roots of the concepts of the sanctity of place has drawn attention to some important dichotomies in various Biblical strata such as that between a sacred place where God dwells and where he reveals himself to humankind, or that between the sanctuary-based localized and hierarchically organized sanctity of 'God's dwelling' and its 'mobile' sanctity version of the Tabernacle,[36] the latter raising the crucial question whether any geographical site of divine revelation can be considered inherently sacred and/or its sanctity can achieve some permanence through the maintenance of worship.[37] Motivated by the eventual centralization of sacred space in the Temple in Jerusalem, the theological justification of the transition from the principles of 'mobility and impermanence' to 'stability and permanence' proceeded also with various rhetorical strategies to extend the sanctity of the Temple to the city itself.[38] Perceptions and descriptions of the Mediterranean Sea as a 'divine mythological entity', essentially a 'sacred sea', in West Semitic

Press 1997) 311–2; Guy Gedalyah Stroumsa, 'False Prophet, False Messiah and the Religious Scene in Seventh-Century Jerusalem' in Markus Bockmuehl and James C. Paget (eds), *Redemption and Resistance: the Messianic Hopes of Jews and Christians in Antiquity* (T & T Clark 2009) 292–3.

35 Seth Kunin, 'Judaism' in Holm and Bowker, *Sacred Place*, 115–48.

36 Sara Japhet, 'Some Biblical Concepts of Sacred Place' in Kedar and Werblowsky, *Sacred Space*, 55–72.

37 Sara Japhet, 'Some Biblical Concepts of Sacred Place', 69–70.

38 Sara Japhet, 'Some Biblical Concepts of Sacred Place', 70.

(Amorite/Canaanite) traditions and their resonances in Biblical and Talmudic literature has also begun to attract some scholarly attention.[39] Apart from the study of the theological implications of the sources for the chronology and evolution of such Biblical notions of the sanctity of sites of God's dwelling and revelation (which need also to be treated against the background of the dichotomy of the two crucial facets of sacrality – immanence and transcendence), more historically oriented research has highlighted the changing and conflicting conceptualization of the Temple in Jerusalem during Hellenistic and Roman rule in Palestine and the Near East. During these periods the cultic space of the local temples of the colonized peoples served as repositories of their ethno-religious heritage and identity and thus possessed national and political dimensions and potential which the Hellenistic and Roman rulers endeavored to neutralize in a variety of ways and with different strategies. In the case of Jerusalem, the growing role of its temple as a 'native local holy space'[40] was challenged by the Hellenizers' attempts to universalize it, while during his reign Herod (37–4 BCE) attempted to implement at the Temple Mount 'a Jewish kind of universalism'[41] within the framework of the Jewish diaspora. The resultant politicization of the holy space of the Temple and Jerusalem had major religio-political implications and consequences.

Further interesting research questions regarding the spacialization of belief in the normative monotheisms of early Judaism and Christianity, on one hand, and contemporaneous polytheistic religions, on the other, are posed by the evident contrast and interfaces between the recognition of only one centre for required pilgrimage in the former, and the 'inbuilt multiplicity of pilgrimage centres' in the latter.[42] Other areas of inquiry of increasing importance to the study of spatiality and sacrality in Judaism, Christianity and Islam include the networks and hierarchical interrelations between the key and paradigmatic holy places of the Abrahamic faiths and sacred sites of local and regional significance. This field is also related to the theory and practice of transposition of sacred space in ancient, late antique and medieval cultures (which could also mark, especially in the sphere of religious experience, the transfer of sanctity from a permanently sacred centre to a ritually sanctified place of temporary sacrality),[43] and the consequent 'Jerusalemization' of sacred spaces in Christendom.[44] The extension

39 See, for example, Abraham Malamat, 'The Sacred Sea' in Kedar and Werblowsky, *Sacred Space*, 45–54.

40 Doron Mendels, 'The Temple in the Hellenistic Period and in Judaism' in Kedar and Werblowsky, *Sacred Space*, 77.

41 Mendels, 'The Temple in the Hellenistic Period', 79.

42 R.J. Zwi Werblowsky, 'Introduction: Mindscape and Landscape' in Kedar and Werblowsky, *Sacred Space*, 14.

43 Jonathan Z. Smith, 'Constructing a Place' in Kedar and Werblowsky, *Sacred Space*, 24–5.

44 See, for example, the contributions in A. Lidov (ed.), *New Jerusalems. The Translations of Sacred Spaces in Christian Cultures/Novye Ierusalimy. Perenesenie sakralnykh prostranstv v. khristiianskoi kul'ture* (Indrik 2006).

of sanctity from the respective sacred place or cultic site to the city, area, landscape or the whole land in which it is located is also a phenomenon which is recurrently attested in Abrahamic religious contexts and merits further close investigation. Finally, the transfer of 'Holy Land' and 'Promised Land' vocabulary and imagery in the creation of the theoretical and practical territoriality of the 'secular sacred spaces' or 'hallowed lands' in modern nationalist ideologies (and their antecedents in medieval Christian political theologies)[45] has also been attracting increasing attention across a range of disciplines, ranging from religious history to political science.

Apart from this expanding research into the roots and *Nachleben* of Biblical models of holy space in the other Abrahamic faiths, investigation of such non-biblically derived models in normative, mystical and popular Christian and Muslim traditions has also been developing, enriching our understanding of the plurality of sources for the sacral spatial dimension in Christianity and Islam. Notwithstanding this growing and cross-disciplinary interest in this problematic, it has not developed sufficiently as yet for more detailed historical typologies of the use of sacred space in Judaism, Islam and Christianity to be proposed for scholarly debate. Furthermore, while remaining important for the disciplines of phenomenology and history of religions, the categories of sacred space and places rarely enjoy any currency in the analyses of religious behaviour coming from social anthropology and sociology of religion which have not been conducive to either inter-disciplinary investigation of the problematic or to enhancing its status within the study of religion. Indeed archaeologists, heritage experts, anthropologists and sociologists working respectively on the archaeology, heritage preservation and site management and intercommunal relations at sacred places frequently find it difficult to accept and employ, in the various concrete dimensions of their work, the theological and phenomenological definitions of and approaches to sacred space. Doubts about the usefulness and applicability of theological interpretations of holy space (with all the ensuing epistemological and ontological issues) in the various methodological frameworks have led to the adoption of more sociologically oriented interpretative perspectives on the spatial dimension of religion, further enriched by the abundant and diverse material accumulated in the last century by the multi-disciplinary study of sacred sites of non-Abrahamic world religions and indigenous peoples around the globe. Such perspectives usually draw on the sociological approach to and definition of sacrality of Émile Durkheim (1858–1917) in which it is a relational descriptive category referring to 'things set apart and forbidden',[46] whose quality of sacredness is not intrinsic but reflects the judgement of the respective group

45 For example, on the notion of 'Holy Russia' in pre-Petrine Russia as being centered on the Holy Land, both in terms of earthly geography and spiritual reality, see Richard M. Price, 'The Holy Land in Old Russian Culture' in R.N. Swanson (ed.), *The Holy Land, Holy Lands, and Christian Culture* (The Boydell Press 2000) 250–262.

46 Émile Durkheim, *The Elementary Forms of the Religious Life* (The Free Press 1967 [1912]) 62.

or society.[47] Being thus 'metaphysically neutral',[48] the Durkheimian sociological notion of sacrality has been seen by a number of archaeologists and anthropologists as a better classificatory and categorization tool in their work on material culture related to the archaeology and anthropology of religion and cult (especially in spheres such as the use of exclusive and inclusive space) or the restrictions on and regulations of human behaviour at sites set apart and separated from the surrounding landscape due to a special religious or other significance attached to them.[49]

It seems evident that the variety of concerns and methods in the existing theological, anthropological and sociological approaches to sacred sites display characteristic interpretative and methodological ambiguities which arise out of the multiple religious, spiritual, social and political functions ascribed to them in human societies and cultures. This highlights the need for a more inter-disciplinary approach which may balance these perspectives and complement the existing and emerging legal discourses, initiatives and guidelines regarding sacred space and sites and give them extra dimension and depth.

47 See the analysis of Durkheim's approach to and definition of the sacred in W. Paden, 'Before "the Sacred" Became Theological: Rereading the Durkheimian Legacy' [1991] *Method and Theory in the Study of Religion*, 10–23.

48 Paden, 'Before "the Sacred" Became Theological', 16.

49 See, for example, Jane Hubert, 'Sacred Beliefs and Beliefs of Sacredness' in David L. Carmichael, Jane Hubert, Brian Reeves and Audhild Schanche (eds), *Sacred Sites, Sacred Places* (Routledge, 1994) 8–19.

Chapter 4
General Problems of International Law Concerning Sacred Places[1]

Umberto Leanza

Introduction

Throughout history, members of various communities all the world over have often associated a particular significant historical or allegorical event that occurred in the past with a particular site. Such a site was regarded as holy and was venerated in shared rites and traditions passed from generation to generation. This explains why members of local communities have long since been competing with one another over the possession, conditions of access to and worship rights over holy places.

All the holy places – such as Jerusalem, the Vatican, Mecca, Mount Athos and the Orthodox holy places of Kosovo – of the three main monotheistic religions have a very complex and articulated history which is often marked by the exercise of sovereign functions by different powers succeeding each other in the control of the territory where these holy places are located. But the foundation of nation-states in Europe, the colonisation of entire continents by most of the European States, the collapse of the Ottoman Empire after the First World War and lastly the decolonisation process starting from the Second World War gave a new dimension to claims of sovereignty over some holy places, while these claims became stronger and stronger.

---

1 This study aims at identifying the main aspects and the most immediate problems of each holy place and tries to trace out some ideas for a possible solution. It is the result of the work of a research group coordinated by Professor Umberto Leanza – former Professor of International Law at the University of Rome 'Tor Vergata' and now *Jean Monnet* Chair at the II University of Naples. The research group is composed of Professor David Attard, University of Malta; Professor Mariano Aznar, University of Castellòn (Spain); and Professor Ida Caracciolo, II University of Naples. On account of Professor Sico's unexpected demise, Professor Talitha Vassalli di Dachenhausen of the University of Naples 'Federico II' has joined the group. Ms Stefania Lucente, Ph.D. student at the II University of Naples, has helped in researching the legal documentation. Concerning the organization of the research within the group, Professor Leanza is responsible for the analysis of multilateral agreements of a universal character; Professor Attard is responsible for the analysis of bilateral agreements; Professor Aznar is responsible for the analysis of multilateral agreements at the European level; Professor Caracciolo is responsible for the analysis of unilateral State acts and decisions; and Professor Vassalli is responsible for historical reconstruction.

In particular the general acceptance of the concept of the full sovereignty of the State within its territory and the recognition of the right to self-determination of any population under an alien or racial sway gave, and gives, rise to opposite actions: on the one hand the maintenance of the acquired sovereignty and on the other hand the effort to gain self-government and thus to revolt against the territorial State.

For some holy places – where these two opposite tendencies occur – this situation logically undermines opportunities to reach an accepted solution by the parties concerned. Similarly at risk are attempts to establish *ad hoc* regimes not based on the principle of sovereignty but, on the contrary, on some kinds of self-government or self-administration in order to guarantee free access to and free utilisation of the holy places as well as freedom of religion.

Framework, Structure and Aim of this Chapter

This chapter aims to analyse the existing regime for each holy place, namely the Vatican, Mount Athos, Mecca (or Makka), the holy places of Kosovo and Jerusalem in the light of international law.

Secondly, the study will ascertain whether the existing regimes present some grey areas and, if this is the case, it will deal with such specific legal problems and their consequences for peaceful relations within a certain geographic area or for international peace and security.

Thirdly, this chapter will envisage possible solutions (either a single solution or different ones, given the particular problems on the ground) which may allow a holy place to maintain and develop its religious function and eventually to help pacification between different ethnic or religious groups. These solutions could be based on existing international agreements. This seems to be the easiest solution, especially when the contrasts on a certain holy place are particularly intense. The possibility of suggesting new provisions cannot anyway be excluded.

Holy Places and International Law *de jure condendo*

Today contemporary international law requires – less by means of consuetudinary laws and very much via multilateral agreements – a series of limits to state sovereignty in order to protect some values that are considered fundamental by the international community, such as human rights, the environment or the common heritage of humankind. These 'new' limits to state sovereignty indirectly provide 'stronger' protection for the holy places from various viewpoints that belong to the reasoning behind these limitations of sovereignty.

As holy places are places where religious faith is expressed, the international protection of human rights, and among these of freedom of religion, is significant. The objective of guaranteeing that these holy places can continue to exercise their high religious function is pursued by means of these rights.

It is well known that at the universal level the 1948 Universal Declaration of Human Rights (whose consuetudinary scope is now agreed) and the 1966 International Covenant on Civil and Political Rights, and some agreements at the regional level such as the 1950 European Convention on Human Rights, recognise and defend not only freedom of religion but also the right to manifest one's religion or belief in teaching, practice, worship and observance whether individually and collectively, in public or in private.

Scholars unanimously recognise that there are no interpretative doubts as regards the meaning of freedom of religion, although uncertainty may arise regarding the so-called neighbouring rights, such as respect for the freedom of assembly or freedom of association. Beyond that, however, it is evident that respect of religious freedom is the responsibility of the territorial State. This means that such respect can be jeopardised when the State's attitude favours a limitative interpretation of religious freedom (for example, bearing in mind reasons connected to national security), or where religious freedom is violated.

In situations of this type it is therefore necessary to provide ad hoc regimes with more or less intense limitations on the sovereignty of the territorial State in order to guarantee a more autonomous regime for the holy places.

In holy places monuments have often been built over the centuries to praise and worship God. Many provide great examples of human ingenuity, and they are representative of a fundamental cultural phase of architecture, painting and so on.

This type of cultural heritage is often protected by the 1972 UNESCO Convention concerning the Protection of the World Cultural and Natural Heritage, which establishes a regime of protection through the inscription of the heritage sites on a special list. The territorial State is responsible for any UNESCO World Cultural and Natural Heritage site within its borders and has a series of obligations to preserve and protect the site so that it can be handed down to the future generations (without excluding the State's right of enjoyment of the site). These obligations are carefully monitored by the UNESCO World Heritage Committee. Alongside these obligations there are important mechanisms of financial aid for the territorial State.

It is significant that Jerusalem (in 1982), the painted churches of the Cyprus region of Troodos (in 1985), Mount Athos (in 1988), the Vatican (in 1988–1900) and some monasteries in Kosovo – such as the Dečani Monastery (in 2004–06) – and the Church of the Nativity of Jesus Christ and the Pilgrim's Route (in 2012) were all inserted in the system of protection provided for by the Convention of 1972 and they can therefore today be considered as World Heritage sites. At the same time, however, it seems clear that the religious significance of such sites in relation to their insertion on the list is virtually nil: when Jerusalem was included, one of the reasons mentioned was its importance for some lifestyles. Religious faith has thus been reduced to a 'lifestyle' with implicit reference to the three great monotheistic religions.

However, UNESCO today also protects intangible cultural heritage and cultural diversity, through the Conventions of 2003 and of 2005 respectively. Even though these two agreements do not expressly safeguard religions as such (through the express will of excluding them from the legal provision) the agreements are nevertheless suitable for protecting some manifestations of religious faith that are culturally felt as bonds for a certain human community (for instance, a type of religious procession that has been held for centuries on certain anniversaries or forms of transmission of religious faith). Here too, then, a certain – albeit indirect – protection is provided to holy places by means of religions that express themselves in such places or through the ways in which the religious faith and its transmission is manifested.

Finally, it is necessary to remember that this regime, specific to peacetime, is supported by an international system of protection of cultural heritage in time of war which is expressed in the 1954 Hague Convention and its protocols – the last of which was adopted in 1999. The aim of this 1999 Protocol is to reinforce the mechanisms of protection already in force, which is completed with the incrimination as a war crime (by international consuetudinary law) of the intentional destruction of religious buildings (1907 Hague Convention IV). In this regard, the Vatican, with Italy's full consent, was inserted on the – very limited – list of heritage that enjoys special protection under the terms of the 1954 Convention on protecting cultural heritage during armed conflicts.

It is a pity, however, that the destruction of religious buildings in order to annihilate wholly or in part a national, ethnic, racial or religious group is not expressed as a crime of genocide according to the Convention on Genocide of 1948. Indeed this possibility was explicitly excluded, as emerges from the work preparatory to the Protocol.

Such protection prohibiting the destruction of religious buildings, among others, whose violation entails responsibility for war crimes, exists not only in the case of international armed conflicts, but also for internal armed conflicts which today are more numerous. It seems evident that also this regime for times of war contributes towards protecting holy places, as religious heritage, placing them outside military objectives and providing for the graver responsibility of the State ordering the attack and of the agents of the attack.

Description of the Existing Legal Situations of Holy Places and Identification of Recurrent Legal Problems

For the abovementioned reasons, contemporary international law does not provide for a common or unique regime for holy places. Therefore some heterogeneous solutions have been found to guarantee freedom of access to the holy places and freedom of religion. In some cases the regime of a holy place is determined by a bilateral agreement between the relevant religious entity and the territorial State concerned, in other cases by unilateral determinations and the following internal rules and regulations discretionally adopted by the territorial State concerned.

In this context the absence of regimes established by multilateral agreements or by international organisations resolutions – either regional or universal – has to be underlined. At this level few results have been attained and just several proposals have been put forward towards the adoption of a specific regime for holy places. Therefore some general rules contained in several multilateral agreements, already in force, can be easily applicable to holy places, reducing the risk of lacunae.

The Vatican

The creation of the current Vatican State descends from the Lateran Treaty of 11 February 1929, between the Kingdom of Italy and the Holy See. The treaty settled the question of the relations between Italy and the Holy See. Known as the Roman Question, this problem arose in 1870 when the newly formed kingdom of Italy annexed the Papal State. In 1871 the Italian government granted to Pope Pius IX and his successors the use of the Vatican and the Lateran palaces as well as a yearly income of 3,250,000 Lira as indemnity for the loss of sovereignty and territory. The Church, claiming the necessity for independence from any political power in its exercise of spiritual jurisdiction, rejected this settlement, and popes thereafter considered themselves prisoners in the Vatican, a small, limited area inside Rome.

Negotiations for the settlement of the Roman Question began in 1926 between the government of Italy and the Holy See, and in 1929 they culminated in an agreement known as the Lateran Treaty, signed on behalf of King Victor Emmanuel III of Italy by Prime Minister Benito Mussolini and on behalf of Pope Pius XI by Pietro Cardinal Gasparri, Papal Secretary of State. These agreements included a political treaty, the so-called Conciliation Treaty, which created the State of the Vatican City and guaranteed full and independent sovereignty to the Holy See. The Pope was pledged to perpetual neutrality in international affairs and to abstention from mediation except when specifically requested by all parties to a dispute. Also agreed on were a Concordat establishing Roman Catholicism as Italy's official religion and a financial arrangement awarding a monetary compensation to the Holy See as a way to settle all its claims against Italy arising from the loss of temporal power in 1870. In 1984 a revised treaty was signed, the so-called Villa Madama Agreement that, among other things, ended the Church's status as the State-supported religion of Italy.

Concerning sovereignty, with Article 3 of the Conciliation Treaty Italy recognizes the full ownership and the sovereign authority and jurisdiction of the Holy See over the Vatican, whose boundaries are set forth in a map called Annex I. As a consequence, Article 4 forbids any intervention in the Vatican City on the part of the Italian government, or any authority other than that of the Holy See. Moreover, under Article 12 Italy recognizes the right of the Holy See to passive and active legation, according to the general rules of international law and all privileges and immunities. Relating to passive legation, foreign diplomats accredited to the Holy See have privileges and immunities recognized by Italy within the Italian territory. But full sovereignty is also recognized towards individuals. As a matter of fact all persons having permanent residence within the

Vatican City are subject to the sovereignty of the Holy See (Article 9). Specific provisions concern the cooperation in judicial matters, the protection of the Pontiff and the status of cardinals.

At the same time the two Contracting Parties undertake to establish normal diplomatic relations with each other, by accrediting an Italian ambassador to the Holy See and a Papal Nuncio to Italy, who is the doyen of the diplomatic corps.

According to Article 24, the Holy See can exercise its sovereignty in international matters, but it shall not take part in any temporal rivalries between other States, nor in any international congresses, save and except in the event of such parties making a mutual appeal to the pacific mission of the Holy See. The Vatican City has to be considered as a neutral and inviolable territory.

Concerning properties and their regime, they shall enjoy, according to the treaty, the status of extraterritoriality (Articles 13–16). Some of these properties are: the Basilica of St John Lateran (*Basilica di San Giovanni in Laterano*); the Basilica of St Mary Major (*Basilica di Santa Maria Maggiore*); the Lateran Palace, university and adjoining buildings; certain buildings on the Gianicolo Hill, among them the Bambino Gesù Hospital; some ancient palaces in Rome; some areas and buildings outside Rome: the Pontifical Palace, in the town of Castel Gandolfo, and the area of Santa Maria di Galeria, where the antennas of Radio Vaticana are located. The area was donated by Italy to the Holy See in the 1950s. Each of those two areas is actually larger than the Vatican City itself. Three basilicas outside Rome have been ceded to the Holy See but they do not enjoy any extraterritorial status according to Article 27 of the Concordat. These are the Basilica of the Holy House at Loreto; the Basilica of St Francis at Assisi and the Basilica of St Anthony at Padua.

It should be remembered that the Fundamental Agreement, signed in 1993, grants the Holy See functional sovereign rights over various Christian holy sites in Israel. This agreement is nowadays in course of renegotiation.

Concerning the use of the holy areas within the Vatican City, first of all, freedom of access to the Vatican City has been fully recognized for St Peter's Square which continues to be normally open to the public and is subject to supervision by the Italian police authorities. But should the Holy See consider it necessary to temporarily prohibit the public from free access to St Peter's Square, for the purpose of special ceremonies, the Italian authorities must withdraw beyond the outer lines of Bernini's Colonnade and the extension thereof (Article 3). The artistic and scientific treasures existing within the Vatican City and the Lateran Palace are open to scholars and visitors, although the Holy See is free to regulate the admission of the public thereto (Article 17). Secondly, the territory forming the Vatican City is free from any charge and from possible occupants.

At the same time, Italy provides for an adequate water supply to the Vatican City; for connection with the State railways; for direct connection with other States by means of telegraph, telephone, wireless, broadcasting and postal services in the Vatican City (Article 5). In accordance with the provisions of international law, it is also forbidden for aircraft of any kind whatsoever to fly over Vatican territory (Article 7). The goods arriving from abroad for destinations within the Vatican City, or outwith its boundaries for institutions or offices of the Holy See, are allowed transit over Italian territory free of payment of any customs (Article 20).

At the same time, the Concordat – signed in 1929 together with the Conciliation Treaty – regulates religious aspects, and all its provisions are centred on the recognition of free exercise by the Catholic Church of its spiritual power to be guaranteed also by the duty for Italy to impede in Rome whatsoever may be inconsistent with its status of centre of the Catholic world and place of pilgrimage (Article 1). That means again freedom of access to the Holy places in Rome and the full exercise of the religious functions of the Catholic Church without any interference by the Italian government. Very detailed provisions regulate the status of ecclesiastics and ecclesiastical entities (Articles 2–8, and Article 29). Other provisions concern the effect of religious marriages in Italy and the teaching of the Catholic religion in schools (Articles 34–7).

The Villa Madama Agreement of 1984 does not change this situation substantially. It renews the statement of the full sovereignty and reciprocal independence of both Italy and the Catholic Church, and the recognition of the function of evangelization of the Catholic Church in the world and all related freedoms (Articles 1 and 2). On these bases some changes were introduced in the specific discipline of marriages and in the treatment of ecclesiastical entities.

The aforementioned discipline descending from bilateral agreements was incorporated into the Constitution of the Italian Republic in 1947. The Constitution recognises a specific legal character to the Lateran Treaty and consequently does not consider it as an ordinary international treaty. The same provisions were inserted in the basic rules of the Vatican City State (Fundamental Law of 7 June 1929 replaced some years ago by the Fundamental Law of 26 November 2000). Furthermore, the rules of the Vatican City State often make reference to the Lateran Treaty, as it contains the basic framework provisions for this State in connection with Italy.

Other agreements regulate various aspects and matters concerning the relations between Italy and the Holy See.

More recently, in 2001, the European Union concluded a monetary convention with the Vatican City State in order to adapt the existing regime to the entry into force of the European Monetary Union. In particular the Convention was stipulated by Italy on behalf of the European Union. The European Commission and the European Central Bank were associated in the negotiations. According to this agreement Euros can be utilised as official currency within the territory of the Vatican City State and it can issue Euros, having legal circulation within the European Monetary Union.

Lastly, in 1988–1990 the Vatican was registered in the World Cultural Heritage List.

In conclusion, the bilateral system that regulates the status of the Catholic holy places in Italy can be considered a good solution, taking into account two elements: on the one hand, the geographical situation of the Vatican City State as an *enclave* State within the Italian territory, so that the duty to guarantee its independence and freedom of exercise of the high functions of the Catholic Church can rest only on

Italy; and on the other hand, the fact that the Vatican holy places are situated in a State like Italy where the dominant religion is Catholicism and which has a fully Catholic tradition. This latter aspect enables the system to function well. Therefore the necessity to enlarge the legal basis of the discipline at the multilateral level does not actually exist.

Mount Athos

The administration of the Holy Mountain throughout its centuries-long history, from the time when monastic life there was officially organised by the issuing of the Typikon of the Byzantine Emperor John Tsimiskes in 972 down to the present, has always been governed by a *sui generis* political and ecclesiastical arrangement. This can be seen very clearly from imperial chrysobulls (decrees) and 'Typika', Patriarchal sigillia (documents), the firmans of Sultans, the 'General Regulations' of the Ecumenical Patriarchate and all subsequent legislation.

Nowadays, by virtue of the Treaties of Neuilly of 1919 (Articles 42–7), Sèvres of 1920 (Article 27) and Lausanne of 1923 (Article 2), Greek sovereignty over Mount Athos officially replaced Bulgarian sovereignty. All that remained was to settle Greece's relations with the Holy Mountain and to draw up an internal arrangement for the administration of the monastic community. Some years later, in 1925 the Charter for the Holy Mountain of Athos was adopted. It was originally drafted by a five-member committee in May 1924 and was adopted by the Extra-ordinary Double Synaxis of the twenty Ruling Monasteries. It was then submitted to the Greek government which, after deferring it for further elaboration to a special committee that took into account the amendments proposed by the Ecumenical Patriarchate, proceeded to its ratification by the Legislative Decree of 10–16 September 1926. This decree contains other provisions regulating the organisation, the administration and the exercise of justice on the Holy Mountain.

To sum up, the 'Charter for the Holy Mountain of Athos' codifies regulations and administrative dispositions stemming not only from written sources but also from tradition and custom. This is the case of: i) the provisions of imperial chrysobulls, the Patriarchal sigillia, the Firmans of the sultans and so on which have not been rescinded by the Charter; ii) the provisions of the Extra-ordinary Twenty-Member Synaxis. These provisions are issued following relevant delegation by the Greek government, but in order to enter into force they have first to be submitted to the Governor of the Holy Mountain and then be ratified by the Minister of Foreign Affairs, unless such provisions deal with matters of a purely spiritual nature, in which case they are submitted to the Ecumenical Patriarchate for approval; iii) the Internal Regulations of the monasteries and sketes (monastic settlements), which are approved by the Holy Community and the Ruling Monasteries, provided, of course, that they are not inconsistent with the provisions of the Charter of the Holy Mountain; and iv) customs which have not been abolished.

While these rules were incorporated into Greek legislation, the general principles governing the status of Mount Athos were incorporated into the 1927

Greek Constitution. Today, Article 105 of the Greek Constitution of 1975/1986, currently in force, reproduces the contents of existing provisions on the status of Mount Athos.

Therefore, concerning sovereignty, according to Article 105, the Mount Athos peninsula – extending beyond Megali Vigla and constituting the region of Aghion Oros – is subject to Greek sovereignty but, in accordance with its ancient privileged status, is a self-governed part of the Greek State.

But Greek sovereignty is limited by some conditions; first of all the prohibition of any expropriation. Secondly, the administration of all the monasteries is attributed to their representatives constituting the Holy Community.

At the same time, freedom of religion – referred to through the word 'spiritually' in Article 105 – is subject to the direct jurisdiction of the Ecumenical Patriarchate. All people leading a monastic life thereon acquire Greek citizenship without further formalities, upon admission as novices or monks. Administrative aspects of the life within the monasteries are under the supervision of the Greek State.

Concerning the internal administration of Mount Athos, the Holy Mountain is administered – according to the status which it enjoys – by the twenty Ruling Monasteries, among which the whole of the Mount Athos Peninsula, whose territory is not subject to expropriation, is divided up.

These monasteries are termed 'Ruling' not only because this is the name which they are given on the Holy Mountain and because they govern themselves in accordance with their own Internal Regulations, but because subject to them are all the dependencies on the Holy Mountain. They are called 'Royal and Patriarchal' because they were either founded or they were put under the protection of kings or patriarchs, and 'Stavropegic' because a cross sent by the Ecumenical Patriarchate is located in them. Thus the monasteries are ranked in a hierarchical order, which cannot be changed. It should be underlined that one monastery is Serbian and another one is Bulgarian.

The administration is carried out by representatives of the monasteries, who make up the Holy Community. The Holy Community of the Holy Mountain, which has its seat at Karyes, is a permanent body which consists of a representative of each of the twenty Ruling Monasteries. These representatives are elected by the monasteries from which they come in accordance with their Internal Regulations, at the latest within the first two weeks of the month of January every year. Candidates for the office of representative must be drawn from among the brothers of the monastery, be at least 30 years of age and be known for the blamelessness of their lives, preference always being given to those with theological training and a general education. Their term of office is one year, but this may be extended if their monastery re-elects them. The Holy Community meets in regular session three times a week, and in extraordinary session as the need arises.

No change is allowed in the system of administration or in the number of the monasteries, nor in their rank in the hierarchy or their position in regard to their dependencies. It is prohibited for heterodox or schismatics to live on the Holy Mountain.

The detailed determination of the Athonite institutions and of the manner of their operation is settled by the Charter of the Holy Mountain which, in consultation with the representative of the State, is drawn up and voted for by the twenty Ruling Monasteries and ratified by the Ecumenical Patriarchate and the Greek parliament.

The observance of Athonite institutions is, in spiritual matters, under the supreme supervision of the Ecumenical Patriarchate and, in administrative matters, under the supervision of the State, which is exclusively responsible for the maintenance of public order and security. The abovementioned powers of the State are exercised by a governor, whose rights and duties are determined by law. Also determined by law is judicial power, exercised by the monastic authorities and the Holy Community, as well as the customs and tax privileges enjoyed by the Holy Mountain (Article 105 of the 1975/86 Constitution).

Thus, by virtue of this provision of the Constitution, two administrative authorities must coexist on the Holy Mountain: a civil administrative authority and a monastic administrative authority. To the first belongs the Governor of the Holy Mountain, who is appointed by a Legislative Decree originating from the Minister for Foreign Affairs, under whose jurisdiction he/she is placed. The Governor's supervision extends not only to those matters which concern public order and security, but also to the observance of the Charter of the Holy Mountain. He/she also draws the attention of the Holy Community to infringements committed by any monastic authority on the Holy Mountain. In the exercise of these duties, the Governor comes into contact with the Holy Community and the other monastic authorities by correspondence. In the event of his absence or of some impediment to the performance of his duties, his secretary acts for him. The Governor is also responsible for the work carried out by the officials within his jurisdiction, that is, the police force and the Governor's staff in the execution of the decisions of the Holy Community and of the monastic authorities (Articles 3–5, Legislative Decree 10/16 September 1926).

The individual administrative organs and the collective organs of each of the twenty Ruling Monasteries are subject to the monastic administrative authority, with a view to safeguarding the self-administration which the Holy Mountain enjoys. The general administrative organs of the Holy Mountain are the Holy Community, the Holy Epistasia and the Extra-ordinary Twenty-Member Synaxis.

In earlier times, these monasteries were divided into 'coenobitic' and 'idiorrhythmic', depending upon the way they were organised and administered. Today they continue not only to govern themselves, in accordance with the provisions of their Internal Regulations which are adopted by the monasteries themselves and ratified by the Holy Community (the supervisory authority), but also to manage their own property and financial affairs. Today, all the monasteries of the Holy Mountain, with no exception, are coenobia.

The particular status of Mount Athos is dealt with by a joint declaration annexed to the Final Act of the Treaty of Accession of Greece to the European Community. This Joint Declaration gives relevance to this status at the European level by recognizing it and assuring that Member States will take it into consideration due to its spiritual and religious nature. An analogous joint declaration concerning Mount Athos was delivered at the time of the Greek signature of the Schengen Agreement of 1985 and the Convention of 1990, having the same contents as the previous one.

In 1988 Mount Athos was registered in the World Cultural Heritage List.

In conclusion, the status of Mount Athos is particularly well structured. On the one hand, it is characterized by Greek sovereignty under certain limitations. This sovereignty has been established by multilateral peace treaties after the First World War, when Greece replaced the Bulgarian Kingdom and the Ottoman Empire in exercising sovereign powers in certain territories. So it is based on a multilateral acceptance and recognition. This sovereignty has always been reiterated (also in the Greek constitutions) and the reason for this reiteration lies in the necessity to confirm and formalize it definitively to territories which were previously under the power of other States. On the other hand, to guarantee freedom of religion and in particular freedom of organization of the monastic life – according to ancient rules and customs developed along the centuries – a sort of administrative autonomy has been awarded to the twenty Ruling Monasteries of Mount Athos. The legal framework for this administrative autonomy is enshrined in internal rules or internal arrangements between the monastic entities and the Greek government. But these internal rules and arrangements were in a certain way 'communitarised' when Greece became a member of the European Community.

Mecca (or Makkah)

The most sacred place in Islam is the city of Mecca (or Makkah), which is located in the western part of Saudi Arabia about 121 kilometres inland from the port city of Jidda in the Hejaz province. Although it was clearly a sacred place for centuries before the time of Muhammad (c.570–632 C.E.) and includes the famous Ka'ba, a cube-shaped building said to have been built by the Hebrew patriarch Abraham and in whose south-eastern corner the venerated 'Black Stone' can be found, supposedly given to Abraham by the Angel Gabriel, the city's sacredness in Islam derives primarily from the fact that it was the Prophet's birthplace.

The revelations contained in the Koran include the 'Five Pillars of Islam', one of which asserts that every Muslim should make a pilgrimage, called the *hajj*, to Mecca at least once in his or her lifetime. Thus the city annually hosts two million Muslims from all over the world. Wearing a white robe called an *ihram*, the pilgrims are expected to circle the Ka'ba seven times, to run another seven times between two hills, Safa and Marwa, to spend from noon until sunset on a hill in the valley of Arafat, to throw stones at the devil in the valley of Mina and to sacrifice sheep and goats.

Since the time of King Abdulaziz (1876–1953), the Saudi monarchy has worked at the improvement and extension of the Mecca Holy Mosque and the Prophet Mosque to cope with the increasing numbers of pilgrims.

The full management of the holy places in Mecca is carried out by the Saudi government as the Custodian of the two Holy Mosques. It also oversees the printing of the Koran and gives top priority to initiatives to benefit Muslims all over the world. Actually it makes this kind of support available through specialized agencies established for this reason, namely the International Islamic Aid Agency, the International Islamic World Assembly, the Two Holy Mosques Establishment and the Saudi Agency for collecting the donations.

In particular, Article 24 of the Saudi Arabia Basic Law (a sort of constitution) states that it is up to the State to maintain and serve the two Holy Mosques. It must ensure the security and safety of all those who visit them so that they may be able to visit or perform the pilgrimage and 'Umrah' (minor pilgrimage) in comfort and ease.

Under Saudi law, non-Muslims are not permitted to enter Mecca. The Saudi government uses a verse of the Koran as confirmation for this law. According to this verse, non-Muslims must be prevented from entering Mecca as they are considered to be impure (Koran, 9:28).

In conclusion, in the case of Mecca we face a completely unilateral regime, deriving from the Basic Law of Saudi Arabia and the Koran. The situation is explained by the continuous control by Muslim powers (in the past and nowadays) over the holy places of Mecca and by the fact that Saudi Arabia still is a theocratic State where religious prescriptions are at the same time legal rules.

The Kosovar Monasteries

The medieval monasteries in Kosovo and Metohia represent the most notable example of the Orthodox culture of Serbs. The most ancient buildings are characterized by two styles: the Western Romanic and the Eastern Byzantine. Among them the most famous is the Monastery of Dečani, 12 kilometres outside Peć. Its cathedral is the biggest medieval church in the Balkan area and it has the biggest Byzantine fresco conserved up to recent times.

Until the humanitarian catastrophe in the second half of the 1990s, these monasteries did not have a special status within the Serbian State. The situation changed dramatically after 1999 with the deployment of NATO troops in the context of the peace-support operations known as KFOR to help maintain a safe and secure environment and freedom of movement for all citizens, irrespective of their ethnic origin. After NATO forces drove out Yugoslav troops amid deadly fighting with the majority ethnic Albanian population, the UN Interim Administration Mission (UNMIK) took over in 1999. It carries out many functions, including those related to the dialogue with Serbia on provisions concerning six areas: police, courts, customs, transport and infrastructure, boundaries and Serbian patrimony.

The recent independence of Kosovo, declared on 17 February 2008, changed the legal situation again. Following the declaration of independence, NATO reaffirmed that KFOR had to remain in Kosovo on the basis of UN Security Council Resolution 1244, unless the United Nations Security Council decides otherwise. In June 2008, NATO agreed to take on new tasks in Kosovo to support the development of professional, democratic and multi-ethnic security structures. Throughout Kosovo, NATO and KFOR continue to work with the authorities and, bearing in mind its operational mandate, KFOR cooperates with and assists the UN (UNMIK), the EU – in particular EULEX, the EU Rule of Law mission in Kosovo – and other international actors, as appropriate, to support the development of a stable, democratic, multi-ethnic and peaceful Kosovo.

Consequently the protection of monasteries of Kosovo still falls within the tasks of KFOR nowadays, even though some new provisions have been inserted into the new Constitution of Kosovo.

Initially, KFOR's mandate (based on UN Security Council Resolution (UNSCR) 1244 of 10 June 1999 and the Military-Technical Agreement (MTA) between NATO and the Federal Republic of Yugoslavia and Serbia) was put in place to deter renewed hostility and threats against Kosovo by Yugoslav and Serb forces; establish a secure environment and ensure public safety and order; demilitarize the Kosovo Liberation Army; support the international humanitarian effort; and coordinate with and support the international civil presence. KFOR's presence has been crucial in maintaining safety and security for all individuals and communities in Kosovo. Today, KFOR continues to contribute to maintaining a safe and secure environment in Kosovo for the benefit of all citizens.

In particular, KFOR's tasks initially included assistance with the return or relocation of displaced persons and refugees; reconstruction and demining; medical assistance; security and public order; security of ethnic minorities; protection of cultural heritage sites; border security; interdiction of cross-border weapons smuggling; implementation of a Kosovo-wide weapons, ammunition and explosives amnesty programme; weapons destruction; and support for the establishment of civilian institutions, law and order, the judicial and penal system, the electoral process and other aspects of the political, economic and social life of the province.

Special attention continues to be paid by KFOR to the protection of minorities. This includes the protection of cultural heritage sites such as monasteries and donations including food, clothes and school supplies.

The same task consisting of protection of cultural heritage led to the insertion of the Dečani Monastery in the World Cultural Heritage List of UNESCO in 2004. Following this registration, the Provisional UN administration for Kosovo (UNMIK) established a special UNMIK Reporting Zone in April 2005 around the Dečani Monastery where KFOR continues to control the existing road and where the municipal authorities have to take measures to protect the monastery in full conformity with the provisions contained in the UNESCO Convention of 1972.

The 2007 Proposal for the Settlement of Kosovo, which subsequently failed, paid particular attention to the protection of the cultural and religious heritage in Kosovo. In particular, under the Settlement, Kosovo would have no official religion. The Settlement provided also for the autonomy and protection of all religious denominations, their property and their sites; and for additional security and certain other forms of protection, rights, privileges and immunities, including guarantees against expropriation, full discretion in the management of their property, property reconstruction and access to their premises for orthodox monasteries.

To this end the Settlement stated that the international military presence would continue to provide security for the nine major Serbian religious and historic sites until a decision is made to transfer this responsibility to the Kosovo Police Service. Lastly, the Settlement established 45 protective zones around the most prominent churches and monasteries, as well as historical monuments, while a monitoring council with local and international participation was established to monitor and facilitate implementation of the Settlement.

Independence was declared by Kosovo in 2008 after a very exhaustive series of negotiations under which the aforementioned Settlement brokered by the UN Special Envoy failed to be agreed on because Serbia was not able to countenance the principle of Kosovo independence, even with the degree of international supervision and limitations envisaged in the UN Special Envoy's proposal.

Most of the provisions contained in the aforementioned Settlement have been accepted and therefore incorporated into the Constitution of the newly independent Kosovo. While this Constitution recognizes the full sovereignty of Kosovo, at the same time it has a duty to preserve the cultural and religious heritage (Articles 2 and 9). In other words the religious heritage is put under Kosovo's sovereignty but this State formally commits itself to protect it. It is evident that any real effort to protect this cultural heritage is fully discretionary for Kosovo except in the case of obligations internationally assumed. In this regard the insertion of the Dečani Monastery in the UNESCO List is very important because it grants to the UNESCO Committee for the World Cultural and Natural Heritage a sort of control on the fulfillment of the duty to protect.

Moreover Articles 38 and 39 of the Constitution recognize freedom of religion and the protection of religious autonomy and religious monuments. Therefore they aim at guaranteeing freedom of access to the holy places as well as freedom of use thereof.

In conclusion, the regime for holy places in Kosovo and Metohia, even though its roots are in a UN Security Council Resolution, appears to be slightly weak for various reasons. First of all, the contents of the regime have to be taken into consideration: a simple duty to preserve religious monuments and to maintain them in their current conditions and nothing more is different from what we have seen before for the Vatican or for Mount Athos. Secondly, it should be considered that no international binding instrument (either bilateral or multilateral) – except the UNESCO Convention of 1972 – establishes a discipline for these religious monuments meaning that the effectiveness of protection may be at risk. Thirdly, the situation in the field, after massive violations of human rights in a sort of ethnic cleansing, is very delicate and maybe only the deployment of KFOR can avert possible attacks or the destruction of the Orthodox monuments.

Jerusalem

The situation of Jerusalem is an exceptional one in that it is far from being solved due to the contemporary presence of different claims to sovereignty by Israel,

Jordan and the Palestinian Authority and, at the same time, the tentative solutions of the conflict between Israel and the Palestinian Authority drafted by the United Nations.

As is well known, in 1517 Jerusalem and its environs were conquered by the Ottoman Turks, who kept control of the area until 1917. During almost the entire Ottoman period Jerusalem remained a provincial, though religiously important, centre as it did not lie on the main trade route between Damascus and Cairo.

In 1917, after the Battle of Jerusalem, the British Army occupied the city and at the Conference of Lausanne in 1922 the League of Nations entrusted the United Kingdom with administering the Mandate for Palestine. The situation between Arabs and Jews in Palestine was not peaceful: in Jerusalem, in particular, riots occurred in 1920 and in 1929.

As the British Mandate for Palestine was expiring, the 1947 UN Partition Plan recommended 'the creation of a special international regime in the City of Jerusalem, constituting it as a *corpus separatum* under the administration of the United Nations'. The international regime (which also included the city of Bethlehem) was to remain in force for a period of ten years, whereupon a referendum was to be held in which the residents were to decide the future regime of their city.

However, this plan was not implemented as the 1948 war erupted, the British withdrew from Palestine and Israel declared its independence. Israel and Jordan concluded an Armistice Agreement, dividing Jerusalem into two parts. After the establishment of the State of Israel, Jerusalem was declared its capital. Jordan formally annexed East Jerusalem in 1950, subjecting it to Jordanian law. Only the United Kingdom and Pakistan formally recognized such annexation which, with regard to Jerusalem, was on a *de facto* basis. Jordan assumed control of the holy places in the Old City. Contrary to the terms of the agreement, Israelis were denied access to Jewish holy sites, many of which were desecrated. Jordan allowed only very limited access to Christian holy sites.

After Israel occupied East Jerusalem in the 1967 Six-Day War, access to Jewish and Christian holy sites was restored, while the Temple Mount remained under the jurisdiction of an Islamic *waqf*. The Moroccan Quarter, which was located adjacent to the Western Wall, was vacated and razed to make way for a plaza for those visiting the walls. Since the war, Israel has expanded the city's boundaries and established a ring of Jewish neighbourhoods on vacant land east of the Green Line.

However, the takeover of East Jerusalem met with international criticism. Following the passing of Israel's Jerusalem Law which declared Jerusalem, 'complete and united', capital of Israel, the UN Security Council passed a resolution that declared such a law 'a violation of international law' and requested all Member States to withdraw all remaining embassies from the city. The *status* of the city, and especially its Holy Places, remains a core issue in the Israeli-Palestinian conflict. Jewish settlers have taken over historic sites and built on land confiscated from Arabs in order to expand the Jewish presence in East Jerusalem, while prominent Islamic leaders have made claims that Jews have no historical connection to Jerusalem, alleging that the 2,500 year-old Western Wall was constructed as part of a mosque. Palestinian Arabs envisage East Jerusalem as the capital of a future Palestinian state and the city's borders have been the subject of bilateral talks.

It is interesting to focus on the international regime envisaged by the aforementioned UNGA Resolution 181.

Concerning the status of Jerusalem and its holy places, the Resolution considers them as a *corpus separatum* located neither in Israel, nor in Jordan. So it envisages a sort of *sui generis* regime strictly defined by international law and strictly subjected to international control. Therefore the Resolution excludes any form of State sovereignty in favour of an international regime.

In more detailed terms, this Resolution tries to maintain the *status quo* by providing that the existing rights in respect of holy places and religious buildings or sites shall not be denied or impaired and specifically recognises full liberty of access, visits and transit in the holy places, in conformity with existing rights, to all residents and citizens of another State and of the City of Jerusalem, as well as to aliens, without distinction as to nationality, subject to requirements of national security, public order and decorum. Similarly, freedom of worship is guaranteed in conformity with existing rights, subject to the maintenance of public order and decorum.

For the same reason, the Resolution states that the holy places and religious buildings or sites must be preserved with their sacred character. If at any time it appears to the government that any particular holy place, religious, building or site is in need of urgent repair, the government may call upon the community or communities concerned to carry out such repairs. The government may carry it out itself at the expense of the community or communities concerned if no action is taken within a reasonable time.

The Resolution deals with the problem of taxation, excluding any taxation in respect of any holy place, religious building or site which was exempt from taxation on the date of the creation of the State and provides that no change in the incidence of such taxation must be made which would either discriminate between the owners or occupiers of holy places, religious buildings or sites, or would place such owners or occupiers in a position less favourable in relation to the general incidence of taxation that existed at the time of the adoption of the UNGA's recommendations.

Moreover the Resolution recognises, *inter alia*, freedom of conscience and the free exercise of all forms of worship, subject only to the maintenance of public order and morals, the right of each community to maintain its own schools for the education of its own members in its own language and to prohibit any kind of discrimination between the inhabitants on the grounds of race, religion, language or sex.

Consequently, except as may be required for the maintenance of public order and good government, no measure must be taken to obstruct or interfere with the activity of religious or charitable bodies of all faiths or to discriminate against any representative or member of these bodies on the ground of his/her religion or nationality.

No expropriation of land owned by an Arab in the Jewish State (by a Jew in the Arab State) is allowed according to the Resolution except for public purposes. In all cases of expropriation full compensation as fixed by the Supreme Court shall be paid previous to dispossession.

The central figure within this system is the Governor, to be appointed by the Trusteeship Council and accountable to it. He/she must be selected on the basis of special qualifications and without regard to nationality. He/she cannot, however, be a citizen of either State in Palestine. The Governor represents the United Nations in Jerusalem and exercises on their behalf all powers of administration, including the conduct of external affairs. He/she is assisted by an administrative staff classed as international officers as per Article 100 of the Charter and chosen whenever practicable from the residents of the city and of the rest of Palestine on a non-discriminatory basis. A detailed plan for the organization of the administration of the city would have been submitted by the Governor to the Trusteeship Council and duly approved by it.

Concerning the holy places, the Governor of the City of Jerusalem has the right to determine whether the provisions of the Constitution of the State in relation to holy places, religious buildings and sites within the borders of the State and the religious rights appertaining thereto are being properly applied and respected, and to make decisions on the basis of existing rights in cases of disputes which may arise between the different religious communities or the rites of a religious community with respect to such places, buildings and sites. He/she must receive full cooperation and such privileges and immunities as are necessary for the exercise of his functions in the State.

It is well known that the Resolution has never been applied and that the International Peace Conference of Madrid in 1993 did not reach any solution on the regime of Jerusalem. As a matter of fact the Conference excluded this aspect from negotiations.

In this context, Jerusalem was registered in the UNESCO World Cultural Heritage List in 1982 following a request for registration advanced by Jordan. Further, Jerusalem is not registered under either the Jordanian or Israeli cultural heritage.

For its part, the Holy See concluded agreements with Israel (on December 30, 1993) and the Palestinian Authority (on 15 February 2000) respectively to protect the rights of Catholics.

The effective management and control of the holy places in Jerusalem is carried out, therefore, by the Israeli government which adopted the Protection of holy places Law in 1967 and nowadays the sovereignty on the holy places in Jerusalem is exercised by Israel. The aim of the 1967 law is to criminalize certain actions in order to protect the holy places from desecration and any other violation and from anything likely to violate freedom of access to members of different religions to the places that are sacred to them or their feelings.

Among the various regimes concerning holy places, the most problematic has always been Jerusalem, mainly because it has become an important component of the more general problem of self-determination and independence in the light of international law. But this problem is also connected with ethnic, cultural and religious differences. If other regimes seem to work positively, the situation of holy places in Jerusalem is at odds with any form of peaceful coexistence and it represents a risk in the maintenance of peace and international security.

Some Preliminary Reflections on a New Legal Framework for the Regulation of Holy Places

From the viewpoint of international law, the main weakness of the legal choices on the status of holy places consists of their fragmentation and diversity (those in force and those not yet in force), so determining quite different legal regimes holy placeeven though all holy places perform the same role of places of worship. It should also be noted that these differences depend on the different contexts of each holy place and that diversified regimes can better take into account the particular features and problems of each one. What proposals can be put forward by an international lawyer, bearing in mind, most importantly, the unresolved and disputed situation of the holy places in Jerusalem and the risk of new ethnic conflicts over the control of the Orthodox monasteries in Kosovo?

Several solutions can be envisaged. The best one in terms of the effectiveness and incisiveness of the regime is certainly that of arriving at bilateral agreements between the interested States as regards freedom of access and forms of shared management of the sites themselves in order to guarantee religious freedom. The achievement of these bilateral agreements is by no means simple. It should come about via the diplomatic mediation of the United Nations or of the European Union, organizations that could also assume the role of 'guaranteeing powers' for the respect of the obligations. The 'guaranteeing powers' should monitor their observance to prevent the bilateral agreements from giving rise in the future to forms of 'creeping sovereignty' that could lead to further territorial and/or inter-ethnic conflicts.

An alternative would be a multilateral agreement whose purpose would be the specific protection of holy places and sites, in virtue of their full religious significance. On the theoretical level, holy place international law serving these holy places would act as mediator between claims to sovereignty, claims to self-determination, the right to religious freedom and the protection of religious heritage which would culminate above all as cultural heritage. On the practical level, this objective would be achieved only by protecting the following: the integrity of the holy places and sites; their enjoyment; their holy character; the freedom to administrate them; the bonds between believers, holy places and places of worship; and the resolution of conflicts regarding the use of holy places and sites.

From this standpoint, the internationalization of the holy places and sites would appear to be the preferable solution. Nevertheless, internationalization would entail the choice of the regime to be applied to that heritage only from those that already exist – which are not suitable for holy places and sites. An alternative option is the definition of a new regime whose application would be entrusted to an international organization or to a body with a high spiritual profile. The idea of establishing a sort of common general regime for the entire category of holy places should be taken into consideration. As a matter of fact, it is worth considering if a good solution would be to define the category of holy places by determining their features and characteristics, and establishing a common regime for them. This common regime could be the basis either for the development of more precise and detailed regimes for each holy place or for the completion of the existing regimes, thus avoiding any *lacunae legis*. Therefore, a solution could be the drafting of a new multilateral treaty under the auspices of UNESCO, dedicated to the protection of holy places. In fact, if we consider that none of the UNESCO Conventions deals with religious heritage expressly, it seems possible to cover this gap via a new conventional instrument.

But at the same time this solution could prove very hard to pursue. The debates on the concept of religion during the negotiation of the UNESCO Convention on Intangible Cultural Heritage of 2003 are still fresh in our minds and they remind us of the different opinions of States on the subject. Moreover the consequences, on a political level, stemming from the inclusion of a place in the category of holy places can be wide-ranging and can alter a certain fragile balance of powers. And, finally, what about the regime? Would it be a regime to protect the buildings and the surrounding areas or a regime to protect certain religious customs and practices? In this case there is the risk of opening a Pandora's Box.

So do different solutions seem more persuasive? According to this approach, the concept of the common heritage of mankind and, in particular, the concept of world cultural heritage could be applied to holy places as outlined by the UNESCO Convention of 1972, without any formal treaty modification. In favour of this solution there is also the fact that all the above-examined holy places – except Mecca – are already included in the World Cultural Heritage List under the UNESCO Convention of 1972.

This solution could be a development of the 'New Global Strategy' adopted by UNESCO in 1994 in order to broaden the definition of World Heritage to better reflect the full spectrum of the world's cultural and natural treasures and to provide for a comprehensive framework and operational methodology for implementing the World Heritage Convention. This new vision goes beyond the narrow definition of heritage and strives to recognise and protect sites that are outstanding demonstrations of human coexistence with the land as well as human interactions, cultural coexistence, spirituality and creative expression. This broad definition would also include those sites whose monumental impact is not particularly evident, but which testify to the fundamental steps of human coexistence, or of particularly tragic moments in human history. In this way, for example, inclusion in the list was justified for Auschwitz Birkenau, a German Nazi Concentration and Extermination Camp (which is without architectural merit but which is of enormous significance) and for the Island of Le Morne, which signifies the period of the slave trade. Nevertheless, in recent years this practice by the World Heritage Committee has been criticised. This practice is – rightly – considered as a deviation from the objectives of the 1972 Convention. At the same time, as it is a stratagem, it reduces the symbolic impact of the heritage, which in some way has to be 'disguised' as a monument.

More specifically, the drafting and the adoption of a single protocol on holy places as cultural heritage can be proposed. As an alternative to this, the adoption of various protocols – one for each holy place – could be suggested. One or more protocols could provide for a more complete and detailed regime for holy places than that already established by the UNESCO Convention of 1972 itself. As is well known, the regime under the aforementioned Convention is quite weak and is very respectful of States' sovereignty since the main duty of States Parties is to maintain all cultural and natural heritage sites/places registered on the List and to endeavour by all appropriate means, and in particular by educational and information programmes, to strengthen appreciation and respect by their peoples. At the same time States have to keep the public broadly informed and to report to the World Heritage Committee any dangers threatening this heritage as well as the activities carried out in pursuance of this Convention.

In particular the protocol(s) could set the rules on access, use and protection of every holy place and, if necessary, could also establish a responsible body (for example a board or council) to guarantee public security and public order as well as the administration of the single holy place.

The regime could be applicable both in times of peace and in war. UNESCO should be the competent UN agency but it is also possible to envisage a role for the European Union and/or the United Nations. The role of a 'Protecting Power' could also be considered – taking inspiration from the past and in particular from the law of armed conflicts. This Power could be called upon to guarantee and monitor the respect of the engagements assumed. This role could also be played by an *inter partes* entity, such as the Order of Malta, especially as far as the protection of the Christian holy places in Jerusalem is concerned.

Another solution, which might be even easier to achieve than the others would be to broaden the application Guidelines of the 1972 UNESCO Convention, as these Guidelines are periodically changed. It would be possible to insert into these Guidelines a 'Global Strategy on holy places and sites' whose aim would be to guarantee the full recognition of their specific values and build stronger specific protection. This solution would be lesser than the others, but it would certainly be more immediate.

Finally, the most ambitious objective would be to guarantee freedom of access to holy places, their special function, freedom of religion, the safeguarding of these places for future generations and the peaceful coexistence between local communities and pilgrims.

Chapter 5

Finding a Grammar of Consent for 'Soft Law' Guidelines on Sacred Places: The Legal Protection of Sacred Places within the Existing Public International Law Instruments and Grass-root Approaches[1]

Peter Petkoff

> But will God indeed dwell on the earth? Behold, the heaven and heaven of heavens cannot contain thee; how much less this house that I have builded?
>
> 1 Kings 8:27, KJB

Introduction

There are multiple legal tools under international law designed to define sacred places, to protect their physical integrity, their function and freedom of access to them. Yet, very few of these tools have proved particularly successful in protecting such places, nor has an attempt been made to elaborate a comprehensive public policy for their protection which integrates rather than isolates these different tools. This chapter explores the benefits of developing a soft law approach[2] to the

1 An expanded version of this chapter is published in *Law and Justice* [2011] 167, 24

2 Soft law instruments range from treaties, which include only soft obligations ('legal soft law'), to non-binding or voluntary resolutions and codes of conduct formulated and accepted by international and regional organisations ('non-legal soft law'), to statements prepared by individuals in a non-governmental capacity but which purport to lay down international principles. The Universal Declaration of the Rights of Peoples, adopted 4 July 1976, for example, was drafted and adopted not by States but by eminent international lawyers from diverse legal cultures. Section 3 of this Declaration is on economic rights and includes rights to permanent sovereignty, the common heritage of mankind, equity in international trade and the right of peoples to choose freely their own path to development. A number of definitions of soft law have been suggested. Some writers refer only to norms in hard law form, usually a treaty but with vague or weak requirements, and characterize this as 'legal soft law', while others concentrate on instruments in non-legal form, for example resolutions of international organisations and codes of conduct, termed 'non-legal soft law'. For the purposes of this chapter the author refers to soft law in the sense of

protection of sacred places and assesses the existing legal instruments in order to consider the possible shape and direction that such a soft law approach might take.

Sacred Places as a Distinct Category

Because of the inherent uniqueness of sacred places, developing a taxonomy of sacred places is virtually impossible in the same way that creating an exhaustive list of types of religion or belief or religious symbols is also impossible. Sacred places range from those with very clearly defined borders and physical specifications, to geographical areas, national parks, processions, pilgrimages, sacramental places and places where the faithful congregate and their spiritual leaders teach. Whether they are static or dynamic, it appears almost impossible to identify patterns to fit these randomly selected types of sacred place into broader categories. It does not come as a surprise, therefore, that law is generally uncomfortable with developing comprehensive regimes of sacred places. The existing regimes are very specific or relate to specific places and do not attempt to develop comprehensive uniform standards of protection of 'the Sacred'. The most prominent form of protection is given to places of worship, that is, places where religious communities congregate. I have purposefully departed from the use of 'places of worship' as the centre of my enquiry and have chosen a non-legal term 'sacred/holy places'. In this way I am able to enquire into forms of protection of places which do not necessarily fit, or fall outside, the category of places of worship and/or of the category of a place and yet may be associated with features which various legal tools often attribute to places of worship. Defining what might be a holy/sacred place/space is probably the topic of a different article.

For the purposes of this chapter I will be concentrating on places, spaces and events which may be perceived in some way as extensions of the legal category of places of worship but are often approached through the lens of legal tools other than freedom of religion or belief, for example. In order to do this I have introduced into the discussion a wider concept of 'sacred place/space/event' as an object of *worshipful* significance for believers and/or non-believers which is sometimes identical or similar to, and sometimes extends beyond, the level of veneration associated with a place of worship and therefore extends beyond the legal category of a place of worship. In doing so this chapter enquires to what extent such objects of worshipful veneration are approached differently from and similarly to places of worship from different perspectives of international law and whether they should be approached primarily through the lens of existing legal

statements prepared by individuals in a non-governmental capacity which systematize and reconceptualise the existing international legal tools relevant for the protection of sacred places, as well as the very concept of sacred places with a view to producing a voluntary code(s) in the area of legal protection of sacred places.

tools or whether a new form of protection reflecting the existence of a separate object of protection would be necessary instead.

Therefore this chapter provides an overview of relevant existing international legal instruments and enquires into similarities and differences in the protection of sacred places such as events: pilgimage routes/processions (which are frequently perceived through the lens of freedom of manifestation of religion or belief), unique sacred shrines (Jerusalem, Mecca, Mount Athos, the Vatican City State and so on), sacred landscape and places more generally perceived as places of worship in the strict sense (churches, mosques, synagogues, prayer rooms). The author feels that approaches which distinguish sacred places for their uniqueness (Mecca, Jerusalem) and places of worship for their communality (churches, mosques, synagogues, prayer rooms) is a false distinction and is not particularly helpful since every sacred place may be perceived as a place of worship and some places of worship may also be perceived as sacred places. As a result the text continuously tries to avoid a definition of sacred place and instead introduces a broader (not necessarily legal) category which absorbs different forms of legal protection of places and events which could be construed as sacred places in the wider sense; enquires into the ways these different forms of protection relate to one another and to the wider concept of sacred places; and asks whether a more transparent picture of these different and yet interconnected forms could serve as a possible blueprint of a soft law for protection of sacred places broadly understood through existing and perhaps new legal tools.

The chapter does not necessarily present a case for a new category of protection under international law. Instead it is in the first place an enquiry into the ways in which different, and sometimes overlapping, legal tools are applied in the protection of different, and sometimes overlapping, objects which could be broadly described as sacred places. Secondly it enquires into the ways in which these different, and yet related, approaches could be made more transparent through a form of soft law for the protection of a broader category of sacred places, which would provide a systematic overview of the existing hard law legal tools and the way they may interconnect in a multi-layered fashion in the area of legal protection of sacred places.

Multiple identities of sacred places and their complex relationships (religious, cultural, civic or even strategic), often triggering conflicting and contested horizontal and vertical sovereignty claims, are not easy to explain as legal entities. Considerations such as whether sacred places should be taxed, audited, dependent on planning laws or insurance laws, included in the register of listed heritage sites or subsidized by the annual budget of the state are no longer dependent on the law, but to a large extent on the commitment the political community chooses to articulate in relation to such places – can it afford to have them tax-exempt and to let the communities in charge of such sites develop a considerable level of autonomy which will make the general rules about social security, public safety and planning laws non-binding for such communities? A list of further questions often emerges in the context of such deliberations:

- How does a holy place differ from a place of worship?
- Should the law take into account any such difference?
- Should access to a holy place be administered in the same way as more general places of worship?
- Should access to holy places for multiple religions be different from access to places of worship of one religion?
- What about access to places of worship of one religion built on ground considered holy by other religions?
- Should religious law be taken into account when considering access to places of worship v sharing places of worship?
- Should soft law deal with the complex difficulty that principles of religious law cannot normally override mandatory provisions of primary legislation?
- What is the balance between religious autonomy and state interference in legal protection of holy places?
- Are idiosyncratic legal narratives, which take into account the different ways holy places/places of worship could be perceived, appropriate?
- Can it afford to treat all sacred places equally or should some places be granted special status? And why?

The answers to such questions are often driven by security concerns, concern for heritage protection, human rights arguments or arguments of religious autonomy. Very rarely special cases, such as Jerusalem, the Vatican and Mount Athos, are regulated by eclectic legal norms, which reflect the complexities of their legal status.

In the effort to reduce the nature of sacred places to one or another aspect of their multiple identities, international as well as municipal law conditions their legal status to a specific substantive definition, category of place or area of law. This definition could be shaped by the way in which international or municipal law categorizes a particular subject matter or by a particular policy-driven agenda to place such subject matter within or outside the specific concern of the law.

There has not, however, been an attempt to develop a non-binding narrative by way of guidelines which would approach sacred places through their multiple identities and serve as a model for legal reasoning that would see these identities in conjunction and not in isolation. In this chapter I wish to show how many of the available tools under international law, and some of the legal tools tangential to, but connected with, international law, could serve to develop such guidelines, which could generate a model for integrated multi-dimensional perspectives in policy-making in relation to legal protection of sacred places.

There has not been a clear and transparent way to integrate the existing International law instruments. It is not clear how they relate to one another even to international lawyers and it is not clear whether they could or should be applied in conjunction. A soft law could propose a way in which these different and sometimes competing approaches could be applied in conjunction. There is evidence that there will not be a sufficient consensus for developing a ‘Freedom of Religion or Belief' convention for the protection of places of worship under international law. The guidelines for teaching religion in schools and drafting law on religion commissioned by the OSCE (Organization for Security and Co-operation in Europe) are good examples of the way forward in this respect.[3] These guidelines are not legally binding and, despite being controversial, have been immensely influential in Member States for suggesting how a particular issue can be approached through the lens of international law. In the context of sacred places, a soft law by way of a systematic commentary on existing approaches from within the existing legal instruments, as well as from within theoretical perspectives on sacred places and their legal status, could set out in a clear and transparent way a narrative of how sacred places can be perceived by law and could perform a function similar to that of the OSCE guidelines.

A soft law text, without harmonizing the different practices, could suggest an intellectual framework within which legal issues relating to sacred places could be approached in a broader and more comprehensive manner, in the first instance as an intellectual tool and only secondarily as a possible future legal framework. Various forms of soft law, by way of guidelines rather than declarations, are more likely to achieve change, transforming legal thinking at the level of the judiciary, executive and legislature.

Thus this chapter will present available tools and the ways they relate or should relate to one another in a wider soft law narrative. The starting premise will be that it protects any places where freedom or religion or belief is exercised and perhaps shared – from the very obvious sacrificial places to the family home as a sacred place/sacred space.

Legal Tools for Protecting Sacred Spaces

Freedom of Religion or Belief

The available legal tools under international law which articulate available sacred places' protection vocabulary through the lens of freedom of religion or belief as a fundamental right can be found in the International Covenant on Civil and Political Rights (ICCPR),[4] the European Convention on Human Rights (ECHR),[5] the American Convention on Human Rights (ACHR),[6] the African Charter on Human and Peoples' Rights[7] and in the Universal Declaration of Human Rights

3 OSCE 'Toledo Guiding Principles on Teaching About Religions and Beliefs in Public Schools'; 'Guidelines For Review Of Legislation Pertaining To Religion Or Belief'<www.osce.org/odihr/13993> accessed 19 July 2011.

4 ICCPR 1966 999 UNTS 171 (ICCPR).

5 ECHR 1950 213 UNTS 221 (ECHR).

6 ACHR (n 10) Article12.

7 African Charter (n 10) Article8.

(UDHR),[8] as well as the 1981 Declaration on the Elimination of All Forms of Intolerance and Discrimination Based on Religion or Belief (1981 Declaration on Religious Intolerance).[9]

The right to freedom of religion positively includes the right to manifest one's faith in worship 'alone or in community'. The concept of a protected place of worship appears to be articulated through the legal tools aimed at protecting freedom of association and manifestation in the ICCPR. The General Comment No. 22 on freedom of religion issued by the Human Rights Committee refers to 'the concept of worship ... including the building of places of worship'.[10]

Article VI in the 1981 Declaration includes the right to worship and assemble and 'to establish and maintain places for these purposes'. It is nevertheless a first attempt to speak of centres of religious devotion in broader terms, avoiding the use of culturally specific terms such as holy, sacred and of worship. The text speaks exclusively of places, thus delineating the intangible dimension of sacred spaces for the purposes of legal protection under international law.

UDHR specifically delineates the right to freedom of religion or belief in Article 18. The *forum externum* aspect of Article 18 includes 'freedom, either alone or in community with others and in public or private, to manifest his religion or belief in teaching, practice, worship and observance', a mild concession to group rights.

Despite the fact that the Declaration has the status of soft law, the widespread acceptance of the UDHR shows that many of its provisions have achieved the status of international customary law.

As a further development from UDHR, Article 18(1) of the ICCPR protects the individual and collective manifestations of a religion, placing particular emphasis on four forms:

- worship
- observance
- practice and
- teaching.

Similarly to UDHR, active exercise of this right is usually exercised in 'public' in the sense of the outside world and thus it is basically subject to limitations.

General Comment No. 22 attempted to relate the text of Article 18 ICCPR to sacred places:

> The concept of worship extends to ritual and ceremonial acts giving direct expression to belief, as well as various practices integral to such acts, including the building of places of worship, the use of ritual formulas and objects, the display of symbols and the observance of holidays and days of rest.

8 UDHR (adopted 10 December 1948) UNGA Res 217 A(III) (UDHR).

9 Declaration 1981, UNGA Res 36/55 (25 November 1981) UN Doc A/RES/36/55.

10 UNCHR 'General Comment 22 (1994) UN Doc HRI/GEN/1/Rev.7 [4].

The most powerful legal tool for enforcement of freedom of religion or belief remains Article 9 ECHR. With regard to protection of sacred sites, the ECtHR requested states to prevent discriminatory practices against some religions.[11] 'The Court emphasized far more rigorously than the European institutions themselves ever have, the positive obligation on states to protect these rights and freedoms by effective, reasonable, and appropriate measures'.[12] Protection of Scared Places and Minority protection

Having had an international human right as our starting point one 'almost naturally' moves to minority protection as an approach which is next in line with individual human rights protection.

The phrase 'religious minority' applies to any group adhering to a defined set of religious beliefs.[13]

Relevant forms of minority protection are outlined in Article 27 ICCPR, the General Comment No 23,[14] the Declaration on the Rights of Persons belonging to National or Ethnic, Religious, or Linguistic Minorities (1992 Declaration) 1992,[15] the Genocide Convention,[16] Article 14 ECHR[17] and in the European Framework Convention for the Protection of National Minorities (European Framework Convention).[18]

The principles those legal tools provide include an obligation for State Parties not to deny persons belonging to minorities the common 'practice of their religion' because 'minority rights enrich the fabric of society as a whole',[19] common 'enjoyment of their cultural life', the common 'practice of their religion' and the common 'use of their language', the promotion of minority identity, participatory rights in 'cultural, religious, social, economic and public life' and establishment of minorities' associations. Such principles underpin the collective dimension of those rights with encouragement of the communal enjoyment of

---

11 *Metropolitan Church of Bessarabia and Others v Moldova* (2002) 35 EHRR 306; *Canea Catholic Church v Greece* (1999) 27 EHRR 521; *Holy Monasteries v Greece* (App no 13092/87, 13984/88) (1995) Series A no 301; *Manoussakis and others v Greece* (1997) 23 EHRR 387 [47]; *Agga v Greece* (App no 50776/99, 52912/99) ECHR 7 October 2002 [52, 53]; *Cyprus v Turkey* (2002) 35 EHRR 731 [246].

12 Paul M. Taylor, *Freedom of Religion: UN and European Human Rights Law and Practice* (CUP 2005) 244.

13 Yoram Dinstein, 'Freedom of Religion and the Protection of Religious Minorities', in David A. Reidy and Mortimer N.S. Sellers (eds), *Universal Human Rights: Moral Order in a Divided World* (Rowman & Littlefield 2005) 147–9.

14 UNCHR 'General Comment 23' (2004) UN Doc HRI/GEN/1/Rev 7 [1].

15 UNGA Res 47/135 (18 December 1992) UN Doc A/Res/47/135.

16 Convention on the Prevention and Punishment of the Crime of Genocide 1948 78 UNTS 277 (Genocide Convention).

17 ECHR (n 10) Article14.

18 European Framework Convention for the Protection of National Minorities (signed at Strasbourg 1.II.1995) ETS no 157.

19 UNCHR 'General Comment 23(1994) UN Doc HRI/GEN/1/Rev.7.

rights without discrimination. Case law and General Comment on Article 27 require the protection of minority identity and the valuing of diversity as part of the essential 'fabric' of communities and states. Nowak argues that Article 27 provides minorities with a *lex specialis* to practise their religion, publish their own literature and found cultural institutions.[20] Sacred Places, Humanitarian Law, Rules of War and Heritage Protection.

Another prominent approach in connection with the protection of places of worship which focuses specifically on the fabric of sacred sites is the notion that the state preserves sacred sites in order to maintain peace and to prevent religious hatred. Taken in isolation this approach reverses the perspectives of religious freedom and focuses on protection of religion and sacred sites, not because religious freedom is good but because people burn each other's houses because of their religion and the state has a duty to prevent religious violence.

Protection of Sacred Sites as Protecting Cultural Sites

In international humanitarian law, places of worship are included in the protection of cultural properties during armed conflicts.

The 1954 Hague Convention expands upon the norms of the 1907 Hague Convention, which established that in bombardments by naval forces all the necessary measures must be taken by the commander to spare, as far as possible, sacred edifices, buildings used for artistic, scientific purposes and historical monuments by adding several new features to the law of cultural property.[21] It defines cultural property as movable or immovable property of great importance to the cultural heritage of every people, such as monuments of architecture, art or history, whether religious or secular. An 'International Register of Cultural Property under Special Protection'[22] was created, featuring monuments of particular importance that qualify for special protection. There are three categories of property to which special protection is to be given:

- a limited number of refuges intended to shelter movable cultural property in the event of armed conflict;
- centres containing monuments;
- other immovable cultural property of very great importance.

20 Manfred Nowak, *UN Covenant on Civil and Political Rights: CCPR Commentary* (NP Engel 1993) 505.

21 David Meyer, 'The 1954 Hague Cultural Property Convention and Its Emergence into Customary International Law' [1993] B U INT'L L J 349, 352. Convention for the Protection of Cultural Property in the Event of Armed Conflict (adopted 14 May 1954, entered into force 7 August 1956) 249 UNTS 240 (The Hague Convention 1954) Article 1.

22 Hague Convention 1954 (n 237) Article 8.

These properties can be placed under special protection if two conditions are fulfilled and respected:

- the protected property must be situated at an adequate distance[23] from any large industrial centre or from any important military objective;
- the protected property must not be used for military purposes.[24]

To date, cultural sites in four states (the Vatican City, 18 January 1960; Austria, 17 November 1967; Germany, 22 April 1978; and the Netherlands, 12 May 1969) have been entered in the register at the request of those states, a total number of eight refuges as well as the whole of the Vatican City State.[25]

The Geneva Conventions Relative to the Protection of Civilian Persons in Time of War, 1949 (hereafter the Geneva Convention), had a fundamental influence on the drafting of the 1954 Convention and prohibits:[26]

> (a) to commit any acts of hostility directed against the historic monuments, works of art or *places of worship* which constitute the cultural or spiritual heritage of peoples;
>
> (b) to use such objects in support of the military effort;
>
> (c) to make such objects the objects of reprisals.[27]

Protocol I prohibits acts of hostility directed at properties which constitute the 'cultural or spiritual heritage' of peoples and extends protection to a number of sacred sites.[28] At the insistence of a large number of states, however, 'places of worship' was returned and supplemented with the current language of 'cultural or spiritual heritage'. The ICRC noted that spiritual importance may exist even in the absence of cultural importance, and that 'spiritual' was written into Protocol I to cover such situations, but not to extend protection to local churches or mosques.[29] Protocol II also covers situations of non-international armed conflict and contains

23 Ibid. Article 8(1)a.

24 Ibid. Article 8(1)b.

25 UNESCO, 'International Register of Cultural Property under Special Protection' <http://unesdoc.unesco.org/images/0014/001407/140792E.pdf> accessed 15 July 2011.

26 Ibid. 21.

27 Protocol Additional to the Geneva Conventions of 12 August 1949, and relating to the Protection of Victims of International Armed Conflicts 1977 UNYB 95.

28 Article 53, the Protocol Additional to the Geneva Conventions of 12 August 1949, and relating to the Protection of Victims of International Armed Conflicts (Protocol I), 8 June 1977.

29 International Committee of the Red Cross, *Commentary on the Additional Protocols of 8 June 1977 to the Geneva Conventions of 12 August 1949* (ICRC, Geneva 1987) 646.

a provision for the protection of cultural property. It prohibits 'any acts of hostility directed against historic monuments, works of art or *places of worship* which constitute the cultural or spiritual heritage of peoples, and to use them in support of the military effort'.[30]

The Second Protocol to The Hague Convention expands the existing legal tools by providing 'enhanced protection' available for immovable and movable cultural property, and a regime of criminal sanctions. It identifies two categories of war crimes specifically relating to cultural property and introduces a 12-person inter-governmental committee[31] for the Protection of Cultural Property in the Event of Armed Conflict, which is empowered 'to establish, maintain and promote the List of Cultural Property under Enhanced Protection'.[32]

The Declaration Concerning the International Destruction of Cultural Heritage was adopted by the General Conference of UNESCO in 2003[33] as a follow-up to the resolution entitled Acts Constituting a Crime against the Common Heritage of Humanity.[34] This declaration advances the cause for framing a convention which specifically sets out the provisions for the protection of sacred sites at all times.

Property Rights

Private property rights play a central part in the assertion of a stable legal status of sacred places. Right to property is stated as a fundamental right only under the UDHR[35] and has failed to find a place in the international human rights covenants such as the ICCPR and the ICESCR.[36] This was partly due to the failure among the State Parties to reach any agreement on an acceptable text.[37] Article 17(2) points out that property rights are not absolute and under certain circumstances this right could be withdrawn, though not arbitrarily. However, the regional human rights treaties[38] have incorporated the right to property as a fundamental right, without any unjust interference from the State as to its use. Forms of state interference in the free exercise of property rights relevant to sacred places fall within the following categories:

---

30 Protocol Additional to the Geneva Conventions of 12 August 1949, and Relating to the Protection of Victims of Non-International Armed Conflicts 1977, 16; Gregory M. Mose, 'The Destruction of Churches and Mosques in Bosnia-Herzegovina: Seeking a Rights-Based Approach to the Protection of Religious Cultural Property' [1996] *Buff J Int'l L* 180, 185.

31 Second Hague Protocol 1999, Article 24(1).

32 Ibid. Article 27(1)(b).

33 UNESCO 32nd Session (2003) 32 C/Res 33 Annex.

34 UNESCO 31st Session (2001) 31 C/Res 26.

35 UDHR (n 23) Article 17.

36 ICESCR 1966 993 UNTS 3 (ICESCR).

37 UNGA 'Report of the Secretary-General' 2929 (1955) UN Doc A/2929, 65–7.

38 Article 1 of the First Protocol to the ECHR, Article 21 ACHR and Article 14 AFCHPR cover the protection of rights to property.

- Curtailing access to sacred sites for adherents of a particular religion, and in many States, these procedures are used to restrict the constitutive – both tangible and intangible – aspects of religious practice, which are not necessarily explicitly covered by rights-based mechanisms; these aspects may combine teaching, practice and observance as well as a relationship with a particular place and time, static and dynamic, including processions and pilgrimages;
- Using planning permission;
- Registration procedures to limit the free exercise of religious faith through worship on sacred sites;
- Creating national parks on the site of private religious foundations which transforms the nature of holy places/places of worship.[39]

Many conventions and declarations have mentioned the right to property of various groups.[40]

European, Inter-American and African Charters contain provisions on the right to property.[41] Article 1 in Protocol I to the ECHR guarantees the right to property by providing for:[42]

- The principle of peaceful enjoyment of property;
- The prohibition on deprivation of possessions except in the public interest, and subject to 'the conditions provided by law and by the general principles of international law';
- Recognition that the State is entitled to control the use of property in accordance with the 'general interest'.

Article 21 ACHR states that everyone has the right to the use and enjoyment of their property but these can be deprived for reasons of public utility or social interests and 'according to the forms established by law'.[43] Both the Inter-American Court on Human Rights (IACrtHR) and the Inter-American Commission on Human

---

39 Paul M. Taylor, *Freedom of Religion*, 242.

40 International Convention on the Elimination of All Forms of Racial Discrimination 1965 660 UNTS 195 Article 5; Declaration on the Elimination of Discrimination against Women 1967 UNGA Resolution 2263 (XXII) Article 6; Convention on the Elimination of All Forms of Discrimination Against Women 1979 1249 UNTS 13 Articles 15 and 16; ILO Convention (No. 107) Concerning the Protection and Integration of Indigenous and Other Tribal and Semi-Tribal Populations in Independent Countries 1957 328 UNTS 247; ILO Convention (No 169) Concerning Indigenous and Tribal Peoples in Independent Countries 72 ILO Bulletin 59 1989.

41 Protocol I ECHR Article 1, ACHR Article 21 and AFCHPR Article 14.

42 *Marckx v Belgium* (App no 6833/74) (1979) 2 ECHR 330.

43 ACHR Article 21(1).

Rights (IACHR) have ensured the rights of Indigenous people to claim their property rights over sacred lands.[44] Eclectic Approaches.

In addition to approaches which stem from the use of specific instruments from within public international law there are also more idiosyncratic, eclectic forms of regulation of the legal status of sacred places which stems from the specific cultural, historical and legal background. The obvious case studies which come to mind are spiritual centres of particular significance for one particular religion, several religions or several divided branches of the same religion. In the Mediterranean the obvious case studies are the Vatican, Mount Athos, Jerusalem and Mecca. Apart from the familiar international law instruments, those places are governed by domestic law and by Jewish, Islamic and Canon law as well as by bilateral treaties. In a similar fashion Islamic law and public law operate in Mecca. International law, Italian public and civil law, Canon law and particularly public ecclesiastical law (*ius publicum ecclesiasticum*) cover the status of the Holy See, while Canon law and Greek public law and civil law shape the status of Mount Athos. This overlap between international law, constitutional law and religious law is not uncontroversial but provides, in some cases, an important perspective on the protection of places of worship. A careful study of the strengths and weaknesses of these regimes is a good starting premise to study the different legal systems. Parallel claims of sovereignty, different legal mechanisms and different rights are perceived from different, coexisting and often competing positions. These regimes seem to share a perception of the protection of sacred places as a multi-layered, often multi-jurisdictional, legal phenomenon, which has been achieved through the effort and concession of all parties involved. While international law is equipped for this purpose, it has failed to achieve such a multi-layered approach in relation to sacred places.

Grass-root Approaches

Another approach regarding protection of places of worship is that of grass-roots transitional justice (Rwanda, Sri Lanka, Northern Ireland, South Africa, Mozambique, Guatemala, East Timor), which seeks to develop a grammar of consent which each party could accept.

New approaches of the grass-root/traditional justice have identified the relationship between religious language, the language of religious freedom and

44 *Mayagna (Sumo) Indigenous Community of Awas Tingni v Nicaragua* Judgment of 31 August 2001 Inter-Am Ct HR (Ser C) no 79 (2001); *Maya Indigenous Communities of the Toledo District v Belize* Case no 12.053 Report no 40/04, Inter-Am CHR (12 October 2004) OEA/Ser.L/V/II.122 Doc 5 Rev 1; Peter W. Edge, *Religion and Law: An Introduction* (Ashgate 2006) 129. Edge brings out the nature of the sacred sites of indigenous people as these sites are not bounded and the religious community is not in the traditional relationship with the land as that attributed to a landowner.

the language of reconciliation in cases in which traditional concepts are used to develop a grammar of consent where international law or constitutional law have failed (in the case of colonialism, and totalitarian or authoritarian domestic regimes with otherwise fully functioning legal systems): traditional 'religious' laws and traditional 'religious' normativity shape the transition, the new legislation and influence other actors within the reconciliation process.

A grass-root traditional approach to dispute resolution was introduced based on traditional religious beliefs and the authority of the *lisan* in East Timor. The Community of Sant'Egidio helped the peace talks and the promotion of an amnesty which would foster forgiveness and reconciliation following conflict in Mozambique and Guatemala. In Guatemala the Catholic Church participated actively in the peace talks. In South Africa the traditional African concept of *ubuntu* was recalled in the provisional constitution as an ethical concept which transcends established and failed political categories. *Magamba* spirits and ceremonies in Mozambique and the *Acholi* rituals in Northern Uganda played a central part in the process of reconciliation.[45]

The grass-roots approach has potential and limitations because it depends largely on the consent of the parties involved. But so does international law. While such an approach can be implemented mostly in communities that already have a common wealth/culture, this is no less the case for the implementation of international law.

These unconventional legal tools seem to be very effective in establishing a normative common ground. While this is not necessarily a solution, they create a common environment and connections in areas where international or constitutional law need to regain a lost legitimacy. These grass-root approaches did not undermine international law but added a new dimension to international law in transitional societies as promoting justice and peace and international human rights standards. Such approaches marked a departure from the application of international law as a due diligence check and developed a grammar of consent, which did not abolish the reception of international law or a concept of constitutional law, but was able to embrace them more confidently.

From religious perspectives soft law tends to be controversial and treated with suspicion and yet at the same time would seem to be familiar territory. What we consider today to be soft law is what shaped the early history of Canon law, as well as Jewish and Islamic jurisprudence, and is the format within which major religious legal traditions still operate. Soft laws tend to propose practices but do not necessarily introduce monolithic legal structures. Moreover such soft law presents legal tools with which religious groups are likely to be more familiar, a non-codified variety of legal strategies ranging from techniques for legal reasoning to manuals for litigation. After all, these forms are what different legal traditions

45 Rinaldo Cristofori, *Il fattore religioso nella giustizia di transizione* (Tesi di Dottorato di Ricerca, Università degli Studi di Milano, Scuola di Dottorato Filosofia del diritto, 2010).

share with pre-13th-century European law, Roman law, Islamic law, Jewish law and Canon law. Christian legal thinking is only too familiar with it from its great canonical collections, which, at least until *Liber extra*, are effectively a soft law. The law to be applied was not to be found in any defined corpus of texts and the applicable precepts might be found anywhere throughout the inherited Mosaic and Christian tradition.[46] Even if one could find the relevant passages, they often appeared to speak in discordant voices. The ultimate authority of the law of the Church rested on the continuous operation of a Legislator whose purposes were beyond judicial reasoning, and whose judgements could not be identified precisely with those of any of His ministers. His supreme command, constantly reasserted, was to love one's neighbour as oneself. The authority of God's agents derived from the invisible operation of grace, which had to be supposed to underpin their formal competence but in practice might not. 'Christ's grace is so free that it cannot be defined by any merit or office held by men, but pours itself out where it will, how it will and to whom it will'.[47] To find God's law then, one might search across a boundless sea of texts, of customs or sacred narrative, yet end in the unknowable depths of His will.[48]

The legal tools I have discussed so far have not brought us closer to defining sacred places as a legal category. Each of the legal tools has been shown to have its own potential and limits in dealing with this category. This only reinforces the need for multiple legal tools to deal with the question of legal protection of places of worship.

It is imperative to find a new narrative towards a complex approach to determine the appropriate legal tools for protection of sacred places – whether this particular sacred place should be viewed through the lens of belief-manifestation (as a place of worship) or whether it would be more appropriate to view it as a more complex entity which may have legal existence beyond the belief-expression perspectives of freedom of religion or belief and may include other relevant areas of law. If the private property dimension is emphasized, could restrictions be imposed through standard private property derogations – through planning law, health and safety, environmental law and so on? Would a freedom of religion or belief claim + manifestation + private property + minority protection argument be more likely to address the complexity of a particular legal challenge? In an attempt to do all this, a soft law approach seems to be in a stronger position to articulate comprehensive, versatile and inclusive applications of the existing legal instruments. This could take several forms – a comprehensive commentary of exiting international and other relevant legal tools, taking into account what believers have to say about

46 Martin Brett, 'Finding the law: the sources of canonical authority before Gratian', in Per Andersen, Helle Vogt and Mia Munster-Swendsen (eds), *Law before Gratian: Law in Western Europe c. 500–1100: Proceedings of the Third Carlsberg Academy Conference on Medieval Legal History 2006* (DJOF Pub 2007) 51–5.

47 Ibid.

48 Ibid.

places of worship (theological statements or evidence of a genuine belief that a place is sacred), expert witness reports whether a place is sacred, judicial activism and so on. However, there is always a potential challenge to perceptions that one place is more sacred than the other – a temple *vis-a vis* a chapel, a religious building where sacramental worship takes place v a building where the congregation merely prays and the preacher teaches (synagogue, mosque), a place v an event (festival, pilgrimage), a building v space (Sacred World, Sacred Landscape). Despite the inherent suspicion of religious communities in relation to any form of legal protection and potential interference on behalf of the State, pending the resolution of uneasy questions such as why should a secular State provide special accommodation for sacred places or how far such accommodation should extend considering that sacred places could in some circumstances be considered as specific as the private family home, a soft law approach would at least begin to contemplate obvious and less obvious difficulties in articulating such possible tensions and project obvious and less obvious solutions.

We are unlikely to develop a universal taxonomy of legal protection of holy places due to the unique nature of the subject matter. In this respect any exercise will be an effort to present a train of thought about possible approaches in the context of legal protection of sacred places. It may show the ways a problem could be approached but will not necessarily tell us a specific way of resolving the problem. It does, however, outline the ways certain things could or could not be approached. What it does not do and should not do is to simplify and generalize the meaning of a religious community in order to leave the doors open for other and new forms of the sacred to enter and to be protected. It is unlikely that our notions, intuitions and concepts of the sacred will meet with existing legal frameworks. But there is no point in waiting for this to happen either. This is why a soft law in a narrative form of a general comprehensive commentary of existing legal tools is an important step towards changing perceptions, changing forms of political and judicial reasoning without which any future hard law for protection of sacred places is likely to fail in exactly the same way it has failed in the past.

PART II
Sacred Places and Religious Traditions

Chapter 6

Sharing Sacred Spaces: A Jewish Perspective

Jack Bemporad

Investigating what constitutes a sacred space and how sacred spaces are viewed within each particular religion may be one of the most effective ways of enhancing and realizing better interfaith understanding.

Each religion has its own doctrine of what constitutes a sacred space. In Judaism, we find such discussion first and foremost in the Hebrew Bible, but also in a variety and great number of rabbinic and Jewish philosophical and mystical texts. A brief review of these texts may help to orient us with respect to the variety of problems that we are facing, but also provide a foundation for our recognizing that we must take seriously the sacred space views of other religions.

The Ideal of Humanity that Comes from Religious Monotheism

The concept of humanity, which comes from the monotheistic religions, must underlie all our discussions (including the examination of the ethical foundation of our legal frameworks) and is a contribution that religion makes to ethics. It is by making explicit what monotheistic religions imply – what it means to be a human being when Jews and Christians say that man is made in the image of God, or when Jews and Muslims say that a person who saves one life saves the whole world and that he who destroys one life destroys the whole world – that builds up the universal dimension which must be acknowledged in each person.

Within the context of monotheistic religions the ideal of humanity is foundational, since it is a basis for respecting 'the Other'. Hermann Cohen has cogently argued that monotheism is not simply the rejection of many gods but rather the rejection of many peoples. It is a rejection of the multiple deities which have the same vices as human beings in conflict with each other, lording it over one another and thus separating peoples, nations and religions. That God creates all human beings, male and female, in the divine image, that each individual is a soul that connects them to the Divine, thereby giving them intrinsic worth, makes all human beings united as a human family.[1]

1 Hermann Cohen, *Religion of Reason* (Scholars Press 1995) 238.

It is monotheism that makes it possible to conceive of a world at peace, as is clear from the teaching of the Prophets Isaiah and Micah:[2] 'They shall beat their swords into ploughshares, their spears into pruning hooks, nation shall not lift sword against nation nor learn war any more' (Isaiah 2:4; Micah 4:3). Malachi summarizes this when he states, 'Have we not all one father, hath not one God created us, why do we deal treacherously brother against brother?' (Malachi 2:10).

Without such a monotheistic foundation, the very respect for 'the Other' would be impossible. As Psalm 82 delegitimizes the deities for their immorality, so God must be a God who is the model for justice and righteousness.

When the Bible states in the book of Leviticus that one should love one's neighbour for he is like you (Lev 19:18), what it basically says is that one should investigate one's own inner self, one's own inner reality, and recognize that that reality is also part and parcel of the reality of the Other. It means that one should love, value and care for the Other as one strives to know, value and care for oneself. In doing this, one begins to recognize the Other in a new and different manner. It is not simply the following of what Hillel said when he stated, 'don't judge your fellow human being until you stand in his or her place'. What he said was that you have to look at the Other from the point of view that he looks at you. By standing in the place of the Other, you see yourself in the way the Other views you, and by recognizing this, one can have a foundation for proper understanding and dialogue.

Moving from the concept of one humanity (and not many different peoples), the idea of sacred (or holy) spaces can be used as a means of reconciliation, since every religion has a view of sacred spaces, and provides doctrines as to what constitutes a sacred space and how such spaces fit into its own religious understanding.

To start, all human beings have a sense of the sacred. There is the need to worship, to adore, to cherish, to sense a reality that we cannot even imagine, let alone fully grasp with our own minds. The question then arises as to how we understand our own, and especially the Other's understanding of this concept of sacred space, and how these spaces can be used as symbols of reconciliation. For instance, Pope John Paul II's revolutionary visit to a Roman synagogue in 1986 was a landmark advance in the recognition of 'the Other's' sacred space.

In another example, spaces were shared for common ends in the civil rights movement, not simply in meeting halls, but also in sanctuaries. It is no surprise then that the prophet Isaiah proclaimed, 'My house shall be called a house of prayer for all peoples' (Isaiah 56:7).

Another key issue in recognizing the sacred is the relationship between the particular and the universal. Since this can have significant meaning, we have to emphasise and clarify what we mean by the particular element and the universal element.

2 Excerpts from the Bible are taken from *The Holy Bible*, Revised Standard Edition (Oxford University Press 2002).

It is only by cooperating and working together for the common good that we can achieve the peace that is so necessary for all of us. I also think that one of the universal elements in any debate, on whatever topic, must be this primary human condition: we are all human beings, we all need help, not only from one another, but also in religious terms, from God, from The Divine, from the supernatural and from all that transcends us. For instance, all of us face the dimension of the sacred in our lives and the incapacity to be connected to it is one of the greatest tragedies that can befall human beings. This was clearly enunciated by Amos (Chapter 8: 11–12) when he indicated:

> I will send a famine on the land, not a famine of bread nor a thirst for water, but of hearing the words of the Lord. They shall wander from sea to sea and from north to east, they shall run to and fro to seek the word of the Lord, but they shall not find it.

We can see for every religion that the word 'sacred' is a precious heritage, and we cannot allow ourselves to be robbed of it, for the word 'sacred', and all associated with it, has a precise meaning, and these meanings have evocative powers that proceed from the part they have played in the history of humanity: and this constitutes the particular element, which also often contains the universal element. Surprisingly, Edward Caird's words relating to nationalism can also be applied to the sacred:[3]

> … there is needed a common history, the memory of great deeds done, great trials undergone, great experiences of sorrow and joy encountered together. Thus the saying: 'Happy is the nation which has no history,' is almost self-contradictory; for a people without history can never rise to any real national unity. The ties of nationality have generally been welded not in peace but in the storm of battle, not in rest and enjoyment but in much effort and suffering. A nation is not born in a day, nor without the long and severe throes which attend all spiritual birth. It is a slow and continuous struggle with the natural obstacles of its position, with other nations, and with the elements of division in itself, by which a people gradually grows conscious of itself, of its independent life, and of the line of thought and action which is peculiarly its own.

On the one hand, we must give proper due to and strengthen the universal, while, on the other, we must not minimize the radical particularity of a religious tradition. In this connection I would like to comment on the nature of the sacred. When we talk about the sacred, we are talking about a religious term that transcends many categories. It is not something we can play with, or something that we can easily control or manipulate or easily categorize. It is something that we devote ourselves to in many respects; that has the feature of giving us a foundation and helps us

3 Edward Caird, *Lay Sermons* (James MacLehose and Sons 1907) 101.

recognize ourselves. So we see that we should not minimize its power and its meaning!

It is the sacred that is at work in the evaluation of those aspects that give a meaning to life. We ask the questions, 'What is truly Sacred to us? What is the sacred that we share as human beings?' I think that when we talk about the sacred, we are speaking about something that ranges beyond pleasure or use, something that cannot be reduced to the contingent and the practical. When we become aware of it, we perceive something that is ultimate, which defines reality and which enables us to transcend the ordinary daily life of the appetites and the senses.

I believe it is the sacred, or, as in Judaism, we can call it the holy, that produces in both ethics and aesthetics a dimension that would otherwise not be there. For example, my professor, Hans Jonas, discussing personal sacrifice, said something that I believe to be essential. He said:[4]

> We must, in other words, distinguish between moral obligation and the much larger sphere of moral value. (This, incidentally, shows up the error in the widely-held view of value theory that the higher a value, the stronger its claim and the greater the duty to realize it. The highest are in a region beyond duty and claim.) The ethical dimension far exceeds that of the moral law and reaches into the sublime solitude of dedication and ultimate commitment, away from all reckoning and rule – in short, into the sphere of the holy. From there alone can the offer of self-sacrifice genuinely spring, and this source of it must be honored religiously.

This means that the sacred not only defines where we reach the highest, but it also gives ethics its absolute dimension.

The Two Elements of the Sacred

But we must draw a distinction between two elements of the sacred. Without this we shall not manage to understand it fully.

The first element is what John Oman, in his great work *The Natural and Supernatural*, calls 'awesome holy'.[5] A description of this would be the seminal work by Rudolf Otto, *The Idea of the Holy*, in which he speaks about the numinous, the fascinating, the terrible, the frightening, recognizing what it is that is awesome and dangerous. And he tried, together with other elements of the sacred, to incorporate them into the awesome holy. The other element is the ethical

---

4 Hans Jonas, *Philosophical Essays From Ancient Creed to Technological Man* (University of Chicago Press, Midway reprint 1980) 119; see also Jonas, *Mortality and Morality. A Search for the Good after Auschwitz* (edited by L. Vogel, Northwestern University Press 1992).

5 John Oman, *The Natural And The Supernatural* (Cambridge University Press 1931).

holy. Both John Oman and A.A. Bowman have criticized Otto for being overly concerned with the awesome holy, not recognizing sufficiently the degree to which the ethical holy transcends and incorporates it.

While it is true that Otto himself acknowledges the ethical holy, he does not give it the dimension as do those who see the ethical holy as the main thrust of monotheistic religions. Otto clearly states that the awesome holy does not fully reflect the Biblical view. He says:

> The venerable religion of Moses marks the beginning of a process which from that onwards proceeds with ever increasing momentum by which the numinous is throughout rationalized and moralized, i.e., charged with ethical import, until it becomes the "holy" in the fullest sense of the word. The culmination of the process is found in the prophets and the Gospels.[6]

In criticizing Otto, Bowman explains:

> Holiness combines morality with religious awe. But if so, it is difficult to think of morality as an absolutely independent ingredient, mechanically compounded with the other ingredient, and itself devoid of numinous significance. To treat it as such is to render its associations with the numinous for ever [sic] unintelligible and to reduce religion to a meaningless and indefensible collocation of unrelated constituents. The question forces itself irresistibly to the forefront: Is not this absolute distinction between morality represented as altogether rational and the numinous conceived as altogether non-rational, the product of abstract analysis, and of a certain confusion between the theoretical standpoint of ethics and the practical standpoint of morality? May it not be (and does not the whole logic of the argument compel us to assume) that the moral life itself, as distinct from any reasoned system of morality, is something into which the numinous enters directly with all the awfulness that characterizes man's sense of deity in the world of his experience?[7]

Oman clearly shows that in the awesome sacred, sentiment determines value, while in the ethical sacred it is value that determines sentiment (Oman, 1931: 66). Oman states: 'Was it not precisely by an appeal to a higher sense of the holy that the prophets set up against it the first truly rational and ethical religion?' (Ibid.: 63).

Indeed, it is Oman's great insight that progress in religion comes with the recognition of the false sense of the holy. The starkest confrontation of the awesome and ethical holy is seen in the Prophet Micah (6:6–8):

6 Rudolf Otto, *The Idea of the Holy* (translator John N. Harvey, Oxford University Press 1923) 111.

7 Archibald A. Bowman, *Studies in the Philosophy of Religion* (Vol. I, MacMillan 1938) 240–41.

> [6] 'With what shall I come before the LORD, and bow myself before God on high? Shall I come before him with burnt offerings, with calves a year old?
>
> [7] Will the LORD be pleased with thousands of rams, with ten thousands of rivers of oil? Shall I give my first-born for my transgression, the fruit of my body for the sin of my soul?'
>
> [8] He has showed you, O man, what is good; and what does the LORD require of you but to do justice, and to love kindness, and to walk humbly with your God?

The burden of Oman's book is to indicate in what way the progress of religion is an attempt at transforming (while at the same time preserving), the awesome holy into the ethical holy (Oman, 1931: 444):

> Nor does any progress wholly deliver from something of awe in reverence or from some dependence upon material embodiments of the sacred, though the former should be exalted to the sublime and the latter to the symbolical. The Old Testament is, on the whole, a record of progress in both.[8]

Sacred Spaces: A Jewish Perspective

As mentioned above, it is the monotheistic religions that make central the ethical holy, and envision it as incorporating and qualifying the awesome holy.

Since in Judaism the same Hebrew word, *Kadosh*, in its various conjugations, is sometimes translated holy and sometimes derivatively translated Sacred, or Sanctify, confusions may arise. The root, *kuf daled shin*, can be translated in many ways, as something, oath, relationship, condition, way of life or set aside for a special purpose. In this sense, it is often translated as sacred (Exodus 30:25; Deuteronomy 26:13 and so on), or to sanctify (Numbers 27:14; sanctify is used to give proper respect). It is important (and confusing, as well) to note that the same root is used with respect to idolatrous practices. So II Kings 10:20 states, 'sanctify a solemn assembly for Baal' (Cf. Isaiah 66:17).

However, what is more significant and unique in both Biblical and rabbinic Judaism, is the devastating critique of of what can be characterized as the 'awesome' holy. For example, there are numerous situations in which one would expect 'reverence, respect, or fear' of the awesome, and yet none is exhibited. In Genesis, Laban is pursuing Jacob, since his 'household gods' are missing. It appears Rachel has hidden them under her saddle; in short, she is sitting on them. Hardly an appropriate way to treat gods of any kind!

There are several passages I would like to point to, among many, where the awesome and numinous character of the situation is clearly manifest, but where the

8 See Oman, op. cit. Appendix A as well as 59–73.

response is totally unexpected. In the first, Jacob is fleeing from his brother. He stops to rest. He has a dream where all the promises of his future destiny are enumerated. He wakes up and a numinous situation is described. How awesome is this place. God is present and I did not know it. The response in Genesis 28:10–22 is amazing:

> [10] Jacob left Beer-sheba, and went toward Haran. [11] And he came to a certain place, and stayed there that night, because the sun had set. Taking one of the stones of the place, he put it under his head and lay down in that place to sleep. [12] And he dreamed that there was a ladder set up on the earth, and the top of it reached to heaven; and behold, the angels of God were ascending and descending on it! [13] And behold, the Lord stood above it and said, 'I am the Lord, the God of Abraham your father and the God of Isaac; the land on which you lie I will give to you and to your descendants; [14] and your descendants shall be like the dust of the earth, and you shall spread abroad to the west and to the east and to the north and to the south; and by you and your descendants shall all the families of the earth bless themselves. [15] Behold, I am with you and will keep you wherever you go, and will bring you back to this land; for I will not leave you until I have done that of which I have spoken to you'. [16] Then Jacob awoke from his sleep and said 'Surely the Lord is in this place; and I did not know it.'[17] And he was afraid, and said, 'How awesome is this place! This is none other than the house of God, and this is the gate of heaven.'
>
> [18] So Jacob arose early in the morning, and he took the stone which he had put under his head and set it up for a pillar and poured oil on the top of it. [19] He called the name of that place Bethel; but the name of the city was Luz at the first. [20] Then Jacob made a vow, saying, 'If God will be with me, and will keep me in this way that I go, and will give me bread to eat and clothing to wear,[21] so that I come again to my father's house in peace, then the Lord shall be my God,[22] and this stone, which I have set up for a pillar, shall be God's house; and of all that thou givest me I will give the tenth to thee'.

Instead of being overwhelmed by the awesomeness of the situation, Jacob begins to bargain with God and give him 10 per cent of what he receives. There is not much awe in his reaction.

In a second example, Moses encounters something miraculous – a bush that burns and is not consumed. He is told to take off his shoes, because the land upon which he stands is holy ground, and God speaks to him. God reveals himself to Moses, imploring him to go to Pharaoh and save the Children of Israel from their suffering. The setting is awesome indeed, but here again, the response in Exodus 3:11–4:17 is amazing. Moses exhibits no fear or trembling, but instead offers a number of excuses as to why he is not willing to take the task upon himself until God overpowers him.

In yet another example, Abraham recognizes that in relation to God he, Abraham, is but 'dust and ashes', (Genesis 18:27). Nonetheless, when God appears revealing His awesome intention to destroy Sodom and Gomorrah, Abraham asks, even challenges (18:25), 'Shall not the judge of the world act righteously?'

Again, in Numbers 14, the situation is tense. The people are rebelling and God intercedes on behalf of Moses, who is about to be stoned. God says He will destroy His people and make a great nation out of Moses. Moses' response is a challenge, not acquiescence. Moses not only states that it will appear that God is not able to keep his promises, but, more significantly, states that the power of God consists not in destroying, but in forgiving, since forgiveness is God's greatest attribute and character.

Finally, the contrast between the awesome holy and ethical holy is fully manifest in the Book of Job. Eliphaz's speech (Job 4:12–17) is a splendid example of the awesome holy and is strongly rejected by Job. In fact in the spirit of questioning, Job asks for an umpire between him and God to judge his case (Job 9:33) and finally defends his integrity unto death, crying out: 'I will take my flesh in my teeth and put my life in my hand. Behold, He will slay me; I have no hope; yet I will defend my ways to his face. This will be my salvation that a godless man will not come before Him' (13:14–16).

Job is criticizing his 'friends', in effect asking, 'Do you mean to defend falsehoods on behalf of God, to uphold untruths for his sake?' The epilogue clearly vindicates Job against the friends when God, angry at the friends, says to them, 'you have not spoken of me what is right as my servant Job has' (Job 42:7).[9]

Prof. Andrea Poma has portrayed this contrast and critique from the perspective of monotheism by categorically separating the sacred and the holy, indicating that the holy is really a new category that devalues and basically rejects the sacred. In his distinction between the sacred and the holy he states:

> I maintain that Judeo-Christian monotheism is the largest and most enduring cultural tradition that has rejected the sacred and engaged in a multi-millenial struggle against it in the name of an alternative and opposing solution, which, once again without reference to any etymological, philological, or historical consideration, I indicate with the term 'holy'.
>
> There have been other cultural traditions that have intentionally distanced themselves from the conception of the sacred. One of these is classical Greek philosophy – and I note that I believe this is one of the elements that facilitated the synthesis between Judeo-Christian monotheism and Greek philosophy. It however seems to me that no other tradition engaged itself so radically in the struggle to eliminate the sacred and replace it with the holy.[10]

---

9 See Jack Bemporad, 'A New Look at The Book of Job' [2011] Centro Pro Unione Bulletin 21.

10 *Andrea Poma Holy vs Sacred: Elements for Reflection* (Paper presented at the Interdisciplinary Conference on Sharing Sacred Spaces Conference: Legal, Theological

What Biblical Judaism has done is to have consistently devalued or outright rejected what was claimed to be sacred or revered in the surrounding religions. So, a fundamental principle of both Biblical and rabbinic Judaism is the rejection of idolatry, paganism and the sacred of the surrounding religions. A clear example of this in the Bible is the ridiculing of Balaam the seer, who, having been hired to destroy Israel with a curse, needs a sword to kill his own donkey and who, supposedly a 'seer', cannot even see the angel brandishing a sword in his path, which his donkey plainly sees (Numbers 22:30–34).

There are numerous places in rabbinic literature that reject idolatry. So the Mechilta gives the example of a discussion:

> A certain philosopher asked R. Gamaliel: It is written in your Torah: 'For I the Lord thy God am a jealous God'. But is there any power in the idol that it should arouse jealousy? A hero is jealous of another hero, a wise man is jealous of another wise man, a rich man is jealous of another rich man, but has the idol any power that one should be jealous of it? R. Gamaliel said to him: Suppose a man would call his dog by the name of his father, so that when taking a vow he would vow: 'By the life of this dog'. Against whom would the father be incensed? Against the son or the dog? Said the philosopher to him: Some idols are worth while. 'What makes you think so?' asked R. Gamaliel. Said the philosopher: There raged a fire in a certain province but the temple of the idol was saved. Was it not because the idol could take care of itself? Said R. Gamaliel to him: I will give you a parable: To what is this comparable? To the conduct of a king of flesh and blood when he goes out to war. Against whom does he wage war, against the living or against the dead? The philosopher then said: 'Indeed, only against the living'. Then he said again: But if there is no usefulness in any of them, why does He not annihilate them? Said R. Gamaliel to him: But is it only one object that you worship? Behold, you worship the sun, the moon, the stars and the planets, the mountains and the hills, the springs and the glens, and even human beings. Shall he destroy His world because of fools? 'Shall I utterly consume all things from off the face of the earth? Saith the Lord' (Zeph. 1.2). – The philosopher also said to him: Since it causes the wicked to stumble, why does God not remove it from the world? – But R. Gamaliel continued saying: Because of fools? If so, then since they also worship human beings: 'Shall I cut off man from off the face of the earth?'[11]

As illustrated, what could legitimately be seen as sacred from a Biblical perspective was put in a context that stressed the ethical in earlier references to Abraham, Moses and Job. Perhaps the clearest example of this was the desacralization of the

---

and Sociological Perspectives, St Thomas Aquinas University – Angelicum, Rome 14–15 December 2011).

11 Jacob Z. Lauterbach, *Mekilta* (vol. II, The Jewish Publication Society of America 1933) 244–6.

temple in the prophetic teaching of the Prophet Jeremiah, and most prominently in his temple sermon (Chapter 7:1–10, 14; 26:9).

The word that came to Jeremiah from the LORD:

> [2] "Stand in the gate of the LORD's house, and proclaim there this word, and say, Hear the word of the LORD, all you men of Judah who enter these gates to worship the LORD'. [3] Thus says the LORD of hosts, the God of Israel, Amend your ways and your doings, and I will let you dwell in this place. [4] Do not trust in these deceptive words: 'This is the temple of the LORD, the temple of the LORD, the temple of the LORD'. [5] 'For if you truly amend your ways and your doings, if you truly execute justice one with another', [6] if you do not oppress the alien, the fatherless or the widow, or shed innocent blood in this place, and if you do not go after other gods to your own hurt, [7] then I will let you dwell in this place, in the land that I gave of old to your fathers for ever. [8] 'Behold, you trust in deceptive words to no avail'. [9] Will you steal, murder, commit adultery, swear falsely, burn incense to Ba'al, and go after other gods that you have not known, [10] and then come and stand before me in this house, which is called by my name, and say, 'We are delivered!' – only to go on doing all these abominations? [11] Has this house, which is called by my name, become a den of robbers in your eyes?"

Generally, holy has the meaning of separation from the ordinary; more specifically from all that is defiling, degenerating, unworthy or, significantly, idolatrous, since the battle with idolatry and all that it implies is central to Judaism. The leitmotif can be seen in Exodus 12:12 where God brings judgement on the gods of Egypt and there is the categorical rejection of any ruler who makes himself a god (see Ezekiel's criticism of the Prince of Tyre, Ch. 28:2,9). Further, God specifically rejects all that is identified with the immorality of the pagan cults (Deuteronomy 18:9–14):

> [9] When you come into the land which the LORD your God gives you, you shall not learn to follow the abominable practices of those nations. [10] There shall not be found among you any one who burns his son or his daughter as an offering, any one who practices divination, a soothsayer, or an augur, or a sorcerer, [11] or a charmer, or a medium, or a wizard, or a necromancer. [12] For whoever does these things is an abomination to the LORD; and because of these abominable practices the LORD your God is driving them out before you. [13] You shall be blameless before the LORD your God. [14] For these nations, which you are about to dispossess, give heed to soothsayers and to diviners; but as for you, the LORD your God has not allowed you so to do.

Of course, the Bible does not invent the world that it describes. It inherited a tribal, polytheistic worldview and there are remnants of these elements, such as second Samuel 6:6–9 or II Kings 3:26–7. Furthermore, as mentioned above, the Bible uses similar words for the pagan and Jewish sacred objects. The Bible inherited and incorporates sacred places of worship, places, utensils, vestments and so on (see in particular the Priestly material in Exodus, Leviticus and Numbers).

The most significant Biblical passage with respect to the ethical holy is found in Leviticus 19:2: 'Say to all the congregation of the people of Israel, You shall be holy; for I the Lord your God am holy'.

The chapter itself combines ritual and ethics but the ethics is prominent and central because it details what it means to be holy. The Jewish tradition has interpreted this passage in term of holiness as separation. Urbach, in his landmark work *The Sages*, clearly expresses this on page 482:[12]

> In the Pentateuchal section 'on which most of the essential parts of the Torah are dependent' the Lord said to Moses: 'Go say to the Children Of Israel: My children, just as I am abstinent, so must you abstain (from sin); just as I am holy, so must you be holy'. Holiness and abstinence are attributes of God and it is His will that his creatures should (also) cleave to them, and He even helps them, if they begin to walk in His ways. A similar exposition was given to the verse, 'May He send forth thy help from the sanctuary' [qodesh, literally holiness] – 'on account of the hallowed deeds you have performed; 'and support thee out of Zion' (Psalms 20 verse 3 [2]) – on account of the distinguished acts you have done.

Then, on page 368, Urbach states:

> When the omnipresent enjoins a new precept upon Israel, He endows them with new holiness. Holiness means abstinence, as is stated in the Sifra: 'Ye shall be holy' means: Ye shall be abstinent' … 'the formulation of the benediction 'who sanctified us by His commandments and commanded us …' The sanctity is, as it were, withdrawn from the precept itself and transferred to the act of the precept and to him that performs it. The commandment is thus voided not only of any magical-mythical quality, but also of its very ritual-cultic basis.

Hermann Cohen, in *Religion of Reason* on page 343 explains:

> 'Blessed art thou O Eternal our God, King of the Universe, who has sanctified us by his commandments'. This wording might seem to suggest that it is through obedience to the commandments themselves that our holiness is brought about. With this, however, the commandments would lose their symbolic character and assume that of the sacrifice. However, in another place in the prayer it says: 'Sanctify us with Thy commandments and purify our heart'. Here again the symbolic character is made unmistakenly clear. The power of sanctification is not in the commandments themselves; instead God is asked to further our sanctification and let it be achieved through the commandments.

12 Ephraim E. Urbach, *The Sages: Their Concepts and Beliefs* (Harvard University Press 1987).

The clearest description of Holiness as separation is found in Roth's excellent chapter entitled 'Imitatio Dei and the Idea of Holiness' in his *Is There a Jewish Philosophy?*.[13]

Roth, being philosophically sophisticated, is very careful to interpret *Imitatio Dei* with respect to holiness in a manner that does not compromise God's transcendence. Roth here, citing more sources than Urbach, writes in the spirit of Maimonides and also Hermann Cohen, a view made explicit by Poma:[14]

> The first and fundamental originality brought by monotheism is the faith in one God, who absolutely transcends the world, created by Him. Such a God, in his [sic] sovereign liberty, sometimes makes himself [sic] present to man, who can praise, thank, and invoke Him, but can never constrain Him with his rites. All of creation is entrusted to man, both individual and collective, so that he can assume full responsibility for it. This new perspective, in which God transcends the world and the world is fully entrusted to man's responsible action, is what I refer to with the notion of the 'holy', which I again use as a working sense, without claiming to justify it, as should be done, from the etymological, philological, historical, and scientific perspectives. The 'sacred' is the perspective by which man is continually anguished by the possible effects of powers that are immanent in the world and superior to him, so that he must therefore seek, through rites, the possibility of persuading or constraining such powers to desist from possible harmful effects and instead support him in the pursuit of his own ends. The 'holy' is a radically different, indeed opposed perspective, by which man, on the basis of his faith in the absolutely transcendent God, is entirely free and autonomous in his action in the world, and recognizes himself as the only one responsible for his own actions and their effects, and does not recognize any political, economic, religious, or natural power above himself that does not come from God. For this reason, the categories by which man measures himself and his dignity in the sacral perspective are 'purity' and 'impurity', by which he is either able or not to ritually enter into the interested exchange with the divine. The categories by which man measures himself in the perspective of holiness are 'good' and 'evil': 'He has told you, O man, what is good' (Micah 6.8). 'Holiness, which is uniquely attributed to God, is, on the other hand, the archetype and ideal for man's moral action: 'Be holy, because I, your Lord am Holy' (Leviticus 19.2).

In his article on Cohen's Doctrine of the Holy Spirit, Poma quotes Cohen:[15]

> … when commenting on God's command in the biblical expressions: 'I will be hallowed among the children if Israel' (Leviticus 22:32), 'Ye shall sanctify me',

---

13 Leon Roth, *Is There a Jewish Philosophy?* (Vallentine Mitchell & Co., Ltd. 1999) 16–19 and, especially, 25.

14 Andrea Poma, *Holy vs Sacred: Elements for Reflection*, op. cit.

15 Andrea Poma, *Yearning for Form and Other Essays On Hermann Cohen's Thought* (Springer 2006) 308.

> 'Him shall ye sanctify' (Isaiah 8:13), 'Sanctify yourselves ... and be ye holy' (Leviticus 11:44), Cohen wrote: 'The holy spirit in man becomes alive insofar as man sanctifies himself. And in this self-sanctification he accomplishes the sanctification of God. For what could holiness in God mean if it were not the archetype (Urbild) for the action of man?'

Perhaps the most exhaustive discussion of the problem of the holy in Jewish perspective is in the fine book of Menachem Kellner, *Maimonides' Confrontation with Mysticism*.[16] Here Kellner traces the distinction between the substantial or intrinsic holy, which can be related to the awesome holy, and the functional or designated holy, which is akin to the ethical. On page 88, Kellner maintains that the intrinsic or substantial holy is

> ... the idea that, however it becomes holy, a holy place, person, time, or object is, once holy, objectively different from profane places, persons, times, and objects ... sanctity is real, it inheres in sacred places, etc., it is intrinsic to them; it is, one might say, part of their metaphysical make-up ... Holy places, persons, times, and objects are ontologically distinct from (and religiously superior to) profane places, persons, times, and objects. This distinction is part of the universe.
>
> In contrast Maimonides held a different view of holiness, a view which we believe is the predominant view in Judaism. Holy places, persons, times, and objects are in no objective way distinct from profane places, persons, times, and objects. Holiness is the name given to a certain class of people, objects, times, and places which the Torah marks off. According to this view holiness is a status, not a quality of existence. It is a challenge, not a given; normative, not descriptive. It is institutional (in the sense of being part of a system of laws) and hence contingent. This sort of holiness does not reflect objective reality; it helps constitute social reality. Holy places, persons, times and objects are indubitably holy and must be treated with all due respect, but they are, in and of themselves, like all other places, persons, times, and objects. What is different about them is the way in which the Torah commands that they be treated. Their sanctity derives from the uses to which they are put, in that sense, it is teleological ...

Kellner summarizes this position on page 90 in one short sentence:

> 'Israel is holy when it behaves in certain ways. Holiness on this view is a challenge and not a gift'. (Kellner's footnote: 'Even 2 Sam. 6 and 1 Chron. 13, often thought of as teaching that the ark of the covenant had some sort of inherent and dangerous holiness, do not teach that. Uzziah's death was not an automatic consequence of his having touched the holy ark; it was a punishment

16 Menachem Kellner, *Maimonides' Confrontation with Mysticism* (The Littman Library of Jewish Civilization 2006).

by God for having done so. Similarly, with the account in 1 Sam 5: the sufferings of the Philistines were inflicted by God as punishment and warning. There is nothing of Indiana Jones in the biblical text itself'.)

Stephen Schwartzchild, in his influential paper on 'Shekhinah and Eschatology',[17] stresses this distinction, taking the side of Maimonides and Cohen:

> There can be no doubt that also throughout Jewish history the temptation to veer toward such literalist understanding has often exercised its dubious charms, especially among more mystically inclined religionists – e.g., in Gnosticism, Philo, Christianity, Kabbalah, Sabbateanism ... Not only do such tendencies take what should be used as poetic metaphors literally; in the process they also hypostatize them, i.e., the shekhinah as a term of art for God's love, care, and nearness becomes a 'meta-physical' ontic entity that, if it is not actually a part, or aspect, of God, insinuates itself as an intermediary between God and humanity. The Talmud itself warns of such hypostatization – for example, by adding the cautionary term 'kivyakhol' – 'as it were', etc. It was normatively understood that otherwise both Judaism's theological transcendence as well as its absolute monotheism are at risk.

I think that Roth's categorical affirmation that holy refers to a cautionary rather than expressly positive action is due to the same concern that Poma and Maimonides have to safeguard the Transcendent character of the Deity. But it also stems from a more critical interpretation of the texts cited by Schechter,[18] who, in his masterful study of rabbinic thought, views the negative character of holiness as secondary to the positive, which simply repeats rabbinic references which speak of God performing specific acts, such as visiting the sick, burying the dead and so on, which can be imitated. I do not think there need be any contradiction, since the Rabbis specifically state that the Scriptures speak in the language of man and qualify such blatant anthropomorphisms with such expressions as kivyakhol (as if to say) and l'havdil (to make a basic distinction). Schechter would be the last to view such statements as anything but ways in which human beings are enjoined to behave. Holiness thus is to separate from everything that is degrading, idolatrous, unethical.

Working to Turn Sacred Places into Places of Reconciliation

What we have to try to do here, then, is to find a way of integrating these two elements, the awesome holy and the ethical holy, and to find ways that the sacred places can also be a place of reconciliation. It is to the great credit of the Bible

17 Menachem Kellner (ed.), *The Pursuit of the Ideal Jewish Writings of Steven Schwarzschild* (State University of New York Press 1990) 238–9.

18 Solomon Schechter, *Aspects of Rabbinic Theology* (Schoken Books 1961) 202–5.

to have joined the ethical and the holy, so that if something is holy, it cannot be unethical, and if something is ethical, it has the dimensions of the holy.

Oman has clearly summarized the true nature of the holy:

> Thus a right response to the highest and a right search for the real sacred – the true, the beautiful and the good, in the wide meaning we have given the words – are necessarily inseparable … all absoluteness, without which truth is mere useful information, morals mere expedient action, beauty mere pleasing of the senses, is from being in the Supernatural. By no matter of addition of natural values of pleasure and profit can they become sacred and by no manner of exalting natural feelings can they be holy. Nor can we say, 'Treat everyone as an end in himself', unless there is a sphere in which he has this worth: for manifestly he is not so in the merely natural.

In this perspective, I would like to add this: I remember when I was studying for the rabbinate in 1954, and at the time I had a confirmation service in my congregation. Everyone invited their friends to the religious ceremony, but not one of their non-Jewish friends attended. At that time, ministers of religion, whether Protestant or Catholic, rarely spoke to each other, nor would they ever set foot in a synagogue. That was just not done! In reality, the first time that ministers of religion spoke to each other in large measure in the United States was during the civil rights movement, and later on with the movement protesting nuclear tests.

What brought about a radical change was the decision taken by Pope John Paul II to visit a synagogue. That gave rise to an interesting dialogue. Some people said that the Pope should not enter the synagogue wearing a cross. John Paul II replied, 'If you want me to come and sit down on a seat without the cross, I will come. And it will be a personal visit. But if you want me to come to you as the Pope, how could I do that without the cross?'

In a flash, a synagogue became a place everyone could go to. It was a place that was recognised or re-cognized in a wholly new manner in every sense of the term. I think that it was this that laid the foundations for the path of reconciliation.

I am profoundly convinced that we must work hard to find the way to enable a sacred place to become a place of reconciliation. Is it so strange to think that the world's religious leaders might find common paths by going together to visit various sacred sites and saying to one another, 'We *re-cognize* the Other'?

Such reconciliation, I believe, will be achieved much quicker and more easily if the functional designative manner of interpreting the Holy takes precedence over the intrinsic ontological Holy. Finally, whatever part the numinous, awesome holy still retains, and it must retain aspects of it, is completely subservient to the ethical holy.

To the extent that there exists a common humanity, and insofar as we recognize sacred sites for ourselves, and that by doing so we cannot deny others their own sacred places, let us go together to seek the path of reconciliation. That is the task awaiting us.

Chapter 7
Sacred Places in the Christian Tradition

Pier *Francesco* Fumagalli

By revising topics already incorporated into the Jewish tradition, the *corpus* of the Christian New Testament presents a series of complementary concepts about sacred or 'holy' places, consistent with the literary genre, the time and those people to whom the texts were addressed. The *corpus* ranges from the Gospels, with editions of texts subsequent to the destruction of the Temple in the year 70 AD, to the *Letter to the Hebrews* which clearly presupposes the holiness of the Temple, to the *Epistles* of Paul didactic and exhortative, aimed at building the first Christian communities between the years 45 and 65 A.D., ending with the *Apocalypse*, which, in the midst of persecution around the year 100 A.D., set its gaze full of hope towards ultimate truths and the City of God, with no temple besides that of the sacrificed and resurrected Lamb.

These multiform and meaningful visions, in which the traditional Jewish concept is constantly present – expressed, implied, reinterpreted or polemically contrasted – sustained the faith of the first communities who had to deal both with being rejected by the Synagogue and with the pagans' destruction of the Temple. *In this dramatic context*, Jesus's words to the Samaritan woman may be the best way of summarizing the Christian position: 'Believe me, woman, a time is coming when you will worship the Father neither on this mountain nor in Jerusalem. You Samaritans worship what you do not know; we worship what we do know, for salvation is from the Jews. Yet a time is coming and has now come when the true worshippers will worship the Father in spirit and truth, for they are the kind of worshippers the Father seeks. God is spirit, and his worshippers must worship in spirit and in truth' (John 4:21–25).

Aspects of the Christian Tradition and Problems which Remain Unsolved

In the two centuries following the generation of the Apostles, until the turning point when Constantine the Great (274–337) granted freedom of religion, Christianity quickly spread throughout the Roman Empire; but it was above all after the initiative of Helena, Emperor Constantine's mother, in 324, that the Holy Land and the holy places of Christianity began to beregarded in a different light. With her pilgrimage to Jerusalem, Helena gave a decisive boost to the building of its churches, of which the basilica of Bethlehem, still in existence, is an eloquent example. On the other hand, the Ecumenical Council of Nicaea, summoned by

Constantine in 325 A.D., expresses two opposing concepts at the same time. The first is the necessity to venerate the physical and historical places relating to the central event of redemption – the incarnation, passion, death and resurrection of Jesus Christ. The second is the disdainful dismissal of the historical places connected with the previous Jewish tradition, which is repudiated in its entirety as a result of the accusation of Deicide formulated against the Jews as a people.[1]

The dichotomy that separates Christian holy places from Jewish ones was to last for approximately 17 centuries. It can be considered as essentially overcome thanks to the turning point represented by the Second Vatican Council (1962–65), summarized in paragraph 4 of the Declaration *Nostra Aetate* ('In Our Time'- 28 October 1965) on non-Christian religions. Alongside this dichotomy, which is a consequence of the millenary Christian-Jewish controversy, we must not forget the other and no less significant one that continues to separate sacred and profane places according to the classical Roman and Greek tradition, which implies an unresolved tension between Greek-Platonic anthropology and the Jewish-Christian conception of Salvation that becomes 'flesh and blood' (*basar wa-dam*).

A Spiritual Temple

Examining these different conceptions of holy places, from ancient times to nowadays, we would like to find a common thread that could unite – in a Christian interpretation – these views that can sometimes appear so distant from one another. A possible unifying interpretation may be found in the idea of the Church as a community in which each believer can be compared to a living stone of a holy place, and the heart of the believer becomes the tent chosen by God in which to dwell. Similar comparisons are frequent in Biblical literature, from the Prophets of Israel (Isaiah 60; Jeremiah 30–31; Ezekiel 36–7), to New Testament writings (Jews 10:5–10; Ephesians 2:20–22; 1 Peter 2:1–10 and parallel passages), up to the *Apocalypse* (chapters 21–2). They can be found in the Church Fathers of the first centuries and also in the medieval Jewish, Christian and Muslim mystics, from Ibn Paquda to Al-Ghazali.

A sacred place is always connected to a further mystery, to a divine Presence that can never be confined to any one place, according to the classical thesis of God's ineffability, the Absolutely Other, sung in a Jewish liturgical poem: *We-Hu a-Maqom shel maqom / we-en la-Maqom meqomo* (God is the Place of the Temple / and the Temple without a place). This may be why there was nothing but emptiness in the Holy of Holies in the Temple at Jerusalem, as in the Holy

1 The famous *Map of Madaba* – a wonderful 6th-century mosaic portraying the cities and sanctuaries of the Holy Land, drawing inspiration from Eusebius of Caesarea's *Onomasticon*, composed in 330 – is one of the most expressive visual documents of the conception of time as regards holy places; cf. M Piccirillo and E Alliata (eds) *The Madaba Map Centenary 1897–1997*.

Sepulchre of Christ, and this may also be why the apophatic and aniconic tradition of both Jews and Muslims directs towards such absoluteness, so akin to the Buddhist vacuity (*sunyata*) and to Taoist *tai kong* or 'Great Void'. All of these different aspects converge in the impossibility of containing the divine presence, the 'Glory of Him who moves all things', or *Shekhinà*.

According to a universally accepted sacred anthropology, thus physical places are, on the one hand, allusive and symbolic of a divine presence, while on the other hand – in the Abrahamic tradition that brings together Jews, Christians and Muslims – separated from a historical and ethical dimension ultimately founded on the centrality of the human person that has been created in the image of God and as such has been called to holiness of life in freedom, brotherhood, dignity, mercy, justice and love. Finally, the very physical reality of the holy place, while referring at the same time to a non-place, also refers in a complementary way to a tangible community, to a historical revelation, to a tradition with its own rituals, authorities and cultural norms; without this basis of tradition, the individual believer would lack the vital *humus* required to fully express his or her social and essential existential dimension. From its very origin, then,three dimensions intertwine within the sacred place: a spiritual-symbolic dimension, an ethical dimension and a historical-social-normative one. This bond creates great tension, as it could be said that all the Earth is sacred, while a specific land and those that inhabit it – the land 'of Holiness' (*Eretz ha-Qodesh*) – where the history of salvation manifested itself to humanity, share this holiness, which is testified by the pages of the Jewish and Christian Bible, by the Gospels and by the Koran. At the same time, however, as a consequence of this universally symbolic value, each specific place refers to all the other infinite places of humanity, and is an invitation to respect and make sacred all lives and all things, in accordance with the One, the living God.

'Inclusive' Sacredness

Contemporary experience and the historical experience of the past testify that it is not easy to attribute holiness to a place in an inclusive way. Indeed the most widespread trend is the opposite, whereby a sacred place – or parts of it – is preferred as one group's exclusive possession instead of a heritagethat can be enjoyed together. Inclusiveness should be increasingly widespread, as a typical expression of the universality of Catholicism, but it is often contradicted by practice. Apart from the most widely known cases, such as the separation of parts of the Holy Sepulchre and of the Basilica of the Nativity and its attribution to different Christian denominations that sometimes have fierce disputes over them, let us remember the example of the Tombs of the Patriarchs and of the Matriarchs at Hebron – venerated by Jews, Christians and Muslims – where an agonizing longing for unity can be felt, while the atmosphere remains full of dramatic tension.

In contrast to these cases there are other examples of silent meditation, like those which can be found in the 'meditation chapels' of modern airports where, on the other hand, we can experience a real, respectful and inclusive plurality, and where there is no pretence of reserving an exclusive and univocal symbol for any specific group or place. That is maybe why the principal holy places of Christianity originally remained outside of any sacred space: the 'Hill of the Skull' (*Golgotha*), memorial of the place of atrocious torment and death of Jesus of Nazareth, was an impure spot far from the Temple of Jerusalem; nearby, in what was a funerary garden, the Holy Sepulchre of Christ was itself also an anonymous and sad place, save for the glory of the Resurrected One who made the life of all humanity flourish again. Not far away, in the Biblical land of Ephrathah near the Tomb of Rachel, is another humble cave Sumptuously decorated later by Constantine, this cave was the birthplace of Jesus, reminding us of the womb of the Virgin Mary, the true holy place of the Incarnation of the Word, the Father's only begotten Son. Following this path that is both at the same time physical and spiritual, we are invited to reach the heart of the 'sacred place' that is characterized by the fullness of the Holy Spirit that the announcing angel reveals to Mary of Nazareth. Thus holiness is brought back to its own anthropological, ecclesiological and theological roots, the source of all the symbols of holiness that touch physical places, transforming them within and enabling them to participate in the manifestation of divine love that knows no boundaries in humankind and in the universe.

The Change Brought About by the Second Vatican Council (1962–65) and its Consequences

The pastoral and theological renovation of the Church that started with the Second Vatican Council and that is still in progress has fostered the emergence of some important new aspects emphasized in the discussion concerning holy places. Increasingly important to this discussion nowadays are ecumenical points of view, of the dialogue between Christians and Jews and among other religions, and the reception of the anthropological, sociological and historical points of view typical of the contemporary era.[2] In particular, we can observe that theological, social and political issues are tightly intertwined when we reflect on the holy places venerated by Judaism, Christianity and Islam together, as is the case of Hebron or Jerusalem.[3]

2 These different points of view can be seen in many of the interventions in the II International Training Course and the interdisciplinary Advanced Training Course, now published in Caterina Foppa Pedretti, *Per una cultura di pace in Terra Santa (Towards a culture of peace in the Holy Land* (Edizioni Terra Santa, 2010).

3 Cf. *Jerusalem and Rome. Two Cities in the Mirror of History*, in *Italy – Israel: the Last 150 Years* (Conference proceedings, Jerusalem 16th–17th May 2011, Corriere della Sera Foundation 2012) 25–31, 327–33; and the conference *The City of God and its People* (Gazzada, 3 September 2012).

In the last few decades the Catholic Church has become more receptive to the many voices coming from the cultures and the religions in the world. The Church heeds and collaborates with Judaism, especially as regards the Holy Land and the holy places: Jerusalem, Bethlehem, Nazareth and all the places of Judeo-Christian revelation in general. In 2001 this cooperation bore fruit with a Common Declaration on Holy Places. This was the result of the dialogue that had been going on for 40 years between Christians and Jews, and it does not only concern the monotheistic Mediterranean religious traditions, but also all the religious traditions of the world. The International Catholic-Jewish Liaison Committee that assembled in New York had expressed the hope that believers of all religions could cooperate and protect religious freedom and holy places for all faiths.[4] The ecumenical and interreligious inspiration that pervades this text brings it very close to the universalist spirit that we can recognise in some of the texts of the Second Vatican Council, and in particular in *Nostra Aetate*.

The *Preamble* reminds us that:

> In recent years, inter-religious and anti-religious violence have been on the rise. In some places thousands of people have been killed and thousands more left homeless or even made refugees. Assassination of religious leaders and lay workers has become a frequent occurrence. Shrines, monuments and houses of worship have come under attack, been damaged or destroyed. The rights of many hundreds of thousands of believers have been violated. The offenders are occasionally individuals. More often they have been groups, whether mobs, terrorist organizations, or people with authority: police, military personnel or even governments. We are troubled by assaults on religious freedom wherever they occur. We are all the more disturbed when members of our own religious communities have been the offenders. Assembled for this International Catholic-Jewish Liaison Committee meeting, we affirm once again before God and the world community our common commitment to the protection of religious freedom and to the security of holy places.

The joint document then stresses the serious perils that can derive from hostility that uses religious diversity as a pretext:

> Tragically, as religious communities fall into estrangement or antagonism, the holy places of each community often become the target of violence or vengeance instead of veneration and reverence. People act out their contempt and anger through various forms of violation: occupation, desecration, even destruction. So too, when holy sites are used for military purposes, their sacred character is

4 Cf. *Protecting religious freedom and holy sites*, a Declaration of the International Catholic-Jewish Liaison Committee, New York, 4 May 2001 <www.vatican.va/roman_curia/pontifical_councils/chrstuni/relations-jews-docs/rc_pc_chrstuni_doc_20010504_new-york-meeting_en.html> accessed 29 April 2013.

> defiled. One group can take physical possession of the holy place of another and eradicate traces of its earlier identity. Objects of veneration can be defaced. Holy places have been reduced to rubble.

It is for this reason that Jews and Christians have made it a common goal to protect religious freedom and the rights that this entails, by stating that:

> Religious freedom is realized through the exercise of specific rights. Among these are: freedom of worship, liberty in public manifestation of one's belief and the practice of one's religion, the freedom of religious communities to organize themselves and conduct their own affairs without interference, the right to express the social implications of one's beliefs, the right to hold meetings, and the right to establish educational, charitable, cultural and social organizations in keeping with the religious orientation of one's own religious tradition.

Finally, we can unite in making a specific appeal to the authorities, not only religious but also civil and military, for the universal benefit of any religious family and for peace:

> Governments and political authorities bear special responsibility for protecting human and religious rights. Those responsible for law, order and public security should feel themselves obliged to defend religious minorities and to use available legal remedies against those who commit crimes against religious liberty and the sanctity of holy places. Just as they are prohibited from engaging in anti-religious acts, governments must likewise be vigilant lest by inaction they effectively tolerate religious hatred or provide impunity for the perpetrators of anti-religious actions. Armed forces should be vigilant in avoiding violent action against religious minorities and attacks against places of worship and holy sites. In the interest of securing religious liberty, in times of conflict, armed personnel should be trained to respect the rights of religious minorities and holy sites and held accountable for their actions. Should conflicts arise between legitimate defense needs and religious immunity, ways must be found to avoid, or at least, minimize the infringement of religious rights.

How important it is for the children of Abraham that all believers, without distinction, be allowed to freely and peacefully practice their faith is expressed in the final invocation:

> In continuous prayer, we look forward to the time when all people shall enjoy the right to lead their religious lives unmolested and in peace. We long for the time when the holy places of all religious traditions will be secure and when all people treat one another's holy places with reciprocal respect.

The same subject, with special reference to Jerusalem and to the Holy places, is frequently dealt with also in the meetings of the International Dialogue Committee that brings together the Holy See's Committee for Religious Relations and the Chief Rabbinate of the State of Israel. Their work started in the summer of 2002 under the joint presidency of Cardinal Jorge Mejía and the Chief Rabbi of Haifa, Shear-Yashuv Cohen, and it has already achieved significant progress over the last 10 years.[5]

Holy Places and Secular Pilgrimage

Another opportunity to express the Christian position on holy places in a new way was the Great Jubilee in the year 2000. In anticipation of this event, a papal document specifically proposed a reflection on pilgrimage and holy places, combining secular and religious points of view. In this text it is pointed out that when we examine social phenomena, even if we do not do so from a specific religious perspective, we must acknowledge that always and everywhere in the world other sacred times and spaces co-exist, and these correspond to numerous and different conceptions of the human and of the divine.

It is possible to consider as places of pilgrimage and meditation not only Jerusalem and Rome, Mecca and Benares, Luang Prabang and Lhasa, but also memorials of terrible tragedies like Auschwitz, Hiroshima or Ground Zero, not to speak of the new possibilities of connecting with virtual places on the internet.[6] The fact that so many different examples of 'holy cities' and holy places exist both throughout the history of humanity and nowadays, all of them expressions of different ideas of the relationship of man with divinity raises questions for both anthropologists and believers, whatever their creed. It is useful at least to reflect on some of the different perspectives that lead to different ways of considering the holiness of a city or a place. The thoughts that Saint Augustine expressed in *De Civitate Dei* (City of God), referred to in the previously cited *Pilgrimage in the Great Jubilee of 2000*, are once more relevant, together with the subject of *peregrinatio* (pilgrimage) as applied to the current path of humankind today:

> A true and real network of itineraries is therefore extending throughout our planet. Some are religious in the most direct sense of the term. Their goals are cities and

---

5 Cf. Walter Kasper, 'The Commission for religious relations with the Jews and the International Catholic-Jewish Liaison Committee', in Philip A. Cunningham, Norbert J. Hofmann and Joseph Sievers (eds), *The Catholic Church and the Jewish People. Recent Reflections from Rome* (Fordham University Press 2007).

6 See chapter V of *The Pilgrimage in the Great Jubilee 2000*, Pontifical Council for the pastoral care of migrants and itinerant people (25 April 1998) <www.vatican.va/roman_curia/pontifical_councils/migrants/documents/rc_pc_migrants_doc_19980425_pilgrimage_en.htm> accessed 29 April 2013.

shrines, monasteries and historical centers. In other cases, the search for spiritual values is manifested by going towards natural sites of rare beauty, islands or deserts, summits or depths of marine abysses. This complex geography of the movement of humankind contains in itself the germ of a radical desire for a transcendent horizon of truth, justice and peace; it gives witness to a restlessness which has for its port the infinity of God, where people may refresh themselves from their anguish. The march of humankind, therefore, notwithstanding its tensions and contradictions, participates in the inevitable pilgrimage towards the Kingdom of God, which the Church is committed to announce and fulfill with courage, loyalty and perseverance, being called by his Lord to be salt, leaven, lamp and city on the mountaintop. Only in this way would open paths in which 'love and loyalty now meet, righteousness and peace now embrace'. In this itinerary, the Church becomes a pilgrim with all men and women who search with a sincere heart for truth, justice, peace; and even with those who wander elsewhere because – as Paul, citing Isaiah, recalls – God affirmed: 'I have been found by those who did not seek me, and have revealed myself to those who did not consult me'. All peoples and all individuals can therefore direct themselves towards this aim of the Kingdom. They may also express their adhesion by means of the explicit and symbolic gesture of a pilgrimage to the various 'holy cities' on Earth, that is, to the places of the spirit where the message of transcendence and brotherhood resounds strongest. Among these cities should also be included those places desecrated by people's sin and later on, almost out of an instinct of reparation, consecrated by pilgrimages. Let us think for instance of Auschwitz, emblematic place of torture of the Hebraic people in Europe, the *Shoà*, or of Hiroshima and Nagasaki, land devastated by the horror of atomic war. But, as previously stated, two cities acquire the value of a sign, not only for Christians but for everyone: Rome, symbol of the universal mission of the Church; and Jerusalem, holy place and venerated by all those who follow the way of the Abrahamic religions, the city from which the Law and the oracle of Yahweh will go out. This indicates the final destination of the pilgrimage of the whole humankind, that is, 'the holy city … coming down from God out of heaven'. We shall advance towards it in hope singing: 'We are a people that is walking / and walking together we want to reach / a city that will never end, / without pain or sadness, / city of eternity'. Just as the Church appreciates the poverty of the Buddhist pilgrim monk, the contemplative way of the Tao, the sacred itinerary of Hinduism in Benares, the 'pillar' of pilgrimage to the sources of his faith characteristic of the Moslem, and every other itinerary towards the Absolute and towards his brothers, She joins all those who, in a fervent and sincere way, dedicate themselves to the service of the weak, the refugees, the exiles, the oppressed, and undertake with them a 'pilgrimage of brotherhood'.[7]

7 The pilgrimage in the Great Jubilee 2000, op. cit., nn. 30–31.

The Holiness of Zion

We could continue to reflect on the subject of Jerusalem, the holy city, by starting with an appropriate prophetic text by Jeremiah:

> Return, O faithless children, says the LORD; for I am your master; I will take you, one from a city and two from a family, and I will bring you to Zion. And I will give you pastors after my own heart, who shall feed you with knowledge and understanding. And when you have multiplied and increased in the land, in those days, says the LORD, they shall no more say, 'The ark of the covenant of the LORD'. It shall not come to mind, or be remembered, or missed; it shall not be made again. At that time Jerusalem shall be called the throne of the LORD, and all nations shall gather, in the name of the LORD in Jerusalem, and they shall no more stubbornly follow their own evil hearts. In those days the house of Judah shall join the house of Israel, and together they shall come from the land of the north to the land that I gave your fathers for a heritage.
>
> Jeremiah 3:14–18

Jeremiah's appeal aimed above all at the conversion of all of Israel and Judea away from sin and injustice. The meeting of all peoples in Jerusalem is linked to this condition, and it is a subject that will reappear later on, with various nuances, also in the Christian and Muslim traditions. The Jewish people, who have now returned to the land of their Fathers and have re-established national independence there, consider this and similar prophecies as having been partially fulfilled as the 'beginning of the flourishing of our redemption' (*reshit tzemikhat geullatenu*). Saint Paul's reflection, on which the Christian conception of the Holy Land was based in subsequent centuries, was to have a strong influence on the Church Fathers. These included Saint Gregory of Nyssa (d. 394) who, in his treatise 'The ideal of the perfect Christian', applies Saint Paul's text in Ephesians 2 to the Christians, new men that have been reborn in Christ, so as to become 'abodes of peace': 'we ourselves will embody peace and we will show that this epithet of Christ is true and authentic also within ourselves' (PG 46:259–62). Starting from the same Pauline text, Saint Augustine instead refers to the Church, temple and city of God: 'He made two peoples into one Church and became for them its cornerstone, and thus was truly a peace-maker.' (*Comment on the Psalms*, Psalm 126:2, CCL 40, 1857–58). Later on, Muslim interpretation was to echo some of these points of view about Jerusalem, but particularly highlighting the relationship of Jerusalem with the Last Judgement and with the Paradise of believers.

Alongside these traditional positions, which are rooted in the Mediterranean environment, there are nowadays other schools of Western philosophy, as well as other cosmologies and other cultural and spiritual views, be they Buddhist, Indian or Chinese; they are becoming increasingly important in the fact that to a certain extent they reveal interesting analogies and differences with respect to these views of Jerusalem. Nonetheless, neither the traditional Mediterranean views nor analogous ones that emerge in other cultures of the world appear to respond adequately and satisfactorily to all the aspirations for peace and justice that they in fact have in common beyond their specific differences. It could thus be concluded that the ideal of a reconciled Jerusalem, a place of holiness and peace open to all peoples, may remain unfulfilled and may even be Utopian. However, if we try to grasp the values and the most relevant aspects of all these different concepts of the world, of the city of God and of mankind as well as of the meaning of history, we may perhaps consider this ethical dimension as the guarantee that this ideal should no longer be Utopian: it is meant to become a concrete hope, capable of lighting the ways of peoples towards the way to peace, joy, truth and justice, towards sharing and reciprocity, in which the city of God and the city of man are actually achieved. Saint Augustine's thought on pilgrimage cited in the above-mentioned *Pilgrimage in the Great Jubilee of 2000*, with the subject of *peregrinatio,* can now be applied to modern timesand apply to the path of mankind today; it could inspire new legal formulas capable of more adequately interpreting the safeguarding of specific 'holy places'. Cardinal Carlo Maria Martini, pastor and father of the Ambrosian Church for over two decades, as well as a deeply serious scholar and praying pilgrim in Jerusalem, dedicated this passionate prayer to this city that stands between the earth and the sky:

> Between new skies and new earth stands the new Jerusalem that we do not build but which comes from God, and it is splendid, described as the beloved spouse, the abode of God and men. For this new Jerusalem the Lord is truly a citizen of mankind as we are his: 'They will be His people and He will be the God-with-them'. It is the formula of the alliance brought to its fullness, of an alliance that has been fulfilled at last, and that is proven once again with the words: 'I will be his God and he will be my son'. This alliance implies that God, going back to the words of David, announces to everyone in the divine birth of Jesus. [...] *O Lord, let us welcome the celestial Jerusalem that comes from you. Make it so that, by praying together for the peace of the earthly Jerusalem, we can see the holy city that comes from the sky and for which God is God-with-us.*[8]

8 Carlo Maria Martini, *Verso Gerusalemme (Towards Jerusalem)* (Feltrinelli 2002) 156–7.

Chapter 8

'God has made the earth like a carpet': The Sacred Places in the Islamic Tradition

Yahya Pallavicini

'God has made the earth like a carpet'.[1] This verse from the Islamic Revelation can symbolically represent something that Islamic doctrine teaches about the sacredness of space: considering every place on earth as a possible sacred space for the ritual worship of God, the Lord of the Worlds (*rabb al-'âlamîn*). Furthermore, in a tradition, Prophet Muhammad says that God has made the earth a 'place of prostration' (*masjid*) and a 'means for purification' (*tahûr*)[2] for the Muslim community: the world as a whole is a sacred place where the believers can worship God. This profound symbolism should not be interpreted as a political slogan towards the Islamization of the world, but rather as a reminder to consider the whole earth as a sacred space in which every living being, faithful to the sacred law of his/her religious community, must follow his path of ritual consecration and existential sacralization and discover spiritual communion in the immanence of the Creator.

The land was covered with a carpet to dignify the adoration of believers, who thus become responsible both for the earth and for the carpet: just as they must honour the responsibilities of life, together with the rituals of their religion. As we shall see in the symbolism of the mosque, there are places that assume a value that is suitable for withdrawal, ritual communion and spiritual contemplation, and they are distinguished from other areas and from other more outward forms and levels like a house, a street, a school, a park, an office, a mountain, a hospital, a sea, a cemetery or the sky. In these spaces, a Muslim shares moments in time and experiences with other beings of other faiths who, in their different ways, all contribute to the growth of knowledge and to working together for the good of all humanity.

Study and work, and sickness and health are actions and situations that follow each other in the places of the earth that welcome us. According to the teaching of Muslim masters, actions inspired by right intention are holy actions: they sanctify whoever carries them out and make holy the places in which these actions are performed, as mentioned by a fundamental prophetic saying, 'Actions have value

1 The Koran, 71:19.
2 Collected by Al-Bukhârî in his Sahîh.

only according to their intentions'.[3] Situations like poverty, wealth, youth or old age are sent by God to test us and are opportunities to change and mature, restoring a more purified and higher sanctity in both people and the land where they live. The Koran says:

> He is Who created Death and Life, that He may try which of you is best in deed: and He is the Exalted in Might, Oft-Forgiving.[4]

Sacred space is space that follows a divine order of hospitality. This divine order is not a merely passive hospitality, but has made Man a guest on earth, carrying out an activity that ensures the communication and the handing on of all that is vital in the sacred, at all times, in all places. When Man follows this traditional situation, he comes into harmony with sacred cosmology, but when, instead, he forgets the sacred nature of the earth, of his own life and of the lives of other people, he becomes part of the cause of human disorder.

All this happens for a sacred reason that links Man to the earth or to the clay from which he is made, but, above all, links him to the presence of the breath of the divine spirit (*ar-rûh*) that gave life to Man. The Koran talks several times about this divine breath in Man that makes him created 'according to the Merciful's form' (*'alâ sûrat ar-Rahmân*),[5] that gives him the possibility and ability to know God and the essence of everything. For example, it is said in the sura of Prostration:

> Such is He, the Knower of all things, visible and invisible, the Exalted (in power), the Merciful; He Who has made everything which He has created most good. He began the creation of man with (nothing more than) clay, and made his progeny from a quintessence of the nature of a fluid despised: but He fashioned him in due proportion, and breathed into him something of His Spirit, and He gave you hearing and sight and hearts: little thanks do you give![6]

That is why also the masters make a comparison between sacred place and human constitution, and say that the body of the one who has realized the divine presence in himself is a temple. But when Man denies the sanctity of the spirit, he denies the matrix of life itself and considers the earth as though it were mere clay: the ignorant man thinks that the world has always existed, or that it was created accidentally, without any sacred quality.

The Islamic Revelation teaches Muslims that the earth and man were created from nothing but the holy will of Allah. According to traditional Islamic teaching, Man is the administrator of the earth's sacred hospitality. A Muslim 'dwells' on the

---

3 Collected by Al-Bukhârî and Muslim in their *Sahîh*.

4 The Koran, 67:2.

5 Collected by Ahmad ibn Hanbal in his *Musnad*. Another version, better known, states that 'God has created Adam according to His form'.

6 The Koran, 32:6–9.

earth, according to the meanings expressed in the Koran with the word *sakana*: he circumscribes his own space in which he offers his intention to be of service within his sacred jurisdiction. His jurisdiction is limited to this circumscription which, in time, coincides with the cycle of his existence in religion and, in space, coincides with every place he has lived on earth, where he has carried the sacred presence of the spirit that is within him. The space is not sacred because it corresponds to a religious jurisdiction or because it is inhabited by a believer, but because it is inhabited by the Spirit guarded within the sacred space of the faithful servant who, in turn, is guarded within the earth that he dwells in, *sakana*. The root *s-k-n* is also the origin of the Koranic term *sakîna*, which has a parallel in the Hebrew *shékhinah* and, in both languages, assumes the meaning of the sacred immanence of God, of God's calming presence in the heart of the believers as well as on the earth:

> And He helps thee with a powerful help. It is He Who sent down great Peace (as-sakîna) into the hearts of the Believers, that they may add faith to their faith; for to God belong the Forces of the heavens and the earth; and God is Full of Knowledge and Wisdom.[7]

It is this presence alone, in the stillness of true peace, that can ensure the full sanctity of every place.[8] The same term is also the origin of the phonetic symbol *sukûn* which, in Koranic grammar, indicates the non-vocalization of a letter, and exactly represents the effort and sacrifice that Man must make: to silence earthly passions in order to make the Holy Word resound throughout every place. In reality, every place and every aspect in the existence is full of the divine presence and mercy; nothing can exist outside of the sacred order of the Holy Word of God. The Koran states:

> To God belong the East and the West: Whithersoever you turn, there is the Face of God. God is all-Pervading, all-Knowing.[9] In another verse, God says: 'I am with you anywhere you are'.[10]

The famous Muslim theologian and mystic Abû Hâmid Al-Ghazâlî (1058–1111) used to say that there is nothing, in the whole of existence, but God's Qualities

---

7 The Koran, 48:3–4.

8 It is interesting to note that some Islamic traditions tell that when Abraham and Ismail were rebuilding the Ka'ba in Mecca, as God had commanded them to do, they began to dig the earth until they found the antique and primordial foundations of the temple that Adam's descendants had built in their time. God manifested His *sakîna* with a cloud in the sky whose shadow covered the original temple traces. In other versions, the *sakîna* has the form of a swirling wind that shows Abraham where he must rebuild the Ka'ba, by rolling itself up like a snake around the foundations of the original temple.

9 The Koran, 2:115.

10 The Koran, 57:4.

and Actions: each part of the Creation is an expression, a 'sign' (*âya*) of God's Omniscience, All-Mightiness and Wisdom. Another great Muslim teacher and philosopher, Al-Fârâbî (872–950), paraphrasing some Koranic verses, wrote: 'The Creator – excellent is His greatness – is the ruler of the world and nothing can escape His knowledge, not even a grain of mustard, and His providence does not neglect any part of the world'.

For many people, going into a mosque and discovering how Muslims live in today's world is to walk between modernity and the sacred, between prejudices and cultures and between stories in the news and oriental exotica. The results of this visit and of these meetings depend largely on our willingness to open up, to engage with each other and overcome our preconceptions, our imaginings and our psychological reservations, to truly enter into an Islamic sacred place and to get to know at first hand the principal aspects of what it means to be a Muslim.

The Universality of the Islamic Ritual Space

In the East, mosques are as common as churches in the West and we can easily recognize a variety of styles, sizes and construction techniques according to the historical, artistic and cultural period of the time. This succession of historical periods and architectural styles is further enriched by the deep cultural diversity that has been a feature of the construction of every mosque outside the Arab world in Turkey, Persia, the Indian subcontinent, in Southeast Asia, in Sub-Saharan Africa and even in Europe and America. Just like Muslim cultures worldwide, Islamic mosque art features a variety of interpretations and languages that exactly represent the universality of Islam: a religion based on precise and identical doctrinal principles for all the faithful, but fully respecting the different historical, legal and political contexts in its application.

So not all mosques are the same, but all Muslims pray following the same basic rules in whatever mosque they find themselves. A mosque can be simply the outline of a series of stone markers open to the sky for the prayers of nomads in their stops in the desert, or be built on piles in Malaysia, have the typical shape of a traditional Chinese pagoda, be simple or finely decorated with mosaics and Persian ceramic tiles. A mosque can be built with straw and mud in Central Africa, or be inside the temple of the Pharaohs in Luxor, inspire the style of the cathedrals in Spain, be carried out by Moroccan workers during the last century in Paris or become a wonder of the world and a symbol of eternal love, like the Taj Mahal in India.

In Fez, Tunis, Kairouan, Dakar, Jerusalem, Baghdad, Damascus, Aleppo, Jakarta, Kuala Lumpur, Granada, Cordoba, Sarajevo, Istanbul, Kazan, Tehran, Qom, Islamabad and, especially, in Cairo, Medina and Mecca, mosques have been built that have included areas for the study and analysis of Islamic doctrine. It is the work carried out for centuries by masters and their pupils and by teachers and students in these areas that has helped to spread the development of traditional

Islamic sciences throughout the world and, in many cases, to create a network of knowledge that connects the wisdom of the East to the West. In these cases, mosques are not simply a ritualistic meeting place for Muslims but, outside prayer times, they are home to Koranic schools, universities, places known internationally for intellectual debate, theological training schools and centres for spiritual guidance.

The Symbolism of the Mosque

Large courtyards with beautiful fountains are placed before the main entrance for the faithful in many mosques in the East. These are spaces within the mosque area that are separate from the prayer hall because it is here that the faithful must perform their ritual ablutions: the washing of certain parts of the body in order to purify a Muslim and make him/her ready for prayer. These courtyards are, to some extent, a passage zone: we are inside the mosque complex but still outside the hall of the mosque.

The faithful have left the world of daily responsibilities outside the mosque's courtyard walls and are about to enter the world of spiritual communication in the prayer hall. The courtyard and the ablutions represent the place and the necessary action for leaving the cares of this world and preparing oneself for contact with the Other world, the higher world, the world of the Lord of the Worlds. The water which the hands use to moisten the mouth, nose, face, arms, head, ears, neck and feet symbolically cleanses impurities from the main parts of the body of the believer.

Soon after, he will hear and recite the sounds of the sacred language, move his hands, arms, head and feet, carrying out a series of movements that together constitute the second pillar of Islam, ritual prayer (*al-salât*): the most evident of the daily practices of a Muslim.[11] After prayer, when he leaves the hall, a Muslim finds himself in the same courtyard from which he has entered and, every now and then, he feels the need to stop in silent reflection or start a conversation with other members of the community and to accompany them to the exit, paving the way for the practical effect of the grace received during the ceremony that will inspire him in his return to his public and private duties. If ritual prayer is central for every believer's spiritual life, ritual worship without reflection and meditation risk being a purely mechanical action deprived of any spiritual involvement, because the inner concentration helps the believer to inspire all his life and not only his prayer

11 According to a famous tradition the practice of Islam is based on five pillars which are: testifying (*al-shahâdah*) that there is no god but God and that Muhammad is the messenger of God; daily prayer (*al-salât*); almsgiving (*al-zakât*); fasting during Ramadan (*al-sawm*); the pilgrimage to Mecca (*al-hajj*) for those who have the capacity. The *salât*, second pillar of Islamic worship, is more than an individual prayer. It is a precise ritual action related to spiritual elevation and intimacy with the Lord of the Worlds. Prophet Muhammad said that 'the *salât* is the spiritual ascension (*mi'râj*) of the believer'. He also pointed out this degree of contemplation and inner-peace: 'The freshness of my eye is in the *salât*'.

in accordance with the Will of God. So the Prophet Muhammad stated that 'an hour of meditation is better than seventy years of worship'.[12]

The Symbolism of a Muslim

Every believer can pray alone or in a group, at home, at work or in a mosque. An Islamic tradition reminds the faithful of the major spiritual benefits that are received when the prayer is done collectively in a mosque.[13] Scholars advise Muslims, when possible, to make the effort to go to some specially prepared prayer place nearby to do their prayers. During the prayers, they recommend finding a sense of belonging to the community of believers, of going beyond their normal horizons, to share a fraternal sense of the coming together of people who do not know each other but who, in brief moments of prayer, are linked together by the duty of worshipping the One God and by the desire for His Mercy.

> Verily, this community of yours is a single community, and I am your Lord, therefore adore Me![14]

The depersonalization of the individual in common prayer is able to put the personal point of view into perspective and bring each individual believer to the recognition of a dimension that goes beyond the individual. This is not to artificially interrupt their own occupations, but to change their providential integration within a rhythm that is confirmed by that intense spiritual concentration that every Muslim feels particularly during his five ritual prayers at home, alone or with the family, or with colleagues in the workplace or places of study or in the mosque next to an indefinite number of people of different races and cultures that, for a few brief moments of that day or all one's life, become companions in prayer. A Muslim's companions in prayer can be friends or relatives but, once they enter a mosque, they too spread themselves out among the faithful to pray next to another person, often a stranger who, just like him, at that moment of the day, has heard the call of the *muezzin*, and interrupted his business, gone into the courtyard for ritual ablutions and entered the mosque to pray to God in the way of Islam.

Empty Space and Sacred Presence

Inside the mosque, the prayer hall can be an open space or can be decorated with columns or without arches and, especially, must not have seats. Symbolically, the interior of a mosque must be empty, because all the available spaces will be filled

12 Collected by Al-Suyûtî.

13 The Messenger of God said: 'Prayer in congregation is better than the prayer of a man by himself by twenty-seven degrees'. Collected by Mâlik, *Al-Muwatta'*.

14 The Koran, 21:92.

by the faithful during prayer. Physically, the mosque is a place that is filled by the faithful doing their prayers in parallel rows:

> 'Verily, God loves those who fight in His Cause in rows (ranks) as if they were as solid structure'.[15]

> 'By those who range themselves in ranks! And by those who are strong in repelling (evil)! And by those who proclaim the Remembrance (of God)!'[16]

The disposition of Muslims in their ritual common prayers, in ranks behind the imam, is modelled on the disposition of the angels behind the Spirit of God in the heavens. Spiritually, the mosque and the faithful is a blessed place where the Word of God resounds with the reading of the verses of the divine Revelation contained in the Holy Koran.

From childhood onwards, every Muslim learns some parts of the Koran by heart in the same sacred language that Allah, the name of God in Islam, used. The Koran is therefore the Word and Language of God, and Muslims who recite the Koran are repeating the same sounds of the divine language. During the five daily prayers, every Muslim gives new voice to the Revelation and recalls for his own sake, for the community united together and for the place they are gathered, the spiritual presence of the Revealer, the presence of Allah.

When an Islamic space is used exclusively as an empty receptacle to accommodate Muslims in prayer and when these faithful empty themselves of their personal concerns in order to invoke the presence of God, this space is called a mosque. What fills the mosque is the faithful, what fills the faithful in the mosque is the presence of God who answers the calls and prayers of His servants.

In Islam, any space that contains a sign of the divine Revelation is sacred, any place where the presence of God is invoked, any place where there is a devout believer or a simple being. The life of every person is sacred and, if this person acts consciously and responsibly because of this honour, his own actions are sacred. When a Muslim decides to honour his divine origin by giving himself to a moment of ritual devotion, the place where he finds himself, of course, becomes consecrated. The mosque and the man who prays there are both sacred spaces that give themselves up to the reaffirmation of the miracle of the religious message, the gift of the Word of God as revealed to the Prophet and passed on to his community of followers.

As we said before, every Muslim can perform his ritual prayers anywhere, as long as it is clean and free of human images.[17] The bedroom or the living

15 The Koran, 61:4

16 The Koran, 37:1–3.

17 According to a statement of Prophet Muhammad, 'Angels do not enter in a place where there are images of living beings'. The Masters of Islam explain that this prohibition aims at avoiding risks of distraction of the worshipper from the Presence of the Unique God by images that might be taken as idols.

room of the house can become a sacred space at the time of prayer; a room in the workplace can be used if necessary. In other words, there is no absolute necessity for a Muslim to only pray in a mosque, considering it as the only sacred place where ritual prayer can be done. If there were to be a preference, it is still subject to the natural order of public and private duties that believers must still be sure of fulfilling in the society in which they live.

Every place and every action is sacred in Islam if done in obedience to a religious perspective, if it has a right and conscious intention. To be a good Muslim, it is not sufficient just to go to the mosque to pray, particularly if you spend the rest of your time not living a life of respect and spiritual sensitivity: nor is it acceptable to cause disorder or confusion by forcing your prayers on others in places and situations that are not suitable for prayer.

The sacredness of places in Islam involves not only a space dedicated to prayer, but also a dimension of the believer that bears witness to the sacredness of life at all times and in all places. Within this perspective, Muslims dedicate at least five moments of their day to their ritual duty, entering a state of interior and exterior consecration. As we have seen, the sacredness of a person and a place comes from the desire to invoke the presence of God in the person praying and in the place in which he performs his daily worship. So, his bedroom or the room in which he finds himself, or the mosque he has gone to, become holy and worthy of being the place for his ritual prostrations, his *sujûd*, the *Masjid*, the Mosque.

Macrocosm and Microcosm: Relating and Hospitality

With this perspective clear, the life of the faithful inside the mosque assumes the quality of a natural religiousness in which, before or after the prayers, the young and the old, and women and children can pause, alone or with others, to meditate in silence, to read the Holy Book, to study, to converse and even to eat and play. Without either confusing the more intimate character of the rituals or failing to participate in all the specific areas of contemporary society, the members of the Islamic community are used to spending time in the mosque several times a week, and this partly brings together many aspects of daily life and renews the very sacredness of all these aspects of life, without artificial barriers between what is inside the mosque and what is outside the mosque. This is not to confuse the mosque with a school, a house, a restaurant or with a cultural or social centre, but it would be a mistake to see it as a temple cut off from the world, indifferent to changes in the country and strictly confined to a monastic seclusion.

On the other hand, as I wrote 15 years ago, the first city of Medina itself took its present name only after the arrival of the Prophet Muhammad: until just shortly before, it was known as the oasis of Yathrib. It was the sacred presence of the Prophet that inspired the development of a new civilization and a new city, and a new time and a new sacred place where families, nomadic and sedentary peoples and various religious communities came together in emulation and cooperation in brotherhood, mutual respect and spiritual harmony, both in time of war and in time of peace. For years now, we have been seeing the formalist and apologetic ideologization of this universal model of Medina, with a literal interpretation promoted by those who are convinced that it is enough to artificially rebuild exclusively confessional neighbourhoods or Islamic ghettos in order to give a sacred character to an area and its inhabitants. Moreover, this is nothing less than making a complete sacrilege of history, of place, of religion and of the faithful.

Sacred Symbols

It is important to say that religious symbols stand for spiritual meanings that must not be denied, belittled or distorted just because someone wants to exploit them for political, ideological or personal power. For what cannot be tolerated is the exploitation of the sacred value of the symbolic universe of religions for worldly ends like the manipulation of consensus and power. Symbols are the signs by which the transcendent becomes immanent and, at the same time, the way and means that, from the order of creation, lead us back to spiritual reality, which would be otherwise impossible to interpret because of its super-rational character. Symbols are a basis for a synthetic knowledge that allows believers to ascend spiritually and intellectually from the multiplicity of creation to the unity of the Creator:

> God doth guide whom He will to His Light: God doth set forth Parables for men: and God doth know all things.[18]

To go further into the Islamic teachings concerning the sacredness of space, we cannot forget that some particular sacred spaces have a special importance among the others. The basis of sacredness is the possibility of worship, and therefore, as we described, the symbolism of the Muslim and that of the mosque are the model for the consideration of sacredness of space in general. A teaching of the Prophet says, 'Do not prepare yourself for a journey except to three Mosques: the Sacred Mosque (*al-Masjid al-Harâm*), the Faraway Mosque (*al-Masjid al-Aqsâ*) and my Mosque (*Masjidî*)'.[19] The 'Sacred Mosque' is the Temple of Mecca, also called the House of God (*bayt Allâh*), the Faraway Mosque is the sanctuary in Jerusalem where the Koran says the ascension of the Prophet started, and finally the Mosque of the Prophet is the Great Mosque in Medina. Mecca, Medina and Jerusalem are the three main Holy Cities in Islam.

---

18 The Koran, 24:35. An example of Islamic perspective towards symbols can be seen in Al-Ghazâlî's work *Mishkât al-anwâr*, 'The tabernacle of lights', where he describes the different levels of meaning and the correspondences from the formal and outward dimension to the spiritual and inward one.

19 Related by Al-Bukhârî.

Mecca, the Primordial Temple

Mecca, or the Noble Mecca (*makkah al-mukarramah*), is the place where the pilgrimage (*al-hajj*), fifth pillar of Islam, takes place. Indeed it is there that the temple to the one God is located, known as the Kaaba and established by Abraham in a valley that the Muslim tradition states to be the same place where Adam, first prophet and man, built the first temple for divine worship on earth after the fall from Paradise. The Koran says, 'The first temple ever set up for mankind was indeed the one at Bakkah: rich in blessings and a source of guidance to the worlds'.[20] The Prophet Abraham, along with his son Ishmael, built the new temple in the same place as the first, its structure inspired by the *Sakîna*, the sanctifying and peaceful presence of Allah that is so present in that place. This reminds us that the establishment of a sacred place must be carried out under the inspiration of the holy presence.

Mecca represents the centre of the world, the place in which the spiritual axis that supports creation is manifested. It is a primordial place, where the believer can taste the transcendence and absoluteness of his Lord. This taste can be accessed through the ritual of the great and the small pilgrimage (*'umrah*). In the *tawâf*, the circumambulation of the Kaaba, the pilgrim captures the ontological status of creature that is submitted (*muslim*) and that circulates with all other beings around the divine centre. In the *say'*, the ritual run between the hills of Safa and Marwa, the believer learns the science of the rhythm of spiritual invocation that unites and ties the interior with the exterior. In the drinking from the spring of Zam Zam, which miraculously emerged at the feet of the young Ishmael thanks to an angelic intervention, the believer discovers that he can have access to an inexhaustible spiritual fountain that flows from the centre of the world.

As for this sacred place, being present within it for the pilgrimage demands a particular ritual condition. Whoever intends to go to Mecca for *Hajj* or *'Umrah*, there being no other reason to go there since the exclusive presence of Allah is the purpose of the place, must enter a particular sacred state (*ihram*) before even approaching the land where the temple is to be found. It is a state that consists of abandoning ordinary clothes and shoes in exchange for a dress composed of two sheets of white cloth that are not sewn. This ritual, sacred state is an analogous form of the moment in which the believer enters the state of canonical prayer that, wherever it may be performed, is always oriented towards the Kaaba.

This place and these rites are the sites in which the believer finds the primordiality of the religion (*dîn al-fitrah*) and the eternity of God, that is shown in His unity and absoluteness. It is also the same place where the Prophet Muhammad was born and where the Revelation was sent down to his pure heart during *Laylat al-Qadr*, the night of Destiny, the event that marked the start of the cycle of manifestations of the Seal of Prophecy and of the traditional form brought about by it, namely Islam. Close to the valley of the Sacred Mosque, within the *haram* of Mecca, is

20 The Koran, 3:96.

Jabal an-Nûr, the Mount of Light, where the cave of *Hira* can be found. It was in this cave that the Prophet Muhammad was in spiritual retreat when the Koran was revealed through Jibrîl, Gabriel. The cave is a symbol of the heart, the centre of the being where direct communication occurs between creature and the Lord of the worlds (*rabbu al-alamîn*).

Medina, the City of the Prophet

If the character of the sacred Mosque of Mecca is determined by the concentration of the absoluteness of the one God, the Mosque of the Prophet (*al-masjid an-nabawî*) in Medina gathers the light of the divine immanence that radiates from its chosen and blessed receptacle, the Prophet Muhammad: hence the name 'the Radiant City' (*al-madînah al-munawwarah*). The current mosque covers the entire extension of the Yathrib oasis at the time in which the Prophet Muhammad had chosen it as the place for his emigration (*al-hijrah*) and refuge from the persecution that he was being subjected to in Mecca. Within this mosque there is the old mosque of the Prophet, including the pulpit (*minbar*) from which he held the Friday sermon, as well as his tomb which, according to his own request to be buried in the place where he died, was the abode of his wife, Aisha.

Pilgrims coming from Mecca after completing the rituals of *Hajj* or *'Umrah* find in the visit and the greeting of the Prophet a renewed fullness of the divine radiance that follows the concentration experienced in Mecca. If Mecca was the metaphysical anticipation of the Last Day and the annihilation before the divine Majesty, the presence of the Prophet in his city is the access to the dimension of immanence, of the divine richness and forgiveness that radiate from the entire universe, revivifying the life of the believers in all its aspects. In a very well-known verse of the Koran, God addresses the Prophet, saying:

> We have not sent you except as mercy (rahma) to the worlds.[21]

The presence of the Prophet is understood as true spiritual influence (*barakah*) and not merely as a memory, a presence that the believer continues to understand as a sign of the possibility of guidance, of protection and of radiance that God bestows upon the believers. Between the home of the Prophet and his *minbar* (pulpit) there is a place, now found inside the mosque, known as *rawda*, literally 'garden', that according to the very words of the Prophet is 'a piece of paradise on earth'. The pilgrims arrive at the *rawda* from the right, the place where the pulpit can be found. A few at a time, they reach it to carry out the ritual prayer of greeting to the place (*tahiyyat al-masjid*), facing towards Mecca, with the pulpit of the Prophet to their right and the Prophet himself resting near his companions, Abu Bakr and 'Umar, to their left.

21 The Koran, 21:107.

Jerusalem, 'The Holy'

Jerusalem is the third sacred city of Islam. In Arabic it is known either as *bayt al-maqdîs*, the 'home of sanctity', or simply as *al-Quds*, 'the Holy'. Like Mecca, there is a convergence of various events in sacred history: the Rock of the Sacrifice of Abraham, the location on earth that God promised the people of Moses and Aaron, the temple ordered by God to David and built by Solomon, the presence and the teaching of the prophets sent amongst the children of Israel, up to Zakaria, the Virgin Mary and the preaching of John the Baptist and Jesus.

However, in the Muslim tradition Jerusalem is especially linked to the Prophet Muhammad's night journey and celestial ascension (*al-isrâ' wa-l-mirâj*). One night the Prophet was woken up by the angel Gabriel while he was in the sacred mosque in Mecca. He was led to Jerusalem where he began his vertical ascension through the heavens up until being in God's presence, at the distance of 'two arches or less',[22] to then return to earth in the reverse order. For Muslims, this journey represents the model spiritual journey that was completed by the Seal of the Prophets, the complete spiritual realization that is the most elevated goal to which the believers can aspire.

The connections between the places of this journey with the places of the sacred history are significant. The end point of the horizontal journey, that is also the starting point of the vertical ascension, corresponds to the small cave hidden beneath the rock of Abraham's sacrifice, upon which the Dome of the Rock (*qubbat al-sakhra*) can now be found. The Dome stands on the esplanade of the mosques, its west side aligned with the Temple of Solomon which was destroyed by the Romans in the year 70 after Christ.

More explicitly than other places, Jerusalem represents convergence towards the unity of the Revelations and of the believers of Abrahamic monotheism. This is not only for the providential convergence of the signs of the sacred history that preceded the Seal of Prophecy, but also because Jerusalem is the symbolic place of the eschatological events: for the coming of the Messiah that, for Christians and Muslims, will coincide with the second coming of Christ; the place of the final battle between the believers of the end of time and the Antichrist; and the beginning of the events that will close the former cycle of humanity in order to open the one that will follow.

The Sacredness of Creation

Although it is possible for the believer to participate in the presence and the communication with the Lord of the Worlds in all the mosques and in every corner of the earth where God has made a carpet upon which to worship Him, the Muslim knows that the very same Creator has chosen certain places above others to manifest some of His signs, like in Mecca, Jerusalem and Medina. Creation

22 The Koran 53:9.

belongs to God and for this reason it is sacred in its entirety. Some masters compare the world to a mirror in which God reflects Himself 'to manifest to Himself His mystery'.[23] For a Muslim, wanting to artificially separate the creation from the Creator, without recognizing the sacredness that He has bestowed upon creation, would be to misunderstand God in His immanence, in His mirror.

However, this does not mean that all spaces are equal. Every place, just like every time, manifests a specific providential character that distinguishes it from others. Complete sacredness does not mean simplicity or uniformity. Following the maieutic of Revelation, the believer learns to deal with complexity as a providential richness, recognizing that the varieties of the differences of creation reflect divine infinity without exhausting it. If God is always the owner of every place, His presence is accessible to believers at various levels and in various ways. In Islam the level and nature of sacredness are universally determined by the Revelation. In the sacred places of Islam, the stages of sacred history find convergence with the believers' rituals of worship. These become the means by which the teachings and spiritual blessings can be accessed and brought alive by the lived presence of the prophets and saints in those places. The right intention of believers allows the sacredness of a place or of a symbol to become functional rather than merely being an imaginary projection, an idol.

In a sacred hadith God says, 'I was a hidden treasure and I wanted to be known, so I created the world'. If the sacred space is a space that follows a divine order of hospitability, then creation is the space of His knowledge, the very purpose of human life. In this symbolic and spiritual perspective, the sacred places in the entire sacredness of creation are seen as signs that reveal something about the nature of the world, of ourselves and of our Lord, conforming to the Koranic verse:

> We will show them Our signs in the horizons and within themselves until it becomes clear to them that it is the truth. But is it not sufficient concerning your Lord that He is, over all things, a Witness?

The holy cities are an example of the sacred symbolism of space, and the visit by the pilgrim is a way not only to discover the blessings of each of them, but also to know the science of space in the footsteps of the Prophets. It is nevertheless important to stress that we cannot take the symbolism in a schematic way, merely associating Mecca with the transcendence of God, Medina with the immanence of the Prophet, and Jerusalem with the eschatological call of the End of Time. Allah is everywhere the same, and everywhere He is the One who must be worshipped, not the single differences or the places: we must not associate anything with Him:

> To God belong the east and the west. Wherever you turn, there is the Face of God. Witness, God is Infinite, All-knowing.[24]

23 In particular Muhyi al-Din Ibn 'Arabi, in *The Wisdom of the Prophets*.
24 The Koran, 41:53.

Universal Meaning of the Three Holy Cities and Sacred Jurisdiction

Mecca, Medina and Jerusalem are not the only sacred places or the only mosques that are particularly transparent to spiritual radiance. The spiritual blessings radiate from the entirety of the traditional meanings and symbols. Amongst these signs, the sages are fundamental, the 'people of the Remembrance of God' (*ahl al-dhikr)*, recognized by Muslims as inheritors of the prophets, as guides and models for the Muslim community. Through the numerous saints in different places and times and from various populations and languages,[25] God has allowed the maintenance of the constant radiation of light and knowledge in various temples and places from Orient to Occident. The places where these saints lived and taught, and where their bodies now rest, have become centres of the radiation of sacred knowledge. Damascus, Kairouan, Fez, Cairo, Baghdad, Istanbul, Konya, Nishapur, Qom, Najaf, Karbala, Delhi, Singapore and many others have constituted centres of radiation of traditional knowledge.

One must bear in mind that the holy places and cities display universal meanings that transcend local and religious specificities and therefore they cannot become vehicles for forms of exclusivity. The sacredness of the space and of time occurs when the intention and concentration are turned solely towards God, regardless of the place or the circumstances in which one finds oneself, in order to carry out the tasks that we are responsible for in this world. The challenge of our time is to find the way to relate, in a conscious and constructive way, to the various jurisdictions of the sacred, those of religious forms, spaces and times, without relativism, without exclusiveness and without indifference. In this task, what can be of help for finding the correct orientation is the capacity to discover a three-dimensional order of reality. A spiritual jurisdiction depends on the breadth and the levels of radiance of spiritual blessing. If, on the one hand, there cannot simply be a material, mechanical or spatial understanding, on the other there has to be an understanding that such blessings can be effective and concrete for the local and temporal context in which the believers live.

Moreover, we cannot forget that Mecca, Jerusalem and Medina are places of permanent residence for few people. For the majority of the believers in this world these places are the destination of pilgrimages, and they continue to represent interior 'spiritual abodes' (*manâzil*) in which the most sincere aspire to remain even when they live, work and pray in Milan, Rome or elsewhere. Physical and temporal distances from central places are nothing but a test for the believers from their Lord.

The sacred dynamic of the pilgrimage also teaches the importance of the movement, from which the understanding of the space cannot be separated. The three sacred cities mentioned here highlight the sacredness of these places, thanks to a different particular movement for each and yet necessary to all. For Mecca,

---

25 The Koran says, 'We have not sent any messenger except speaking the language of his people', Koran 14:4.

the House of Allah is both the place in which God descends from Heaven to Earth and is the centre around which the believer walks and then runs, turning in circles and approaching the centre; whereas Safa and Marwa show their character thanks only to the ritual run between them. Jerusalem is the place where the spiritual journey becomes vertical. Medina is the city that welcomed the Prophet from his emigration, from the rescission of tribal ties and coming under the protection of an exclusively spiritual community. The movement occurs in space but also in time and therefore there are three dimensions that cannot be separated from one another in order to reach the objective of knowledge and action in the times and spaces that the believers find themselves in. The proof of knowing how to gather the value of space and time is that of knowing how to move in harmony with their character, to know how to behave as vicegerents (*khalîfa*) of Allah on earth, being actual symbols of the spiritual realities and of the superior truths that belong to God and at the same time radiating their beneficial influence.

The attempt to sever the constitutive relationship between Earth and Heaven, and between Man and God by separating what is ontologically united derives from an anti-traditional perspective designed to oppose the spiritual currents that have given life to symbolic and genuine artistic forms from the beginning of time.

It is therefore necessary to rediscover the deeper meaning of traditional symbolism and, at the same time, be able to interact constructively with the pluralism of religions, ideas and men. As regards the issue of Islam in Italy, it would then not only be a question of encouraging the positive integration of immigrant communities towards achieving full citizenship, but also a question of recognizing the official, authentic and native presence of the Italian Islamic community so that it can organize its own worship and sacred places without discrimination.

In this perspective, we are glad that our Al-Wahid Mosque in Milan has been selected as a model of best practices by the Islam Committee of the Italian Ministry of the Interior as we consider this recognition also as a model for the respect of new sacred spaces owned and managed by the recent European Muslim community. *COREIS Italiana* (the Italian Islamic Religious Community), together with the *European Council of Religious Leaders* (ECRL), fully supported the 'Universal Code on Holy Sites' adopted at the international conference 'Holy Sites' in Trondheim, organized by the *Center for Peace and Human Rights* in Oslo in July 2009 and participated in March 2011 in the meeting hosted by the European Commission in Brussels and organised by the Sovereign Order of Malta on 'Protecting the sacred spaces in the Mediterranean'. Following this initiative we fully support the 'Declaration on the Protection and Enhancement of Sacred Places in the Mediterranean area'[26] and the responsibilities religious communities and public authorities share on this important issue.

26 Annexed to this book.

PART III
The Sacred Places of the Mediterranean

Chapter 9
Jerusalem's Holy Sites in Israeli Law

Marshall J. Breger

Introduction: The Boundaries of Jerusalem[1]

This chapter considers legal issues related to the holy places in Jerusalem. Preliminary to this discussion one must consider the boundaries of Israel or *Eretz Yisrael* (biblical Israel). As one commentator has pointed out:

> Where is Eretz Israel? The answer to this question is different for the religious and national camps since they draw on different sources to support their definitions. The former draws solely on Biblical sources while the nationalists' approach stems primarily from the borders of the British Mandate, borders which were formulated in the aftermath of the Versailles Conference in 1919. One was defined in Genesis and in other places in traditional religious texts, the other was essentially the outcome of political negotiations between the imperial powers of Britain and France after the ravages of World War I.[2]

One must also consider the boundaries of secular Jerusalem. These boundaries have shifted over time. The 'core' is similar for all the Abrahamic religions – the Old City – which is the area within the historic city walls. But the city grew outside of the walls in the 1840s with Arab areas like Sheikh Jarrah and Jewish areas like Meah Shearim and later Rechavia. After the 1967 War, the Israeli military sent an officer with a jeep to circle Jerusalem with instructions of

---

1 This chapter draws considerably from a paper written by Marshall J. Breger and Leonard Hammer, 'Legal Issues of the Holy Places', in Marshall J. Breger, Yitzhak Reiter and Leonard Hammer (eds), *Holy Places in the Israel-Palestine Conflict: Confrontation and Coexistence* (Routledge Kegan Paul, 2009) and from Marshall J. Breger and Thomas A. Idinopulos, *Jerusalem's Holy Places and the Peace Process* (Washington Institute for Near East Policy 1998). Much of my thinking in this area has been informed by my ongoing transatlantic dialogue with Leonard Hammer. I thank both Prof. Hammer and Prof. Indinopulous for their instructive insights. My work in this area has for some years been supported by the Royal Norwegian Ministry of Foreign Affairs whom I thank for their willingness to support theoretical work with practical consequences.

2 Colin Shindler, 'Likud and the Search for Eretz Israel: From the Bible to the Twenty-First Century' (2001) *Israeli Affairs* 92.

'maximum land, minimum Arabs'. It is hard to view the results of that historical accident as sacred.[3]

The 'metes and bounds' of sacred Jerusalem is also a concept 'in play'. For some, it is particular churches, synagogues or mosques that are *makam*, sacred space. For others, it is the entire city that is holy. And for yet others, it is the entire land of Israel (or Palestine). These latter maximalist views suggest the difficulty of managing Jerusalem in an inclusive manner. Indeed, one needs to reflect on what geographical boundaries specifically encompass the holiness — in Hebrew, the *Kedusha* — of Jerusalem for Muslims, Christians, and Jews, as well as on what geographical boundaries symbolize these groups' respective nationalist aspirations.

Further, the urban reality is that after 1967, the city grew out into its hinterland to functionally encompass areas that were formally part of the West Bank. This porousness between Israel and Palestine makes discussions of Jerusalem even more difficult.

This chapter does not pretend to discuss every site in Jerusalem holy to one of the Abrahamic religions. Rather, it tries to bring out general principles and focus on some of the more important sites. It will end with some proposals about issues to be considered when dealing with holy places.

What is the Definition of Holy Places in Israel and Palestine?

The Encyclopedia of Public International Law defines holy places as

> … geographically determined localities to which one or more religious communities attribute extraordinary religious significance or consider a subject of divine consecration. Holy Places may consist of man-made structures (churches, temples, graves, etc.) or natural objects (trees, groves, hills, rivers, etc.).[4]

Traditionally, the holy places in Israel and Palestine were understood as those sites listed in the so-called Ottoman *Status Quo*, whose goal was to ensure protection for a variety of key Christian sites and lessen tension among the religious populace.

We should note that there is no definition of a holy place in Israeli law. The term is referred to in the 1967 Law for the Protection of Holy Places[5] without explanation.

---

3 For the religious basis see, Genesis 15:18–21; Numbers, 14:1–4; Numbers 12:1–4; I Samuel, 24:2; I Kings, 5:5. This is not an exhaustive list of sources.

4 Christian Rumpf, 'Holy Places', in Rudolf Bernhardt (ed.), *Encyclopedia of Public International Law* (vol. 2, Max-Plank-Institut für Ausländisches Öffentliches Recht und Völkerrecht 1995) 863–6.

5 Protection of Holy Places Law 1967, trans. in Ruth Lapidoth and Moshe Hirsch, *The Jerusalem Question and Its Resolution: Selected Documents* (Kluwer 1994) 169.

What are the Number of Holy Sites in the Greater Jerusalem Area?

The number of holy sites in Jerusalem depends, of course, on one's definition of Jerusalem. Most holy sites are found in the Old City of Jerusalem which describes the area within the walls built in 1453 by Sultan Suleiman the Magnificent. Other holy sites can be found in an area called the 'historic basin' (sometimes called the Holy Basin) which encompasses an area ranging from the Mount of Olives to the City of David.[6] Other definitions of Jerusalem's holy sites have extended to areas presently within the area 'controlled' by the Palestinian Authority (PA) including Rachel's Tomb, The Church of the Nativity and other Christian sites in Bethlehem.

The Ottoman *Status Quo* listed five Christian holy places.[7] In this definitive, if not exhaustive, study of holy places for the Mandate authorities, Lionel Cust, however, added two Jewish sites to the *Status Quo*, namely the Western Wall and Rachel's Tomb, but did not address Islamic sites given the Mandate's policy of non-interference with Muslim institutions.[8] A 1949 United Nations map enumerated 30 Holy Places in the Jerusalem area.[9]

A 1950 Israeli inter-ministerial committee, established to study the manner by which the new State of Israel might protect the holy places, listed at least 300 holy sites for the Christian, Muslim and Jewish religions, although this was an expansive list including all places of worship and cemeteries.[10] The ensuing regulations that were issued following the 1967 Holy Places Law included 15 Jewish holy sites.[11] On an informal level, however, the Department for Holy

---

6 The so-called Historic Basin, which has been defined as including not only the Old City, but also its environs like Mount Zion, City of David, Kidron Stream and Mount of Olives. See Wendy Pullen and Maxmilian Steinberg, 'The Making of Jerusalem's Holy Basin', (2012) 23 *Planning Perspectives*, 225–48. See also Ruth Lapidoth and Amnon Ramon, *The Historic Basin of Jerusalem, Problems and Possible Solutions* (Jerusalem: The Institute for Israel Studies, 2006).

7 Lionel G.A. Cust, *The Status Quo in the Holy Places* (Government of Palestine 1930).

8 Ibid.

9 'Central Portion of the Jerusalem Area: Principle of Holy Places', United Nations Map, no. 229 (Nov. 1949); see also Elihu Lauterpacht, *Jerusalem and the Holy Places* (n. 1, The Anglo-Israel Association 1968) 5.

10 Israeli Archives 2397/3 – Holy Places, 25/5/50. The list was compiled to determine the viability of certain structures that had been abandoned and the financial possibilities for protecting the sites. The authorities closed many churches and mosques due to problems of decay or abandonment, with the remainder receiving some form of protection or having posted guards.

11 The first regulations drafted in 1968 related to the manner of decorum to be imposed at the gravesite of Rabbi Shimon bar Yochai in Meron, Kovetz Takanot 2182, from 9/2/68, at 828, followed in 1969 by additional sites where the rules of decorum were to apply – Cave of Simon the Just and the Small Sanhedrin in Jerusalem, Graves of Rabbi

Places deems itself responsible for close to 160 Jewish sites throughout the country. According to a list prepared in 2000 by three authors, an Israeli Jew, an American Christian and a Palestinian Muslim, there were 326 noted holy places in Jerusalem.[12] The Islamic organization Al-Aqsa Association for Protection and Maintenance of Islamic *Waqf* Properties has catalogued hundreds of abandoned and disused Muslim sites throughout the country.[13] There is no 'official' list of Christian sites as the Custos of the Holy Land (the Franciscan order charged with custody of holy sites for Catholics) considers a formal list to be inappropriate as it may 'close off' additions in the future.

We should note that in 2003 the Foundation for the Culture of Peace also proposed a similar open-ended list for holy places in all of Israel, pursuant to the norms of the common heritage of mankind.[14] There are specific lists of holy places in the Peace Treaty with Jordan,[15] the various Oslo Accords[16] and the Vatican-Israel Fundamental Agreement.[17] But these lists are certainly not exclusive and do not exhaust the possible holy places in Israel and the Palestinian Authority controlled areas. For example, the Israeli Holy Places Authority lists over 140 sacred places,[18] yet does not include the site holy to Jews and Muslims known as Har ha-Bayit (the Temple Mount) to Jews or Al-Haram al-Qudsi al-Sharif (the Noble Sanctuary) to Muslims.[19]

Ovadiah of Bartenura, Zechariah the Prophet and Absalom in Jerusalem, the Cave of Elijah in Haifa and the Grave of Maimonides, Cave of Rabbi Akiva, Cave of Rabbi Chiya and Sons all in Tiberias, Kovetz Takanot 2387, from 8/5/69 (in Hebrew), at 1438.

12 See Y. Reiter, M. Eordegian and M. Abu Khalaf, 'Between Divine and Human: The Complexity of Holy Places in Jerusalem' in Moshe Ma'oz and Sari Nusseibeh (eds), *Jerusalem: Points of Friction – and Beyond* (Kluwer Law International) 95–7, 109–10. They use two criteria to develop a definition of holy places: first, 'the relationship between the public and the place', and second, 'the function of the place itself'. With these criteria they have prepared an exhaustive list. The authors distinguished between different levels of sites and concluded that holy places should be split into five groups: sanctuaries, holy sites, places of worship, religious buildings and religious sites.

13 See discussion infra. See also Noga Collins-Kreiner, 'Pilgrimage Holy Sites: A Classification of Jewish Holy Sites in Israel', (2000) *Journal of Cultural Geography* 57.

14 Holy Places – Common Heritage of Mankind, 27 September, 2003, Foundation for the Culture of Peace Madrid, Spain, at Annex III, paras 1–3 (on file with author).

15 Treaty of Peace between Israel and the Hashemite Kingdom of Jordan, 26 October 1994 <www.mfa.gov.il/mfa> accessed 30 April 2013.

16 Israeli-Palestinian Interim Agreement on the West Bank and Gaza Strip, Annex III, Schedule 4.

17 Fundamental Agreement between the Holy See and the State of Israel, 30 December, 1993, Vatican-Israel, ILM, 1994, vol. 33, 153 (hereinafter Fundamental Agreement).

18 Official list compiled by the Holy Sites Authority as of 12 April 2003 (on file with author).

19 But see 3338/99 *Pakovich v. State of Israel* 54 (3) Piskei Din 667 (2000) (in Hebrew) where the Israeli High Court found that it was obvious that the Temple Mount was a holy place, even if not listed as such.

What Domestic Laws Govern Holy Sites?

The Six-Day War in 1967 resulted in Israeli conquest of 'Jordanian' Jerusalem. It immediately doubled the area of Jerusalem to an area including the Old City and beyond. Shortly thereafter, Israel passed the Protection of Holy Places Law, 1967. That law states:

1. The Holy Places shall be protected from desecration and any other violation and from anything likely to violate the freedom of access of the members of the different religions to the places sacred to them or their feelings with regard to those places.
2. a) Whosoever desecrates or otherwise violates a Holy Place shall be liable to imprisonment for a term of seven years.
   b) Whosoever does anything likely to violate the freedom of access of the members of the different religions to the places sacred to them or their feelings with regard to those places shall be liable to imprisonment for a term of five years.
3. This law shall add to and derogate from any other law.[20]

Other Israeli statutes include provisions that impact on holy sites law and sites which are used for prayers and other religious purposes.[21] As an example, Section 146 of the Criminal Code Ordinance 1936, makes it an offence to cause damage to any place of worship or to any object sacred to any religion, with the intention of affronting the religion of any class of persons. Section 148 imposes penal sanctions for trespassing on places of worship and burial, for indignity to corpses and for disturbances at funeral ceremonies. In *Wagner v Attorney General*[22] it was held that this section applies not to opinion but to action (the difference in American 1st Amendment nomenclature between "speech" and "acts").

20 Protection of Holy Places Law 1967, supra note 73. The first paragraph of this law was adopted in the Basic Law: Jerusalem, Capital of Israel, 1980. See generally, Ruth Lapidoth and Moshe Hirsch (eds), *The Basic Law: Jerusalem, Capital of Israel* (repr. in *The Arab-Israel Conflict and its Resolution*, Martinus Nijhoff Publishing 1999) 255.

21 See, as an example, Section 22 of the Drainage and Flood Control Law, 1957; Section 70 of the Water Law, 1959; Section 8(1)(a) of the Mines Ordinance. Section 3 of the Local Authorities (Vesting of Public Property) Law, 1958, excludes property used for religious purposes and services from that which a local authority is empowered to acquire compulsorily for public purposes.

22 H.C. 4/64 18 (1) *Piskei Din* 29. See Section 2 of the Protection of Holy Places Law 1967, which makes it an offence to violate a Holy Place. Under Section 37(2) of the Police Ordinance, it is one of the duties of a police officer to maintain public order 'in the neighborhood of places … of public worship'.

What Archeological Statutes Govern Holy Places?

The British Mandate made a distinction between historical sites that have sacred aspects and sacred sites that are still in use (or 'living' sites).[23] The 1929 Antiquities Ordinance distinguished between historical monuments 'whether moveable or immovable or part of the soil' and 'antiquities of religious use or devoted to a religious purpose which are the property of a religious or ecclesiastical body'.[24] The effort was to distinguish, in the words of a British government memorandum, between monuments 'that are not of a merely archeological character, but are also … "living" monuments, that is to say monuments still in use for religious purposes'.[25]

Israel passed its own Antiquities Act in 1978.[26] The legislation defines an antiquity in Article 1 as an object, either detached or attached, which was made by a person prior to 1700 CE, including anything added to it that constitutes an integral part of it. In the spirit of the times, a change was made in this definition in Article 2, according to which an object made in 1700 CE or thereafter could be an antiquity if it possessed historical value and the Minister of Education had declared it to be an antiquity. There is no written definition of what constitutes 'an object of historical value', and thus its definition is left exclusively in the hands of the Minister of Education, who is responsible for the implementation of the law.[27] The Minister acts through the Director of the Department of Antiquities who has authority to declare a particular place an antiquity site.[28]

What Regulations Govern Holy Sites?

The regulation of holy sites in Israel has been a virtual kaleidoscope. The Ministry of Religious Affairs was originally charged with the implementation of the 1967 law. After consultation with representatives of the religions concerned, the Ministry of Religious Affairs was to draft regulations for various sites that the Ministry of Justice must then approve. On the demand of the secular Shinui Party, the Ministry of Religious Affairs was dissolved in early 2004 and its functions distributed among the other ministries and the National Authority for Religious Services was located in the

23 Antiquities Ordinance 1929, 1 Laws of Palestine 28.

24 Ibid.

25 See Naidha Abu El-Haj, 'Producing (Arti) Facts: Archeology and Power During the British Mandate of Palestine' (2002) *Israel Studies* 41.

26 Article 29 (iii), 885 Sefer Chukim 76, 1978 (in Hebrew).

27 See for example Meron Benvenisti, *Sacred Landscape: The Buried History of the Holy Land Since 1948* (University of California Press 2000) 305. See also Shoshana Berman, 'Antiquities in Israel in a Maze of Controversy' (1987) *Case Western Reserve Journal of International Law* 346–47.

28 1978 Antiquity Law at § 49(b). See also Meron Benvenisti, *Sacred Landscape*, op. cit., 346.

prime minister's office.[29] But by early January 2008, the political map had changed once again, and in what many viewed as a nod to the religious political party, Shas, the cabinet approved the resurrection of the Ministry of Religious Affairs.[30]

Further, while the 1967 statute declared that holy places were protected, it did not provide a list of the protected sites. The Ministry of Religious Affairs was charged with developing such a list. In 1968 the Ministry began the process of drafting regulations regarding holy sites, starting in Meron with the grave of Rabbi Shimon Bar Yochai, one of the most eminent disciples of Rabbi Akiva, attributed by many with the authorship of the Zohar ('The Brightness'), the chief work of Jewish mysticism, who lived in the era of the Tannaim (scholars of the Mishnah) during the Roman period after the destruction of the Second Temple in 70 CE. In 1981, the Religious Affairs Ministry promulgated regulations designating the Western Wall and surrounding sites as holy places.[31] Additionally, after 1967, the Organization for Holy Places[32] was created and funded by the Minister of Religious

---

29 See Zvi Zrahiya, 'It's Official – Religious Affairs Ministry to be Dissolved Sunday', *Haaretz* (Tel Aviv, 3 March 2004) A1 col 2 (in Hebrew) which states: 'Responsibility for non-Jewish groups will be transferred to the Interior Ministry, while the department that deals with religious councils will be moved to the Prime Minister's Office. The Center for the Development of Holy Sites will be the responsibility of the Tourism Ministry, the rabbinic courts will be under the control of the Justice Ministry, and the Rabbi of the Holy Sites and the Western Wall will be under the supervision of the Chief Rabbinate. Civil Service Commissioner Shmuel Hollander called the move historic, saying it was correct from an administrative point of view'. See also, Aryeh Dayan, 'Carving Up the Religious Affairs Ministry', *Haaretz* (Tel Aviv, 23 December 2003); Gideon Alon, 'Knesset Votes to Dismantle Religious Affairs Ministry', *Haaretz* (Tel Aviv 25 December 2003) (in Hebrew).

30 Roni Sofer, 'Ministry of Religious Affairs Reestablished' (2008) <www.YnetNews.com> accessed 6 January 2008.

31 Including, for example, the Cave of Simon the Just, the small Sanhedrin Cave (near the former), the Tomb of Rabbi Ovadiah of Bartenura (at the Mount of Olives cemetery) and Zechariah's Tomb and Absalom's Monument in the Kidron Valley. See Kovetz Takanot 4252 from 16/7/81 (in Hebrew), at 1212 for a list of the 'officially declared' sites in the regulations. See also Appendix 1 to Regulations for Protection of Jewish Holy Places 1981, where sites are listed for Jerusalem, Haifa, Tiberias, Meron and Peki'in. These designated sites are a far cry from the 160+ sites that the Holy Places Authority oversees on an unofficial basis, as discussed infra. See also Ruth Lapidoth, *The Basic Law: Jerusalem, Capital of Israel* (The Harry and Michael Sacher Center for Legislative Research and Comparative Law, the Hebrew University of Jerusalem 1999) 56 (in Hebrew). In 1995, the Ministry of Religious Affairs proposed to add to the list the following: David's Tomb on Mount Zion, the Cave of the Prophets Haggai and Malachi (on the western slopes of the Mount of Olives), the Tomb of the Prophetess Hulda (at the top of the Mount of Olives), Jehoshaphat's Cave and the Grave of the Sons of Hezir in the Kidron valley, the Siloam Tunnel and Spring, the large Sanhedrin Cave (now situated in the Sanhedria Park), Jeremiah's Cave (Hatzar Hamatarah) (near the central bus station of East Jerusalem), Zedekiah's Cave (near the Nablus Gate), the Kings' Tombs in Saladin Street and the synagogues in the Old City. This proposal was not approved.

32 Sometimes this is translated as 'the Observer of Holy Places'.

Affairs to care for and tend to Jewish holy sites. In 1988, the Ministry reorganized this body into the Office of Religious Affairs, which in 1989 went on to create a public organization, the Organization for the Development of the Holy Places. The list prepared by the Organization in 1989 is informal and includes any site with a link to a Jewish personality, synagogue or places of historical significance to the Jewish people. It now lists 162 sites and, where necessary, tends to their upkeep.

Based on this criterion, it would be difficult to 'create' a new holy site if the place has not been in continuous use or was not recognized as such.[33] In 2000, the Ministerof Religious Affairs attempted to delineate the criteria for designating holy sites, recognizing the potential for abuse by political and nationalist-religious forces. Although the regulations were never promulgated, the draft notes that not all synagogues or graves are automatically deemed holy;[34] there must be specific reference to the site in the rabbinic literature. Furthermore, even with such a reference, the site must be subject to some form of continuous 'use', such as for prayer and pilgrimage.

Inexplicably the Ministry has never issued – in draft or otherwise – a list of Muslim holy sites. The reason for the failure of the Ministry to develop a list is clearly political. Many Muslim holy sites were treated by the Israeli government as abandoned property after 1948 and were often (legally or otherwise) converted for other purposes. Israeli officials fear that listing Muslim holy sites will open a Pandora's Box of claims related to decisions under the Abandoned Property Law.[35] As an example, legal (and political) controversy followed the efforts of Muslim groups to reclaim the 'Large' mosque in Beersheva. When the mosque was abandoned in 1948, the municipality used it as a court and then a prison. Recently the city proposed to turn the 'Large' Mosque into a museum against the objections of local Muslims who sought to reclaim it for use as a mosque. The Israeli Supreme Court rejected that request but determined that the museum should be dedicated to Islamic culture rather than a general museum.[36] At the time of writing this the city does not appear to have bowed to the Court's ruling.[37]

---

33 Official list compiled by the Holy Sites Authority as of 12 April 2003 (on file with author). The organization actively tends to around 140 sites.

34 The draft, prepared on 23 July 2000 (hereinafter Draft Report), was submitted by Rabbi Shmuel Rabinowitz, then the Rabbi of the Holy Places in Israel and now the Rabbi of the Western Wall (on file with author).

35 Abandoned Property Law, 1950, Sefer Ha-Chukim, 14/3/50, p. 86 (in Hebrew).

36 Jack Khoury, 'High Court Rules Be'er Sheva Mosque to Be Used as Islamic Museum', *Haaretz* (Tel Aviv, 23 June 2011) Ilana Curiel, 'Beersheva Mosque to Become Islam Museum' (2011) <www.ynetnews.com/articles/0,7340, L-4086545,00.html> accessed 30 April 2013.

37 In fact, in September, 2012 the city planned a wine festival in the mosque's courtyard. After President Shimon Peres called the Mayor the city agreed to move the event outside the mosque's perimeter. Yanir Yagna, 'Israeli Mayor Moves Be'er Sheeva Wine Festival off Grounds of Muslim Mosque', *Haaretz* (Tel Aviv, 5 September 2012).

In November 2004, Adalah, an NGO operating on behalf of the Arab minority in Israel, filed a petition before the Israel Supreme Court, requesting that the Ministry of Interior (the replacement for the disbanded Ministry of Religion) draft regulations concerning Muslim holy places.[38] The petition contended that the absence of such regulations is discriminatory to the minority Arab population and a violation of the Basic Law: Human Dignity, of freedom of religion and the concept of equality.[39]

What International Instruments Govern Holy Places?

General Observations

There is a difference of opinion regarding the status of international instruments relevant to Jerusalem. It is generally agreed that the following international instruments govern holy places in Jerusalem: the Hague Convention for the Protection of Cultural Property in the Event of Armed Conflict[40] of 1954;[41] the UNESCO World Heritage Convention;[42] and the International Covenant on Civil

38 See 'Press Release: Adalah Petitions Supreme Court in Name of Muslim Religious Leaders Demanding Legal Recognition for Muslim Holy Sites in Israel' <www.adalah.org/eng/pressreleases/pr.php?file=04_11_23> accessed 23 November 2004) (hereinafter: Adalah Press Release). The petition was officially filed on 21 November 2004. For a copy of the petition (in Hebrew) see Adalah Newsletter, vol. 39 <www.adalah.org/newsletter/eng/aug07/6.php> accessed 21 November 2004 (hereinafter: Adalah Newsletter).

39 See Adalah Press Release. Ibid. The most recent development occurred in August 2007 when the Israel Supreme Court ordered the State to explain why there was no protection for Muslim holy sites and to provide appropriate funding for protection. For a copy of the Order, see Adalah Newsletter.

40 24/5/54, 249 UNTS 215. The Hague Convention was reaffirmed in the 1977 Additional Protocols to the Geneva Conventions of 12/8/49 Relating to the Protection of Victims of International Armed Conflicts, 8/6/77, 1125 UNTS 3, at Article 53, providing that, as regards the: 'protection of cultural objects and of places of worship 'Without prejudice to the provisions of the Hague Convention for the Protection of Cultural Property in the Event of Armed Conflict of 14 May 1954, and of other relevant international instruments, it is prohibited: (a) to commit any acts of hostility directed against the historic monuments, works of art or places of worship which constitute the cultural or spiritual heritage of peoples; (b) to use such objects in support of the military effort; (c) to make such objects the object of reprisals'. Israel has not ratified the Additional Protocols. Note as well that military necessity can mandate the use of cultural objects for military purposes, if no other alternative exists. See Geoffrey Corn, 'Snipers in the Minaret-What is the Rule? The Law of War and the Protection of Cultural Property: A complex Equation' (2005) Army Lawyer, 28–40.

41 See 1954 Hague Convention for the Protection of Cultural Property in the Event of Armed Conflict, 249 UNTS 215 (24 May 1954).

42 UNESCO World Heritage Convention <http://whc.unesco.org/en/conventiontext> accessed 21 August 2008.

and Political Rights (ICCPR).[43] Israel also has bilateral agreements with both the PA and Jordan.

However, we should note that while Israel views Jerusalem as effectively 'annexed' to Israel,[44] Palestinians view Jerusalem as 'occupied territory' and therefore that the Geneva Convention rules regarding 'belligerent occupation' would apply.[45] In response to world criticism regarding its activity in Jerusalem,[46] Israel, in 1980, passed the *Basic Law: Jerusalem as the Capital of Israel*.[47] While

43 See Article 18, 999 UNTS 171 (16 December 1966). The Human Rights Committee, the body charged with overseeing the treaty, applies the convention to areas under control by Israel, including the West Bank. See Human Rights Committee, General Comment 31, Nature of the General Legal Obligation on States Parties to the Covenant, UN Doc. CCPR/C/21/Rev.1/Add.13 (2004) <www1.umn.edu/humanrts/gencomm/hrcom31.html> accessed August 4 2008. See also, Universal Declaration of Human Rights, Article 18, UNGA Res. 217 (III 1948) <www.un.org/Overview/rights.html> accessed 29 May 2008.

44 For discussion of the precise legal status see, Ian S. Lustick, 'Has Israel Annexed Jerusalem?' (1997) *Middle East Policy* 34; Terry Rempel, 'The Significance of Israel's Partial Annexation of East Jerusalem' (1997) *Middle East Journal* 520; and Michael Dumper, 'Jerusalem's Infrastructure: Is Annexation Irreversible?' (1993) *Journal of Palestine Studies* 78. See note 51 *infra*.

45 For 'belligerent occupation' see generally, Yoram Dinstein, *The International Law of Belligerent Occupation* (Cambridge University Press 2009).

46 Criticism from the UN has been ongoing and continuous since 1967. In particular, note United Nations Security Council Resolutions regarding the city of Jerusalem, 252 (1968), 267 (1969) and 298 (1971), resolution 476 (1980), in which the Security Council expressed its regret over Israel's persistence in changing the urban nature, the demographic composition, the institutions and the position of Jerusalem, and resolution 478 (1980), in which it called upon United Nations Member States that have diplomatic missions in Jerusalem to withdraw those missions from the Holy City. GA Resolutions concerning Jerusalem include resolutions 2253 and 2264 (1967) (and subsequently 36/120, 35/207, and 36/226) deploring Israel's failure to implement General Assembly resolutions on Jerusalem.

47 Basic Law: Jerusalem, Capital of Israel, 30/7/1980, Hatzaot Chok 1464, 5740, reprinted in Ruth Lapidoth, *The Basic Law*, op. cit., 139. The Jerusalem Basic Law and the international reaction is discussed in Note, 'Middle East: Status of Jerusalem' (1980) *Harv. Int. L. J.* 784. See also, Shlomo Slonim, 'The United States and the Status of Jerusalem, 1947–1984' (1984) *Isr. L. Rev.* 179, 243–44 (noting that Israel adopted the Basic Law in response to Security Council Resolution 465 of 1 March 1980, which called for the dismantling of settlements 'in the Arab territories occupied since 1967, including Jerusalem'); Bernard Wasserstein, *Divided Jerusalem* (Yale University Press, 2001) 241–3 (indicating that the Basic Law was enacted in response to diplomatic pressure and Arab propaganda about Jerusalem). Note that while the Basic Laws are meant to serve as the framework for an eventual written constitution, they are essentially equivalent to any other law; only entrenched provisions within the Basic Laws that require a special majority vote by the Knesset (Parliament) prior to any change are accorded a form of elevated status above other laws. Stephen Goldstein, 'Protection of Human Rights By Judges: the Israeli Experience' (1994) *St. L. L. R.* 605–6. The Basic Law: Jerusalem, discussed infra, does not contain such an entrenchment clause.

mostly a symbolic step,[48] the law defined Jerusalem as the 'complete … united … capital of Israel'.[49] The text of the Basic Law does not state that eastern Jerusalem is annexed to Israel. The question whether these steps are legally tantamount to annexation has been one of considerable debate.[50]

What is the So-called 'Status Quo'?

In the 18th and 19th centuries, the Ottoman Empire issued *firmans*, providing Christian denominations with rights over selected holy places. Most important of these were the *firmans* of 1757 and 1852. These *firmans* collectively became known as the *Status Quo*. They were enshrined in international law through the 1878 Treaty of Berlin[51] and various other legal instruments and affirmed by the British in 1923 after they took over the Mandate.[52]

---

48 GA Res. 35/169 (1980) strongly deplored Israel's passing the Basic Law on Jerusalem.

49 In 2000, in an effort to make changes in the legal status of Jerusalem more difficult, amendments were made to the Basic Law that provided that Jerusalem may not be transferred to a foreign entity and that any subsequent changes to the Jerusalem Basic Law must derive from another Basic Law passed by a majority of the Knesset, for example 61 in favour, not merely a majority of those voting. The Laws of the State of Israel no. 1760 (5761/2000) at 28.

In November 2007 there was a vote on a proposal to amend this Basic Law, requiring a majority of 80 Knesset members (instead of 61) to make any changes to the status of Jerusalem. While the coalition was split on this matter, it is not clear how far the proposal will actually go in becoming a law, given the serious implications it can have on a future peace agreements. See Shaha Ilan and Zvi Zrahia, 'Amendment to Basic Law on Jerusalem shakes up coalition', *Haaretz-online* (15 November 2007) <www.haaretz.com/hasen/spages/924441.html> accessed 4 August 2008.

50 In particular, see Ruth Lapidoth, *The Basic Law*, op. cit., 64–71, 110 (the Basic Law understands the city to be 'one unit' as it has been since 1967). Lapidoth concludes that the Basic Law: Jerusalem does not amount to a formal form of annexation. See also, Ian S. Lustick, 'Has Israel Annexed Jerusalem?' op. cit., and Asher Maoz, 'Application of Israeli Law to the Golan Heights is Annexation' (1994) *Brook. J. Int'l L.* 355, 359–66 (finding that Israel had, in fact, annexed East Jerusalem prior to the creation of the Basic Law). In 283/69 *Ravidi v. Military Court, Hebron Zone*, 24(ii) P.D. 419 (1969), the Israel Supreme Court held that a local antique merchant from the Silwan Valley could be deemed to have removed antiquities from Hebron to East Jerusalem contrary to a Jordanian law that prohibited removal of antiquities outside the borders of Jordan. The Court reached this conclusion based on the reality of the facts (that is, that Jordanian law did not apply to East Jerusalem) and did not decide, per se, that East Jerusalem was 'formally' annexed to Israel, even though Israeli law did apply to the area and it was treated as a different (Israeli) legal zone than Hebron (which was under formal military command and subject to Jordanian law from 1967).

51 1878 Treaty of Berlin, repr. in Fred L. Israel (ed.), *Major Peace Treaties of Modern History 1648–1967* (Chelsea House Publishers 1976) 975.

52 Mandate for Palestine, together with a note by the Secretary-General to its Application to the Territory of Trans-Jordan, League of Nations, Cmd. 1785, December

In an effort to better understand the *Status Quo*, the British Military Administration tasked L.G.A. Cust, a British soldier with a classical education, to compile and classify the elusive *Status Quo* arrangements as they had evolved over the centuries. Cust operated without the aid of the Ottoman Archives, which had been removed from Jerusalem when the Ottomans retreated in 1918, and, thus, hc at times contradicted himself. Nonetheless, his is still the best (if not the only) codification of States Quo principles. The different religious communities have, of course, supplemented (or substituted for) Cust's text from their own archives where useful to them. Cust's study *The Status Quo in the Holy Places* was published in 1929.[53] Nonetheless, this 'Shulhan Arukh', so to speak, of the *Status Quo* became the touchstone of Britain's holy places policy.

It is important to note that the Mandate interpreted holy places in a broader sense than did the 1757 and 1852 Ottoman *firmans*. While the British adhered to the *Status Quo*, they extended the *Status Quo* principles to the Western Wall and Rachel's Tomb.[54] Cust himself noted the application of regulations tracking the *Status Quo* beyond the five Christian *Status Quo* sites to include the Milk Grotto, Shepherds' Field, the Western Wall and Rachel's Tomb.[55] The *Status Quo* was also affirmed in the 1993 Vatican-Israel Fundamental Agreement which noted:

> § 1. The State of Israel affirms its continuing commitment to maintain and respect the '*Status quo*' [sic] in the Christian Holy Places to which it applies and the respective rights of the Christian communities there under. The Holy See affirms the Catholic Church's continuing commitment to respect the aforementioned '*Status quo*' [sic] and the said rights.[56]

As Raymond Cohen shows, however, the 'exact' legal authority of the Ottoman *Status Quo* is unclear. The Ottomans viewed the *firmans* as an extension of privileges granted by the Sultans. In contrast, the Christian communities viewed them as having the quality of rights. Cohen makes clear, however, that the essence of the *Status Quo* is the authority of tradition. Once a particular religious community places a ladder in a church corridor, absent of any objection, it has the right to do so again in the future. Also relevant are Ottoman laws stating

---

1922, in Ruth Lapidoth and Moshe Hirsch (eds), *The Arab-Israel Conflict and its Resolution*, op. cit., 25–32. For the intricacies of the *Status Quo*, see for example Marlen Eordegian, 'British and Israeli Maintenance of the Status Quo in the Holy Places of Christendom' (2003) *International Journal of Middle East Studies* 307; Peter Berger, 'The Internationalization of Jerusalem' (1950) *Jurist* 362–8.

53 See generally, Lionel G.A. Cust, *The Status Quo in the Holy Places*, op. cit.

54 Marlen Eordegian, 'British and Israeli Maintenance of the Status Quo in the Holy Places of Christendom', op. cit., 311.

55 Lionel G.A. Cust, *The Status Quo in the Holy Places*, op. cit.

56 Fundamental Agreement at Article 1. It was also reaffirmed in the Basic Agreement between the Holy See and the Palestine Liberation Organization on 15 February 2000, Article 4.

that whoever owned a roof, owned the building below, and a suggestion in Muslim *shari'a* law that 'payment for repairs indicated possession'. This led to numerous situations where the Jordanians would propose repairs and offer to pay, but the religious communities would refuse unless they paid all of the costs themselves.[57]

These three principles make repairs or renovation extremely difficult as every action took on precedential value. If one side did not challenge another church's 'violation', it would lose the 'right' to consent such infringements in the future.

Bi-lateral Treaty Obligations

a) Jordan

As regards Israel and Jordan, the Jordan-Israel Peace Treaty of 26 October 1994 requires that 'Each party will provide freedom of access to places of religious and historical significance'. The Treaty further notes that:

> In this regard, in accordance with the Washington Declaration, Israel respects the present special role of the Hashemite Kingdom of Jordan in Muslim holy shrines in Jerusalem.
>
> When negotiations on permanent status will take place, Israel will give high priority to the Jordanian historic role in these shrines.[58]

The 1994 Treaty of Peace between the State of Israel and the Hashemite Kingdom of Jordan raises two key issues relevant to the Old City and its holy places. They concern access to holy places and the recognition of Jordan as an important actor in administering the *waqf* on the Temple Mount.

Specifically, Article 9 of the Israel-Jordan Peace Treaty provided that:

1. Each party will provide freedom of access to places of religious and historical significance.
2. In this regard, in accordance with the Washington Declaration, Israel respects the present special role of the Hashemite Kingdom of Jordan in Muslim holy shrines in Jerusalem. When negotiations on permanent

57 Raymond Cohen, *Saving the Holy Sepulchre: How Rival Christians Came Together To Rescue Their Holiest Shrine* (Oxford University Press 2008).

58 Israel-Jordan Treaty of Peace (26 October 1994), Article 9, 34 ILM 43–66 (1995). One should note that in the Jordan-Israel Armistice Agreement of 1949, Jordan agreed to allow Israel 'free access for the Holy Places and cultural institutions and use of the cemetery on the Mount of Olives'. Hashemite Jordan Kingdom-Israel General Armistice Agreement, 3 March 1949, 42 UNTS 304 (1949). That agreement was never adhered to.

> status will take place, Israel will give high priority to the Jordanian historic role in these shrines.[59]

The general language of Article 9(1) relating to both religious and historical sites appears to accord access for more than religiously mandated purposes (for example prayer or performance of religious rituals), but also includes access rights for historical investigation or research as well as tourism.[60] This aspect of the Treaty has never been explored.

Additionally, section B(3) of the Washington Declaration signed by Israel and Jordan on 25 July 1994 requires that:

> Israel respects the present special role of the Hashemite Kingdom of Jordan in Muslim holy shrines in Jerusalem. When negotiations on the permanent status will take place, Israel will give high priority to the Jordanian historic role in these shrines. In addition, the two sides have agreed to act together to promote interfaith relations among the three monotheistic religions.[61]

While general in its terms, the provision should be understood as a veiled reference to the Temple Mount, where Jordan maintains continuing administrative duties through financial (and other) support for the *waqf* authorities in the area. It is an important acknowledgment by Israel vis-à-vis Jordan's position in the Old City, and the role that Jordan plays (and continues to play) in supporting the workers of the *waqf*.

---

59 Israel-Jordan Treaty of Peace (26 October 1994) (1995) 34 *Int'l Legal Materials* 43–66 (hereinafter Peace Treaty). Background and commentary on the Treaty can be found in Reuvan Merchav and Rotem M. Giladi, 'The Role of the Hashemite Kingdom of Jordan in a Future Permanent – State Settlement in Jerusalem', in Marshall J. Breger and Ora Ahimeir (eds), *Jerusalem: A City and its Future* (Syracuse University Press, 2001) 175–222. See also, Daniel Reisner, 'Peace on the Jordan' (1995) Justice 3. Article 9 of the Peace Treaty further states that: 'The Parties will act together to promote interfaith relations among the three monotheistic religions, with the aim of working towards religious understanding, moral commitment, freedom of religious worship, and tolerance and peace'.

60 This is an important distinction in the context of the freedom of religion. In customary international law, access to holy sitesis essentially limited solely to manifestations of a religious belief, such as a mandated pilgrimage or to perform a particular required religious ritual. This is arguably a more narrow understanding of access as such when compared to the broad language of Article 9 of the Peace Treaty.

61 Section B(3) of the 29 July 2007 Washington Declaration <www.mfa.gov.il/MFA/Peace%20Process/Guide%20to%20the%20Peace%20Process/The%20Washington%20Declaration> accessed 30 April 2013. This section was noted in Article 9 of the Peace Treaty, supra note 204, where the parties expanded upon the language of the Declaration.

b) Vatican

After the signing of the Oslo Accords,[62] between Israel and the Palestinian Authority, the Catholic Church moved rapidly to conclude an "'agreement'" for mutual recognition with Israel. On 30 December 1993, Israel and the Holy See[63] signed the Fundamental Agreement Between the Holy See and the State of Israel.[64] The Fundamental Agreement states in Article 4 that:

1. The State of Israel affirms its continuing commitment to maintain and respect the *Status Quo* in the Christian Holy Places to which it applies and the respective rights of the Christian communities thereunder. The Holy See affirms the Catholic Church's continuing commitment to respect the aforementioned *Status Quo* and the said rights.
2. The above shall apply notwithstanding an interpretation to the contrary of any Aarticle in this Fundamental Agreement.
3. The State of Israel agrees with the Holy See on the obligation of continuing respect for and protection of the character proper to Catholic sacred places, such as churches, monasteries, convents, cemeteries and their like.
4. The State of Israel agrees with the Holy See on the continuing guarantee of the freedom of Catholic worship.

The implication of this language, at s least as understood by Israel, is to the *Status Quo* as it applies in the present, thereby incorporating the changes that have occurred under Israeli rule, such as prayer at the Western Wall.[65] Nonetheless, the "'respective'" rights are meant as a limiting factor to be construed as solely applying to the parties to the Fundamental Agreement. The Israeli government made it clear to the other religious communities in Israel that the Fundamental Agreement would not serve as a basis for changing the legal status of the other Christian denominations in Israel.

Nonetheless we should note that the language 'respective rights of the Christian communities' in Article 4(1) applies to all the Christian communities and not merely the Catholic Church. Thus, in the Fundamental Agreement, the Holy See is not only serving in its capacity as a sovereign entity, but also as a representative of the various Christian communities.

---

62 Formally referred to as: Declaration of Principles on Interim Self-Government Arrangements 13 September 1993, <www.mfa.gov.il/MFA/Peace+Process/Guide+to+the+Peace+Process/Declaration+of+Principles.htm> accessed 30 April 2013.

63 The Vatican and the Holy See have unique positions in international law. The Holy See serves as the government of the Vatican; entering into treaties on its behalf, and engaging in other acts of diplomacy. Stephen E. Young and Alison Shea, 'Separating State from Church: A Research Guide to the Law of the Vatican City State' (2007) Law Libr. J. 589.

64 (1994) 33 *Int'l Legal Materials* 153 (1994).

65 See Leonard Hammer, 'Israel's Understanding of the Fundamental Agreement with the Holy See', in Marshall J. Breger (ed.), *The Vatican Israel Accords: Political, Legal and Theological Contexts* (University of Notre Dame Press 2004) 67–79.

Further, we should note that the Vatican signed a Basic Agreement with the PLO in February 2000 which states the following as regards Jerusalem:

> Calling therefore, for a special status for Jerusalem, internationally guaranteed, which should safeguard the following: a. Freedom of religion and conscience for all; b. The equality before the law of the three monotheistic religions and their institutions and followers in the City; c. The proper identity and sacred character of the City and its universally significance, religious and cultural heritage; d. The Holy Places, the freedom of access to them and of worship in them; e. The Regime of the '*Status quo*' in those Holy Places where it applies.[66]

What Customary International Law Principles Might Apply?

a) Freedom of Religion and the Right of Access

One central aspect of customary international law regarding the holy sites in the Old City is that of freedom of access to the sites. The principle basis for that right of access is Article 18 of the 1966 International Covenant on Civil and Political Rights (ICCPR).[67] Article 18 provides for the right of access only when exercised in the context of an actual manifestation of a religious belief.[68] The capacity to exercise the right is the manifestation of a religion or belief through worship, observance, practice and teaching. Manifestation implies an external action conducted pursuant to the edicts of a religion or belief that mandates a particular form of observance or practice. Article 18 can also include protection for places of worship or practice when an individual or group lays claim to a specific place of worship as essential.[69] Otherwise, the right would be hollow. Thus, if the religion or belief mandates a

66 Leonard Hammer, 'The Basic Agreement Between the Holy See and the Palestine Liberation Organization', in Marshall J. Breger, *The Vatican Israel Accords*, op. cit., 195.

67 The 1981 Declaration on the Elimination of All Forms of Intolerance and of Discrimination Based on Religious Belief does delineate the right somewhat, but it is at best a form of soft law, being a General Assembly Resolution. GA Res. 36/55, 25/11/81.

68 Article 18(1) provides: everyone shall have the right to freedom of thought, conscience and religion. This right shall include freedom to have or to adopt a religion or belief of his/her choice, and freedom, either individually or in community with others and in public or private, to manifest his/her religion or belief in worship, observance, practice and teaching. Thus, a request by West Bank Christians to visit the Church of the Holy Sepulcher would fit under this 'right', but the request of a Palestinian Muslim to visit friends or relatives on the other side of the 'green line' would not, albeit such holiday visits may well be part of local custom. Interview with Bishop Munib Younan, Evangelical Lutheran Church in Jordan and the Holy Land, Jerusalem, 18 December 2007.

69 Note as well the non-binding United Nations Declaration on the Elimination of all Forms of Intolerance and of Discrimination Based on Religion or Belief, GA Res. 55, U.N. GAOR, 36th Sess., Supp. No. 51, at 171, UN Doc. A/36/51 (1981), at Article 6(a), which includes a right to worship and assemble, as well as 'to establish and maintain places for these purposes'.

particular form of practice at a given holy site, access to the site should be upheld as a means of allowing for the manifestation of the right. The trigger, however, is the claim to exercise the right, and not the fact that the site itself deserves protection.

The Human Rights Committee bolstered this interpretation of Article 18, by specifically including the protection of places of worship within the mandate of the Article. General Comment number 22 at paragraph 4 states that places of worship fall within the rubric of Article 18, such that the right to manifest a religion or belief encompasses the protection of places of worship (given their importance to the exercise of the right).[70] It follows that such protection would incorporate religious places, sites and shrines.

The scope of article 18's protection, however, is limited to religious activity that is required by religious doctrine.[71] Thus, the need to protect religious observance or worship may require protection for places of worship. But it does not protect the site for the benefit of the common cultural heritage (although that could be a secondary benefit), but rather to ensure the right to worship or to engage in a specific religious ritual. By way of example, the European Court of Human Rights was confronted with the matter of Greek Cypriots who sought to visit holy sites in North Cyprus.[72] While the parties did not make reference to freedom of religion (Article 9 of the treaty), the Court held that denying access to religious sites violated the human right to freedom of religion (although there was insufficient proof of such to make that finding in the case before the Court.).[73]

Note that in the International Court of Justice (ICJ) Advisory Opinion of 2004, *The Legal Consequences of the Construction of a Wall in the Occupied Palestinian Territory*,[74] the ICJ understood Article VIII of the Jordan-Israel

70 General Comment No. 22: The right to freedom of thought, conscience and religion (Article 18), CCPR/C/21/Rev.1/Add.4, 30 July 1993.

71 See for example General Comment Number 22, at paragraph 4, noting that worship for example extends to 'giving direct expression to belief'.

72 25781/94 *Cyprus v. Turkey* (2001). Note that a variety of rights had been violated such as privacy, property and security.

73 One should also consider the freedom of access and worship provided by the 1994 Agreement on the Gaza Strip and the Jericho Area, see *Agreement on the Gaza Strip and the Jericho Area between Israel and the Palestine Liberation Organization (Cairo Agreement)*, 4 May 1994, UN Doc. A/49/180-S/1994/727 (Annex) of 20 June 1994, reprinted in 33 I.L.M. 622 (1994), and the 1995 Israeli-Palestinian Interim Agreement on the West Bank and the Gaza Strip. *Israeli-Palestinian Interim Agreement on the West Bank and the Gaza Strip (Interim Agreement)*, K.A. 33, 1, *reprinted in* 36 I.L.M. 551 (1997) (excerpts). In the 1995 Interim Agreement, mention is made of the status of graves sacred to Jews in the territories that were to be handed over to the Palestinian Authority (that is, those in Area A). According to the agreement, 'The present situation and the existing practices shall be preserved' (Article V, b). Similar concerns are addressed in the 1997 Protocol Concerning the Redeployment in Hebron. See *Protocol Concerning the Redeployment in Hebron and Note for the Record*, 17 January 1997, 36 I.L.M. 650 (1997).

74 Available at <www.icj-cij.org/docket/files/131/1671.pdf> accessed 30 April 2013.

Armistice Agreement as creating an ongoing obligation on both Israel and Jordan to guarantee freedom of access to the holy places.[75] While the ongoing relevance of the Armistice Agreement after the 1994 Jordan-Israel Peace Treaty is unclear,[76] one can understand the Agreement as entrenching the right to access and acceptance by the parties involved of, at the very least, a general right of access to holy places in the Old City.[77] Moshe Hirsch notes that the ICJ understood the obligations concerning access that derived from the 1994 Peace Treaty as applying to citizens from third party states as well.[78]

b) Pilgrimage

One form of access at time mandated by a religion is pilgrimage. Pilgrimage could be upheld as a manifestation of belief when carried out pursuant to a specific religious directive. The Islamic Hajj for example is an obligatory action required by all Muslims to conduct at least once in their lifetime. When considered within the context of freedom of religion, some scholars have concluded that because the right of access for pilgrims is not explicitly stated, a right as such does not exist.[79] Nevertheless,

---

75 Hirsch, supra note 23, at 312.

76 See for example Shabtai Rosenne, *Israel's Armistice Agreements with the Arab States: A Juridicial Interpretation* (Blumstein Bookstores, Tel Aviv, 1951) 24–6, noting that armistice agreements are temporary agreements to cease hostilities serving as a positive document that was meant to lead towards a more formalized agreement. Rosenne also notes that such agreements usually go beyond cessation of hostilities to include economic and political concerns. In the case of Israel, the Agreements were envisioned as serving a definitive step towards a more permanent peace. Id. at 41. See also H. Levie, 'The Nature and Scope of the Armistice Agreement' 50 (1956) *AJIL* 880 (armistice agreements can be declared null by the parties to the agreement, and if there is a violation, one side may unilaterally nullify the agreement. The author notes that a peace treaty will also remove an armistice agreement, referring specifically, at 892, to the Israeli-Lebanese agreement as an example). See generally Q Wright, 'The Armistices' 13 (1919) *Am. Pol. Sc. Rev.* 128.

77 Israel declared the Armistice Agreement as terminated following the 1967 war, alledging that Jordan had committed acts of aggression against Israel. See Y. Blum, Zion Has Been Redeemed in Accordance with International Law, 27 (1971) *Hapraklit* 315, 320. However, Article XII(2) of the Armistice Agreement deemed it to be in force until a peaceful settlement between the parties is achieved, an event that occurred in 1994.

78 Moshe Hirsch, 'The Impact of the Advisory Opinion on Israel's Future Policy: International Relations Perspective' (2005) *Hebrew University International Law Research Paper* 319, noting that the ICJ implied such an understanding concerning third parties given the seemingly broad intentions of Jordan and Israel, and the fact that the holy places play a significant role for a variety of third parties external to the immediate states. Hirsch refers as well to Article 36(1) of the Vienna Convention on the Law of Treaties relating to obligations to third parties that supports the ICJ's approach. Customary international law will also play a factor regarding the right of access, as discussed infra.

79 See for example Geoffrey Watson, 'Progress for Pilgrims? An Analysis of the Holy See-Israel Fundamental Agreement' in Marshall J. Breger, *The Vatican-Israel Accords*, op. cit., 203.

where the pilgrimage stems from a specific religious requirement, there are strong grounds to assert the customary right of accessto visit specific holy sites.[80]

c) Destruction of Cultural Heritage

The prohibition of destroying cultural heritage derives principally from prohibitions developed during times of conflict. Aside from the 1954 Hague Convention for the Protection of Cultural Property in the Event of Armed Conflict,[81] there exist a number of provisions concerning the destruction of cultural property during conflict. The 1874 Brussels Convention prohibits military action against 'institutions dedicated to religion …', holding the parties responsible for marking their protected landmarks and implying that there is no immunity if use of the area is for military purposes.[82] The 1880 Institute of International Law's Laws of War on Land (referred to as the Oxford Manual), which was meant to serve as a guidebook that codified the (then) customary law, required that warring parties spare buildings dedicated to religion, art or science. Both the 1899 Convention with Respect to the Laws of Custom of War on Land[83] and the 1907 Hague Convention with Respect to the Laws and Customs of War on Land[84] impose a similar requirement.[85] The 1923 Hague Convention on the Rules of Air Warfare, although never ratified, provides protection zones around buildings dedicated to public worship at Articles 25 and 26, provided they are not used for military purposes.

Attention should be paid to the efforts of UNESCO to impact on cultural property and (by derivation) holy places issues in Jerusalem. Deploying the 'soft

80 Moshe Hirsch, 'Freedom of Pilgrimage to Christian Holy Places in Jerusalem under International Law' in Ruth Lapidoth and Ora Ahimeir (eds), *Freedom of Religion in Jerusalem* (Jerusalem Institute for Israel Studies, 1999); Arcot Krishnaswami, 'Study of Discrimination in the Matter of Religious Rights and Practices' (1978) *N.Y.U.J. Int'l L. & Pol.* 227; but see Peter W. Mason, 'Pilgrimage to Religious Shrines: An Essential Element in the Human Right to Freedom of Thought, Conscience, and Religion' (1993) *Case W. Res. J. Int'l L.* 619.

While not establishing a legal right, Article 5 of the Fundamental Agreement requires that '(t)he Holy See and the State of Israel recognize that both have an interest in favoring Christian pilgrimages to the Holy Land'. Fundamental Agreement between the Holy See and the State of Israel, *Acta Apostolicae Sedis* 86 (1994).

81 1954 Hague Convention, *op. cit.*

82 See <www.culturalpolicycouncil.org/Laws%20and%20Conventions/1874%20Brussels%20Delaration.htm> accessed 30 April 2013. See also United States Lieber Code of 1863 that referred to a prohibition of harming cultural property, US War Department, General Order Number 100, Instructions for the Government of the Armies of the United States in the Field, reprinted in *The Laws of Armed Conflict,* 4th edition, eds D. Schindler and J. Toman (Brill 2004).

83 T.S. No. 403 (32 Stat. 1803).

84 T.S. No. 539 (36 Stat. 2227).

85 Note that Israel considers the 1907 Convention to reflect customary international law. The Convention only applies to instances of international armed conflict, unlike the 1954 Hague Convention, discussed supra, to which Israel also is a party.

law' of the Hague Conventions as well as the World Heritage Centre, UNESCO has sought to protect cultural property in Jerusalem that it considers 'the common heritage of mankind'.[86]

While the Palestinians often point to the cultural protection jurisprudence as a source of legal protection, one should not put too much weight on these efforts as Israel has shown a clear 'reluctance to consider a role to UNESCO in the old city'. Indeed, Israel has generally 'refused to allow inspection teams to visit the city or to meet with responsible officials'.[87] In any event, the UNESCO treaties have little, if any, enforcement power.[88]

How are Holy Sites Disputes Adjudicated?

On 25 July 1924 the British promulgated an Order in Council stating that no cause or matter in connection with holy places or religious buildings or sites, pursuant to a site's historical relevance and the degree of veneration accorded to it by humankind in general,[89] shall be heard or determined by any court in Palestine.[90] The Order in Council referred all matters regarding the holy places to the High Commissioner, 'pending the constitution of a Commission charged

86 The term is drawn from the preamble to the 1954 Hague Convention: Convention for the Protection of Cultural Property in the Event of Armed Conflict, The Hague, 24 May 1954 *op.cit.* The term is open-textured and has been said to refer to the shared heritage as well as to heritage important to cultural heritage.

87 Michael Dumper and Craig Lerkin, 'The Politics of Heritage and the Limitation of International Agency in Contested Cities: A Study of the Role of UNESCO in Jerusalem's Old City' (2012) *Review of International Studies* 32.

88 While not in Jerusalem, we should at least note the 2011 dispute over Prime Minister Netanyahu's designation of Rachel's Tomb in Bethlehem and Joseph's Tomb in Nablus as Israeli National Heritage sites. B. Netanyahu, Prime Minister, State of Israel, Address by PM at Herzliya Conference: 'The Only Way to Achieve Peace is to Begin Conducting Negotiations Towards a Peace Settlement', 3 February 2010. Transcript online available at <http://mfa.gov.il/MFA/Government/Speeches+by+Israeli+leaders/2010/PM_Netanyahu_Herzliya_Conference_3-Feb-2010.htm> accessed 30 April 2013; Chaim Levinson, 'Netanyahu: West Bank Sites Added to National Heritage List' (2010) *Haaretz.com* <www.haaretz.com/news/netanyahu-west-bank0sites-added-to-national-heritage-list-1.266037> accessed 30 April 2013. UNESCO opposed this designation in resolutions that underscored that they were/are Islamic heritage sites and ignored their Jewish past. Véronique Chemla, 'Israel and UNESCO' (2010) *American* <www.americanthinker.com/2010/11/israel_and_unesco.html> accessed 30 April 2013. The Netanyahu designation is analysed (from a Palestinian perspective) in Kimberly L. Alderman, 'The Designation of West Bank Mosques as Israeli National Heritage Sites: Using the 1954 Hague Convention to Protect Against In Situ Appropriation of Cultural Sites' (2011) *Creighton L. Rev* 799.

89 See for example Marlen Eordegian, 'British and Israeli Maintenance of the Status Quo in the Holy Places of Christendom', op. cit., 310.

90 Article 2 of Palestine (Holy Places) Order in Council, 1924.

with jurisdiction over the matters set out in the said Article'.[91] While the British adhered to the *Status Quo* for the five key Christian sites, it is important to note that the Mandatory power understood holy places in a broader sense than the 1757 and 1852 Ottoman *firmans* and that they extended similar forms of protection and veneration for arrangements made at the Wailing Wall and Rachel's Tomb.[92]

The practical meaning of the 1924 Order today is that decisions about holy places issues not directly addressed in Israeli law are made by the Executive Branch.[93] As Prof. Ruth Lapidoth has written:

> … the 1924 Palestine (Holy Places) Order in Council is still in force except where it has been superseded by later Israeli legislation, like the 1967 Protection of the Holy Places Law. Therefore, the courts will not rule on questions of substantive rights or claims to 'Holy Places, religious buildings, or sites'. Similarly, in principle, courts do not consider themselves authorized to adjudicate on matters related to the right to worship at Holy Places. It is the government that is authorized to deal both with disputes about rights to Holy Places and with the modalities of worship … On the other hand, the courts consider themselves authorized to deal with all matters mentioned in the Protection of the Holy Places Law, 5727–1967, namely, protection against desecration, against violation of freedom of access, and against the offending of the feelings of the members of a community with regard to the place that is sacred for them. The courts are also authorized to deal with criminal offenses in order to preserve public order at the Holy Places. Even where a dispute actually relates to claims or rights to a Holy Place, the courts may intervene in order to restore possession to a community if it had been deprived of this possession by a recent act. The reason for this rule is that the courts have an obligation to preserve law and order.[94]

Examples of recent use of the Order in Council can be seen in the dispute between Copts and Amharics over a portion of the church of the Holy Sepulchre where the government took the dispute out of the Court and consigned it to a committee which has met twice in the last 40 years.[95] Another example is the dispute over

91 *The Palestine (Holy Places) Order in Council*, 25 July 1924, reprinted in Enrico Molinaro, *Negotiating Jerusalem* (annex 2, PASSIA Publication 2002).

92 Marlen Eordegian, 'British and Israeli Maintenance of the Status Quo in the Holy Places of Christendom', op. cit., 311.

93 The 1967 Protection of the Holy Places Law states at section 3 that the law is to 'add to, and not derogate from, any other law', implying as well the ongoing application of the Order in Council.

94 Ruth Lapidoth, 'Freedom of Religion and Conscience in Israel', in Marshall J. Breger (ed.), *The Vatican-Israel Accords*, op. cit., 249.

95 The tale is told in W. Zander, Jurisdiction and Holiness: Reflections on the Coptic-Ethiopian Case, Israel L. rev. Vol. 17, no. 3, pp. 245-73 (1982).

Nachmanides' Cave in East Jerusalem where the government created a committee of experts who prepared a report denominating the Cave a holy place.[96]

The Question of Freedom of Access to Holy Sites

As noted earlier, the 1967 Protection of Holy Places Act protects access to holy sites for religious purposes. The difficulty comes when there are competing claims to a holy site and competing (as opposed to supplemental) rites used by a specific religion at that holy place. At that point there are competing claims of access that must be negotiated.

There are many examples of this in Jerusalem. Muslims claim that Jews cannot pray on the *Haram* without desecrating its holiness for Muslims. Orthodox Jews claim that Jewish women who wish to pray with a public quorum at the Wall desecrate that holy place. Christian sects battle over which rite to use at what time in the Church of the Holy Sepulchre.

The legal problem is that the Protection of Holy Places Law both protects access and prohibits desecration. In the *Haram* example the protection of its sacred character for Muslims may require excluding Jews from prayer (if not more).

The problem has been navigated by administrative judgments as to who controls the sacred character. Thus as the rabbi of the Western Wall is Orthodox, it is the Orthodox Jewish rite that controls there.

A second issue is: what is desecration? The Supreme Court has interpreted desecration as turning something holy into secular, such that, for example, building another mosque on the Temple Mount was not considered a desecration to Judaism since Muslims have always prayed there.[97] It is, further, not clear legally how we address desecration. Is it not physical damage or some other criteria that can be 'objectively' determined? Or at what point do you look to subjective sensibilities in determining desecration?

Israeli domestic law concerning the right to prayer is particularly relevant when discussing access to the Temple Mount. From a doctrinal perspective the Supreme Court has expanded its jurisdiction to include the right to prayer as part of the right of access.[98] As Justice Izhak Englard suggested, courts have shifted ideologically from rejecting outright an enforceable right to pray on the Temple Mount, to the recognition of an abstract right subject to the needs of public order. Thus, in one recent case, *Gershon Solomon v Yair Yitzchaki*, the Supreme Court wrote, 'The petitioner, like any other person in Israel, enjoys the freedom of conscience, belief, religious observance and practice. This framework provides him with the privilege

96 See text at notes 133-188 *infra.*

97 7128/96 *Temple Mount Faithful v. State of Israel* 51(ii) PD 509 (1997).

98 See for example 292/83 *Temple Mount Faithful v. Commander of Police* 38(ii) PD 449 (1984) where the court notes that the right to worship is a basic human right, subject to certain limitations based on public order and security.

of gaining access to the Temple Mount for purposes of worship'.[99] In principle, then, Jews have the right to pray on the Temple Mount but it is understood as a limited form of this right,[100] especially when weighed against the danger to public security.[101]

According to this view, the law would ensure access contingent upon an executive (that is, police) decision that permitting access would not cause a breakdown in public order. The question is, of course, what constitutes public order. The courts have generally taken a very deferential view of leaving it to the judgment of the police. Thus, public order considerations have included not only exigencies of the moment (for example, the inability to protect worshippers at the time of the request), but also deference to police priorities regarding the deployment of policeforces throughout the city.[102]

---

99 3374/97 *Gershon Solomon v. Yair Yitzchaki, Officer in Charge of East Jerusalem and the Israeli Police*(decided 10 June 1997) (in Hebrew) Online <http://elyon1.court.gov.il/files/97/740/033/E03/97033740.e03.pdf> accessed 30 April 2013.

100 See for example 2697/04 *Solomon v. Commander of East Jerusalem* 58(4) PD 572 (2004), 67/93 *Kach Movement v. Minister of Religion* 47(2) PD 1 (1993).

101 4776/06 *Solomon v. Commander for East Jerusalem* (unpublished, decided 28/12/06) (must balance right of prayer against a justified limitation for public security concerns). Note as well The Protection of Holy Places Law of 1967 that provides for free access in Article 1: the Holy Places shall be protected from desecration and any other violation and from anything likely to violate the freedom of access of the members of the different religions to the places sacred to them or their feelings with regard to those places. (<www.mfa.gov.il/mfa/peace%20process/reference%20documents> accessed 30 April 2013). Additionally, there are jurisdictional limitations imposed on the Court as a result of the Mandate Law. See for example 10450/07 *Temple Mt. Faithful v. Police and others* (unpublished, decided 12 November 2007) (Court refrained from deciding whether movement can light Hanukah candles on the Temple Mount due to lack of jurisdiction), 8666/99 *Temple Mt. Faithful v. Attorney General* 54(1) PD 199 (2000), 7128/96 *Temple Mt. Faithful v. Government* 51(2) PD 509 (1997).

102 Similar considerations are made when addressing the issue of digging on the Temple Mount by the *waqf* authorities. Coupled with the issue of jurisdictional limitations imposed on the Court as a result of Mandate law and governmental policy concerning the *waqf*'s control of the area, the Court also defers to the relevant authorities including the police and the Antiquities Authority. 8666/99 *Temple Mount Faithful v. A. Rubisntein and Others* (decided 11/1/2000) (Justice Cheshin noting as well the need for deference to the government as the Court is an inappropriate place for these decisions), 1868/07 *Temple Mount Faithful v. Government and Others*, unpublished decision, decided 4/6/07) (court recognized presence of archeologists working with *waqf* to supervise digs). In 2007, when Israeli Prime Minister Ehud Olmert granted *waqf* officials permission to conduct excavations under the Al Aqsa Mosque to install new electrical and telephone cables in the mosque, Israeli archeologists expressed outrage. See Aaron Klein, 'Olmert allows Muslims to dig on Temple Mount' (2007) WorldNetDaily <www.worldnetdaily.com/news/article.asp?ARTICLE_ID=56626> accessed 30 April 2013. They claimed that digging the trench violates professional standards for such a sensitive historic site. The Committee Against

The Western Wall

The Western Wall is considered one of the holiest places in Judaism as it was for years the closest space to the Temple accessible to Jews. Archeologists believe it to be a retaining wall of the Temple.

Jews were allowed to pray (albeit with restrictions) at the Wall under the Ottomans and under the British Mandate. While Jerusalem was under Jordanian control (1948–67) they were forbidden access. In 1967 after Israel's conquest of Jordan, 135 buildings across from the Wall in the Mugrabi Quarter were razed and a plaza built to accommodate worshipers.

During the Mandate, the *Waqf* initially kept the keys to all of the gates of access, including the Mugrabi Gate (and charged non-Muslims entrance fees, an important component in *Waqf* income), and maintained autonomous control over most of the Haram. This situation changed abruptly in August 1967, when the soldiers of the IDF rabbinate tried to enter the Mount via the Mugrabi Gate in order to access a small office they had established on the edge of the Mount, only to find the gate locked. In reaction to this incident, Moshe Dayan ordered the keys to the Mugrabi Gate confiscated, and turned them over to the Israeli police. Access through the Mugrabi Gate has remained in Israeli hands ever since.

Regulations were promulgated in 1981 designating the Western Wall plaza (the *Kotel*) as a holy place under the 1967 Protection of Holy Places Law and detailing the rules of behaviour there. The regulations appointed a rabbi to be in charge of the Wall.[103]

However in 1989 after a women's group, Women of the Wall (WOW), began to pray in a public quorum at the Western Wall, the Ministry of Religious Affairs amended those regulations to expressly 'prohibit the conduct of a religious ceremony which is not according to the custom of the place and which injures the sensitivities of the worshiping public towards the place'.[104] The Women of the Wall were consigned to a far corner of the Wall (Robinson's Arch) as the Wall and attendant plaza are run on Orthodox religious lines.

It should be noted that in one sense the legal status of the Western Wall is unclear. While it is clearly a holy place, it has customarily been considered a

---

the Destruction of Antiquities on the Temple Mount petitioned the High Court of Justice to intervene, claiming the dig was being carried out at night to occlude proper archaeological inspection. Id. See also Nadav Shragai, 'The Latest Damage to Antiquities on the Temple Mount' (2008) Jerusalem Center for Public Affairs <www.jpca.org/JCPA/Templates/Showpage> (accessed 30 April 2013) noting the dismissal of the petition.

103 Kovetz Takanot 4252 from 16/7/81, at 1212 (in Hebrew).

104 The Regulation on the Protection of Sacred Spaces for the Jewish People (Amendment), Kovetz Takanot 5237 from 1989 (in Hebrew), at 190, which added in the wording 'which is not according to the custom of the place'. See also, Ruth Halperin-Kaddari, 'Women, Religion and Multiculturalism in Israel', (2000) *UCLA Journal of International Law and Foreign Affairs* 358.

national shrine. Thus, IDF officers, as example, are sworn in in front of the Wall. This issue has become relevant in tensions between the sanctity and custom relevant to an Orthodox holy place and the more inclusive requirements of a public or national scheme. One recent example can be seen in the recent demand by the Rabbi of the Western Wall that the citizenship ceremony for new immigrants traditionally held at the site be gender segregated in accordance with Jewish law.[105]

Furthermore, its ownership status is shrouded. The Wall itself is owned by a *waqf*. However, in 1931 the British determined that there was an easement, allowing Jews to pray under specified conditions.[106] After the 1967 War, Israel expropriated the area adjacent to the Wall (Mughrabi Gate) to build the Western Wall Plaza.[107] And after 1967 Israel created a Western Wall Heritage Foundation to manage the Wall and the plaza next to it.

Adjacent to the Wall is the Western Wall Tunnel built by the Western Wall Heritage Foundation. The *waqf* sees the tunnel as another step of changing the Status Quo, another form of control. Most importantly, they also see it as endangering the different Islamic buildings above and a form of conquering the underground of the Haram al-Sharf. Conversely, Israel sees this as a way to explore the history of underground Jerusalem and to assert Jewish identification with the Temple Mount.

It should be noted that the Western Wall is also a holy site for Muslims as by tradition it is the place where the Prophet's horse Baraq was tethered during his night journey. While in principle Muslims are not forbidden from access to the Wall, in practice they are likely to be forbidden by security personnel.

---

105 Chaan Liphsiz, 'Immigrant groups decry sex segregation at Western Wall Citizenship Ceremonies', *Haaretz* (Tel Aviv, 25 September 2009). The Jewish Agency moved the ceremony to the courtyard of the Jewish Agency, Press Release, The Jewish Agency for Israel, 2000 New Immigrants on 7 flights arrive from around the world on one day, 13 October 2009. The ceremony was resumed at the *kotel* some months later, The Jewish Agency for Israel, Press Release, 10,000 New Immigrants Arriving in Israel this week from all over the World Organized by the Jewish Agency for Israel, 27 July 2010. The issue was both whether the Western Wall was a religious or national site and whether the citizenship ceremony was a religious or national event.

106 Report of the Commission appointed by His Majesty's government in the United Kingdom of Great Britain and Northern Ireland, with the approval of the Council of the League of Nations, to determine the rights and claims of Muslims and Jews in connection with the Western or Wailing Wall of Jerusalem (London HMSO 1931).

107 Shlomo Berkovitz notes that: 'In the map of the expropriation order, and I'm not sure how this happened, the bottom meter of the Wall, that is, its base, is included for the length of 140 meters, which includes all the prayer space at the foot of the Wall and the archaeological excavations there. However, legally and formally, the remaining portion of the Wall still belongs to the Waqf', quoted in Aryeh Dean Cohen, 'Whose Wall Is It Anyway?' *Jerusalem Post* (Jerusalem, 21 November 1997) 3.

The Temple Mount/Haram al Sharif

For Palestinians the Al-Haram al-Sharif has been an Islamic holy site since the 7th century AD, and even the Israelis do not question its holiness to Muslims. In addition to its distinct religious status to Muslims, it includes unique and historical examples of Islamic architecture. Since 1967, al-Haram al-Sharif was not only the holiest place for the Palestinians in Palestine, but also an important symbol for their continued presence in the city in particular, and on the land of Palestine in general. Al-Haram was also a symbol of the spiritual and national relation, which linked the Diaspora Palestinians to their homeland.

For Jews, the same site is where the Solomon and Herodian Temples (the First and the Second Temple) were located. The Second Temple was destroyed in 70 AD by the Roman Titus, and remained in ruins until Umar Bin al-Khattab (the second Caliph of Islam) built the al-Aqsa Mosque. Orthodox Jews believe that it was destroyed as a punishment for the Jewish people disobeying God. Consequently, the site is so sacred that the overwhelming majority of rabbinic opinion has ruled that the site may not even be visited.[108] However, a growing minority of both religious and secular aspire to not only visit the Mount, but to conduct prayers and even to establish a synagogue on its periphery. Those individuals see visits to the Temple Mount as an expression of Jewish nationalism, for example sovereignty not only over the Temple Mount. but over the entire land of Israel.[109] Others see Jewish activity at the Mount as a condition precedent for the coming of the Messiah.

As early as 1968, the Israeli Supreme Court has recognized the Jewish right of access to the Temple Mount, but has consistently placed the authority to allow such visits (particularly for the purposes of prayer) in the hands of the police The police have consistently denied access altogether in times of tension, and completely denied access for purposes of prayer. This has become the subject of perennial lawsuits.

While Israel claims sovereignty over the Temple Mount, this sovereignty is not recognized by the Muslim *waqf* authorities. Security issues aside, the *waqf* manages

---

108 Yair Ettinger, 'Prominent Rabbi to Peres: Jews Forbidden on Temple Mount', *Jerusalem Post* (Jerusalem, 8 October 2009).

109 See for example the recent (25 October 2009) religious Zionists meeting in Jerusalem calling for Jews to ascend the Temple Mount: participants urged Jews to ascend the Temple Mount and disregard the prohibitions of the 'official' religious establishment. They were urged to protest at 'the injury caused to the rabbis' dignity by the inspections at the entrance to the site'. The gathering was hosted by the Organization for Human Rights in the Temple Mount, directed by Yehuda Glick, who has been encouraging Jewish ascent to the Temple Mount for years and endeavouring to prepare the ritual temple utensils. Yair Ettinger, 'Religious Zionist Rabbis: Ascend the Temple Mount', *Haaretz* (Tel Aviv, 26 October 2009); Kobi Nahshoni, 'Jews Urged to Visit Temple Mount Despite Prohibitions' (2009) Ynet <http://www.ynetnews.com/articles/0,7340,L-3795054,00.html> accessed 30 April 2013; Roi Sharon and Roni Malul, 'Tonight: Rabbinical Gathering to Promote Ascent to the Temple Mount', *Ma'ariv* (Tel Aviv, 25 October 2009) (Hebrew).

the property according to its own regulations within the framework of Israeli law. Thus there is no Israeli presence on the Mount itself except for a small inobtrusiveIsraeli police post. Israel does, however, control access to the Mount itself. And Israeli security often severely limits Palestinian access to married men over 40 (or 45) for security reasons. In periods of high tension, Jewish visitors are barred as well. And Israeli law prohibits the *waqf* from preventing Jews access although it defers to the *waqf's* restriction of Jewish prayer on the Mount (following deference to the religious custom of the place as interpreted by the religious authorities in charge). Thus, Jews can enter but any indication of prayer (use of prayer shawls, phylacteries, or physical indications such a bowing and so on) will result in ejection or even arrest.

The *waqf* which manages the *haram* is itself controversial as control was disputed by both the PLO and Jordan. As it presently stands the *waqf* is controlled by Jordan which pays the salaries of *waqf* employees.

One area of significant controversy is the question of archaeological excavations by the *Waqf*: in recent years they have refused to liaise with Israeli archaeology officials. One such controversial excavation was the excavation of Solomon's Stable, an underground area used by the Crusaders as a stable for horses which was turned into a Muslim prayer hall. Jewish groups complained that the *Waqf* was violating Israeli archaeology law. The Israeli Supreme Court found the issue to be delegated to the Executive Branch under the 1924 Order in Council and refused to intervene.[110] Controversy among the Israeli public continues because of claims that Jewish archaeological connections to the site have been destroyed.

At the same time, Muslims are concerned with Israeli archaeological 'digs' adjacent to the Temple Mount. In 2006 the Israeli Antiquities Authority, in partnership with the Western Wall Heritage Foundation, began excavation approximately 100 metres west of the Temple Mount.[111] Archeologists uncovered remains from the First Temple period, including preserved walls of buildings, an ornate personal seal and pottery decorated with ancient Hebrew script.[112] The 'salvage expedition' was carried out ahead of the planned construction of the Western Wall Heritage Generations Center.[113] The state-of-the-art tourist centre at the Western Wall tunnels incorporates ancient and modern Jewish history and includes a light show highlighting discoveries of Jewish ruins.[114]

---

110 See Temple Mount Faithful – *Amust al et al. v. Attorney-General, Inspector-General of the Police, Mayor of Jerusalem, Minister of Education and Culture, Director of the Antiquities Division Muslim Waqf* (23 September 1993) translated at 45 *Catholic University Law Review* 861 (1996).

111 News Press, 'Building remains from First Temple period exposed west of Temple Mount' (2008) WL 5407118.

112 Id.

113 Etgar Lefkovits, 'First Temple remains uncovered in dig near Temple Mount', *Jerusalem Post* (Jerusalem, 17 March 2008).

114 Etgar Lefkovits, 'Israel denies Temple Mount excavation', *Jerusalem Post* (Jerusalem, 3 January 2006).

Another area of controversy concerns proposals to rebuild a ramp at the Mughrabi Gate leading up to the Temple Mount. It is alleged that proposals to rebuild the ramp (which has partially collapsed) threatens various Muslim prayer spaces and has occasioned protests by UNESCO as well as other Arab states, particularly Jordan.

Church of the Holy Sepulchre

The Church of the Holy Sepulchre, considered by Catholics as the site of the crucifixion, has long been a place of legal (as well as actual) controversy. It is 'owned' by a Christian *waqf* but is effectively 'shared' by various Christian denominations under the so-called *Status Quo*. The keys to the church are kept by one Muslim family and the daily opening of the church was entrusted to another family.[115]

Control of the Holy Sepulchre, is shared between three Christian denominations or 'communities', the Greek Orthodox, the Roman Catholics and the Armenians, all of whom have rights of both possession and usage. Three additional sects, the Copts, the Ethiopians and the Syrian Orthodox, are called 'the minor communities' and have rights of usage but not possession. The Protestants came too late to the party and, in any event, believe that most of the events commemorated at the Holy Sepulchre really took place at the Garden Tomb, outside the Old City walls.

The Christian sects dispute over every aspect of their rights under the *Status Quo*. One such dispute is currently being fought out before the Supreme Court, concerning control over the Holy Fire Ceremony in the Church of the Holy Sepulchre. The parties in dispute are the Greek Orthodox Patriarchate and the Armenian Patriarchate.[116]

For years the Christian communities were unable to come together on repairs of the Church of the Holy Sepulchre.[117] It took more than twelve 12 years to agree to paint the dome of the rotunda. Only when Goerge Doty, a Catholic philanthropist from New York offered to front the bill and other denominations accepted was the matter resolved.[118] For years Israeli authorities had sought to secure permission

---

115 Simon Goldhill, *Jerusalem: City of Longing* (Harvard University Press 2008) 12–13.

116 *See The Armenian-Patriarchy of Jerusalem v. the Government of Israel,* HCJ 633/05.

117 See Lisa Pevtzow, 'Holy Squabbles', *Jerusalem Post Magazine* (Jerusalem, 1 April 1994) 6, describing the territorial battles among the six religious denominations housed in the church.

118 See, Mary Curtius, 'Holy Sepulcher Church Paint Job an Act of Faiths', *Los Angeles Times* (Los Angeles, 15 April 1995) A1; see also Michael Krikorian, 'A Simple Cross Ends Decades of Division', *Los Angeles Times* (Los Angeles, 30 December 1995) B4. Haim Shapiro, 'Holy Sepulchre Cupola Unveiled After 68 Years Under Wraps', *Jerusalem Post* (Jerusalem, 3 January 1997) 15, 20. Only after seeking the assistance of the Pontifical

to build a fire exit for safety purposes. While they almost succeeded to forge an agreement for such an exit, but as of today there is still no agreement.[119]

There is open and unfettered access to the Church for residents of Israel and for tourists. Access for Palestinian Christians living beyond the Green Line is limited to persons holding Israeli entry permits, which in practice severely limits Palestinian Christian access.

Other Holy Sites in Jerusalem

Muslim Sites

Muslim holy places are in general owned by religious waqfs.[120] On occasion they are owned by private or family waqfs.[121] Specified Muslim mosques in Jerusalem are likely to be protected in part because there were few mosques in Jewish West Jerusalem before 1948 and largely those in Arab East Jerusalem were most likely never abandoned. There are two significant exceptions. The first is mosques and Muslim holy sites in the Jewish Quarter as the land there, after 1967, was handed over to the Company for the Redevelopment and Reorganization of the Jewish Quarter for reconstruction.

The second is the Mamilla Cemetery, a large cemetery in West Jerusalem, the bulk of which is now a public park. Before building the park, the city of Jerusalem in the 1960s arranged for the cemetery to be declared abandoned by a 'friendly' Qadi in Haifa. The matter was rekindled when the Simon Wisenthal Center of Los Angeles received permission to build a Museum of Tolerance on property which it turned out had been part of the cemetery (the construction dug up numerous bones). While the Israeli Supreme Court has approved the project, it remains highly controversial, not the least because of the museum's purpose.[122]

Mission for Palestine, a social services organization, was Doty able to secure the agreement of all the religious 'stakeholders' to begin the restoration. See Graziano Motta, 'Jerusalem Basilica's Dome Is Restored', *L'Osservatore Romano* (weekly, Vatican City, 8–19 February 1997) 8.

119 See, Deborah Sontag, 'At Riven Holy Sepulchre, Anxiety as Crowds Loom', *New York Times* (New York, 1 December 1999); Motti Friedman, 'Religious Politics Foil Fire Exit at Holy Sepulchre', *USA Today* (Tysons Corner, 20 April 2011).

120 Islamic Endowment (*Waqf*): the Islamic Endowment holds 717 real property units in the Old City; 19.2 per cent of the real property in the old city including 98 units inside al-Haram Al-Sharif.

121 Family Endowments/*Waqf* Thuri (Islamic): they number 1,212 in the Old City which constituted approximately 32.6 per cent of endowments. Some of these family endowments are administered by the Islamic Endowment Department either from the family itself, or the actual revenues from these endowments.

122 The Muslim perspective on this controversy is well laid out in Sheik Ahmed Nafour, *Battle Over Muslim Cemeteries in Israel* and in Marshall J. Breger, Yitzhak Reiter,

Christian Sites

a) The Cenacle

The Cenacle situated on Mount Zion is considered to be the site of the Last Supper. In 1552, the property was taken from the Franciscans and handed over to a Muslim family *waqf*. After 1907 the property came under Israeli control as the Muslim *waqf* was considered abandoned property under the Abandoned Property Laws. The Church maintained an easement over the so-called Upper Chamber on certain Christian holdings. The Vatican is negotiating for the return of, or at least use of, the Cenacle. The matter is controversial as the Cenacle is part of Mount Zion, a site sacred to Jews where tradition claims King David is buried. Mount Zion is also site to the Diaspora Yeshiva which seeks use of all of the land for its own purposes.

The Tomb of David has been held for generations before the 1948 war by the Dajani family and recognized as a Muslim religious *waqf*. The Israeli victory in 1948 created a new reality with complex legal and practical problems. During the 1948 War and for some months thereafter, the Mount Zion area, including King David's Tomb, was a closed military zone to which free access was not permitted. Activity in the area was administered by the military rabbinate in increasing cooperation with the Ministry of Religious Affairs which took over the site at the end of 1949.

b) German Church of St Mary's

The German Church of St Mary's, located in the Old City Jewish Quarter, was leased in perpetuity to the *Aish Hatorah* Yeshiva in 1999 through the Jewish Quarter Development Agency (hereinafter: Agency) without any form of oversight.[123] The lease was successfully challenged and revoked before the Israel Supreme Court,[124] on the grounds that the Agency was established as a governmental corporation to serve a public purpose.[125] As such, the long-term lease is contrary to public policy and was declared void. The central ground for the Court's decision was that the site was a particularly important and unique historical site that should not be altered.[126] For the Agency to allow a private Jewish body like *Aish Hatorah* to build a Jewish building on a noted archeological site was contrary to its underlying purpose.[127]

& Leonard Hammer, eds., *Sacred Space in Israel and Palestine: Religion and Politics* (2012) 168–192.

123 See *Hot Property, Jerusalem Post*, 21 July 2006 at p. 27, col. 1 The Attorney General vehemently opposed the lease, supporting a challenge raised by the Jerusalem Foundation, on the grounds that the lease had inherent administrative deficiencies as the Agency acted *ultra vires* and in an unreasonable manner.

124 4290/00 *Jerusalem Foundation v. Prime Minister and Others*, decision of 26/6/06, unpublished decision.

125 Id. at para. 13.

126 Id. at para. 16.

127 Id. at para. 17–18.

Jewish Sites

a) Old City Synagogues
A 1967 Israeli government report listed 70 destroyed synagogues in the Old City, most of them in the Jewish Quarter. The Quarter is controlled by the Society for the Development and Reorganization of the Jewish Quarter[128] which has made efforts to rebuild as many synagogues as possible throughout the entire area of the Jewish Quarter.

b) Nachmanides' Cave
Nachmanides' Cave (the Cave of the Ramban), is the site where the noted medieval scholar allegedly worshiped when he came to Jerusalem in 1267 and was possibly buried there as well. Apparently the cave initially was used as a cattle shed and then by vagrants and drug users. It came to public attention when a group of Jewish settlers in Wadi Joz, led by MK Benny Elon, a leader in the Moledet Party (a radical right-wing party), sought to pray there. The Arab owners thereupon fenced off the area to prevent access. At that point, the Jewish settlers petitioned the Supreme Court to grant them access.

In accordance with the 1924 Order in Council, then Minister of Religion, Yossi Beilin, appointed a committee to determine whether in fact the cave was to be considered a holy site.[129] The committee reviewed rabbinical sources that mentioned the cave, as well as testimony that Jews had frequented the cave for prayer and study as evidence of continuity.[130] Despite the fact that the cave was not listed as a holy site in the Ministry of Religion's regulation or icritical religious sources,[131] such as the writings of Rabbi Isaac Luria (the ARI),[132] the committee decided that there were enough historical reference to justify deeming the cave a holy site, albeit at a 'low' level. In doing so, it gave '"points' to the importance of

128 See Simona Ricca, *Reinventing Jerusalem: Israel's Reconstruction of the Jewish Quarter After 1967* (I.B. Tauris 2007). The Society was created in 1970. It reports directly to the prime minister and Inter-Ministerial Committee for Jerusalem Affairs. See Michael Dumper, 'Israeli Settlement in the Old City of Jerusalem' (1992) *J. Pal. Studies* 38. The Company is treated as a formalized governmental entity under the Law of Governmental Companies 29/5/73 Hatzaot Chok 1067 at 317 and 4/7/75 Seifer Hachukim 770 at 132.

129 The committee was composed of individuals experienced in these issues including rabbinic officials, the Rabbi of the Holy Places and the Legal Adviser to the Ministry of Religion. The entire affaire is discussed in Michael Wygoda "The Third Kind of Holy Places: The Case of Nachmanides' Cave in Jerusalem" in Marshall Breger, Yitzhak Reiter, and Leonard Hammer eds.) Confederation and Coexistence" in Holy Places; Religious, Political, and Legal Aspects (Rutledge, 2009), 93–104.

130 They did not make use of traditional or modern Muslim scholarship.

131 An example of an important source would be the responsa, known as She'elot u-Teshuvot 'questions and answers' that comprise the body of written decisions and rulings given by poskim ('decisors of Jewish law').

132 See 'Luria, Isaac Ben Solomon', *Encyclopædia Judaica* (1972) vol. 11, 572–8.

the personality involved and accepted the assertion that there had been extended use of the cave through continuous and ongoing visits and prayer.

The committee's decision highlights the problems associated with certifying hholy places. There was ample testimony contradicting the assertions of the Jewish groups regarding the cave. Indeed, the very location of the cave was controversial, a host of sources (Jewish and otherwise) referring to different locations for the cave. Besides that, the cave had not really been subject to 'continuous' use but only sporadic visits (the Arab owners had held the property in their family for over 100 years and had only witnessed recent interest in the cave). The committee began by treating the cave as equivalent in status to a synagogue, but then elevated its status to that of a holy place on a par with unique areas protected by the Holy Places Law and its attendant regulations.

Nonetheless, the *waqf* continued to litigate on the question whether the Cave was a holy site and in 2008 after a court determined it was not, the *waqf* retained ownership and possession[133]

c) The Cave of Shimon Hatzaddik (Simon the Just)

The Cave of Shimon Hatzaddik is located next to the Cave of the Ramban near Sheikh Jarah in East Jerusalem. Today it serves as a synagogue. Tensions have arisen not at the cave itself, but in the residential area surrounding the cave where Jewish settlers claim to have purchased property and are ejecting Muslim residents in order to build a Jewish enclave in the area. While these conflicts are not directly connected to holy sites, they may well roil over into conflicts at holy sites themselves.

d) Mount of Olives

The Mount of Olives contains the most ancient Jewish ceremony in the world. By tradition the Jewish Messiah will first appear at the Mount of Olives. During the period of Jordanian control some 38,000 Jewish gravestones were largely destroyed by Jordanians and many of them used to pave the road to the top.

The land of the cemetery is owned by various Jewish burial societies such as the Sephardic Community Committee and the Jerusalem Community Council. The area around the Mount is under the administrative control of Elad, a settler organization. Access is open to all.

We should note that the churches of Dominus Flevit, Mary Magdalene and the Church of All Nations are on the Mount of Olives and at the foot of the Mount

133 Arutz Sheva, Jews Barred from Nachamanides Cave, Dec. 21, 2008 accessed at http://www.israelnationalnews.com/News/Flash.aspx/157819; Yeshiva World, Ramban's Cave Belongs to Muslim Waqk, Dec. 21, 2008 accessed at http://www.theyeshivaworld.com/news/israel-news/27465/court-rambans-cave-belongs-to-the-muslim-waqf.html. For legal citations *see* Yitzhak Reiter & Lior Lehrs, The Sheik Jarah Affair: The Strategic Implications of Jewish Settlement in An Arab Neighborhood in the Old City, Jerusalem Institute of Israel Studies, (2010) n. 33 at p. 21.

are the Tombs of the Prophet Zachariah, the sons of Hezir (Second Temple High Priests) and Absalom (the son of King David).

e) The City of David

The City of David, just outside the Old City, was the first capital of King David.[134] It has also been the site of an Arab village – Silwan. In recent years, Elad has operated the City of David Archeological Park to promote the heritage of King David and, by inference, the Jewish presence in Jerusalem.[135] It further sought to purchase Arab homes and move Jews into the area. This has created significant tension between settlers and the Arab population with weekly demonstrations by Jewish supporters of 'Arab' rights.[136] f) The National Park System

One development that impacts on the geography and demography of Jerusalem generally and only indirectly on sacred space is the burgeoning national parks system in Jerusalem. While trumpeted as a way to preserve open space and promote cultural heritage, many believe the nascent national park system is designed to hem in Palestinian development and highlight the Jewish relationship to the city. Certainly the park system to date has done little, if anything, to underscore the Christian or Muslim relationship to Jerusalem although the proposed area includes sites of religious significance to both.[137]

The national park does not take title to Christian or Muslim religious property. However, the park designation creates an easement which burdens such religious property outside their walls. The administration of some of the National Parks has been turned over to settler groups, such as ELAD, with little interest in protecting the character of Christian or Muslim populations or institutions. Two national parks, the Old City Walls and the Tzurim Valley Park have been declared. Other proposed parks include Mt. Scopus and the Kings Valley with parks also being considered for the Mt. of Olives, Sheik Jarrah and Bab al-Sahrah.[138]

The municipality of Jerusalem has been affirmatively promoting this plan as have the Israel government planning authoriti. In 2009 the municipality's finance committee approved a budget of NIS 600,000 for the plan, but 88 illegal buildings built by East Jerusalem Arabs got in the way of making progress with park planning. The plan is for the land designation to be changed and part of it be

---

134 See, 1 Kings 11:27; 1 Chronicles 11:8; 11 Samuel 5:8.

135 For Elad see Meron Rapaport, 'The Republic of Elad', *Haaretz* (Tel Aviv, 23 April 2001). For the archaeological park see Melanie Lidman, 'Elad Can Continue to Operate City of David, Court Finds', *Jerusalem Post* (Jerusalem, 28 October 2011).

136 Wendy Pullen and Maximilian Gwiazda, 'Designing the Biblical Present: Jerusalem's "City of David"', in Andrew Webber, Uta Staiger and Henriette Steiner, *Memory Culture and the Contemporary City: Building Sites* (Palgrave Macmillan 2009) 106–25.

137 This is true in particular for the park surrounding the Old City walls, the City of David Park, and the proposed Mt. of Olives Park.

138 An exhaustive critique can be found in BIMKOM, From Public to National: National Parks in East Jerusalem (New Israel Fund,__ 2012).

earmarked for residences and part for development and preservation of open areas. This proposal has proved controversial.[139]

Conclusion

Issues related to the holy places in Jerusalem are sensitive and complex. One of the biggest and continuing issues is land ownership. The ownership rights in the Old City are often difficult to ascertain. They depend on hundreds of years of unregistered titles burdened by varieties of easements. Much *waqf* property in West Jerusalem was declared abandoned property after 1948 and other *waqf* properties in East Jerusalem, for example in the Jewish Quarter, were condemned after 1967 for use by the Society for Redevelopment of the Jewish Quarter. In 1965 the government amended the Absentee Property Law to clearly incorporate *waqf* assets into the domain of the Custodian of Absentee Property.[140] Further, the Knesset passed a 2009 land reform law that allows the state to privatize state-owned lands, including land held by the Custodian for Absentee Property.[141] How this will impact on *waqf* land and holy places held by the Custodian remains to be seen, but it has been deemed by many as a problematic law that endangers rights of the Arab minority.[142]

A number of Christian properties were taken over during the 1948 Arab-Israeli War, such as the Terra Sancta property, and their status is still being negotiated. (Terra Sancta itself as returned to the Franciscans a few years ago.)

A second issue to be considered are there holy places that are in the greater Jerusalem area as opposed to within the geographical boundaries of Jerusalem. This report has not considered such sites which include Rachel's Tomb, Church of the Nativity and Samuel's Tomb. It should be noted that as to these areas, in

---

139 Drawn from Yekutiel Tzafri Malkov, Forecast: International Storm, *Yediot Yerushalayim* (Jerusalem, 26 October 2009) (Hebrew);Melanie Lidman, National Parks in East Jerusalem Stirs Controversy, *Jerusalem Post*, July 12, 2011.

140 Absentee's Property Law (Release and Use of Endowment Property) 2 February 1965 *Sefer ha-Huqqim*, 445 (1965) at 58. The explanatory notes to the law state that the amendment was passed to remove all doubts concerning the Custodian's control over abandoned *waqf* assets.

141 Mazal Mualem, 'Knesset passes land reform and "Mofaz law"' (2009) *Haaretz* online <www.haaretz.com/hasen/spages/1104900tm> accessed 30 April 2013.

142 See for example Adalah Position Paper of 21 September 2009 detailing problems with the law, <www.adallah.org> accessed 30 April 2013. Note as well that while there has been an informal governmental policy not to apply the abandoned property law to East Jerusalem, this policy has been subject to alterations in recent years, particularly for the acquisition of Palestinian properties in the Muslim Quarter. See for example Michelle Oliel, 'Property Rights and Ownership in the Old City of Jerusalem' <http://web2.uwindsor.ca/wsgcms/Projects/JerusalemInitiative/documents/oldcitypropertyrights.pdf> accessed 30 April 2013.

the West Bank proper (i.e. not in Jerusalem), Israeli law does not apply. Pre-1967 Jordanian law applies to these areas as amended by Israeli military regulations and, where applicable, Palestinian legislation and regulations. For their part, the Palestinians argue that international law would apply.

A third issue is the possibility of sharing holy sites. The experience of the Temple Mount/Haram-al-Sharif can only make one pessimistic in this regard. As Ron Hassner has underscored,[143] given the extent to which control of a holy site is intertwined with ideological and nationalist claims, it is very difficult to envision a sharing *modus vivendi*. To emphasize this point, consider the statement of the Rabbi of the Western Wall who, on religious reasons, himself opposes Jews ascending the Temple Mount, yet who recently asserted, 'The Arabs won't dictate to us when to go up to the Temple Mount'.[144]

We must recognize that the problem of access is a central issue for Palestinians. Because of security issues they are not allowed free access to their holy places. And, equally important, there is little effort to develop ways to meet religious needs consonant with security. During the Christmas season special passes are provided for Arab Christians resident in Jerusalem to go to Bethlehem and for Arab Christian residents in the West Bank to attend the services at the Church of the Holy Sepulchre. But there is no recognition of the need to develop ways to do this during the year. Creative efforts can be made to 'square this circle'.[145]

---

143 Ron Hassner, 'The Pessimists' Guide to Religious Coexistence', in Marshall J. Breger, Yitzhak Reiter and Leonard Hammer (eds), *Holy Places in the Israel-Palestine Conflict*, op. cit. 145.

144 Matthew Wagner, 'Rabinovitz: Arabs Will Not Dictate to Us When to Go Up To the Temple Mount', *Jerusalem Post* (Jerusalem, 16 October 2009).

145 One creative example was the decision in December 2007 to establish 'a special passage to Bethlehem for Christian pilgrims before and after Christmas'. Yuval Azoulay and Irit Rosenbaum, 'Pilgrims to Get Quick Entry into Bethlehem', *Haaretz* (Tel Aviv, 21 December 2007) A3 (in Hebrew). Former British Prime Minister Tony Blair made a special request to ease the passage of the thousands of Christians planning to attend Christmas mass in Bethlehem. Due to the numerous security checks at the checkpoint leading to Bethlehem, visitors typically braved long lines when entering the West Bank. Unfortunately, the 'fast-track' checkpoint was open only to Christian pilgrims from abroad. Ibid. Similarly, between 1947–67, Israeli Christians enjoyed passage to Bethlehem during the Christmas and New Year season. See Raphael Israeli, *Jerusalem Divided: The Armistice Regime 1947–1967* (Frank Cass 2002) 101–3. Because Jordanian officials would not accept Israeli passports, Israeli citizens received acceptable documents from the government – called laissez passer – in advance of the holiday. Ibid. By allowing Israeli Christians to participate in Christmas celebrations in Bethlehem, Jordanian officials complied, at least in part, with Article VIII of the Armistice Agreement providing free access to religious sites. Ibid. The Christmas crossings also eased tensions on both sides: 'If on normal days an abnormal vigilance prevailed on both sides, lest someone trespassed into no man's land, on the abnormal day of the Christmas crossing, the place suddenly became normal: people wandered about the square in large numbers, completely unmindful of their proximity to the armistice lines'. Id. 101.

From a sociological perspective, the dispute over Jerusalem is exacerbated by the abundance of overlapping and competing holy sites between different religions. Some form of 'separate administration' may be desirable to ensure long-term stability in the politics of Jerusalem as well as the stability that comes from fairness in site management.

For similar reasons, in order to protect the 'cultural heritage' of all parties, efforts must be made to depoliticize archaeological activity and delegate archaeological decisions to technical experts. Consideration should be given to the implementation of the Israeli-Palestinian Cultural Heritage Agreement by Israel alone or jointly by Israel and the Palestinian Authority. That agreement signed by leading Palestinian and Israeli archaeologists requires that each party be obliged to treat equally all archeological sites in its territory, 'regardless of their ethnic, national or cultural affiliation'.[146] It further requires the creation of a 'Heritage Zone' to include the Old City and additional sites, and specifies that 'archeological sites in the zone would be accessible to anyone, and any research would have to be done with full transparency'.[147] Hopefully, acceptance of this approach by the governing authorities would reduce the belief (and perhaps reality) that holy places are being used to shore up nationalist narratives and deny the connection of other religions to a holy site.

Many of the conflicts regarding the holy places are made worse by the ignorance (or willful rejection) of the narratives of other religions.[148] One of the most useful efforts by the Knights of Malta or other international organizations would be to disseminate information regarding various religious narratives. Such a task should be given to any 'separate administration' or government commission charged with managing the holy sites in Jerusalem.

146 Meron Rapoport, 'A Separate Peace', *Haaretz* (Tel Aviv, 14 April 2006); see also *Israeli-Palestinian Archaeology Working Group Agreement* <www.usc.edu/dept/LAS/religion/arc/sh/agreement.pdf> accessed 10 October 2008, 2.

147 John Bohannon, 'Team Unveils Mideast Archaeology Peace Plan' (2008) *Science* 302; see also *Israeli-Palestinian Archaeology Working Group Agreement*, op. cit., 5.

148 For one example, see Bari Weiss, 'Palestinian Leaders Denies Jewish Tie to Temple', *Wall St Journal* (New York, 25 September 2009). There are numerous equivalent examples of Jewish rejection of Muslim claims, in particular the 'custom' of Orthodox Jews to 'white out' the Dome of the Rock in pictures of Jerusalem.

Chapter 10

Jerusalem as a Holy Place: Christian Sacred Sites in the Holy City

Rafael Palomino

Context: Human Rights Framework

Our approach to the intricate Jerusalem question may begin by remembering the uniqueness of the City if compared with other holy cities in the world. In Jerusalem, different identities and different contested political aspirations converge:

Certainly are other cities of God in the world, such as Rome and Mecca, but none possess the distinctive characteristics of Jerusalem – the historical meeting point of various religions, the place that marks the cross-roads where their paths meet (…) it must be stressed that Jerusalem is different from all other holy cities which attest to the strong links between a place and a religion. Specifically, the historical vocation of Jerusalem is to be the meeting place of three religions, and continually to relaunch the challenge of their peaceful coexistence within the same physical space.[1]

We find in Jerusalem different identities which correspond to different interests. On one hand, the *national identities* – Palestinian and Israeli – contend and affirm the centrality of Jerusalem as the capital city.[2] In this sense, Jerusalem plays a major role in the narrative, history and explanation of two peoples. On the other hand, Jerusalem stands for three *religious identities* – the Jewish, the Muslim and the Christian.[3] For these religions Jerusalem is the *evidence*, the

---

1 Silvio Ferrari, 'The Religious Significance of Jerusalem in the Middle East Peace Process: Some Legal Implications' [1996] *Catholic University of America* 734.

2 'Jerusalem, complete and united, is the capital of Israel'. *Basic Law: Jerusalem, Capital of Israel*, passed by the Knesset on the 17th Av, 5740 (30 July, 1980) and published in Sefer Ha-Chukkim No. 980 of the 23rd Av, 5740 (5 August, 1980), p. 186. 'Jerusalem is the capital of Palestine' Article 3, 2003 Amended Basic Law, Ramallah: 2003. The Palestinian Basic Law: 'The Palestine National Council, in the name of God, and in the name of the Palestinian Arab people, hereby proclaims the establishment of the State of Palestine on our Palestinian territory with its capital Jerusalem (Al-Quds Ash-Sharif)'. Palestinian Declaration of Independence, Algiers, 15 November 1988. <www.al-bab.com/arab/docs/pal/pal3.htm> accessed 24 September 2012.

3 Concerning the different and convergent meaning of Jerusalem for the three religions, *Ebraismo, Cristianesimo, Islam – Dizionario Comparato delle Religioni Monoteistiche* (Piemme 1991) 232–5.

symbol and the *memorial expression* of faith realities. Yet we might identify a third source of identity, a special feature, since the meaning of Jerusalem bursts out its geographical and political boundaries, touching the hearts of millions of people around the world.[4] In this sense Jerusalem purports to have an *international identity* which in the legal sense means that the basic political decisions affecting the City have international impact and dimension,[5] and cannot be adopted unilaterally.

The approach to these identities shifts between two basic perspectives of the same phenomenon.[6] One of these perspectives is *state/territorial*. It gives an account of the Jerusalem issue in terms of national belonging and in terms of statehood tools, like sovereignty, citizenship or frontiers. This first perspective corresponds to the *national identity* claims. The other perspective is the *global/trans-territorial* one and, compared with the former, it gives an account of the Jerusalem question in terms of global interests and international instruments to bring about a satisfactory solution. Not necessarily, but in part, the *religious identity* may move in these terms, as at the same time it is true that the combination of religion and national identity (much stronger among Muslims and Jews) stoutly opts for a state/territorial perspective.

When speaking about Jerusalem we move in two different stages.

The first stage explains the City essentially as a physical space containing a group of sites related to the three monotheistic religions which conveys a special significance for believers or followers of those religions. This significance goes far beyond the sacredness of religious spaces in general (churches, mosques, synagogues) for historical reasons. Being sacred, each of those places requires special legal protection and attention. However, once legal protection is afforded by whatever State or national authority, special needs from the religious and human

4 'The General Assembly (…) *Reaffirming* that the international community, through the United Nations, has a legitimate interest in the question of the City of Jerusalem and the protection of the unique spiritual, religious and cultural dimensions of the city, as foreseen in relevant United Nations resolutions on this matter (…) 2. Stresses that a comprehensive, just and lasting solution to the question of the City of Jerusalem should take into account the legitimate concerns of both the Palestinian and Israeli sides and should include internationally guaranteed provisions to ensure the freedom of religion and of conscience of its inhabitants, as well as permanent, free and unhindered access to the holy places by the people of all religions and nationalities'. Resolution adopted by the General Assembly 63/30. Jerusalem, A/RES/63/30, 23 January 2009.

5 'One of the principal reasons underlying the dispute over Jerusalem is that the controversy exceeds the city's boundaries. In contrast to almost all other cities in the world, the future of Jerusalem is important not only to those who inhabit the city. During the last decades Jerusalem has become a major national and religious symbol for Jews, Muslims, and Christians all over the world. Thus, the main struggle is not for territorial, strategical, or economic gains, but rather for symbols'. Moshe Hirsch, 'The Future Negotiations over Jerusalem, Strategical Factors and Game Theory' [1996] *Catholic University of America Law Review* 705.

6 Enrico Molinaro, *The Holy Places of Jerusalem in Middle East Agreements – The Conflict between Global and State Identities* (Sussex Academic Press 2009).

rights perspectives would be met and then Jerusalem would be basically a physical place without a significant or special legal value. Once the legal interests of each of those single sites are secured and guaranteed, the Jerusalem question itself would have no special meaning from the *international* and *religious* perspective, and it would be a pending issue solely for the *national identity* dimension. In my opinion, this is the perspective adopted by the State of Israel in regulating separately, in two laws, the legal protection which Holy Places deserve on the one hand, and the legal meaning of Jerusalem on the other.[7]

However, if we look carefully at a further stage, related to the City as a whole, Jerusalem is more than a physical space which contains religious Holy Places with special legal requirements on the grounds of freedom of religion. Jerusalem as a unit is a value in itself. Like other Holy Cities, Jerusalem gathers together four main elements:

First, they support an institutional religious hierarchy often graced by the presence of leading clerics who have considerable political influence, locally, nationally, and regionally. Second, holy cities have an administrative apparatus controlling large swathes of property as well as religious, welfare, and educational services that provide the clerics and senior functionaries with an important local constituency and undergird a communal identity. Third, they have an independent financial basis in the form of endowments and donations. This allows holy cities absorbing external funds regardless of the strength or weakness of the local economy, which, in turn, allows them to fund religious personnel and relatively state intervention-free projects. Finally, they can point to an important network of international and diaspora related contacts built up through pilgrimage and educational activities. Such contacts and interactions offer a degree of protection to the clergy and their administrators and can strengthen their immunity from state intervention. Taking all these aspects together, one can see how the sovereignty of a state is to a considerable extent circumscribed in a holy city'.[8]

Besides, the maintenance and vitality of those Holy Places inside the City need the presence of population, traditions, hinterlands … which constitute an essential substrate to preserve the peculiar character of a place which is *holy* but at the same time is a *living* place. In sum:

> Jerusalem contains communities of believers full of life, whose presence the peoples of the whole world regards as a sign and source of hope, specially those who consider the Holy City to be in a certain way their spiritual heritage and a symbol of peace and harmony. Indeed, in so far as the City is the homeland

7 *Basic Law: Jerusalem, Capital of Israel*, passed by the Knesset on the 17th Av, 5740 (30 July 1980) and published in Sefer Ha-Chukkim No. 980 of the 23rd Av, 5740 (5 August 1980), p. 186; the Bill and an Explanatory Note were published in Hatza'ot Chok No. 1464 of 5740, p. 287. *Protection of Holy Places Law*, 5727–1967.

8 Michael Dumper, *The Old City of Jerusalem in the Middle East Conflict* (Lynne Rienner Publishers 2003) 9.

> of the hearts of all the spiritual descendants of Abraham who hold it very dear, and the place where, according to faith, the created things of earth encounter the infinite transcendence of God, Jerusalem stands out as a symbol of coming together to union, and universal peace for the human family. The Holy City, therefore, strongly urges peace for the whole human race, specially for those who worship the one, great God, the merciful Father of the peoples.[9]

Jerusalem is not only the vessel or receptacle of religious spaces but a religious space itself.[10] As a consequence, it is hard – if not impossible – to isolate the religious dimension of the City from certain purely secular aspects. In other words, many political and legal actions of a secular character on the City necessarily have serious consequences on the essential religious dimension of Jerusalem. Therefore, any legal or political action concerning Jerusalem must take into account its religious meaning.

Any reflection on Jerusalem as a Holy City involves basically two different sets of rights and freedoms.

First, there are the freedoms and rights related to the religion of people who belong to those communities worshipping in Jerusalem, namely members of communities of the three monotheistic religions. According to the Universal Declaration of Human Rights, Article 18, '[e]veryone has the right to freedom of thought, conscience and religion; this right includes freedom to change his religion or belief, and freedom, either alone or in community with others and in public or private, to manifest his religion or belief in teaching, practice, worship and observance'. Article 18 of the International Covenant on Civil and Political Rights of 1966 adds that '[n]o one shall be subject to coercion which would impair his freedom to have or to adopt a religion or belief of his choice. Freedom to manifest one's religion or beliefs may be subject only to such limitations as are prescribed by law and are necessary to protect public safety, order, health, or morals or the fundamental rights and freedoms of others'. Finally, the Declaration on the Elimination of All Forms of Intolerance and of Discrimination Based on Religion or Belief of 1981, Article 6, establishes that the right to freedom of thought, conscience, religion or belief shall include, *inter alia*, freedom 'to worship or

---

9 John Paul II, Apostolic Letter *Redemptionis Anno* (20 April 1984), *Acta Apostolicae Sedis* 1984) 626.

10 'For Jews, then, Jerusalem is not a city that encompasses holy places. Rather it is the earthly city itself that is holy, both the land and, as the former Chief Rabbi Kook tells us, even the air. Jerusalem, then, is synonymous with Judaism's entrenchment in the land of Israel. It is the very center of that entrenchment (…) At the same time (…) "[t]he sanctity of Jerusalem in Islam is a fact". It is the original direction for Moslem prayer, 'ula al-qublatheyn, and the al-mi'radj haqq, the place from which the Prophet ascended (some say in a winged mount) to heavenly spheres. It is, moreover, the place that in Moslem tradition those eschatological events harkening the end of the world will commence. Those who try to suggest that al-Quds is less holy to Islam than to Judaism simply are incorrect'. Marshall J. Breger, 'The future of Jerusalem: A Symposium. An Introduction' [1996] *Catholic University of America Law Review* 654.

assemble in connection with a religion or belief, and to establish and maintain places for these purposes'. Consequently, and given the special significance of Holy Places in Jerusalem, they – like Holy Places in general – constitute an integral part of religious freedom.

The second set of rights and freedoms are those related to culture: as is enshrined in Article 27 of the International Declaration of Human Rights of 1948: '[e]veryone has the right freely to participate in the cultural life of the community, to enjoy the arts and to share in scientific advancement and its benefits'. Article 15 of the International Covenant on Economic, Social and Cultural Rights of 1976 establishes that, '[t]he States Parties to the present Covenant recognize the right of everyone to take part in cultural life'. The cultural and historical value of Jerusalem might involve the category of cultural rights as well.

It is not impossible to envisage a clash between these two sets of rights – namely the right to religious freedom and the right to cultural heritage – related to Jerusalem as a Holy City in general and to the Holy Places in particular. Which of them takes precedence? Does the right to cultural heritage of humankind have priority over the right to religious freedom of several individuals or communities? Certainly all the value of Jerusalem and its Holy Places derives primarily from their religious significance. If that peculiar religious significance is absent or blurred, the substantial and profound foundation of the value of Jerusalem would disappear or would be diminished. In consequence, full and complete enjoyment of freedom of religion and related rights must be observed as a guarantee for the enjoyment of the right to cultural heritage which all humankind deserves. Therefore, any legal action concerning the cultural or historical value must yield to the intrinsic religious value and to the religious dimension inherent to Holy Places in general.

Terminology Concerning Holy Places in Jerusalem

For clarification purposes it would be important to address the meaning of terms usually applied to Jerusalem's Holy Places, places of worship and so on since in this particular case:

- not all the Holy Places inside Jerusalem can be identified strictly as 'buildings' (that is, places of worship like churches, mosques or synagogues);
- not all the Holy Places necessarily have the same historical and legal value; and
- not all the Holy Places of the three monotheistic religions are within Jerusalem.

The same clarification purpose may lead to a general historical division of periods of time when dealing with the political and legal framework concerning Holy Places in Jerusalem:

- Ottoman Rule period (1517–1917);
- League of Nations period (British rule, 1917–48);
- United Nations period (which overlapped with the League of Nations Period and extended in time from the logical viewpoint since it stands for the internationalization of the City);
- The proclamation of thc modern State of Israel (1948–67): Jerusalem divided *de facto* into West and East, Israeli and Jordanian rule over parts of the City. Most of the Holy Places were on the Jordanian side;
- The Six-Day War of 1967 to the present. Israeli rule over all Jerusalem.

Holy Places, in general and not specifically for Jerusalem, are 'geographically determined localities to which one or more religious communities attribute extraordinary religious significance or consider as subjects of divine consecration (…) Holy Places may be of juridical importance within the protecting State as well as between States'.[11] Holy Places require as a precondition some sort of 'religious qualification' which bestows on a place or locality a peculiar value.

However, 'Holy place' might not be a religious category itself. Take for instance the case of Christianity and specifically the Catholic Church. According to the law of the Catholic Church, 'Holy Places' is not a legal category stemming from religious law. Rather, it is a conventional term which appears in Article 4 of the Fundamental Agreement between the Holy See and the State of Israel to point out specific places in a historical context[12] (see below *Christian Holy Places*) and in Article 4 of the Basic Agreement between the Holy See and the Palestinian Liberation Organization. The proper term for Canon law to designate a category of special religious places is 'Sacred Places' or *Loca Sacra*, which comprises those places designated for worship or for burial of the faithful (churches, chapels, shrines, altars and cemeteries). That is why the same Article 4 of the Agreement between the Holy See and the State of Israel deals specifically and individually with this other category,[13] conferring on them the expected legal treatment due to places of worship (as a legal secular category). In this sense, it could be important to stress that religious communities have places of worship which are not Holy Places themselves, but places located in a Land which is Holy. And for these places the rights derived from private property are the basic legal guarantee, according to modern constitutional standards, as well as the prerogatives conferred on places of worship in general.

11 Christian Rumpf, 'Holy Places' in *Encyclopedia of Public International Law* (vol. II, Elsevier, 1995) 863.

12 'The State of Israel affirms its continuing commitment to maintain and respect the "Status quo" in the Christian Holy Places to which it applies and the respective rights of the Christian communities thereunder. The Holy See affirms the Catholic Church's continuing commitment to respect the aforementioned 'Status quo' and the said rights'.

13 'The State of Israel agrees with the Holy See on the obligation of continuing respect for and protection of the character proper to Catholic sacred places, such as churches, monasteries, convents, cemeteries and their like'.

Christian Holy Places is a specific category linked to Jerusalem and to other geographical sites close by. It designates the legal status conferred on precise Christian places. 'The technical and legal use of the term *Christian Holy Places* restricts the meaning to specific sites and refers to the practice of certain rites and proprietorship within them'.[14] This category was generated during the Ottoman Empire which issued a number of legal norms to assign or to transfer rights of use and possession between Christian denominations concerning specific Christian places. It is usual to make reference to the *hatty-sharif* (*firmans* or imperial decrees) of 1757 and of 1852.

Though the Ottoman list of Holy Places was restricted to Christian Holy Places, the British Mandate (1922–48) extended the term to include other Christian, Muslim and Jewish Holy Places and sites.[15] The United Nations Special Committee on Palestine (UNSCOP, 1947) and the Conciliation Commission on Palestine (1948) followed that trend and included under the concept of Holy Places, 'a list of recognized holy sites of interest and importance rather than sites to which the *Status Quo* arrangements were applied'.[16]

According to that extensive concept, Holy Places in Jerusalem (and its surroundings) are:[17]

- Christian Holy Places governed by the legal regime of *Status Quo*: the Church of the Holy Sepulchre and its dependencies, such as the Convent of Dayr al-Sultan; the Basilica of the Nativity in Bethlehem, the Tomb of the Virgin Mary.
- Christian Holy Places generally occupied by others but with some rights reserved to the Catholic Church, notably the Cenacle (certain rights reserved to the Franciscan Custody of the Holy Land),[18] the Church of

14 Michael Dumper, op. cit., 108.

15 'A special commission shall be appointed by the Mandatory to study, define and determine the rights and claims in connection with the Holy Places and the rights and claims relating to the different religious communities in Palestine. The method of nomination, the composition and the functions of this Commission shall be submitted to the Council of the League for its approval, and the Commission shall not be appointed or enter upon its functions without the approval of the Council'. Terms of the British Mandate for Palestine, confirmed by the Council of the League of Nations on 24 July 1922, League of Nations Official Journal, August 1922, pp. 1007–12, at 1009. See Ruth Lapidoth and Moshe Hirsch (eds), *The Jerusalem Question and Its resolution: Selected Documents* (Martinus Nijhoff Publishers 1994) 1.

16 Michael Dumper, op. cit., 110. 'The Wailing Wall and Rachel's Tomb, of which the ownership is in dispute between the Moslems and the Jews, are similarly subject to the Status Quo'. Lionel G.A. Cust, *The Status Quo in the Holy Places* (Government of Palestine 1930) 12.

17 See H. Eugene Bovis, *The Jerusalem Question, 1917–1968* (Hoover Press 1971) 142.

18 The Shrine of the Cenacle is not included in Cust's account, because the site was acquired by the Franciscan Order in 1342. It was never occupied by other Christian communities. The Franciscans were expelled from the Cenacle in 1552. 'The Cenacle is not

the Ascension on the Mount of Olives (generally occupied by Muslims with some rights reserved to the Franciscans), Tomb of Lazarus (generally occupied by Muslims with some rights reserved to the Franciscans).

- Christian Holy Places in the possession of Christian Churches: the Church of St Anne, the Church of St James, the Church of St Mark, the House of Caiaphas and the Holy Prison, thc Garden of Gethsemane, the Pool of Bethesda, the Milk Grotto, Shrines in the Shepherds' Fields.
- Muslim Holy Places: notably the Dome of the Rock, the Al-Aqsa Mosque (both in the al-Haram al-Sharif compound), El Burak Esh-Sharif.
- Jewish Holy Places, above all the Western [Wailing] Wall complex (Kotel),[19] but also other places including, for example, the Tomb of Absalom, Bath of Rabbi Ishmael, Pool of Siloam, Cementery of Mt of Olives, Tomb of Zachariah, Tomb of Simon The Just and so on.[20]

Somehow the law leaves the definition of Holy Places to regulations. But as a matter of fact there is neither a Christian Holy Places definition nor a 'State legal' catalogue of those Holy Places, since that could be a 'nationalization' of the Holy Places.[21] In fact Catholics have preferred other sources for regulation: the right

---

a subject of concern to this study, being absolutely under the authority of the Moslem Waqf of Nebi Daud, who however arranges to open it to the many that are anxious to visit a site of such sacred traditions'. Lionel G.A. Cust, op. cit., 7. Yet the Church of the Cenacle is a contested issue, since it passed to the hands of a Jewish entity. After the fist Israeli-Arab war, the State of Israel took possession of the Cenacle and later assigned to itself the title to the property. However, the Custody of the Holy Land has consistently claimed its own property rights in the whole complex of the Cenacle (the Franciscan monastery and the shrine). It is known that this matter is now on the agenda of the negotiations between the Holy See and the State of Israel.

19 It would be preferable to designate it as complex, since the Kotel includes nowadays the cluster of old buildings known as the *Abu Midyan al-Ghawth Waqf* in the Magharib Quarter which was demolished by the Israeli army in 1967 to build a large square before the Western Wall.

20 Some writers include the so-called Tomb of David.

21 Protection of Holy Places Law, 1967. 'The Holy Places shall be protected from desecration and any other violation and from anything likely to violate the freedom of access of the members of the different religions to the places sacred to them or their feelings with regard to those places.

'Whosoever desecrates or otherwise violates a Holy Place shall be liable to imprisonment for a term of seven years.

'Whosoever does anything likely to violate the freedom of access of the members of the different religions to the places sacred to them or their feelings with regard to those places shall be liable to imprisonment for a term of five years.

'This Law shall add to, and not derogate from, any other law.

'The Minister of Religious Affairs is charged with the implementation of this Law, and he may, after consultation with, or upon the proposal of, representatives of the religions

to private property, bilateral treaties between the Holy See and the State of Israel (Article 4), general and specific international laws.

In any case, an Israeli government adviser has opined that: '[t]here are 30 important Holy Places in Jerusalem (in addition to 1072 synagogues, 52 mosques, 65 churches and 72 monasteries)'.[22]

As has been said, among the Christian Holy Places *stricto sensu*, three of them (the Holy Sepulchre and the Tomb of the Virgin Mary in Jerusalem, the Nativity Church in Bethlehem) are regulated by the so-called Status Quo.[23]

The Status Quo designates the complex and detailed rights and traditions, on places, times and actions imposed and sanctioned originally by the Ottoman Empire, mainly derived from the *firmans* of 1757[24] and 1852,[25] comprising

---

concerned and with the consent of the Minister of Justice make regulations as to any matter relating to such implementation.

'This Law shall come into force on the date of its adoption by the Knesset'.

22 Shmuel Berkowitz, 'The Holy Places in Jerusalem: Legal Aspects' [1996] *Justice* 6. The figures on the number of places of worship may change from one author to other. For instance: 'In addition to the more well-known sites on the *Haram* mentioned above, there are many places of worship, among them 65 functional mosques, several sufi lodges, saints' tombs and cemeteries. Furthermore, many sites that served as places of worship or burial grounds that have not operated for many years according to their original purpose have become "cultural properties"'. Yizhak Reiter, *Islamic Institutions in Jerusalem. Palestinian Muslim Organization under Jordanian and Israeli Rule* (Kluwer Law International, Jerusalem Institute for Israel Studies 1997) 87.

23 Also the Ascension shrine, which is a mosque, but this shrine is under the *Status Quo* as far as the Christians are concerned and mentioned in the decree of 1852, with the other three shrines above.

24 'The Capitulations of 1604, 1673, and 1740, confirmed the Latins in the possession of the Holy Sepulchre and Calvary, the Church of the Nativity, and the Church of the Virgin. On the other hand, in 1637 the Patriarch of Jerusalem, Theophanes III, obtained a firman in favour of the Orthodox and finally in 1757, while the European Powers were engaged in continual strife among themselves, this element definitely regained the supremacy'. Lionel G.A. Cust, op. cit., 8.

25 'In 1850 the French representative at Constantinople, General Aupick, on behalf of his Government and the Catholic Kingdoms of Sardinia, Belgium, Spain, and Austria, submitted to the Sublime Porte a demand for the restoration to the Franciscans of the Holy Places they possessed prior to 1757, that is to say, the Rotunda and the Edicule, the Stone of Unction, the Seven Arches of the Virgin and the Prison of Christ, the Courtyard of the Holy Sepulchre, the Church of the Virgin, and the Church of the Nativity. These claims were received with no less powerful opposition on the part of Russia, the Czar threatening to withdraw his representative at the Porte if they were entertained, and the dispute was one of the causes that led to the Crimean War. An important firman issued in 1852 by Sultan Abdul Mejid, after making reference to a careful examination that had been conducted by a Committee appointed by the Porte, rejected the claim put forward by the Latins to the absolute possession of the major shrines, as detailed by General Aupick, and directed that the *Status Quo* be maintained in all these places. This firman constitutes the official Declaration

Christian Communities (Greek Orthodox, Latin, Armenian Orthodox, Coptic, Syrian, Abyssinian) in the Holy Land, mainly in Jerusalem.[26] The 1757 *firman* gave the Greeks majority (not exclusive) possession of the Basilica of Bethlehem and the Tomb of the Virgin, and joint possession, action and use with the Latins of parts of the Basilica of the Holy Sepulchre. After various conflicts, local affairs and international political pressures, in 1852 another *firman* established that the *Status Quo* (that is, that of 1757) had to be maintained.[27] These *firmans* comprise rules concerning actions (like access, maintenance of building, restoration, cleaning works, conduct and timing of services and festivals) and places.[28]

In practice:

> … [t]he main thrust of the firman was to confirm the 'status quo' without providing details of it. The absence of a detailed inventory of practices meant that the possibility for minor encroachments and misunderstandings was endless causing much tension between the established churches. At the same time a written inventory was not welcome because it would have enshrined practices that, although they may have been the prevailing ones, were not consensual and may have been set through *force majeur*. It also meant that the succeeding secular authority did not have a reference document and was often working in the dark.[29]

A significant part of the content of the *Status Quo* was described by L.G.A. Cust in 1930.[30] The relationship between places and actions was synthesized by Cust who explained that:

> For the purpose of defining the Status Quo, the Holy Places and their component parts may be divided into certain categories:
>
> (1) The parts that are accepted to be the common property of the three rites in equal shares;
>
> (2) The parts claimed by one rite as under its exclusive jurisdiction, but in which the other rites claim joint proprietorship;

---

of the *Status Quo* in the Holy Places. Shortly afterwards the Crimean War broke out. The Treaty of Paris at its close in 1855 left the position as it was, the Signatory Powers, including Russia, undertaking to uphold the Status Quo ante bellum'. Lionel G.A. Cust, op. cit., 9.

26 For a juridical and historical assessment of the *Status Quo*, see Bernardin Collin, *Le problème juridique des Lieux-Saints* (Centre d'Etudes Orientales 1956) 179–86.

27 The 1852 *firman* freezed the situation after several acts of violence.

28 Bernardin Collin, *Le problème juridique des Lieux-Saints*, op. cit., 107.

29 Michael Dumper, op. cit., 108.

30 The Cust report does not have objective legal force: it is a report, an account, which helps to know the legal situation at the moment in which he made his report.

(3) The parts of which the ownership is disputed between two rites;

(4) The parts of which one rite has the exclusive use, but qualified by the right of the others to cense and visit it during their offices;

(5) The parts which are in the exclusive jurisdiction of one rite, but are comprised within the ensemble of the Holy Place.[31]

The *Status Quo* was recognized in international treaties such as the Paris Convention of 1856 (after the Crimean War), the Congress of Berlin (1878) and the Versailles Treaty (1919).

As pointed out above, the main problem of the *Status Quo* is its practical frailty, which calls for constant vigilance. It is nothing more and nothing less than a secular settlement of contested rights, caused by external international pressures.

However, the *Status Quo* has been formally accepted on various occasions in recent times by the parties concerned.

From the religious viewpoint, it has been formally accepted in the Memorandum on the Significance of Jerusalem for Christians' 'Legitimate Demands of Christians for Jerusalem' of 14 November 1994 signed in Jerusalem by the Patriarchs and the Heads of Christian Communities – the Greek Orthodox Patriarch, the *Custos* of the Holy Land and the Armenian Patriarch – who are the heads of the three communities principally and directly concerned. But it was also signed by the Coptic Orthodox, Syrian Orthodox and Ethiopian Orthodox Archbishops, whose communities also have concerns, albeit small ones; and by the Latin Patriarch, the Greek Catholic Maronite and the Syrian Catholic Patriarchs or Vicars, as well as the Anglican and Lutheran Bishops who as such have no role with regards to the *Status Quo* in the Holy Places.[32]

Even more significantly, from the international legal viewpoint, the *Status Quo* regime is endorsed in article 4§1 of the Fundamental Agreement between Israel and the Holy See, signed on 30 December 1993 and in Article 4 of the Basic Agreement between the Holy See and the PLO of 15 February 2000.

In sum, '[w]hile this system is far from perfect',[33] as observed by professor Ferrari, it is now agreed by all that it represents achievement of the best system possible in an imperfect world.

31 Lionel G.A. Cust, op.cit., 13.

32 The acceptance of the *Status Quo* was reaffirmed in the Statement 'City of Two Peoples and Three Religions' of 29 September 2006 by the same religious authorities, plus the Armenian Catholic Patriarchal Exarchate.

33 Silvio Ferrari, 'The Religious Significance of Jerusalem in the Middle East Peace Process: Some Legal Implications', op. cit., 738.

What Should be Guaranteed?

In light of the aforementioned considerations and descriptions, we may consider now what requirements should be guaranteed in the case of the Holy City of Jerusalem according both to the historic standards and to the human rights framework.

The Human Rights Perspective

In this case, religious freedom covers a cluster of rights which could be enumerated as follows:

- The right to pilgrimage, as part of freedom of worship.[34] The special character of the Holy City of Jerusalem attracts the attention of believers as a living testimony of their faith. It is true that it is not mandatory for Muslims or Christians to travel regularly (or even once in their lifetime) to Jerusalem, and after the destruction of the Temple (AD 70) it is not even mandatory for Jews to do so. However, it is part of the religious identity of believers to worship and exercise their religion whenever and wherever, especially in the case of places which hold a deep significance, both historically and spiritually, for those believers, of course always respecting the limits of rights.
- The right to religious autonomy. This right basically implies the freedom of religious bodies (communities, churches, denominations and so on) to conduct their internal affairs and concomitant issues without external interference or undue influence coming from the political powers and from secular or other groups.[35] In the case of Jerusalem the right to religious autonomy has deep roots in historical rules, customs and usages, respected by successive States over very long periods of time, even centuries. The right to religious autonomy requires also respecting the 'environmental' conditions which make both the exercise of religion and its autonomy possible.[36]

---

34 It is clearly expressed in Article 6 of the Declaration on the Elimination of All Forms of Intolerance and of Discrimination Based on Religion or Belief, Proclaimed by General Assembly Resolution 36/55 of 25 November 1981: 'In accordance with article 1 of the present Declaration, and subject to the provisions of article 1 § 3, the right to freedom of thought, conscience, religion or belief shall include, inter alia, the following freedoms: (a) To worship or assemble in connection with a religion or belief, and to establish and maintain places for these purposes'.

35 Again it is enshrined in Article 6 of the Declaration on the Elimination of All Forms of Intolerance and of Discrimination Based on Religion or Belief: '(g) To train, appoint, elect or designate by succession appropriate leaders called for by the requirements and standards of any religion or belief (…) (i) To establish and maintain communications with individuals and communities in matters of religion and belief at the national and international levels'.

36 That is why Article 6 of the same Declaration consecrates the right '(b) To establish and maintain appropriate charitable or humanitarian institutions'.

The right to culture embraces the preservation, safeguarding and protection of those places with a special meaning for humankind, making it possible for present and future generations to enjoy and have access to those places in conditions which, in the specific case of Jerusalem, combine the testimony of the history of humankind and at the same time are the living proof of the geographical meeting point of different peoples, languages, ethos, beliefs and so on. In this case, the right to culture points basically to the balance between the preservation of the conditions under which the historical and cultural experience of the Holy City may be safeguarded, while respecting the needs of the ordinary development of the peoples and communities living in the City.

Matters to be Covered

The different matters which have emerged in ancient and recent times to identify specific requirements concerning the status of Jerusalem could be synthesized in the following way.[37]

a. From the substantial viewpoint:

- Preserving the Holy City identity, regarded as equally sacred by the three monotheistic religions. The identity of the City comprises a series of characteristics: historical, material, religious and cultural. Identity also comprehends integrity (of places and of communities). As is well known, this issue is closely connected with the political situation of Jerusalem and with the solution of the 'Jerusalem political question'.[38] The debate has not been solved yet and it seems that clarification is not at hand. What has been clear up to now is that there is a gap between the *de iure* situation (still governed by international instruments which reflect

37 Different sources establish a series of requirements. Take for instance the 'Principles governing the cultural and religious status quo in Jerusalem', in Enrico Molinaro, *The Holy Places of Jerusalem in the Middle East Peace Agreements*, op. cit., 135; Angelo Macchi and Giovanni Rulli, 'Il Futuro di Gierusalemme' [1996] *La Civiltà Cattolica* 555; David Maria A. Jaeger, 'The Multilateral Treaty on the City of Jerusalem and its Environs', ENEC (Europe-Near East Center, Associazione Internazionale per le relazioni col Vicino Oriente) <http://www.enec.it/Multilateral.htm> accessed 27 June 2009; Francisco Utray, 'El problema de los Santos Lugares' [1962] *Revista de Política Internacional* 296.

38 'As for the Jerusalem problem, most of the literature suggesting possible ways to resolve it falls into one of three categories. The first category is administrative, or what some call the municipal solution; the second category is religious; and the third category is political, or what some call the territorial solution. So we have three categories of solutions — three different attempts at a solution — and if one examines each approach, it becomes clear that no single approach will effect a balanced settlement to this explosive issue'. Adnan Abu Odeh, 'Religious Inclusion, Political Inclusion: Jerusalem as an Undivided Capital' [1996] *Catholic University of America Law Review* 690.

the international vocation of the City)[39] and the *de facto*[40] arrangements. Manifold hypothetical solutions have been advanced over time for solving the dispute in its different dimensions.[41] A careful examination of these proposals[42] is beyond the limited scope and purpose of this contribution. However, it seems to be manifest that the solution (that is, a permanent status respecting the singularity of the City) requires a negotiated solution observing international requirements.

- Securing religious freedom in all its aspects, for individuals and communities, according to international standards. The respect for this human right must encompass the combination of equality of all institutions and persons before the law. Obviously, freedom of religion includes freedom to access and visit the respective religious sacred places as part of the right to pilgrimage. Freedom of access must be understood here as a 'civil' right (access and exit) before State authorities,[43] not as a *carte blanche* for access to specific places of worship wherever and whenever, which could be inconsistent with freedom of worship or with specific rules derived from the right to property, ownership or tenure.
- Respect for the Holy Places and protection of them (including protection

39 Those documents are well known. Among others, GA Res. 181 (II), UN GAOR, UN Doc. A/64 (1947), GA Res. 194 (III), UN GAOR (1948), GA Res. 303, UN GAOR (1949); SC Res. 478, UN SCOR, 35th Sess., 2245th mtg at 14, UN Doc. S/INF/36 (1980); GA Res. 35/169E, UN GAOR, 35th Sess., Supp. No. 48, at 208 – 09, UN Doc. A/35/48 (1981).

40 Charalambos Papastathis, 'A New Status for Jerusalem? An Eastern Orthodox Viewpoint', in Marshall G. Breger and Ora Ahimeir, *Jerusalem: A City and Its Future* (Paperback 2002) 723–4.

41 Moshe Hirsch, Deborah Housen-Couriel and Ruth Lapidoth, *Whither Jerusalem? Proposals and Positions Concerning the Future of Jerusalem* (Jerusalem Institute for Israel Studies, Mekhon Yerushalayim le-heker Yiśra'el, Martinus Nihoff Publishers 1985).

42 Spanish Ambassador López de Aguirrebengoa has listed up to 11 models for the solution: 1) Internationalization of all the City, 2) Internationalization of the Old City, 3) Internationalization of the historic part of the City with a special, internationally guaranteed statute, 4) Partition of the City between Israelis and Palestinians, taking as pattern for division the situation before 1967, 5) The 'Condominium' solution, 6) Autonomous municipal administration of the Old City under Israeli sovereignty, 7) Israeli sovereignty and international municipal regime, 8) Segregation of a sector inside the present municipal boundaries to establish the Capital of Palestine, 9) Jerusalem as a capital of two States following the Lateran Treaty of the 1929 Vatican model, 10) Municipal autonomy with a mixed Israeli-Palestinian municipal authority, Israeli sovereignty and extraterritoriality position for Holy Places (*lato sensu*?), 11) special, internationally guaranteed statute with religious communities' administration under Israeli or mixed Palestinian-Israeli sovereignty. See Ramón Armengod, 'Jerusalén y el proceso de paz de Oriente Próximo' [1996] *Política Exterior* 27.

43 United Nations Declaration of Human Rights of 1948, Article 13. '(1) Everyone has the right to freedom of movement and residence within the borders of each state'.

from desecration, expropriation, alteration, exemption from taxation). Moreover, it would be necessary to put on a normal footing the treatment of Holy Places and other places of worship as mainly the private property of the religious communities that own them wherever they in fact do own them. In this sense, nowadays the continuation in different forms of the survival to whatever extent of the 'reservation of jurisdiction to executive power' principle of the 1924 Palestine Holy Places Order in Council[44] is not acceptable, since it deprives the religious bodies concerned of the due process of law. The current legislative situation is not satisfactory either, as, for many issues (if not all) concerning Holy Places, the consent and guidelines of the Minister of Religious Affairs (not the mandatory consultation or consent of the religious communities) are required as a precondition for carrying out certain actions.[45]

- Respect for spiritual, research and welfare activities carried out by religious communities.
- Equality for all persons (both natural and legal), of whatever religion or none, before the law in all respects (individuals, communities, their institutions, activities and places).

b. From the procedural viewpoint:

- Setting up a legal instrument under which all the substantial rights and freedoms are safeguarded.

How Should it be Guaranteed?

It has been proposed that the protection of holy spaces inside Jerusalem be afforded by granting extraterritorial status (limited exercise of sovereignty by the

---

44 '(…) 2. Notwithstanding anything to the contrary in the Palestine Order-in-Council 1922, or in any Ordinance or Law in Palestine, no cause or matter in connection with the Holy Places or religious buildings or sites or the Rights or claims relating to the different religious communities in Palestine shall be heard or determined by any Court in Palestine.

'Provided that nothing herein contained shall affect or limit the exercise by the Religious Courts of the jurisdiction conferred upon them by, or pursuant to, the said Palestine Order in Council.

'3. If any question arises whether any cause or matter comes within the terms of the preceding Article hereof, such question shall, pending the constitution of a Commission [never constituted] charged with jurisdiction over the matters set out in the said Article, be referred to the High Commissioner, who shall decide the question after making due inquiry into the matter in accordance with such instructions as he may receive from one of His Majesty's Principal Secretaries of State (…)' The Palestine (Holy Places) Order in Council, 1924, in Enrico Molinaro, *The Holy Places of Jerusalem in the Middle East Peace Agreements*, op. cit., 133–4.

45 Cf. Shmuel Berkowitz, 'The Holy Places in Jerusalem: Legal Aspects', op. cit., 6.

State).[46] However, that solution does not respond to the needs either theoretically or practically. As may be supposed from the previous considerations, the full and satisfactory protection of the sacred spaces inside Jerusalem cannot be isolated from the Holy City as a whole.

Manifold problems then appear on the scene. It is common to refer to at least two of them: the boundaries of the City and sovereignty.

Concerning the boundaries, at first glance it would be really easy to establish the boundaries of protected places according to the Old City limits[47] or to the General Assembly of the United Nations Resolution 181 (II) (including, among other places, Abu Dis, to the East; Bethlehem, South; Ain Karen, West; Shufat, North). This approach establishes *material* boundaries. However, it is important to underline that the hinterlands around these physical limits (population, culture and so on) must be taken into account as well. Environs must play a role of some sort of 'easement' related to special rules on zoning law, population stability and so on.

Concerning sovereignty, it is well known that the question still remains open. The discussion started with the idea of a pending international solution of sovereignty, which has not been solved as yet,[48] and has developed into the idea of a 'vacuum' of sovereignty which was filled by Israel in 1948 and 1967 (in an act of self-defence),[49] or even a pending right of the Palestinian people to land and Jerusalem as a Capital. The UN Resolution 181 aspirations and goals have not been carried out due to the subsequent hostilities. The international community has not recognized the successive annexations made by Jordan and Israel. While it is true that the main actors for reaching a permanent solution for the Jerusalem question are the Israelis and the Palestinians, it is also true that Israel and Palestine cannot decide Jerusalem by themselves without taking into account the spirit and purpose of the existing international legal instruments in force.[50]

---

46 Silvio Ferrari, 'The Religious Significance of Jerusalem in the Middle East Peace Process: Some Legal Implications', op. cit., 737–8.

47 Michael Dumper, op. cit., 7; Adnan Abu Odeh, 'Religious Inclusion, Political Inclusion: Jerusalem as an Undivided Capital' [1996] *Catholic University of America Law Review* 693.

48 John Quigley, 'Sovereignty in Jerusalem' [1996] *Catholic University Law Review* 767–8.

49 However, '[a] state that occupies territory while acting in its defense does not thereby gain sovereignty'. John Quigley, 'Sovereignty in Jerusalem', op. cit., 780.

50 This is the spirit recognized in the Preamble of the Basic Agreement between the Holy See and the Palestine Liberation Organization, AAS (2000) 853–61: 'The Holy See, the Sovereign Authority of the Catholic Church, and the Palestine Liberation Organization (hereinafter: PLO), the Representative of the Palestinian People working for the benefit and on behalf of the Palestinian Authority (…) Declaring that an equitable solution for the issue of Jerusalem, based on international resolutions, is fundamental for a just and lasting peace in the Middle East, and that unilateral decisions and actions altering the specific character and status of Jerusalem are morally and legally unacceptable'.

International Instruments

The peculiar nature of the City of Jerusalem might suggest that it would be necessary to include the Holy City in the international multilateral instruments for the protection of the universal cultural heritage. Indeed in 1981 the Old City and Walls[51] were included in the World Heritage List under Article 11 of the Convention Concerning the Protection of the World Cultural and Natural Heritage, adopted by the UNESCO General Conference at its 17th session (Paris, 16 November 1972) to which Jordan was a State Party. Applied to this issue, the Convention may seem interesting in abstract, since it affords international protection for the identification, protection, conservation, presentation and transmission for the future generations of the cultural and natural heritage (Article 4), establishing a system of international co-operation and assistance designed to support States Parties to the Convention in their efforts to conserve and identify that heritage (Article 7) and a source of funding for preservation of important historical and cultural sites and values (Article 15). However, the inclusion of Jerusalem in the World Cultural and Natural Heritage scheme does not constitute any satisfactory solution to the main issues related to the Jerusalem question for the following reasons.

- The Convention does not contain any provision concerning the respect of the human rights concerned, especially freedom of religion; in the case of Jerusalem – as probably in the case of other Holy Cities – the religious freedom issue is crucial. It is necessary to protect holistically the material 'physical cultural heritage' addressed in Article 1 (monuments, groups of buildings, sites) and also the 'human mosaic' of peoples, religions and living cultures. Furthermore, with the Convention we run the risk of reducing the multi-faceted reality of religion to the cultural factor reflected in stones.

51 Jerusalem UNESCO World Heritage List, <http://whc.unesco.org/en/tentativelists/1483/> accessed 29 June 2009. Article 11 § 3 points out that: '3. The inclusion of a property in the World Heritage List requires the consent of the State concerned. The inclusion of a property situated in a territory, sovereignty or jurisdiction over which is claimed by more than one State shall in no way prejudice the rights of the parties to the dispute'. In fact the registry of Jerusalem contains this caveat: 'This concerns the property entitled "Jerusalem – the Old City and Ramparts to include Mount Zion" proposed by Israel as an extension to the "Old City of Jerusalem and its Walls" inscribed on the World Heritage List in 1981, upon proposal by Jordan. The Committee at its 25th Session (Helsinki, 2001) endorsed the recommendation of the 25th session of its Bureau (Paris, June 2001) "to postpone further consideration of this nomination proposal until an agreement on the status of the City of Jerusalem in conformity with International Law is reached, or until the parties concerned submit a joint nomination". It should be noted that the UNESCO General Conference in its Resolutions 32C/39 and 33C/50 affirmed that: "(…) nothing in the present decision, which is aimed at the safeguarding of the cultural heritage of the Old City of Jerusalem, shall in any way affect the relevant United Nations resolutions and decisions, in particular the relevant Security Council resolutions on the legal status of Jerusalem"'.

- Indirectly, promoting the Convention as a source for regulating or partly providing a legal solution to Jerusalem means to take a stand on the dispute on Jerusalem while avoiding any negotiated solution. Only after achieving a stable and internationally recognized solution between Israel and Palestine would it be acceptable to include Jerusalem in the framework of the Convention.[52]
- The Convention does not fully safeguard the rights of private property that religious bodies have in many (if not all) Holy Places, and it does not fit into the complex issue of the religious private property of Christian Holy Places in particular and Holy Places in general. Article 6 § 1 seems to be devised for abstract situations in which property rights are held by individuals or groups under the generic law and rules of a given State.[53] However, in the particular situation of Jerusalem it must be taken into account that even the rule of solving disputes and making arrangements concerning the property of Holy Places is under dispute, since it leaves all the power in the hands of the Israeli executive (mainly the Ministry of Religious Affairs, following the British Mandate system, as explained previously), without the clear-cut common guarantees afforded by the judiciary. Besides, the guarantees afforded by the *Status Quo* imply some sort of autonomy specific to and/or different from the common rules of private property in the State.
- And finally the Convention only gives voice and action to two types of actors: States and the World Heritage Committee. It does not take into account the role of religious communities. It would give a blank check to unilateral actions taken by the State or indeed by the World Heritage Committee whilst ignoring the legitimate interest of religious communities, even where they are the owners of the places and monuments concerned.

It is therefore necessary to look for other ways and legal international instruments to provide a proper umbrella for the solution of the issue of Holy Places in Jerusalem. In any case, that solution must be negotiated and agreed if it is to

52 In this sense it is clear to me that the recent inscription of the *Birthplace of Jesus: Church of the Nativity and the pilgrimage route, Bethlehem, Palestine*, on the List of World Heritage in Danger, despite apparent good intentions and needs, might become the perfect instrumentation of sacred places for political purposes. *Unites Nations Educational, Scientific And Cultural Organization, Convention Concerning The Protection Of The World Cultural And Natural Heritage, World Heritage Committee, Thirty-sixth session: Saint Petersburg, Russian Federation*, 24 June–6 July 2012, WHC-12/36.COM/19, Decision: 36 COM 8B.5 <http://whc.unesco.org/archive/2012/whc12-36com-19e.pdf> accessed 25 September 2012.

53 'Whilst fully respecting the sovereignty of the States on whose territory the cultural and natural heritage mentioned in Articles 1 and 2 is situated, and without prejudice to property rights provided by national legislation, the States Parties to this Convention recognize that such heritage constitutes a world heritage for whose protection it is the duty of the international community as a whole to co-operate'.

produce a lasting result. And putting aside the crucial problem of sovereignty in its different versions, it may be clear that the international aspiration *de iure* of Jerusalem calls for a solution that:[54]

- is multilateral;
- is under the auspices and supervision of the United Nations or of its Mandates;
- may be formalized in a multilateral agreement or treaty, as primary international law, with the possibility of a supplementary application of international law concerning the protection of cultural patrimony or historical sites and monuments, except in those issues modified or regulated by that treaty;
- is subscribed to by the Parties (with international personality) involved (including the Israelis and the Palestinians);
- protects freedom of religion and conscience, including the right to access in a context that safeguards human rights in general (according to international legal standards);
- guarantees equality under the law to all residents, both individuals and communities;
- guarantees the legal regime of the *Status Quo* where it applies;
- provides for a specific organization for the purpose of implementing and following up the implementation of the treaty, with appropriate representation of the parties to the treaty;
- provides for a Religious Leadership Advisory Board and an Environmental and Cultural Advisory Board; and
- defers the matter of territorial sovereignty to resolution in accordance with international law on appropriate terms.

54 I follow here the suggestions made by David Maria A. Jaeger, through his proposal 'The Multilateral Treaty on the City of Jerusalem and Its Environs', op. cit.

Chapter 11
The Haram Al-Sharif in Jerusalem: An Israeli Law Perspective

Moussa Abou Ramadan

Introduction

The idea of the existence of Islamic holy places in Jerusalem is connected to the approach of Islam to the heavenly monotheistic religions: Judaism and Christianity. Most Islamic scholars consider that the prophets of the heavenly religions were Muslims, and in this way they see them as part of the Islamic faith.[1] Because of this view, places that are holy for Jews and Christians are deemed as such also for Islam. The Koran considers the *Bilad al-Sham* (Syria and Palestine) as holy land. This is clearly shown by the way the Koran deals with the religious narrative of the other religions. Concerning the entering of Bani Israel (People of Israel) into the Land of Canaan, it says: 'O my people! Enter the holy land (Palestine) which Allah has assigned to you, and turn not back (in flight) for then you will be returned as losers'.[2] These concepts are also applied to the holy places in Jerusalem as most of the holy places for Muslims in Jerusalem are connected with the religious narratives of the other religions according to the Islamic narrative. These places are given new Islamic features that distinguish them from those given to them by other religions.

1 This belief originated from the Koran itself, where we find several verses that imply that Moslems have existed since the time of Abraham. Verse N. 78 of al-Hajj (Pilgrimage), says: 'He has chosen you (to convey His Message of Islamic Monotheism to mankind by inviting them to His religion, Islam), and has not laid upon you in religion any hardship, it is the religion of your father Ibrahim (Abraham) (Islamic Monotheism). It is He (Allah) Who has named you Muslims both before and in this (the Koran), that the Messenger (Muhammad) may be a witness over you and you be witnesses over mankind!'. Verse 3.67 of Surat Al Imran emphasizes that Abraham was a Moslem. Abraham was not a Jew nor yet a Christian; but he was true in Faith, and bowed his will to Allah (Who is Islam). Similarly, the people of Jesus and the Hawareen who followed are also considered Moslems. 'And when I (Allah) put in the hearts of *Al-Hawarieen* (the disciples) [of 'Iesa (Jesus)] to believe in Me and My Messenger, they said: "We believe. And bear witness that we are Muslims"' (*Table Spread with Food*, 111).

2 *Koran, Table Spread with Food*, verse 21. For English translation of the Koran see <www.dar-us-salam.com/TheNobleQuran> accessed 30 April 2013.

It is possible to divide holy places for Muslims in Jerusalem into two categories. The first consists of the places located in the square that has come to be known as al-Haram al-Qudsi al-Sharif (the Noble Sanctuary). The second consists of the holy places located in other areas in Jerusalem, and which are connected to prophets or prominent persons from the early period of Islamic history, or to sites linked to events to take place in the afterlife. In this chapter we will concentrate on the legal status of the Haram al-Sharif in Israeli law, but before that I will provide some very brief elements on the significance of Haram al-Sharif from an Islamic perspective.

The Establishment of the al-Aqsa Mosque

Although al-Aqsa was built during the period of the Umayyad Caliph al-Walid bin Abdul-Malik bin Marwan,[3] we find some interpreters and jurists who lived in the Umayyad period who think that the mosque was built during the era of Bani Israel in order to lend legitimacy to it in light of the Koran verses that talk about Bani Israel. This is affirmed by the interpreters who lived in the Umayyad period on the assumption that the al-Aqsa Mosque is a holy place because it was built by the prophets. For example, the interpreter and jurist Mujahid bin Jaber (d. 720)[4] argued that the al-Aqsa Mosque was built by the Prophet Solomon as a main centre for the worship and purification of people from sins.[5] It should be noted that in later periods some Muslim historians raised doubts regarding these versions that maintain that King Solomon is the one who built the al-Aqsa Mosque. Al-Maliki Jurist Ibn Khaldoun maintained that the 'al-Aqsa Mosque was built in the days of Sabians as a site for the Temple of the al-Zahra, and they were offering oil to it, and pour oil on the rock there'.[6]

The Story of Isra' and Mi'raj (Night Journey/Ascension and Diversion) and its Connection to the al-Aqsa Mosque in Bayt al-Maqdis

We find also that some jurists in the Umayyad period linked many of the Koran verses with the al-Aqsa Mosque in al-Quds. The Umayyad jurist and interpreter Qatada bin Da'ama al-Sadousi (680–735)[7] translated the Koran verse which says 'Exalted is He who took His Servant by night from al-Masjid al-Haram to

3 Ibn Khaloun, *Muqadduma* (Dar a-Fajr 2004) 432.

4 He was a mawla of Abdulla bin al-Saeb, who was considered one of the dignitaries of Mecca. He is considered as one of the jurists of asceticism who lived in Mecca. He was well known for his jurisprudence in spite of his asceticism and piety.

5 Mohammad bin Ahmad al-Qurtubi, *al-Jami' Li Ahkam al-Koran* (vol 4, Dar al-Sha'ab 1961) 138–9.

6 Ibn Khaldoun, *Muqaddima*, op. cit., 430.

7 An Umayyad jurist and interpreter who lived in al-Basra. See Omar Kahhalah, *Mujam al-Mu'allifn* (vol. 8) 127.

al-Masjid al-Aqsa, whose surroundings We have blessed, to show him of Our signs. Indeed, He is the Hearing, the Seeing',[8] saying that Allah took the Prophet Mohammad from the site of al-Ka'ba to the site of the al-Aqsa Mosque in al-Quds, where the Prophet Mohammad prayed as the imam of the prophets.[9]

However, this great status that was given to the al-Aqsa Mosque during the Umayyad period began to decline somewhat after the Umayyad rule ended and the centre of Islamic authority moved to other places. With the coming of the Abbasid dynasty to authority and the shift of the centres of government from al-Sham to Iraq, we find that there was an attempt by some jurists to decrease the degree of holiness of al-Aqsa. For example, the Iraqi jurist Sufian al-Thawri (716–78)[10] argued that the Prophet Mohammad did not reach the al-Aqsa Mosque because if the Prophet had prayed at al-Aqsa, he would have ordered Muslims to pray in it.[11] However, the jurist and muhaddith Abu Bakr bin Ayyash (d. 809), who lived during the days of Haron al-Rashid, and is considered one of his favourites,[12] stresses that the prophet did not even dismount al-Buraq and his feet did not tread al-Aqsa Mosque, and he cites certain traditions (hadiths) that are ascribed to the Prophet's companion, (Sahabi) Hudhaifa bin al-Yaman, who mocks the versions that say that the Prophet prayed at the al-Aqsa Mosque.[13]

The Dome of the Rock

The Dome is considered one of the buildings that Abdul-Malik ibn Marwan built in al-Quds, and which became one of the holy places for Muslims in al-Sham. Some historians agree that it was built for purely political reasons, as the Shafi'i Damascene historian Ibn Kathir states:

> The reason for it was that Abdullah Ibn al-Zubayr had taken over Mecca, and was giving his speeches during the days of Mina and Arafa and during the people's stay in Mecca. He was attacking Abdul-Malik Ibn Marwan, recalling the vices of Bani Marwan and saying that the Prophet, God's peace be upon him, cursed the

8 Verse n. 1 of *Surat al-Israa*.

9 Mohammad bin Jarir al-Tabari *Jami' al-Bayan fi Ta'wil al-Quran* (vol. 17, Mu'assasat al-Risalah 2000) 331–2.

10 An Iraqi jurist and a Muhaddith, who lived in al-Kufa and died in al-Basra. He wrote several books on jurisprudence and Hadith. Some of these works reached us through other jurisprudence books (Kahhalah, *Mu'jam al-Mu'allifin*, vol. 4, 234).

11 Mohammad bin Jarir al-Tabari, *Jami' al-Bayan*, op. cit.

12 He lived in al-Kufa and was a mawla of Bani Asad. Al-Dhahabi, *Siyar A'laam al-Nubala*, vol. 8, p. 495. He had some contacts with Haroun al-Rashid. Ibn Ya'ish described the Abbsid rule as a religious one, unlike the Umayyad rule. For this saying, al-Rashid gave him a large prize of money. Al-Dhahabi, *Siyar A'laam al-Nubala*, vol. 8, p. 498. Yet, several Islamic versions describe him as a pious and ascetic person who prefers afterlife to this earthly life. Al-Dhahabi, *Siyar A'laam al-Nubala* (vol. 8) 499.

13 Mohammad bin Jarir al-Tabari, *Jami' al-Bayan*, op.cit. (vol. 17) 349.

> regime and what it brought, and that he was chased by the Messenger of God and his damned one, as he used to call himself, and was so eloquent that the majority of the people of al-Sham were inclined to follow him. This became known to Abdul-Malik and he prevented people from making pilgrimage to Mecca, and they protested strongly. So he built them the Dome over the Rock and the al-Aqsa Mosque to divert their thinking and feeling from making a pilgrimage to Mecca, and to win their hearts. People used to stop by the Rock and move around it, as they do around the Ka'ba and they make sacrifices on the Sacrificing Day and shave their heads. This gave the opportunity to Ibn al-Zubayr to defame him as he started to slander him in Mecca by comparing this enterprise to what a Persian King did, by building a palace and moving the circling (Tawaf) from the House of God (i.e. Mecca) to the *qibla* of Bani Israel, and so on.[14]

It is worth noting that in that historical period non-Muslims, like Christians and Jews, were also allowed to visit the Dome of the Rock and pray in it. There is a tradition that says, 'and other people like the serving Jews, who made glass lights and cups and *bazaqat* and other things, were exempted from paying tribute'.[15]

The Legal Status of Haram al-Sharif in Israeli Law

Though Muslims grant Jerusalem special reverence and holiness, it is incorrect and impossible to analyse its status without taking into account that of the other holy places for Muslims under Israeli law. Therefore, I will firstly describe the legal status of Islamic holy places in general. This analysis is also relevant to the Noble Sanctuary/al-Haram al-Sharif. In the second part, I will try to point out the unique status of Jerusalem for both the legal status and the special sensitivity of this holy site.

Each of the monotheistic religions in Israel has a different legal status.[16] The explanation for this can be found in the historical development of each religion and in the character of the State of Israel. Beyond that, each Christian community has a different legal status. However, the Jewish religion has a special status in Israel, which is legally defined as a 'Jewish State'. In this context, it should be noted that in Israel there is no separation between State and religion. Consequently, and in many aspects, Judaism is considered to be the 'Religion of the State'. Practically, the significance of this conclusion is that State authorities are committed not only to preventing any harm to the Jewish religion, but to being active in various areas

14 Ismael Ibn Kathir al-Dimashqi, *al-Bidaya wa al-Nihaya* (vol. 12, Dar Hajar 1998) 41. The Muslims who do the pilgrimage to Mecca have to go around the Ka'aba (a Holy stone in Mecca). Instead of going around the Ka'aba in Mecca, Marwan wanted Muslims to go around the al-Aqsa.

15 Al-Musharraf Ibn al-Murajjaal-Maqdisi, *Fada'il Bayt al Maqdis* (Dar al-Kutub al-'Ilmiyah 2002) 62.

16 This applies also to relatively small communities such as the Druze community.

to develop, enhance and consolidate it by giving it priority and preference over other religions.

The other two religions, Christianity and Islam, do not get similar treatment. For example, Christianity has a special status due to the fact that it is protected through the special status that Israel gave to the different churches. This status gives the different Christian communities special protection that is preserved in the different agreements between Israel and these churches. Evidence of that is the commitment of the State of Israel to preserve the status quo that has existed since the Ottoman era. Israel corroborated this recognition in the international agreement that it signed with the Holy See in 1993.

However, Islamic holy places have been granted lesser protection in comparison with other religions and they have been treated with suspicion by the Israeli authorities. Therefore they were sometimes subjected to hostile treatment by the Israeli authorities for various reasons. First, Islam is the religion of the majority of the Palestinians who lived in this area before the establishment of the State of Israel. This fact put Islam at the centre of the Israeli-Palestinian conflict. Second, the State of Israel saw Islam as a competing component with Judaism, and much more dominant in Palestine than Christianity. Third, and as a result of these two reasons, the State of Israel saw Islam and Muslims as a direct threat to the idea of the homogeneity of the Jewish religion and people in the State of Israel.

Yet, and because of the special importance of this area from a religious point of view, Israel chose to grant freedom of worship to the different religions and give protection to their holy places. However, as will be explained, this protection is modular and varies from one religion to the other. As I will show, this treatment does not only vary from one religion to the other, but also from one place to the other, even when the holy places belong to the same religion. For example, the status of Islamic holy places in Israel is different from the status of al-Haram al-Sharif in al-Quds.

This introductory exposition aims to shed light on the legal status of al-Haram al-Sharif as a holy place according to Israeli law. However, this analysis requires a preliminary explanation of the complexity of the definition of 'holy place' according to the Israeli legal system. On the assumption that al-Haram al-Sharif can be defined as a holy place, it is appropriate to present the status of al-Haram al-Sharif within the general context of the status of the Islamic holy places under Israeli law. Presenting al-Haram al-Sharif in this way is essential to the understanding of the uniqueness of al-Haram al-Sharif, on the one hand, and the complications in the conduct of the authorities of the State of Israel in general and the courts in particular regarding al-Haram al-Sharif, on the other.

Definition of 'Holy Place'

Classification of a certain place as 'holy' is pertinent to granting it the position of 'special status', which implies a series of rules and forms of protection that are provided in various laws related to 'holy places'. Despite the importance of such a definition, surprisingly Israeli law does not have a definition of 'holy place'.

A partial explanation of this aspect lies in the fact that the concept of 'a holy place' is basically a religious one. Being so, such a definition is a complicated issue that includes profound religious, historical and social components. Therefore, the job of the law that aspires to give clear definitions turns out to be not easy at all. This complexity appears in the verdict of the Israeli Supreme Court on the restriction imposed on Israeli courts on disputes related to holy places.

The Supreme Court of Justice defined a 'holy place' as 'a place that the people considered for a specific period of time as a holy place, or alternatively, as aforementioned, because the place is so visible and seen that the court has formulated a legal idea regarding the character of the place as a holy place'.[17]

This definition makes courts dependent upon religious sources in order to conduct a sociological-factual analysis, and verify how a certain place is conceived by the relevant community.

Dependence on religious and social sources is foreseen also in the law on the protection of holy places of 1967. According to this law, which we will deal with later in detail, the Minister of Religious Affairs, who is in charge of enforcing the law, is allowed to draw up regulations that guarantee its enforcement, 'after consultation with representatives of the relevant religions, or according to their proposal, and the agreement of the Ministry of Justice'.[18]

The way in which the authority of the minister is exercised is very useful to our study. The Minister of Justice has actually used his authority, and issued regulations with a detailed list of holy places, but the holy places he listed are related or are supposed to be related to Jews only.[19]

This absolute disregard for other religions in regulations is not accidental; it is related to both the definition of the State of Israel as a Jewish State and to the Israeli-Palestinian conflict, which is known to have a strong religious side too. As is known, and as a result of the 1948 War, most Palestinians, who were mainly Muslims, were evacuated from their homeland. The cities and villages were destroyed and, consequently, Islamic holy places were abandoned. Within this context, a number of Israeli researchers suggest the removal of the aspect of 'holiness' from these places, and propose to consider any place as 'holy' only if it is 'alive' and 'active', which means that religious rituals are being held there at present.[20]

This proposal is intended in a clear way to prefer Jewish holy places to the holy places of other religions, especially Islam.[21]

---

17 I.E 492/79 PD 45, pp. 157, 161.

18 Article 4, *The Protection of Holy Places Law*, 1967.

19 *Regulations for the Protection of Holy Places to the Jews*, 1981.

20 Shmuel Berkovitz, *The Legal Status of the Holy Places in Jerusalem* (Jerusalem Center for Israeli Studies 1997) 18.

21 Ibid., p. 41.

As mentioned previously, the attempts to decrease the degree of holiness of holy places do not apply to al-Haram al-Sharif, as the holiness of the place is an agreed fact, even by Israeli law, as will be explained in detail later.

However, at the same time, there are many places in Israel, including al-Haram al-Sharif, that raise an opposite problem related to places that are considered holy by other religions simultaneously. Such a situation constitutes an additional source of tension and disputes. A strong example to this is the Western Wall, which constitutes a source of considerable conflict between Muslims and Jews.

Given the national conflict between Jews and Arabs, a heated dispute broke out regarding the status of the Western Wall, which the Muslims call 'The Wall of Tears'. This conflict started during the British Mandate on Palestine, and was discussed and clarified by the International Investigation Committee that the British appointed[22] (henceforth, Report of the Western Wall). After thorough investigation, the Committee decided the following:

- the Western Wall is holy for the Muslims because according to the Islamic belief, Prophet Mohammad tied his horse to the Western Wall;[23]
- the Western Wall is holy for the Jews also because it is the last remnant of their Temple,[24] according to their belief;
- Muslims are the exclusive owners of the Western Wall and the adjacent yard that is connected to it;[25]
- the Jews have the right to pray at the Western Wall.

The conclusions of the Western Wall Committee are enshrined in the law (The King's Order in the Council of Palestine [Land of Israel] [Western Wall], 1931). This law also protected the exclusive right of Jews to pray at this place as part of the status quo. After the establishment of the State of Israel this law lost its effectiveness, and after the 1967 War and the occupation of East Jerusalem, the Western Wall turned into a holy place for the Jews only, both practically and legally.[26] It is worth mentioning that in order to legitimize the Western Wall as a praying place for Jews, the State of Israel confiscated the Moghrabi Quarter and destroyed all the houses where Palestinians lived.

From the above information, we can say that Israeli law, the State ministries and authorities deny *de facto* (practically), and *de jure* (theoretically) any holiness

22 *Report of the Commission* appointed by His Majesty's Government in the United Kingdom of Great Britain and Northern Ireland, with the approval of the Council of the League of Nations, to determine the rights and claims of Moslems and Jews in connection with the Western or Wailing Wall at Jerusalem, 1930 (printed and published by his Majesty's Stationery Office 1931) 18.

23 Ibid., 41.

24 Ibid., 42–3.

25 Ibid., 38–41.

26 *Regulations for the Protection of Holy Places to the Jews*, 1981.

of the Wall for Muslims. On the other hand, other parts of al-Haram al-Sharif acquired the recognition of the authorities of the State as 'holy' for Muslims. This recognition is very important and relevant in order to apply to al-Haram al-Sharif the rules and protection that are granted by Israeli law to holy places in general.

Protection of Holy Places of all Religions Under Israeli Law

Before we present Israeli law on the protection of rights connected to holy places, it is important to mention that this analysis is related only to the actual condition of things as they are reflected in Israeli law and in the verdicts of Israeli courts. This remark is needed given the fact that there is a wide gap between the legal condition and the real condition in this matter. It is also true that we can argue that such a gap can be found on every issue. However, in this specific issue, the gap is not only quite wide, and more significant than in other cases, but it is inherent to the political and legal system of the State of Israel, which is related to its definition as a Jewish State and to the Israeli-Palestinian conflict that has been going on for many decades. Therefore, and in order to give a complete picture, the actual situation in the field is briefly described after this chapter.

The Regulations on the Protection of Holy Places, 1967

This is the central law that deals with the general protection of holy places according to Israeli law.

Article (1) of the law states: 'the religious places will be protected against desecration and any other offense and against anything that is likely to form an obstacle to the access of the believers of the other religion to their holy places, or their feelings towards the same places'. The article adds that any violator of these prohibitions can be sentenced to heavy punishment or imprisonment.[27]

It should be noted that the above protection is quite broad and is not limited to the protection against desecration of a holy place as it includes protection against other offences.

Despite the broad protection it grants, this law raises a number of problems even from a logical point of view. First, as was pointed out before, there is no clear legal definition of 'holy place'. The absence of a clear definition is even more serious as we are dealing with a law that entails criminal sanctions. Second, though the law gives the Minister of Religious Affairs authority to pass regulations and rules, the only regulations that the Minister issued to apply this law are related to the Jewish holy places alone, with clear and absolute disregard for other religions. In addition, there are difficulties in applying the law in a context where there are tensions between competitive rights between different religions or different

27 Seven years for anyone who desecrates a holy place or 5 years for anyone who harms freedom of access to holy places – Article 2 of the law.

sects of the same religion. The issue is so complicated, especially with regard to the sensitive conditions at a number of holy places. For example, al-Haram al-Sharif and the Macphela Cave in Hebron/al-Khalil are holy for both Muslims and Jews. Since the customs of each religion are different from the others, this might create tension and conflict between identical rights. Thus, for example, Jews were forbidden to drink wine inside the Macphela Cave as the place also serves as a mosque. Similarly, Muslims are forbidden to hold funerals as the place serves also as a synagogue.[28]

A further tension that emerged as a result of the interpretation of this law is reflected in the issue of Jewish ladies who asked to pray at the Western Wall. Such a request is likely to harm the religious feelings of the Orthodox current in Judaism. The petitions of these women were rejected but the decision of the court, despite its different views, expresses the difficulty involved in reconciling these opposite rights.[29]

Penal Law

Israeli penal law establishes a number of offences whose purpose is to guarantee the protection of holy places, as part of the protection of freedom of worship. Article 170 of the penal law provides for a punishment of three years for anyone who 'destroys, damages, or desecrates a place of worship … that is held holy for a crowd of people, with the purpose to desecrate their religion, or if he knows that they are likely to consider his action as humiliation to their religion'. Article 171 of this law inflicts a punishment of three years imprisonment on anyone who 'deliberately bothers a congregation of people who gathered legally to perform a religious worship …' Article 172 inflicts punishment of three years imprisonment on anyone who enters a place of worship without permission or a burial place and behaves in a way that shows 'a purpose to injure the feelings of a person or desecrate his religion'.

Law of Antiquities

Since a large number of holy places have also a historical and archeological value, they mostly enjoy the protection that is given to antiquities in the Law of Antiquities (1978). Article 29(a) of this law prohibits building, paving, quarrying, burying or performing other activities without written permission by the Director of the Antiquities Service. Beyond that, according to Article 29(c), the law says: 'When an antiquity site is used for religious requirements or devoted to a religious purpose, the Director shall not approve digging or any of the operations enumerated in subsection (a) save with the approval of a Committee of Ministers consisting

28 High Court of Justice Decision 223/67 *Israeli court rulings* Kof Bet (1) 440, 448.

29 High Court of Justice Decision 257/89, 2410/90 *Israeli court rulings* Mem Het (2) 256, 354.

of the Minister as chairman, the Minister of Religious Affairs and the Minister of Justice'. In addition, the Law decides penal sanctions in Article 37 against anyone who breaks the provisions of Article 29.

As detailed below, this law constituted a legal basis for the numerous litigations that are related to works that the waqf (Islamic religious endowment trust) made in the halls below al-Haram al-Sharif.

General Protection of Freedom of Worship in Israeli Law

Freedom of worship was recognized in the Israel Declaration of Independence, where the State of Israel took the commitment to guarantee 'freedom of religion'. It was decided that 'freedom of worship is one of the basic liberties that are recognized according to our legal system and they constitute part of it. Ways of expression of the mentioned liberty are of course, in their essence, in the freedom of religious expression and practicing'.[30]

In spite of the fact that there is no written constitution in Israel, freedom of worship was recognized as a right that has a legal value. Besides, and differently from other basic rights, it was decided that protection of freedom of worship, except for criminal prisoners, will be in the hands of the executive authority, and will be taken out of the realms of possible interference by courts. This exception is based on Provision 2 of the King's Order regarding holy places in 1924, which excludes from the scope of courts, 'every issue or legal case that are connected to the holy places or buildings or religious sites in Palestine (Land of Israel) …' The Supreme Court interpreted this order as excluding the protection of freedom of worship from the authority of courts, except for enforcement of the law in guarding the holy places. This view was supported already in 1968 in the first court verdict that dealt with fulfillment of the rights of Jews to pray at the Temple Mount.[31] It was decided that the right to pray is different from free access to holy places, since the right to pray is not foreseen in the law on holy places. In view of this, courts have no authority to deal with this issue; only the executive authority has the jurisdiction to do so. Courts confirmed this position in a long series of verdicts, in which many petitions submitted by Jews to pray on the Temple Mount were rejected.

In another verdict that was given in the early 1990s, we see how the Supreme Court restricted this sweeping viewpoint by determining that another interpretation is possible when it is related to an individual person who is requesting to pray at al-Haram al-Sharif. In this case, it seems that the court thinks that it is possible to recognize the right of the individual as part of his/her right of free access.[32]

30 High Court of Justice Decision 650/88. *Israeli court rulings*, Mem Bet (3) 377, 381.

31 *Israeli court rulings*, Kof Dalet (2) 141.

32 High Court of Justice Decision 67/93. Kakh Movement, and the League for Jewish Defense, The Minister of Religion and One, *Israeli court rulings*, Mem Zayen (2), 1.

Legal Status and Actual Condition of Islamic Holy Places

In light of the general protection of holy places as mentioned above, it is appropriate to evaluate the status of the holy places for Muslims in a more specific way. This assessment should address two aspects: the legal aspect and reality.

From the legal point of view, the relevant law is the Absentee Property Law of 1950, which is one of the most significant and controversial laws regarding the relationship between the State of Israel and the Palestinian minority living in it, especially regarding Palestinian properties in Israel. It should be pointed out that this law is not applicable to al-Haram al-Sharif. However, opinion is divided among the authorities in Israel whether to apply this law in East Jerusalem too or not.

The Absentee Property Law basically deals with the property of Palestinians who left the area as a result of the 1948 Palestine War and turned into refugees. Besides, the law applies to a quarter of the Palestinians who became citizens of Israel after the war. To their misfortune these people were present at the time of war in areas where, according to Israeli claims, there were forces that fought against the Israeli forces. According to this law, their properties were 'absentee property', and therefore they were confiscated by the State of Israel and moved to the administration of a governmental body that was established accordingly, called the Custodian of Absentee Property. This is a huge amount of property, which is basically individual property that includes lands and houses. Part of this property is made up of public institutes, including religious holy places that belong to Muslims. Regarding religious places, the law provided a special arrangement. It was decided that religious property should be run either by the Custodian of Absentee Property or a Committee of Trustees that was set up according to the law. In addition, special rules provided that this property must be run to the benefit of the Muslim population. It should be pointed out that in the case of religious property the law does not decide that special protection should be given to it. However, the law establishes the prohibition of selling mosques.[33]

Actually, the management of the property is characterized by neglect, and the selling of this property[34] is a common phenomenon. Lands that served as Muslim cemeteries were sold as pieces of real estate.[35] Thus, for example, the Muslim cemetery of al-Jamusin was sold. The cemetery was located north of the promenade in Tel Aviv. Even cemeteries in use were sold without any interference by the Israeli authorities and their selling was approved by the Supreme Court in Israel.

33 Article 29(c) (Gemel) of the Law of Absentee's Assets.

34 *Reports of the State Controller: Annual Report*, No. 24 (1974), P. 1980\-190, *Annual Report*, No. 34 (1984), 73–80, *Annual Report*, No. 38 (1988), 83–90, *Annual Report*, No. 45 (1994).

35 Ayen Alef עא3997/91, *The Committee of the Islamic Waqf*, N Yosi An Investment Company Ltd. PD 49, 788 (5).

Mosques, though there is a legal prohibition to their selling, were exposed to similar bleak conditions. Many mosques were so neglected that they had to be demolished. Some mosques were turned into places for purposes that have nothing to do with religious rites or services. An illustrative example is the story of the big mosque in Ber Sheva. The mosque served as a museum for the history of the Negev for years. When the museum was closed and the building was abandoned, Muslim people in the Negev asked to reuse the building as an active mosque. Their application was refused and they had to appeal to the Supreme Court which ruled that the building could be turned into a Muslim museum.

Beyond legal activity, the actual situation indicates constant attempts to harm the holy places of the Palestinian residents in Israel in general and the Muslims in particular. A report that was written by the Arab Association for Human Rights shows a worrying practice of desecration of Islamic and Christian holy places in Israel: the report details many incidents in which Israeli Arab citizens were forbidden to enter their neglected holy places, thus undermining the attempts of the Arabs to restore sites of worship alongside a systematic desecration of cemeteries, especially those of Muslims.[36]

The Legal Status of al-Haram al-Sharif

The Occupation and Annexation of Jerusalem and the Application of the Israeli Law on East Jerusalem

Immediately after the Six Day War in 1967, Israel made legal changes that were intended to apply Israeli law to East Jerusalem, including al-Haram al-Sharif. The order of the arrangements of government and law of 1967, and the decree of arrangements of government and law (No. 1) were amended in a way that could allow the application of Israeli law to East Jerusalem. The order of the municipality (amendment No. 6, 1967) was also amended in a way that allowed the annexation of large areas. The area of Jerusalem increased from 38,100 dunams to 108,500 dunams. Regarding al-Haram al-Sharif, on 11 June 1967 the Military Government transferred responsibility for the Muslim community to the hands of the Ministry of Religious Affairs. The Ministry took immediate measures that were intended to concretize the annexation of East Jerusalem to Israel. Thus, for example, the representatives of the Ministry of Religious Affairs requested to take control over the property of the Islamic waqf and started practicing direct inspection, control and censorship on the Friday sermon at the al-Aqsa Mosque.[37] After severe protests by Muslim religious leaders, a compromise was finally reached, which

36 www.arabhra.org/Hra/Pages/PopupTemplatePage.aspx?PopupTemplate=142> accessed 30 April 2013.

37 Shmuel Berkovitz, *The Wars of the Holy Places* (Jerusalem Institute for Israeli Studies 2000) 261.

has constituted a kind of delicate status quo. As a result, responsibility for keeping order and security is in the hands of the Israeli security forces, mainly the Israeli police, while responsibility for internal and religious arrangement remains in the hands of the waqf people, who had been in charge of al-Haram al-Sharif before the Israeli occupation of Jerusalem.[38]

The occupation of Jerusalem has not been recognized by the international community, and the United Nations considered the unilateral steps taken by Israel as illegal, void and invalid.[39]

In spite of that, in 1980 the State of Israel passed a basic law which declares that united Jerusalem is the capital of Israel. This law, too, received severe criticism from the international community, and it was decided that it is against international law and constitutes an obstacle in the attempts to achieve peace in the Middle East.[40]

Thus, East Jerusalem, including al-Haram al-Sharif, is an occupied area from the point of view of international law with all its implications, and according to the Geneva Convention, the laws of an occupied area apply to Jerusalem and al-Haram al-Sharif.

This international condition implies that it is not easy to deal with the legal status of al-Haram al-Sharif according to Israeli law. Here are some examples that illustrate the complications of this issue.

First, the Palestinians have never recognized or accepted the occupation of East Jerusalem and the control by the Israeli authorities of al-Haram al-Sharif. This strong resistance explains the fact why Palestinians in general and the waqf people who are running al-Haram al-Sharif, in particular, traditionally refuse to approach the Israeli courts in order to realize and implement their religious and national rights. It is understood that this avoidance and abstention stems from the absence of basic trust of Palestinians in the Israeli legal system.

In addition to this, and although this is out of context, it should be noted that the Israeli control of al-Haram al-Sharif limits to a large extent the rights of the Muslims to pray at the place. For example, for years Israel has limited the rights of the Palestinians who are not citizens of Jerusalem (or Israeli citizens) to pray at the place. This is a severe limitation that impacts and offends millions of Palestinians who live in the West Bank and Gaza Strip.

Second, even Israel does not deal with East Jerusalem and al-Haram al-Sharif as an Israeli area. Israel's attitude to this place is ambivalent. On the one hand, Israel has taken unilateral legal and aggressive measures in order to assert and concretize its military control and domination on the area. For example, Israel took over the Western Wall by destroying an entire quarter near the Wall. On the other hand, Israel tries to be very careful and avoids absolute control over the mosque

38 Yitzhac Reiter, *The Waqf in Jerusalem* (Jerusalem Institute for Israeli Studies 1992).

39 A/Res/2254 (14.7.67); A/Res/2253(4/7/67), S/Res/298; S/Res/271; S/Res/252.

40 A/S/Res/478.

site and the Dome of the Rock, but allows a certain autonomous administration by the Islamic waqf people, who practically run the site of al-Haram al-Sharif.

As Israeli authorities are in charge of security in the whole area, and because their desire is to keep this responsibility, they prevent activities by different Jewish circles who ask to pray in the site of al-Haram al-Sharif, and, by doing so, threaten to spark off a religious war in the region.

All this above indicates that a considerable part of the legal issues that arise regarding al-Haram al-Sharif revolve around this complexity.

Two basic major issues have reached the courts in recent years, and they reflect the complexity of the situation that is described above. The first is the issue of Jews who want to pray at al-Haram al-Sharif. The second is related to the various attempts to limit the autonomy of the authorities of the waqf at al-Haram al-Sharif. However, before I deal with these two issues, it is appropriate to shed light on the status quo at al-Haram al-Sharif, after the occupation of East Jerusalem.

The Status Quo in the Area of al-Haram al-Sharif After 1967

Until the 19th century, an Ottoman status quo had been established and fixed in Jerusalem regarding holy places, mainly the Christian ones. This arrangement received international recognition in a number of agreements, and was recognized by the different powers that controlled the region like Britain and Jordan. Before that arrangement, the authorities used to settle the conflicts between the different Christian communities. After the occupation of East Jerusalem, Israel committed itself, along with the Christian communities, to an agreement that the previous arrangement would continue under Israeli law. Thus, and since then, Israeli authorities have dealt with the disputes between the Christian communities regarding holy places. Israel recognized the status quo again in an agreement that was signed with the Vatican in 1993.

However, regarding Muslims, Israel has not recognized the arrangement of the status quo of the British Mandate (as it was decided by the International Investigation Committee that was appointed by the British government to decide the rights of the Jews and the Muslims at the Western Wall). In addition, Israel actually cancelled the arrangement on the Western Wall, which is part of al-Haram al-Sharif. Furthermore, Israeli authorities cancelled prohibiting the entry of Jews to al-Haram al-Sharif and the Macphela Cave and also cancelled the restrictions on the rights of Jews to pray at the Western Wall. Israel also confiscated the area of the Moghrabi Quarter from the Muslim waqf and evacuated the inhabitants from it.

Except for what has been said above, the administration of the internal and religious affairs at al-Haram al-Sharif remained basically in the hands of the waqf.

The Praying of Jews at al-Haram al-Sharif

Since 1967, the State of Israel has forbidden Jews to pray at the Temple Mount for fear of increasing tensions at this sensitive place. Actually, on 20 August 1967 the

Israeli government decided that when Jewish prayers reach the entrance of the Temple Mount, they would be turned to the Western Wall. Both the form of their decision and the discussions that were made before it indicate that it was a temporary decision that was intended to prevent a flare-up which is quite different to an attitude of principle.

This policy was discussed at the Supreme Court after 1967, and since then it has been discussed occasionally at the court. The first appeal about this issue was submitted in 1968 by a group of Jews who asked to pray at al-Haram al-Sharif.[41] The legal question that was raised in this and other petitions was: does the court have authority to discuss such a case in view of Article 2 of the 1924 King's Orders regarding holy places? That article states that 'every issue of trial that are related to the holy places or the building or religious sites in Palestine (Land of Israel)' will be taken out of the authority of the court. In order to be able to discuss this issue, the court should have discussed the status of Provision 2 of the King's Order with regard to the Israeli law.

After disagreement and division of opinions on this question, the court decided that the mandatory law would apply as long as it did not interfere with the provisions of the Israeli law concerning the guarding of holy places. Regarding the right to pray, it was decided that this right is different from the right of access to holy places, which is foreseen in the law on holy places, and therefore this law does not apply to it. Thus, there is no authority for the court to deal with the freedom of Jews to pray at al-Haram al-Sharif.

The court confirmed this view in many subsequent decisions. It should be noted that in all these decisions, the court pointed out the fundamental right of the Jews on al-Haram al-Sharif, and also their right to pray at the place, provided that public order is ensured.

In all these decisions, we find a similar legal argument. Here is a characteristic quotation from one of the verdicts that dealt with this issue:

> The high importance and status of the basic-rights in whose name the appellant asks to go up to the Temple Mount – freedom of expression and worshipping, and also freedom of movement and access to holy places are known and accepted by everyone. The centrality of these rights in our legal system is known to have much importance in formulating the character of our democratic regime. In accordance with this, the main stepping point of the court has been that the right to implement religious rites and even to go up to the Temple Mount is kept for every Jew. Together with that, this right, like other basic rights, is not absolute, and it should retreat in favor of other interests, including the maintenance of public order and the safety of the public and its security. According to the verdict of the court, the right of freedom of expression and worshipping, and right of having access to holy places will retreat if danger is very likely to harm the public order.[42]

41 See also: High Court of Justice 267/9גP.D 43, P.728, P.737 (3) 728, 737.

42 Verdict of the judge (as his title was then) Barak at the Supreme Court 83/292: Trustees of Temple Mount N. Commander of the Police – Jerusalem Region, 449, High

From time to time, Jewish associations submit appeals to the court in which they ask the court to order the waqf to stop works at the Temple Mount site. An example of such petitions is the one called the Case of Orot Shlomo, which refers to the underground halls that exist under al-Haram al-Sharif and that were restored as a mosque. In 1996 a Jewish rightist association called the Association of Temple Mount Trustees appealed to the High Court of Justice asking it to stop the works that the Islamic waqf was carrying out there to prevent them from turning the place into a mosque.[43] The claim of the association is interesting. Though the association was a rightist one, it did not try to give national arguments. The appellants argued that the site is an archeological site of antiquities, and therefore the law of antiquities applies to it. This law forbids carrying out building work without the permission or license of the Director of the Authority of Antiquities, and since the place is a religious one, it requires certification from the Committee of Ministers. The High Court rejected the appeal and decided that the works that have been done do not cause any damage to the antiquities, and the works do not need any license as they are internal changes. In addition, the decision of the High Court emphasized the need for strict enforcement of the law due to the importance and sensitivity of the place.

Court of Justice 4776/06, Gershon Solomon, N. Commander of Jerusalem District. Limitation of the Waqf Authorities in al-Haram al-Sharif.

43 High Court of Justice, *Temple Mount and Eretz Yisrael Faithful Movement*, N. Mayor of Jerusalem, N. (4) 241.

Chapter 12

Envisaging a Legal Framework for Ensuring Sustainable Preservation of Holy Places with Regard to the Case of Kosovo and Metohia[1]

Dušan Rakitić

Introduction

Sacral architecture in Kosovo and Metohia, which forms by far the most substantial part of the total Serbian cultural and spiritual heritage, has found itself in a precarious situation since the armed conflict in the province of 1999. The predicament is conceptually complex because a great number of monuments and holy places have already been intentionally destroyed, while the present political and legal circumstances remain conducive to the continuation of such destruction of the remaining ones. In a number of significant cases, the architectural heritage forms a home for live monastic communities and active pilgrimage. The destruction, on the other hand, may only be fully understood by assigning it to the intention of denying the very spiritual, cultural and ethical identity that these monuments provide for the Serbian Orthodox population. The latest events, which transpired in the first months of 2013, particularly the systematic destruction of Serbian cemeteries and repeated attacks on Serbian religious monuments by ethnic Albanians, clearly show that meticulous protection of sacred places is essential.[2]

Armed conflict in the spring of 1999 over Kosovo and Metohia, conducted by NATO and Albanian guerrillas on one side and the Federal Republic of Yugoslavia on the other, was qualified by NATO as 'humanitarian intervention', and by the

1 This chapter has evolved from the booklet *The Predicament of Serbian Orthodox Holy Places in Kosovo and Metohia – Elements for a Historical, Legal and Conservational Understanding*, which I co-authored with Sima Avramović, Mirjana Menković, Vojislav Vasić, Aleksandra Fulgosi and Branko Jokić (Pravni fakultet Univerziteta u Beogradu and Nevladina organizacija Mnemosyne 2010). Whereas the latter also contained a number of case-studies of particular holy places in Kosovo and Metohia, and provided a pronounced conservational perspective on the issue of holy places in Kosovo and Metohia, the present chapter elaborates the historical and legal aspects of the subject matter, including an update of the legal analysis demanded by the pronounced dynamics of developments at the levels of international law and relations in respect of Kosovo and Metohia.

2 'Serb cemeteries, memorials desecrated in Kosovo' (B92, 21 January 2013) <www.b92.net/eng/news/crimes-article.php?mm=1&dd=21&yyyy=2013> accessed 15 March 2013.

FR of Yugoslavia as 'aggression'. It resulted, among other consequences, in the destruction of a number of medieval sacred structures – holy places. The war led to the establishment of a temporary UN administration for the province and in commencement of the process aimed at determining the status, and fulfilment, of certain standards in this territory (UNSC Resolution 1244/99). Since in 1999 the territory formed part of Serbia as one of the two constituents of the FR of Yugoslavia, upon dissolution of the federal state in 2003, independent and internationally recognized Serbia continued to claim the territory. Both on the grounds of the UNSC Resolution 1244 (1999) and in accordance with its Constitution, Serbia considers Kosovo and Metohia part of its sovereign territory, enjoying the status of an autonomous province.

Serbia has not agreed with the unilateral declaration of independence of Kosovo, proclaimed in 2008, and this self-proclaimed independence is therefore not recognised by Serbia or by approximately half of the Member States of the United Nations, as well as five Member States of the European Union. On most of the territory of Kosovo and Metohia, Serbia *de facto* has not been able to exert governmental powers since the end of the hostilities in 1999, including protection and efficient conservation of sacred/holy places.

Most historians are unanimous in designating the area of Kosovo and Metohia as 'the cradle' of Serbian medieval statehood and spirituality. This is where the Serbian medieval state grew to its greatest strength, the seat of the first Serbian Patriarchate was located and numerous Serbian rulers and church leaders lived and were buried.

One of the richest and most concentrated groups of sacred architecture and holy places inherited by the European, contemporary Christian and global cultures from the Christian East is situated on the territory of Kosovo and Metohia. According to the registers of protected cultural assets of 1986 and 1994, there were over 400 protected cultural properties in Kosovo and Metohia, whereby a significant number had been designated as protected prior to 1986. The only monuments in Kosovo and Metohia recognized by UNESCO as part of the world cultural heritage are the Serbian Orthodox sacred/holy places. The Visoki Dečani Monastery was included in the World Cultural Heritage List by UNESCO in 2004, while three other prominent sacred monuments were added in 2006: the Pećka Patrijaršija Monastery (Patriarchate of Peć), Gračanica Monastery and the Church of the Mother of God Ljeviška in Prizren. Their inclusion in the List has confirmed the universal civilizational value of these sacred/holy places. Sadly, they were also included in the List of World Heritage in Danger, a fact clearly showing their precarious status (UNESCO 2006) This heritage belongs to humanity as a whole and needs to be protected and saved regardless of the culture and confession it belongs to, according to the principle of European 'common heritage'.

Kosovo represents the Holy Land to Serbs as well as to neighbouring Christian nations. The Serbian Orthodox Church regards Kosovo and Metohia as crucial for the national, spiritual, cultural and Christian identity of the Serbs (Holy Assembly of Bishops of the Serbian Orthodox Church – SOC, 2003). The map published by the Serbian Orthodox Diocese of Raška and Prizren (Figure 12.1) shows only a few hundred of the most important monasteries and churches built both before and after the fall of Serbian state under the Ottoman rule in the 15th century (Diocese of Raška and Prizren). The Holy Assembly of Bishops of the Serbian Orthodox Church claims 1,300 Serbian Orthodox churches and monasteries in Kosovo and Metohia, dating from the Middle Ages to the present day (Holy Assembly of Bishops of the SOC 2003).

Numerous threats and violent actions against Serbian Orthodox Christian places in Kosovo have persisted since 1999.[3] From 15 June 1999 to 10 May 2003, at least 40 Serbian Orthodox churches and monasteries were completely destroyed, while more than 70 were demolished, plundered and burned (Holy Assembly of Bishops of the SOC 2003). Then, in the March 2004 Pogrom of Serbs, international forces, although armed to the teeth, turned out to be powerless against the well-orchestrated tide of nationalist rage against Serbs. In just two days several dozen monasteries, churches and other Orthodox sacred/holy places were destroyed and devastated.[4] During the March 2004 Pogrom, apart from human casualties, seven Serbian villages were destroyed or depopulated. Thirty-five Serbian Orthodox churches and monasteries, some dating back to the 13th century, were razed to the ground or damaged beyond repair. The (UNMIK) admitted the March Pogrom shocked the mission 'to its foundations'. The rapid spread of the violence 'overwhelmed' UNMIK. It was so widespread and so clearly targeted against Serbian churches and villages that it had to have been coordinated, UNMIK concluded.

The effects of the March Pogrom will thus have a prolonged impact, which had been its very goal: after the unilateral declaration of independence of Kosovo in 2008, Serbian sacred/holy places were suddenly put in a new administrative context that, after the experience of 2004, is viewed by believers and by the Serbian Orthodox Church as hostile and insecure. Occasional attacks on religious objects and pilgrims have continued to take place since.

One of the distinctive characteristics of Orthodox Christian holy places in Kosovo and Metohia is the fact that many people feel a strong connection to them and understand them as their own living history. The Christian Orthodox holy places of Kosovo and Metohia are domestic holy places, watched from the doorsteps of family homes, visited regularly, at holidays and for liturgies, by Orthodox Christians from

---

3 John A. Bold, *Study on the state of the cultural heritage in Kosovo* (Council of Europe/European Commission Project Report 2001); Council of Europe, *Protection of the cultural heritage in Kosovo, Report of a study visit on 9–10 October 2003*, by Eddie O'Hara, General Rapporteur for the Cultural Heritage, Council of Europe Parliamentary Assembly, Committee on Culture, Science and Education, Sub-Committee on the Cultural Heritage (AS/Cult/AA 2003) 14.

4 Technical Co-operation and Consultancy Programme, *Preliminary Technical Assessment Report on the Religious Buildings/Ensembles and Cultural Sites damaged in March 2004 in Kosovo* (AT04 111 rev, 30 April 2004); Id., *Technical Assessment Report on the Religious Buildings/Ensembles and Cultural Sites damaged in March 2004 in Kosovo* (AT04 171 rev, 24 May 2004); Id., *Technical Assessment Report on the Religious Buildings/Ensembles and Cultural Sites damaged in March 2004 in Kosovo* (bis) (AT04 245, 9 July 2004).

various countries, with members of other confessions joining the ranks of Kosovo and Metohia monks. At the same time these are the places of material and spiritual experience of the national history of Serbs and living history since the Middle Ages.

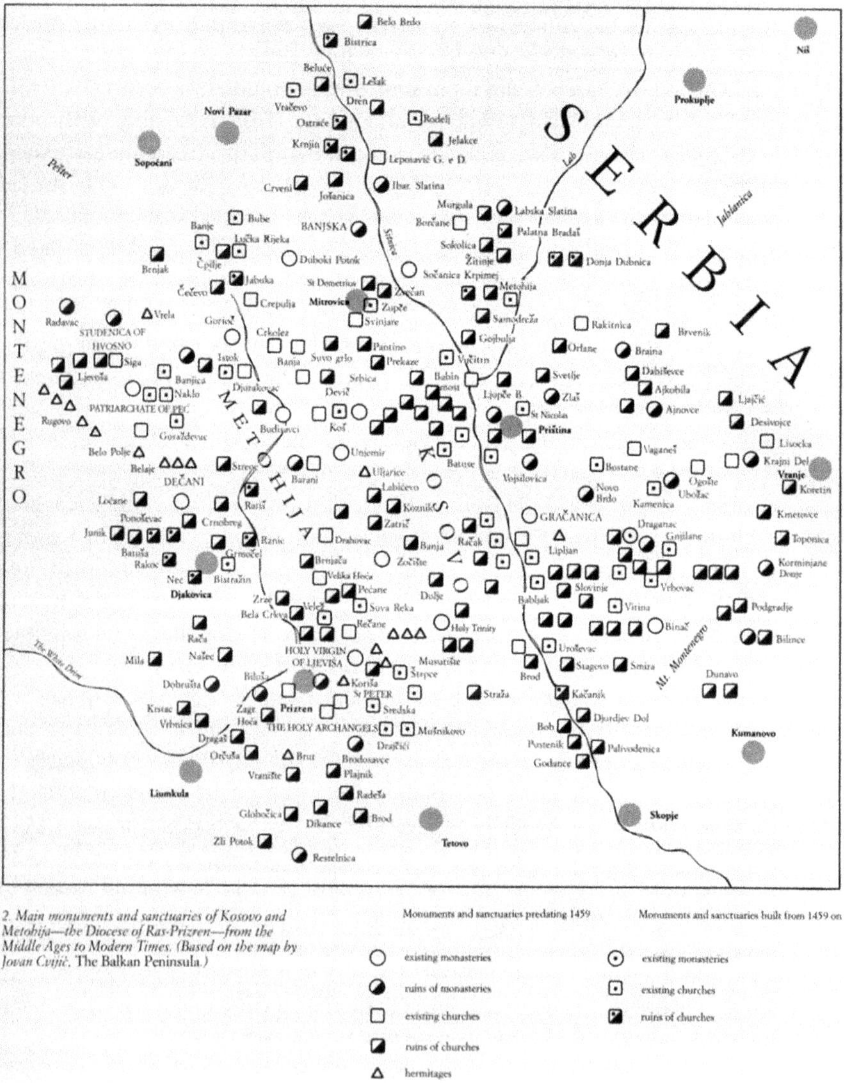

Figure 12.1 The most important monasteries and churches of the Serbian Orthodox Church in Kosovo and Metohia

Source: Serbian Orthodox Diocese of Raska and Prizren, KIM Info Service.

Approach

For the purpose of analysing the status of holy places in Kosovo and Metohia, we have completely abided by this provisional definition:

> A holy place is a public area or an object traditionally and regularly visited by at least several generations of devotees due to its undisputed symbolical, religious, memorial or other spiritual significance, enabling multiple, direct or communicated experience of worship, religious identity, ethnical origin, national history and/or hope for salvation.

Holy (sacred) places have an important role in the history of a religion as its permanent landmarks, contributing to its unique identity by their spiritual, symbolic and social significance. It sounds plausible that the concept of holy or sacred places should also allow for the possibility of broadening its territorial scope within 'sacred zones' or 'sacred areas'. The case of Mount Athos is an example of such a situation, as the whole area of the peninsula is considered to be sacred, not only particular monasteries and other sanctuaries. A similar situation seems to affect the case of Jerusalem, which is also due to the high concentration of sacred sites. A holy place should therefore be viewed, perceived and defined in such a context.

In certain cases, holy places may also include other categories of places of worship, such as cemeteries and shrines. The sacred character of such sites may be grounded in oral tradition, teaching, history, myth, folklore or legend, often being associated with magic and miracles.

Conceptualization of specific problems of conservation of Serbian Orthodox holy places in Kosovo and Metohia has been undertaken in line with the wording and the spirit of applicable international documents, especially the Declaration on Cultural Diversity, the European Convention on Human Rights and the Ministers Committee Declaration on Human Rights, the European Cultural Convention, the World Heritage Convention and the Guidelines for its implementation and also partially the standards of IUCN for Sacred Natural Sites.[5]

Historical Context

Serbs, as one of the Slav tribes, inhabited central parts of the Balkan Peninsula, including the territory of Kosovo and Metohia, approximately starting from the end of the 6th and beginning of the 7th centuries AD, and underwent Christianization in the second half of the 9th century, first due to the influence from the towns

5 Rob Wild and Christopher McLeod (eds), *Sacred Natural Sites: Guidelines for Protected Area Managers* (IUCN 2008).

on the Adriatic coast and then through the work of the Byzantine missionaries[6] Cyril and Methodius.[7] The settlement of Serbs did not entail conflicts with the Indigenous population of nomad shepherds, but instead with the Romanic population of towns and with Byzantium. Having spent several centuries between intermittent loyalty to the Byzantine Empire and then conflicts with it, the Serbian state began taking over Kosovo and Metohia from thc Byzantinc Empire – led by Prince Časlav in the 10th century AD and under Megajupanus Vukan at the end of the 11th century AD, approaching it from the north-west.[8] At the end of the 12th century, after the death of Byzantine Emperor Manuel I Komnenos, Serbian leader Megajupanus Stefan Nemanja, the founder of the Nemanjic dynasty that ruled Serbia in the two centuries that followed, succeeded in establishing his rule in Kosovo and Metohia.[9] Since then the territory formed part of the Serbian medieval state until its fall more than two and half centuries later, in the mid-15th century.[10] However, the state enjoyed greatest vigour and progress under the Nemanjic dynasty, which ruled it until the second half of the 14th century. It was during that time that Kosovo and Metohia were central to the country's politics, commerce and spirituality, which was due to fertile land, great density of population and good communications.[11]

The Kosovo and Metohia towns of Prizren and Priština both served as state capitals during the Nemanjić period and numerous palaces of Serbian kings and emperors were located in the territory. Although the first seat of the Serbian autocephalous archdiocese was in the Žiča Monastery, outside the province, the second archbishop, Arsenius, initiated construction of the second seat, near Peć in Metohia.[12] Peć became the seat of the Serbian Church upon its promotion to the dignity of Patriarchate in 1346. Numerous charters, dating from the 12th century on, show a wide presence of Serbs, mostly as land farmers, throughout the province, as well as a much smaller presence of Vlachs and Albanians in

---

6 Dimitrije Bogdanović, *Knjiga o Kosovu* [The Book on Kosovo] (Srpska književna zadruga 2006) 24–61, 337–52.

7 D Srejović, M Mirković, J Kovačević, et al., *Istorija srpskog naroda, prva knjiga, Od najstarijih vremena do Maričke bitke (1371)* [History of the Serbian Nation, vol. 1, From Earliest Times until the Battle of Marica (1371)] (Srpska književna zadruga 2000) 144–47, 197–99, 212–3, 257–9.

8 Dimitrije Bogdanović, *Knjiga o Kosovu*, op. cit.

9 Ibid.

10 D Bogdanović, M Mihaljčić, M Ćirković, et al., *Istorija srpskog naroda, druga knjiga, Doba borbi za očuvanje i obnovu države (1371–1537) [History of the Serbian Nation, Vol. 2, Period of struggle for preservation and renewal of the state (1371–1537)]* (Srpska književna zadruga 2000) 278–312.

11 Sima Ćirković, 'Srednjovekovna prošlost današnjeg Kosova' ['Medieval past of present-day Kosovo'], in Ivan Jevtić (ed.), *Zadužbine Kosova [Endowments of Kosovo]* (Eparhija Raško-Prizrenska, Bogoslovski fakultet u Beogradu 1987) 553–7.

12 Sima Ćirković, 'Srednjovekovna prošlost današnjeg Kosova', op. cit.

bordering mountains, as shepherds.[13] The Charter granted in 1330 to the Dečani Monastery, which pertained to the largest Church estate in medieval Serbia after that of the Hilandar Monastery, encompassing significant areas of Metohia and present-day northern Albania, shows only 1.8 per cent Albanian-owned properties in its catalogue of assets and subjects of the monastery.[14] Mining had developed since the 12th century in Kosovo and Metohia towns, supplementing the already rich commercial activity that was in the hands of merchants from towns on the Adriatic coast. The most prominent mining town and one of the strongest fortresses throughout the duration of the Serbian medieval state was Novo Brdo.[15] Priština, Prizren, Peć and Novo Brdo remained the largest Serbian towns during most of the time the Serbian medieval state existed.[16]

In 1389 Kosovo was the scene of the second major battle between medieval Serbia and the Ottoman Turks, after the rulers of the Serbian southern provinces were defeated in 1371 in the battle on the river Marica. Although both rulers, Prince Lazar and Sultan Murad I, died in the battle, and both sides incurred substantial losses, the inability to recuperate on the part of Serbia amounted to a defeat. However, in the centuries that followed, in which Serbs were scattered over vast territories of the Balkan Peninsula, from Trieste to Timisoara and from Buda to the Vardar River, living without a nation-state, within the Austrian and Ottoman Empires, the memory of the Battle of Kosovo evolved into a primary designation of the national identity and ethos. The traditional ethnic myth assigned the defeat to Prince Lazar's preference for the Kingdom in Heaven over the Kindgom on Earth, thus inextricably joining this instance of political history with religious and ethical identity.

The Patriarchate of the Serbian Orthodox Church was restored by way of official recognition from the Ottoman sultan in 1557, and its seat was restored to Peć in Metohia. The Patriarchate kept its seat in Peć for most of the Ottoman rule, until 1766 when it was abolished pursuant to a sultan's decree, which also granted jurisdiction over the Serbian Orthodox population to the Ecumenical Patriarchate.

Since the final fall of the remnants of the Serbian medieval state under the Ottoman rule in the mid-15th century, until approximately the end of the 16th and beginning of the 17th centuries, the non-Serbian population remained present in the territory of Kosovo and Metohia in very low numbers, and it was mostly made up of Ottoman Turks in towns.[17] The region was regularly referred to as 'Serbia'

13 Milisav Lutovac, 'Geografski i političko-geografski značaj pokrajine Kosova u Srbiji' ['Geographical and political-geographical importance of province Kosovo for Serbia'] in Ivan Jevtić (ed.), *Zadužbine Kosova*, op. cit. 582–7.

14 Dusan Bataković, *The Kosovo Chronicles* (Plato 1992); Dimitrije Bogdanović, *Knjiga o Kosovu*, op. cit.

15 Sima Ćirković 'Srednjovekovna prošlost današnjeg Kosova', op. cit.

16 Milisav Lutovac, 'Geografski i političko-geografski značaj pokrajine Kosova u Srbiji', op. cit.

17 Dusan Bataković, *The Kosovo Chronicles*, op. cit.

by foreign travel writers throughout the 16th and 17th centuries, while the rivers Beli Drim and Crni Drim were considered to mark the border between Serbia and Albania. From the end of the 16th century, however, the ethnical structure in the western part, Metohia, began to change due to the gradual arrival of Albanian settlers. Albanian settling took place amid constant incursions of Albanian bandit groups from northern Albania.[18]

The end of the 16th century also marks the beginning of a widespread struggle and constant uprisings of the Serbian population against Ottoman rule.[19] The Serbian population rebelled in coordination with Austrian military operations, which resulted in migrations to Austria, the two most notable examples of which were the two Great Migrations – in 1690 and 1738 – in which they fled together with the retreating Austrian armies, fearing retaliation from the Ottomans. The migrations resulted in the weakening of homogeneous Serbian settlements in Kosovo and Metohia, and thus in their loss of capacity to withstand pressure from looters and new settlers. The Ottoman administration, by the same token, had become corrupt and thus unable to maintain law and order, and further developed mistrust in the Serbs' loyalty.[20] At the end of the 17th and beginning of the 18th centuries, Albanian tribes colonized Kosovo and Metohia in more significant numbers, which coincided with the emergence of Islamization pressures on the Serbian population.[21]

The Serbian uprising in 1804 and its successful development into the autonomous Principality of Serbia further incited ethnic Albanian pashas in Kosovo and Metohia, the region's hereditary rulers, towards large-scale oppression aimed at the Serbs living in the region. Notwithstanding all the adverse circumstances, Serbs formed the largest ethnic group in Kosovo and Metohia until the Eastern Crisis (1875–78), when the terror against the Serbian population in the region escalated. The territory of Kosovo and Metohia had been continuously referred to simply as 'Serbia' from the Middle Ages until the fourth decade of the 19th century, when the term 'Old Serbia' was introduced within the Principality of Serbia itself, for the purpose of differentiating the Principality from this historic Serbian region.[22] Approximately 150,000 Serbs fled Kosovo and Metohia between the mid-18th century and 1912, lowering still further the percentage of the Serbian population to around one half of the original volume.[23]

---

18 Milisav Lutovac, 'Geografski i političko-geografski značaj pokrajine Kosova u Srbiji', op. cit.

19 R Samardžić, P Ivić, D Bogdanović et al., *Istorija srpskog naroda, treća knjiga, drugi tom, Srbi pod tuđinskom vlašću 1537–1699 [History of the Serbian Nation, Vol. 3, Part 2, Serbs under Alien Rule 1537–1699]* (Srpska književna zadruga 2000) 67–73.

20 Milisav Lutovac, 'Geografski i političko-geografski značaj pokrajine Kosova u Srbiji', op. cit.

21 Dusan Bataković, *The Kosovo Chronicles*, op. cit.; Milisav Lutovac, 'Geografski i političko-geografski značaj pokrajine Kosova u Srbiji', op. cit.

22 Dusan Bataković, *Kosovo i Metohija – Istorija i ideologija [Kosovo and Metohia – History and Ideology]* (Hrišćanska misao 1998) 7–22, 147–9.

23 Dusan Bataković, *The Kosovo Chronicles*, op. cit.

Kosovo and Metohia became parts of Serbia and Montenegro, respectively, in 1912, as a result of the First Balkan War, and thus became part of the Kingdom of Serbs, Croats and Slovenes, formed in 1918. The new state abolished feudal estates on its territory, which pertained to Kosovo and Metohia as well. Between the two World Wars approximately 10,000 Serbian families, that is, approximately 60,000 people – Serbs from the Kingdom's non-developed and mountainous regions – settled on land properties in Kosovo and Metohia that became available by virtue of agrarian reform.[24]

In World War II ethnic Albanians fought under the flags of Germany and Italy. They used the opportunity created by the occupation of the Kingdom to launch a campaign of terror against the Serbs in Kosovo and Metohia: approximately 10,000 were killed, while more than 100,000 were expelled.[25] The policy of the Communist Party of Yugoslavia towards Kosovo and Metohia had been set at least since the 1920s, when in its official documents the region was identified as Albanian, annexed to the Kingdom of Serbs, Croats and Slovenes by the 'victorius imperialists of the Entente'.[26] Thus when the communists gained power in Yugoslavia at the end of World War II on the heels of the Red Army advance, the new authorities immediately forbade the return of the expelled Serbs to the province and at the same time enacted statutes on the 'revision of assignments of land in Macedonia and Kosovo and Metohia province to colonists', effectively depriving of their land rights those Serbs who had settled in the province after World War I.[27] At the same time, Albanians who had settled in the province during World War II were allowed to remain there, and an open border with Albania was kept until 1948, which encouraged new Albanian settlers to arrive.

In post-World War II communist Yugolavia, Kosovo and Metohia became an autonomous province within Serbia. In accordance with the Communist Party of Yugoslavia's official agenda for quelling 'Serbian hegemonism', Serbia was the only Yugoslav republic whose territory was segmented in this manner. Constitutional changes of 1974 strengthened the autonomy of the province even further, so that its effective powers amounted to those of a federal unit. Until the fall of the Berlin wall and the disintegration of communist Yugoslavia, the province was controlled by the Albanian-dominated Communist Party of Kosovo, which had been providing the aegis for the continued terror against, and persecution of, the non-Albanian population, aimed at its expulsion.[28]

---

24 Kosta Čavoški, *Na rubovima Srpstva [On the Outskirts of Serbdom]* (Tersit 1995) 44–54; Dusan Bataković, *The Kosovo Chronicles*, op. cit.

25 Dusan Bataković, *The Kosovo Chronicles*, op. cit.

26 Kosta Čavoški, *Na rubovima Srpstva*, op. cit.; Dusan Bataković, *Kosovo i Metohija – Istorija i ideologija*, op. cit.

27 Kosta Čavoški, *Na rubovima Srpstva*, op. cit.

28 Dusan Bataković, *The Kosovo Chronicles*, op. cit.

The Meaning of Toponyms Kosovo and Metohia

In most cases reference to the region of 'Kosovo' includes the entire territory of the Autonomous Province of Kosovo and Metohia, as this area is defined by the present Constitution of Serbia, and it had been designated by the previous constitutions of socialist Yugoslavia (1963, 1974). Serbs usually insist on the two-part name 'Kosovo and Metohia' due to geographic and cultural-historical reasons. These are two completely different regions from the climate-landscape and hydrographic perspectives. Metohia (the smaller, south-western/western part of the province) belongs to the divide of the Adriatic Sea and is influenced by the Mediterranean climate. On the other side, Kosovo (the larger, eastern/north-eastern part) belongs to the divide of the Black Sea and is influenced by the continental climate. In an even narrower sense, Serbs use the term 'Kosovo' for the spacious, semi-steppe grassland (without forests) in the lowland plains ('polje' meaning field) in the catchment of the rivers Sitnica and Lab. This includes the immediate and broader vicinity of Priština.

The name 'Metohia' derives from the Greek word *metohion* (pl. *metohia*) denoting monastery estates. In the Middle Ages all the most important Serbian Orthodox monasteries in the region had their estates in Metohia, which is the area with the most fertile land and the mildest (sub-Mediterranean) climate. The word 'Metohia' is particularly important for Serbs as the greatest number of the most important and the oldest holy places are grouped there. Therefore they are particularly sensitive in the case of omission of this part of the name. On the other hand, omitting this part of the region's name cannot be defended from the suspicion that it is aimed at hiding the long-standing historical presence and property rights of the Serbian Orthodox Church.

The communist regime eliminated the traditional name Metohia from the full name of the region due to its policy of suppressing the Serbian presence in Kosovo and Metohia, and due to its general anti-religious attitude. Now the omission continues to be made by provisional authorities formed by Kosovar Albanians, representing one of the forms of negation of the religious importance of the region as a whole. The Albanians and, regretfully, most of the international public, use the shorter term 'Kosovo' (without 'and Metohia'): the former for national propaganda reasons, the latter in most cases due to practical reasons.

The shortening of two-part names is not rare in other areas as well. There is a similar example with the two-part name of Bosnia and Herzegovina, which is widely called just 'Bosnia', and its inhabitants are called 'Bosniaks' (instead of 'Bosniak-Hercegoviniaks' or some other proper term). In the same way, although we usually say just the United Kingdom, the UK, or Britain, instead of the United Kingdom of Great Britain and Northern Ireland, we always keep in mind the special value of the final part 'and Northern Ireland'.

In a romantic fashion the word Kosovo is assumed to derive from the Serb word *kos* (*kos-ovo* – belonging to *kos*) which means a blackbird. The famous battle between the Serbs and the Turks in the 14th century took place at the Field of

Blackbirds (Kosovo Polje). However, it is difficult to imagine that the open field would have got its name from a forest bird that likes shady and moist habitats. There is a toponym, Kosovi Lug (Blackbird's Grove) in Montenegro, but that is not a field. It is much more plausible that the word root *kos-* in *Kosovo polje* stems from the root of the Serbian (Slavic) word *kos-iti* (English *to scythe, to mow*, Russian *kosit'*, *косить*, Polish *kosić*, češ. *kosit*, Slovakian *kositi*, Romanian *cosi*), so that the toponym would mean a place for mowing, a place with good grass, yielding good hay. There are other Serbian toponyms elsewhere (Kosovo in Dalmatia, Koševo in Sarajevo). In the Albanian language the word *kosovo, kosova* has no original meaning, apart from the proper name of the area. It is interesting that the Albanians, after they came to Kosovo, learned the mowing process and manner of use of the requisite tools from Serbs, adopting the Serbian word both for the tool (English *scythe*, Serbian and Russian *kosa*) and for the verb 'to mow', although these two languages are not related. In general, over 90 per cent of terms used in agriculture, names of settlements and geographical names in today's Kosovo are of Serb origin. The names of cities and villages have only their Albanian equivalent of Serb toponyms (Mališevo/Malisheva, Pec/Peja, Prizren/Prizreni, Priština/Prishtine and so on).

Present Legal Status of Kosovo and Metohia

Unilateral Declaration of Independence, its Origins and Consequences

Immediately following the cessation of hostilities that resulted from the NATO military intervention against the FR of Yugoslavia, the UN Security Council enacted Resolution 1244, in which principles of a 'political solution to the Kosovo crisis' were laid out. In addition, the document demanded, *inter alia*, establishment of an international security presence as a transitory step towards establishment of an international civil mission. The principal goals of the latter would include 'promoting the establishment, pending a final settlement, of substantial autonomy and self-government in Kosovo … facilitating a political process designed to determine Kosovo's future status' (Article 11(a), UN S/RES/1244).

Annex I to the Resolution further elaborated certain general principles of the overall political solution to the 'Kosovo crisis', including 'establishment of an interim administration for Kosovo to be decided by the Security Council… to ensure conditions for a peaceful and normal life for all inhabitants in Kosovo; the safe and free return of all refugees and displaced persons … a political process towards the establishment of an interim political framework agreement providing for a substantial self-government for Kosovo, taking full account of the Rambouillet accords and the principles of sovereignty and territorial integrity of the Federal Republic of Yugoslavia and other countries of the region, and the demilitarization of the KLA' (UN S/RES/1244, Annex I).

Annex II to the same Resolution contained 'principles to move towards a political resolution of the Kosovo crisis'. These included the return of 'an agreed number of Yugoslav and Serbian personnel', which would be, *inter alia*, in charge of 'maintaining a presence at Serb patrimonial sites; maintaining a presence at key border crossings', 'limited to a small agreed number (hundreds, not thousands)'. Another principle set forth in Annex II was 'safe and free return of all refugees and displaced persons …' (UN S/RES/1244, Annex I).

The Secretary-General of the UN designed UNMIK. The first Special Representative of the UN Secretary-General promulgated UNMIK Regulation 1999/1, whereby all legislative and executive authority, including administration of justice, is vested in UNMIK and exercised by the Special Representative. By virtue of UNMIK Regulation 1999/24, law applicable in Kosovo and Metohia was defined as 'the regulations promulgated by the Special Representative … and the law in force in Kosovo on 22 March 1989' (ICJ Advisory Opinion 2010, paras 60, 61). Paradoxically, an international mission predominantly influenced by Western democracies thus expressly reinvigorated a legal system that had been in force before the fall of the Iron Curtain in a country then ruled by an authoritarian communist regime.

Division of responsibilities in respect of governance of Kosovo and Metohia between the Special Representative of the UN Secretary-General and the so-called Provisional Institutions of Self-Government of Kosovo (which encompassed the Assembly, President, Government, courts and so on) was set forth in UNMIK Regulation 2001/9 on a Constitutional Framework for Provisional Self-Government (UNMIK 2001).

A series of events of major importance for understanding the nature of the political and social circumstances in Kosovo and Metohia post-1999 took place on 17 and 18 March 2004, when approximately 51,000 ethnic Albanians violently rioted throughout Kosovo and Metohia against Serbs. The riots were provoked by untrue reports that Serbs had been responsible for drowning three Albanian children. There were 33 separate riots in total. According to Human Rights Watch:

> … security structures in Kosovo … completely lost control; the March violence forced out the entire Serb population from dozens of locations-including the capital Pristina – and equally affected Roma and Ashkali communities. According to Human Rights Watch, in a short span of only two days of rioting, at least 550 homes and 27 Orthodox churches and monasteries were burned, leaving approximately 4,100 Serbs, Roma, Ashkali, and other non-Albanian minorities displaced. Some 2,000 persons still remain displaced months later, living in crowded and unsanitary conditions-including in unheated and unfinished apartments, crowded schools, tent camps on KFOR military bases, and even metal trucking containers.[29]

29 Human Rights Watch, *Failure to Protect: Anti-Minority Violence in Kosovo, March 2004* (Human Rights Watch, 26 July 2004) <www.hrw.org/node/11989/section/2> accessed 15 March 2013.

In his address to the UN Security Council in February 2008, the President of Serbia Mr Boris Tadic asserted that 35 churches and monasteries and 800 houses were burned in the March 2004 riots, and that more than 5,000 Serbs and other non-Albanians had fled their homes as result (UNSC S/2008/211).

Human Rights Watch noted numerous instances in which international forces failed to protect the Serbian population, its homes and sacred places from violent attacks:

> In numerous cases, minorities under attack were left entirely unprotected and at the mercy of the rioters. In Svinjare, French KFOR troops failed to come to the assistance of the besieged Serbs, even though their main base was just a few hundred meters away – in fact, the ethnic Albanian crowd had walked right past the base on its way to burning down the village. French KFOR troops similarly failed to respond to the rioting in Vucitrn, which is located in between two major French bases. In Prizren, German KFOR troops failed to deploy to protect the Serb population and the many historic Serbian Orthodox churches, despite calls for assistance from their UNMIK international police counterparts, who later accused German KFOR commanders of cowardice. In Kosovo Polje, UNMIK

Figure 12.2 Prizren – Monastery of Holy Archangels near Prizren (14th century). The monastery was looted and torched in March 2004

Source: The Information Service of the Serbian Orthodox Church.

> and KFOR were nowhere to be seen as Albanian crowds methodically burned Serb homes and sanctuaries. The village of Belo Polje, rebuilt on the outskirts of Pec to house returning Serbs, was burned to the ground even though it was almost adjacent to the main Italian KFOR base. Italian KFOR soldiers refused to approach the besieged Serbs, forcing the Serbs to run for several hundred meters through a hostile Albanian crowd, before KFOR evacuated them.[30]

The Parliamentary Assembly of the Council of Europe asserted that 4,100 Serbs, Roma and other non-Albanians left Kosovo after the events, noting that the return process of displaced persons was thereby reversed.[31]

In 2005, the UN Security Council supported the UN Secretary-General in his intention to commence the political process to determine the future status of Kosovo.[32] The Secretary-General appointed Mr Martti Ahtisaari as his Special Envoy for the status process of Kosovo and Metohia in November 2005. Several rounds of negotiations between the Serbian government and the Albanian-controlled provisional authorities in Kosovo and Metohia took place in the course of 2006. According to the reports of the UN Secretary-General, the parties remained distant on most issues. In February 2007, Mr Ahtisaari addressed them with a comprehensive draft proposal for the Kosovo status settlement. The final round of negotiations took place and ended unsuccessfully the following month. In his report, Mr Ahtisaari expressed his 'firm view that the negotiations' potential to produce any mutually agreeable outcome on Kosovo's status is exhausted'. Having stressed the urgent need for solving the status of Kosovo, Mr Ahtisaari concluded that 'the only viable option for Kosovo is independence, to be supervised for an initial period by the international community'.[33] Together with the report, Mr Ahtisaari submitted 'the Comprehensive Proposal for the Kosovo Status Settlement' – a detailed proposal of key constitutional principles and provisions for the intended independent Kosovo, as well as of the mechanism for the transfer of powers from the international administrative mission to the Kosovo authorities. The plan provided, *inter alia*, for the establishment of protective zones around more than 40 key religious and cultural sites, as well as granting to the Serbian Orthodox Church property rights, exemption from taxes and customs duties and the

30 See supra note 29.

31 Resolution 1375 (2004) Situation in Kosovo. Council of Europe Parliamentary Assembly, 29 April 2004. <http://assembly.coe.int/Main.asp?link=/Documents/AdoptedText/ta04/ERES1375.htm> accessed 15 March 2013.

32 Security Council Presidential Statement Offers Full Support for Start of Political Process to Determine Kosovo's Future Status. Security Council SC/8533 <www.un.org/News/Press/docs/2005/sc8533.doc.htm> accessed 15 March 2013.

33 Letter dated 26 March 2007 from the Secretary-General addressed to the President of the Security Council – Report of the Special Envoy of the Secretary-General on Kosovo's future status. United Nations Security Council. S/2007/168, 26 March 2007 <www.un.org/ga/search/view_doc.asp?symbol=S/2007/168> accessed 15 March 2013.

freedom to maintain links with the Serbian Orthodox Church in Belgrade.[34] In the discussions that followed the submission of the report and proposal of Mr Ahtisaari the Security Council remained unable to reach a decision regarding the future status of Kosovo and Metohia and did not endorse the so-called Ahtisaari Plan.

The so-called Assembly of Kosovo declared the independence of Kosovo on 17 February 2008, vowing full adherence to the Ahtisaari Plan. The President of Serbia, Mr Tadic, informed the UN Secretary-General that 'Serbia had adopted a decision stating that the declaration of independence by Kosovo represents a forceful and unilateral secession of a part of the territory of Serbia, and does not produce any legal effect either in Serbia or in the international legal order'.[35] Serbia demanded and was granted an emergency public meeting of the UN Security Council, at which Mr Tadic denounced the declaration of independence as illegal, as well as a violation of the sovereignty and territorial integrity of Serbia, which had been guaranteed by Security Council Resolution 1244 (1999). President Tadic warned that 250,000 Serbs remained expelled from Kosovo since 1999, and stated that recognition of Kosovo would set a dangerous precedent. Finally, the President of Serbia vowed that Serbia would never recognize Kosovo.[36]

In October 2008 the UN General Assembly backed the request by Serbia that an advisory opinion on the legality of Kosovo's declaration be sought.[37] The question addressed to the ICJ was the following: 'Is the unilateral declaration of independence by the Provisional Institutions of Self-Government of Kosovo in accordance with international law?'[38]

In its opinion, delivered in July 2010, the ICJ based its reasoning on a two-pronged analysis – first, whether the declaration of independence of Kosovo violated general international law, and, second, whether it violated UN Security Council Resolution

---

34 Letter dated 26 March 2007 from the Secretary-General addressed to the President of the Security Council – Addendum – Comprehensive Proposal for the Kosovo Status Settlement. United Nations Security Council. S/2007/168/Add.1, 26 March 2007 <www.unosek.org/docref/Comprehensive_proposal-english.pdf> accessed 15 March 2013.

35 Report of the Secretary-General on the United Nations Interim Administration Mission in Kosovo. UN Security Council. S/2008/211, 28 March 2008 <www.un.org/ga/search/view_doc.asp?symbol=S/2008/211> accessed 15 March 2013.

36 Record of the 5839th meeting of the UN Security Council. S/PV.5839, 18 February 2008 <www.securitycouncilreport.org/atf/cf/%7B65BFCF9B-6D27-4E9C-8CD3-CF6E4FF96FF9%7D/Kos%20S%20PV%205839.pdf> accessed 15 March 2013.

37 Backing request by Serbia, General Assembly decides to seek International Court of Justice ruling on legality of Kosovo's independence. UN General Assembly GA/10764, 8 October 2008 <http://www.un.org/News/Press/docs/2008/ga10764.doc.htm> accessed 15 March 2013.

38 UN A/RES/63/3 2008: request for an advisory opinion of the International Court of Justice on whether the unilateral declaration of independence of Kosovo is in accordance with international law, resolution adopted by the General Assembly 63/3 <http://daccess-dds-ny.un.org/doc/UNDOC/GEN/N08/470/97/PDF/N0847097.pdf?OpenElement> accessed 15 March 2013.

1244. In its negative finding in respect of the former, the ICJ encompassed the assertion that the principle of protection of territorial integrity was not violated by the disputed declaration because the principle mattered only in relations between states. The ICJ furthermore claimed that earlier condemnations of certain unilateral declarations of independence (Southern Rhodesia, Northern Cyprus, Republika Srpska) were not based on the unilaterality of the condemned acts, but 'on the fact that they were, or would have been, connected with the unlawful use of force or other egregious violations of norms of general international law'[39] (paras 80–81). The Court avoided pronouncing on whether Albanians in Kosovo had a right to self-determination in respect of their independence from Serbia, or a right to 'remedial secession', by simply claiming that these questions fell outside of the scope of the question posed by the UN General Assembly (paras 82–3). The Court similarly decided not to pronounce itself on whether Kosovo in fact reached statehood (paras 80–81).

In respect of UN Security Council Resolution 1244, the Court identified as its 'object and purpose … to establish a temporary, exceptional legal regime which, save to the extent that it expressly preserved it, superseded the Serbian legal order and which aimed at the stabilization of Kosovo, and that it was designed to do so on an interim basis' (para. 100). The Court modified the very question it had been requested to answer by noting that 'the authors of the declaration of independence … did not act as one of the Provisional Institutions of Self-Government within the Constitutional Framework, but rather as persons who acted together in their capacity as representatives of the people of Kosovo outside the framework of the interim administration' (para. 109). The Court based this conclusion on the language of the subject declaration, as well as on the silence of the Special Representative of the UN Secretary-General. Although having admitted at one point that the language of Resolution 1244 is ambiguous in this regard, the Court went on to assert that Resolution 1244 did not contain a 'prohibition, binding on the authors of the declaration of independence, against declaring independence'. The Court noted particularly that the collocation 'political settlement', used in Resolution 1244 to express the condition subsequent of the interim status, did not encompass prohibition of a unilateral declaration of independence. The Court failed to provide an explanation for such a tenuous interpretation, in spite of the fact that the interpretation it relied upon contravened the plain and ordinary meaning of the subject collocation (para. 118).

Among academics, the opinion has been criticized mostly for taking an excessively narrow approach and the consequent failure to clarify boundaries between the right to self-determination and the principle of territorial integrity of states.[40] Jovanović

39 International Court of Justice, *Accordance with International Law of the Unilateral Declaration of Independence in Respect of Kosovo*, Advisory Opinion. I.C.J. Reports 2010. <www.icj-cij.org/docket/files/141/15987.pdf> accessed 15 March 2013.

40 Harvard Law Review, 'Recent International Advisory Opinion' [2011] *Harv. L. Rev.* <www.harvardlawreview.org/media/pdf/vol124_kosovo_declaration_of_independence.pdf> accessed 15 March 2013.

has identified a common denominator among both academic and foreign affairs perspectives that argued in favour of Kosovo's independence: the claim was that the case of Kosovo was unique and incapable of setting a precedent for other similar cases around the world. Jovanović systematized a total of four arguments in favour of the uniqueness of the Kosovo case, before rebutting each one.[41] In the aftermath of the unilateral declaration of independence and the Advisory Opinion of the ICJ, the case of Kosovo has retained the potential to seriously transform legal theory pertaining to the dilemma between the declaratory and constitutive effect of state recognitions, criteria of statehood and right to self-determination.[42]

It seems that the reasoning of the Court encompassed two major flaws. Firstly, the Court would not be able to claim accordance of the declaration of independence with the Resolution 1244 had it not first modified the question it was supposed to answer by claiming that it was not Provisional Institutions of Kosovo that enacted the subject declaration, but political representatives of the people of Kosovo instead. Such an assertion seems untenable in the light of the fact that the political structure that proclaimed independence directly originated from the Provisional Institutions. Secondly, the Court's abstention from tackling the perspective of the right to self-determination deprived the Court's conclusion of any substantial grounds, for if the assumption that the body that had enacted the declaration of independence was not in fact identical to one of the Provisional Institutions were true, only a positive finding of the right to self-determination on the part of Kosovo Albanians could serve as valid ground for such a declaration. Such an assessment may rely on the contention of Raič, who claimed that 'Under contemporary international law, the right of self-determination is not only the principal legitimation of statehood, it has also become a crucial factor in the process of formation of States'.[43]

A civil and police mission of the EU, EULEX, assumed responsibility in the area of rule of law in December 2008, taking over from UNMIK, so that UNMIK police completed almost 10 years of active operation in the region.

All references to the Ahtisaari Plan were removed from the so-called Constitution of Kosovo by virtue of amendments thereof in September 2012. The International Steering Group (ISG), which according to the Ahtisaari Plan comprised key international stakeholders and was tasked with appointing the

41 Miodrag Jovanović, 'Is Kosovo and Metohija Indeed a "Unique Case"?' in James Summers (ed.), *Kosovo: A Precedent? The Declaration of Independence, the Advisory Opinion and Implications for Statehood, Self-Determination and Minority Rights* (Leiden 2011) 345–75.

42 Miloš Jovanović, 'Recognition of Kosovo Independence As A Violation of International Law' [2008] *Annals – Belgrade Law Review*, 108–40 <www.ius.bg.ac.rs/Anali/Annals%202008/Annals%202008%20p%20108-140.pdf> accessed 15 March 2013; Jure Vidmar, 'International Legal Responses to Kosovo's Declaration of Independence' [2009] *Vanderbilt Journal of International Law* 779–851 <www.vanderbilt.edu/jotl/manage/wp-content/uploads/Vidmar-cr_final_final1.pdf> accessed 15 March 2013.

43 David Raič, Statehood and the Law of Self-Determination (Martinus Nijhoff Publishers 2002) 68.

International Civilian Representative (ICR), held its final meeting on 10 September 2012, at which it declared the end of the supervised independence of Kosovo.[44]

Key Factors of the Dynamics of the Present Situation

The Constitution of Serbia of 2006 expressly states that the Autonomous Province of Kosovo and Metohia forms part of the territory of Serbia, enjoying an 'essential' autonomy that shall be stipulated in greater detail by virtue of a separate law. Such a law has neither been enacted nor drafted as of February 2013 (Ustav Republike Srbije [Constitution of the Republic of Serbia]).

Accession to the EU has remained a key goal of almost all governments of Serbia following the democratic changes of 2000. However, Serbia is faced with the EU demands to 'improve relations with Kosovo', which should lead to 'full normalization of relations between Serbia and Kosovo'. The demand that Serbia 'respects territorial integrity of Kosovo' has been particularly contentious (Enlargement Strategy 2012, 26). The EU itself remains divided over recognition of Kosovo. Five of its Member States have not recognized it.

The EU has been mediating a dialogue between the government of Serbia and the secessionist authorities of Kosovo since March 2011. So far, the negotiations have resulted in a number of so-called technical agreements: on border management, with the integrated management component in Northern Kosovo and exchange of liaison officers agreed upon in December 2012, as well as on the free flow of people and goods, books and cadastre, customs stamps, the acknowledgment of diplomas and the representation of Kosovo at regional conferences.[45] Just before the 5th round of talks, the presidents of the European Council and of the European Commission, Messrs Van Rompuy and Barroso, stressed that 'the dialogue and the upcoming round in particular were immensely important for Kosovo and Serbia's relations with the EU'.[46] Serbian officials have been maintaining that the EU-mediated dialogue between the Serbian government and the secessionist authorities of Kosovo should be status neutral.[47] The most contentious topics on the dialogue agenda – the support that the government of

44 International Civilian Office Kosovo, *The Comprehensive Status Proposal* <www.ico-kos.org/?id=38> accessed 15 March 2013.

45 Report of the Secretary-General on the United Nations Interim Administration Mission in Kosovo. UN Security Council. S/2012/818, 8 November 2012. http://www.un.org/ga/search/view_doc.asp?symbol=S/2012/818> accessed 15 March 2013.

46 'Belgrade and Pristina open most delicate issue in dialog' (*EurActiv.rs*, 22 February 2013). <www.euractiv.rs/vesti/5469-belgrade-and-pristina-open-most-delicate-issue-in-dialog> accessed 15 March 2013.

47 'Fuele reassures Serbia on Kosovo "territorial integrity"' (*EurActiv.rs*, 11 October 2012). <www.euractiv.com/enlargement/fuele-reassures-serbia-kosovo-te-news-515346> accessed 15 March 2013.

Serbia has been providing to Serb-controlled instututions in Northern Kosovo, as well the status of Serb Orthodox holy places in Kosovo and Metohia – have not been opened as of February 2013.[48]

A solution for the apparently imminent deadlock in the relations between EU and Serbia over recognition of Kosovo is being proposed in the form of a partition of Kosovo and Metohia, which would entail that Northern Kosovo, homogenously inhabited by Serbs, be excluded from the rest of the province. Jovanović defends such a solution on the grounds that it simply represents a consequence of strict application of the principle of right to self-determination.[49]

Internally Displaced Persons

In March 2000, the Serbian Commissariat for Refugees, in cooperation with UNHCR, conducted for the first time registration of internally displaced persons (IDPs) from Kosovo and Metohia, when 187,129 such persons were registered in Serbia. The number of these refugees is not decreasing at all (although the reports of the Temporary Government of Kosovo regularly mention returnees) but, on the contrary, is on the rise. During the period 2000–05, an additional 20,000 persons fled Kosovo and Metohia. In March 2008, the number of IDPs in Serbia was 209,700.[50] This number does not include only Serbs, but also other 'non-Albanians' who looked for safety and help in Serbia and elsewhere. On the other hand, Albanian sources deny such figures and cite a significantly fewer number of refugees and IDPs. The UN Secretary-General admitted that 'return statistics for 2008 show a dramatic decline in the number of voluntary minority returns to Kosovo compared to earlier years … only 582 minority community members returned to Kosovo in 2008, as compared to 1,816 in 2007 and 1,669 in 2006'.[51] In 2011 and 2012 the overall number of minority returnees slightly increased in comparison with 2008, but did not reach the levels of 2007 and 2006: in 2012 a total of 970 returned, while for 2011 the number stood at 1,143.[52] The report of the Secretary-General on the activities of UNMIK between July and October 2012 mentioned 'renewed debates on sustainability of returns to Kosovo', prompted by 'sales of Kosovo Serbs of their properties and their relocation to Serbia'. The Secretary-General referred both to socio-economic reasons, as well

48 See supra note 46.

49 Miodrag Jovanović, 'Final Status for Kosovo – Should We Really be Petrified With the "Partition Option"?' in Miodrag Jovanović and Kristin Henrard (eds), *Sovereigny and Diversity* (Eleven International Publishing 2008) 171.

50 The Commissariat for Refugees, *About us*. <www.kirs.sr.gov.yu/articles/onama.php?lang=ENG> accessed 15 March 2013.

51 Report of the Secretary-General on the United Nations: Interim Administration Mission in Kosovo (United Nations Security Council S/2009/149, 17 March 2009) <www.unmikonline.org/SGReports/S-2009-149.pdf> accessed 15 March 2013.

52 Report of the Secretary-General on the United Nations Interim Administration Mission in Kosovo (UN Security Council. S/2013/72, 4 February 2013) <www.un.org/ga/search/view_doc.asp?symbol=S/2013/72> accessed 15 March 2013.

as to perception of insecurity among returnees, caused by several security incidents in returnee areas, as possible causes of the mentioned relocation process. Cited data suggest that the process of return of displaced persons is virtually non-existent, since an annual rate of return of between 0.1 per cent and 0.5 per cent of the total number of refugees is coupled with new departures.

Profile of Serbian Orthodox Holy Places in Kosovo and Metohia

Places of Gathering and Destinations of Pilgrimage

Most of the sacred/holy places in Kosovo and Metohia are also traditional places of gathering of local, regional or even national significance, in which Serbian Orthodox Christians experience 'sabornost', an important dimension of social, political and religious significance for them [Russian *sobornost*, conciliarism, catholicity, a unity of persons in a loving fellowship in which each member retains freedom and integrity without excessive individualism]. Each of the old and well-known churches represents such a holy gathering place, so that it is irreplaceable for Serbian Orthodox believers who reside both in neighbouring areas as well as further away. Such holy places are called *svetinje* (sanctities). If one of the *svetinje* is destroyed, there are great chances that the local community would depart the region. For that reason such holy places are particularly attractive targets for inflicting damage and destruction.

One of the best examples is Gračanica Monastery (Figure 12.3), where every year on June 28 (according to the Gregorian calendar) several thousands (previously several tens of thousands) of Serbs gather to attend the Vidovdan [St Vitus' day] Divine Service. Vidovdan is one of most important Serbian feasts. Its importance stems primarily from the Battle of Kosovo of 1389, when, according to tradition, Prince Lazarus died on the battlefield and thus favoured the Kingdom in Heaven over the Kingdom on Earth. Since the beginning of the 20th century, St Vitus' Day also became a Church feast in honour of the Holy Martyr Prince Lazarus.

In addition to places of gathering, there is an almost equal number of holy places that represent destinations of pilgrimage for all Orthodox believers in Kosovo and Metohia and other areas, particularly for those who were forced to temporarily leave Kosovo as refugees and displaced persons. It is remarkable that the strong impulse for pilgrimage is felt even by persons who do not consider themselves deeply religious, and even by those who are not Orthodox or Christians at all, most often in association with a hope of being cured from an illness.

One of the best known holy places of pilgrimage is Visoki Dečani. For Serbs, the Dečani Monastery is the third most important destination of pilgrimage, just after Jerusalem and the Hilandar Monastery at Mount Athos. Mass visits began after the canonization of Holy King Stefan Dečanski, just before the mid-14th century, and have not decreased during the last six centuries. Pilgrimage to the Dečani Monastery is most often made in spring and in late summer through to early autumn. Pilgrims usually remain at the monastery for 5 to15 days.

Figure 12.3 Gračanica Monastery (14th century)

Centres of Saints' Cults

Physical remains of the first martyrs for the Christian faith have been respected as sacred since the earliest days of Christianity. The cult of relics had a pronounced growth in the 6th century, when bodies of many holy persons were located and moved around. The theological foundation of respecting the relics was laid by the most prominent fathers of the Church (Ephrem the Syrian, Gregory of Nazianzus, Cyril of Jerusalem), and the dogmatic rules were agreed on during the Seventh Ecumenical Council.

The cult of relics developed among Serbs as an integral part of the holy persons' cults, so the *announced* bodies could belong only to state rulers and heads of the Church. There was an exception with the relics of St Petar Koriški, the only Serbian hermit from the Middle Ages that has been proclaimed a saint. The relics of Serbian holy persons could be in form of bones or entire bodies. Examples of such embalmed bodies were those of King Stefan Prvovenčani, Archbishop Sava Nemanjić, Queen Jelena, King Milutin, King Stefan Uroš III Dečanski, Prince Lazar, archbishops Arsenije and Jevstatiej I. After the announcements, bodies of Serbian holy persons were placed in a shrine called *kivot* (casket-like object with the specific purpose of storing a holy person's relics; the only Middle Ages specimen preserved to this day is the kivot of King Stefan Uroš III Dečanski, which is a representative specimen of artistic woodwork from the 14th century), which was placed in front of the altar in the church of the Visoki Dečani Monastery.

The relics were announced by miracles, and their particularly important feature was their healing power. Exuding of myrrh was only associated with the relics of St Simeon Nemanja, the founder of the Nemanjić dynasty.

The importance of the relics of Serbian holy persons exceeds boundaries of religious practice. In the Middle Ages they were an important element of dynastic ideology, while in the period of Ottoman rule they were a key factor of the preservation of national identity.[53]

The Devič Monastery is the centre of the cult of St Joannicius of Devič.[54] Saint Joannicius was a Serb from Zeta (south-western part of the Serbian medieval state, today mostly conforming to the territory of the Republic of Montenegro). The holy and wonder-working relics of St Joannicius are kept in this monastery. According to tradition, Serbian Prince George Branković brought his mentally ill daughter to the Saint, who then healed her. Out of gratitude, George built a monastery on this spot, known today by the name of Devič. Obviously due to its importance, this holy place is a very common target of attacks and hate-motivated crimes. The monastery was looted in 1999, and set on fire and demolished in 2004 (Figures 12.4 and 12.8).

The Visoki Dečani Monastery[55] is the centre of the cult of Serbian holy man and king Stefan Uroš III Dečanski (c.1285–11 November 1331) who reigned from 1321 to 8 September 1331, the son of King Stefan Uroš II and Anna of Bulgaria. The most significant event of Stefan Uroš III's reign was the Battle of Velbuzhd, in which he defeated the Bulgarian army and killed Emperor Michael Asen III. Dečanski's conquests allowed him to push the borders of Serbia further to the south into Byzantine Macedonia. The Serbian Orthodox Church canonized Stefan Uroš III as a saint-martyr. His remains are kept in the church of the Visoki Dečani Monastery, which was endowed by him.

The church of the Visoki Dečani Monastery hosts also the relics of St Helen, the sister of Stefan Dečanski, who died in the mid-14th century. She 'presented herself' in 1692 through a miracle which prevented the Turks from turning the Dečani church into a mosque.[56]

---

53 SM Ćirković, R Mihaljčić and M Bajalović-Hadži-Pešić (eds), *Leksikon srpskog srednjeg veka [Lexicon of the Serbian Middle Ages]* (Knowledge 1999) 420.

54 Đorde Radojičić, *Janićije Devički* (Glasnik Etnografskog instituta 1952) 173–8.

55 Smilja Marjanović-Dušanić, *Sveti kralj: kult Stefana Dečanskog [Holy King: the cult of Stefan Dečanski]* (Balkanološki institut SANU: Posebna izdanja 2007) 97; Danica Popović, *Pod okriljem svetosti: kult svetih vladara i relikvija u srednjovekovnoj Srbiji [Under the wing of holiness: cult of holy rulers and relics in Medieval Serbia]* (Balkanološki institut SANU: Posebna izdanja 2006) 92; Dragan Vojvodić, *Prilog poznavanju ikonografije i kulta sv. Stefana u Vizantiji i Srbiji [Contribution to knowledge of iconography and cult of St. Stefan in Byzantine and Serbia]* (U: Zidno slikarstvo manastira Dečani: građa i studije, SANU: Odeljenje istorijskih nauka: Posebna izdanja 1995) 537–65.

56 Leontije Pavlović, *Kultovi lica kod Srba i Makedonaca, Istorijsko-etnografska rasprava [Face cults in Serbs and Macedonians, historical-ethnographic debate]* (Narodni muzej, Posebno izdanje 1965) 1.

Figure 12.4 Two Serbian Orthodox Church nuns in front of Devič Monastery after it was burned and torn down in March 2004

Source: The Information Service of the Serbian Orthodox Church.

Places of Miracles and of Healing

The places of miracles and healing are the sacred/holy places in which relics believed to cause unnatural events and phenomena are kept. This group also includes the Monastery of Saint Joannicius at Devič because of the miraculous shrine of its church, as well as the Visoki Dečani Monastery.

The Monastery of Saint Healers Cosmas and Damian at Zočište possessed both healing body relics of the Saint Healers and a spring of water in the monastery yard which had been believed by both Serbs and Albanians to heal eye ailments. However, this was not an obstacle for the violent destruction of the monastery in 1999. The monastery church was rebuilt, and part of the Saints' body relics returned to the monastery in 2004. Today Serbs approach the site mostly escorted by KFOR or Kosovo police, fearing attacks by the local population, while the Albanians are free to visit it at will. However, although the site belongs to the Serbian Orthodox Church, it is now visited by Roman Catholic Albanians.[57]

57 'Prebačene mošti Svetih vrača Kozme i Damjana' ['Body relics of Saint Healers Cosmas and Damian Relocated'] (*Večernje Novosti*, 17 May 2012) <www.novosti.rs/vesti/

Miraculous healings were also recorded at the Devič Monastery and attributed to the relics of St Joannicius. Among the numerous ailments, these relics were reported to be particularly successful with mental illnesses.[58] Pilgrims with mental illnesses, belonging to various ethnicities and religions, visit Devič looking for a cure through the miraculous phenomena of the St Joannicius' relics.

An important dimension of the Devič Monastery is its significance for ending bloody feuds between families in the past. Together with the lay court, a 'mission' of Devič monks visited villages and made peace between the estranged families. They carried 'Devič holy relics' with them in their missions, which seem to have always been successful.[59] There are indications that peace was mediated between estranged Albanian tribes and families as well.

Both Serbs and Albanians believe that crawling under the shrine of the Holy King Stefan Uroš III (as it is raised above ground) at the Visoki Dečani Monastery cures many illnesses, keeps good health and particularly secures an easy delivery of newborns.[60] With the hope of miraculous healing, this monastery is visited by the deaf and mute, blind, mentally ill and patients with ear ailments, as well as by nursing mothers with breast illnesses and mothers bringing ill children.[61]

Figure 12.5 Frescoes of the Gračanica Monastery: the depiction of Queen Simonida with intentionally made scratches on her eyes

Muslims, whose religion forbids depiction of human figures, seemed to believe that frescoes in Serbian monasteries, depicting saints and rulers, had miraculous powers, and seemed to think that mortar and paint dug out of the eyes of the pictured persons would cure poor eyesight or eye ailments. This may be the reason why many of the most beautiful frescoes (Figure 12.5) were stained during the Ottoman occupation. Some

srbija.73.html:380097-Prebacene-mosti-Svetih-vraca-Kozme-i-Damjana> accessed 15 March 2013.

58 Tatomir Vukanović, *Srbi na Kosovu [Serbs in Kosovo]* (Nova Jugoslavija 1986).

59 Tatomir Vukanović, *Srbi na Kosovu*, op. cit.

60 Ibid.

61 Leontije Ninković, *Čudesa sv. Stefana, kralja Dečanskog [Miracles of St. Stefan, King og Dečani]* (Duhovna straža 1929) 1.

people believe that the Turks dug out the eyes from the frescoes as they could not withstand the looks from the holy faces on the church walls.

Patriarchate of Peć

The Monastery of Peć – known as the Patriarchate of Peć due to its status of the historical seat of the Patriarchate of the Serbian Orthodox Church – includes all the traits of a holy place: it is a centre of a Saint's cult, as well as a place of gathering and pilgrimage, and is believed to possess miraculous healing powers.[62]

One of the cults associated with the Patriarchate of Peć belongs to St Arsenije I, who was Serbian archbishop from 1233 to 1263 and who founded the Monastery of Peć. His birthplace was in Srem (north-western Serbia). Several years after his death, miraculous phenomena started happening on his grave. Arsenije I 'appeared' at the Patriarchate of Peć in the form of a strong earthquake that was heard and felt in the church one night. When the monks entered the church, they saw Arsenije's tomb broken apart. Together with Archbishop Sava II, the monks opened the tomb, removed the relics and placed them in a casket in the Church of St Peter and Paul within the monastery.[63]

The first legendary miracle in connection with the relics of St Arsenije I happened when a monk with a throat ailment visited his grave and was cured after touching the relics. Since then, many stories and legends on miraculous healings of ill persons who have touched the relics of this holy person have appeared. Half a century after the death of Arsenije I, a folk cult developed on top of the cult recognized by the Church. Ill and frail people would lie near the shrine for several hours, or would leave parts of their clothing on or around the shrine, sometimes overnight, hoping for cure when they put the clothing on. The monks read prayers in support of the healing.

Extra-Territorial Status and Scope of Self-government

None of the Serbian Orthodox holy places has any kind of extraterritorial status. As for the Special Protective Zones established around the holy places of major importance, it should be understood that secessionist Kosovo institutions are entitled to exercise their powers within these zones. Indeed municipal authorities are responsible for implementing the provisions of the legal regulation of the Special Protective Zones, and the Serbian Orthodox Church is expected to cooperate with the municipalities.[64]

---

62 Sreten Petković, *Manastir Pećka patrijaršija i njegove spahije [Monastery Patriarchy of Peć and its landowners]* (Balcanica 1982–83)13–14, 353–9.

63 Tatomir Vukanović, *Srbi na Kosovu*, op. cit.

64 International Civilan Office (ICO), *Implementation of Special Protective Zones for Religious and Cultural Heritage in Kosovo – Progress Report* (September 2011) <www.

However, while most holy places are surrounded by an Albanian majority, some of them are situated within enclaves of Serbian population. These enclaves are characterized by limited jurisdiction and powers of the Kosovo secessionist authorities, for example Sredačka župa, Velika Hoča near Orahovac[65] and the Gračanica Monastery. The case of Gračanica is paradigmatic – as this holy place is surrounded by the greatest agglomeration of homogeneous Serbian communities. Although encircled by a hostile majority, the Serbs feel safe near the revered monastery. Vice versa, the existence of this community for many centuries has amounted to a guarantee of the safety and survival of the monastery, as well as for its continuous use as a living holy place and not just as a mere tourist attraction.

The Serbian Orthodox religious community disposes of very limited religious freedom within the holy places that are not destroyed and deserted. In the 'living' churches the priests and monks are regularly performing religious services in accordance with the Constitution of the Serbian Orthodox Church and applicable canons. However, devotees have difficulties in reaching most of the holy places. The degree and form of internal autonomy of the active monasteries is defined by the Constitution and other applicable rules of the Serbian Orthodox Church. Rights of self-governance are often reduced to within the monastery walls, as assets outside are often illegally usurped.

References to certain forms of extraterritoriality, as a mechanism for establishing international responsibility for the protection of cultural and religious heritage, appear in some documents. Particularly important is recommendation no. 56 by the UN Special Envoy Kai Eide.[66] The idea of a special status for Serbian Orthodox holy places is also mentioned in Principle no. 5 of the Guiding Principles of the Contact Group for Settlement of the Status of Kosovo.[67]

In accordance with the so-called Ahtisaari Plan, a law was passed in February 2008 whereby special protective zones around 45 religious and cultural sites were

---

ico-kos.org/data/Image/SPZ_Progress_Report_Final_EV.pdf> accessed 15 March 2013.

65 Krsta Vitošević, *Velika Hoča* (Biblioteka Starosrpska sela 1995); Mirjana Menković (ed.), *Velika Hoča: The Pearl of Metohia* (Mnemosyne Center 2003).

66 'There is a need to create a "protective space" around these sites in order to make them less vulnerable to political manipulation. Arrangements should be designed for putting Serbian Orthodox sites in Kosovo and Metohia under a form of international protection. This would need to include guarantees of access, property rights, and community sustainability. It is important not only to protect individual sites as cultural and religious monuments, but also as living communities. The Council of Europe and the United Nations Educational, Scientific and Cultural Organization (UNESCO) have particular expertise in this area and should be invited to play a role in such arrangements'. United Nations Security Council, A comprehensive review of the situation in Kosovo (S/2005/635) <www.unosek.org/docref/KaiEidereport.pdf> accessed 15 March 2013.

67 Contact Group, Guiding principles of the Contact Group for a settlement of the status of Kosovo (2005) <www.unosek.org/docref/Contact%20Group%20-%20Ten%20Guiding%20principles%20for%20Ahtisaari.pdf> accessed 15 March 2013.

formed. However, the results of its implementation are poor and its violations have been frequent, while endangerment of sanctuaries persists, both in the form of actual physical attacks and in the form of various harms to property and identity. The recent attempt by several thousands of Albanians to forcefully enter the Visoki Dečani Monastery, of February 2013,[68] is a typical example of the ineffectiveness of the special protective zones. It is due to their ineffectiveness that the special protective zones have remained virtual and unsuitable for the purpose they had been established for.

An important question that arises is whether religious organizations or state authorities should be allowed undivided sovereignty over the holy places, or a mechanism for sharing sovereignty, similarly to the Mount Athos example, should be more appropriate.

Interaction with the Albanian Community and the Provisional Authorities

Both the Ahtisaari Plan and the Law on Special Protective Zones provided for the formation of Implementation and Monitoring Councils both at the level of the whole of Kosovo and Metohia and for each particular protective zone, with the aim that cooperation between Serbian Orthodox Church and local authorities be institutionalized. However, only cooperation by way of exchange of letters seems to have been realized by September 2011. It also seems, according to the International Civilian Office for Kosovo, that the 'only mechanisms where the SOC and Kosovo authorities formally discuss RCH (religious and cultural heritage) matters directly is in the CoE (Council of Europe) – led Reconstruction and Implementation Commission' (ICO Progress Report 2011, 13). This account shows an extremely limited quality and scope of interaction with local authorities.

Principal Dangers for the Sustainability of Holy Places in Kosovo and Metohia

Violations and Limitations of Ownership, Duty of Maintenance

Property of the Serbian Orthodox Church was appropriated on a large scale during the communist rule, which consequently jeopardized in the medium and long run the sustainability of the very sacred/holy places. Appropriation transpired in the form of nationalization, land reform and other types of forced deprivation of assets, as well as through infringements of religious rights, including attacks and pressures on clergy. Both the international missions to Kosovo and the secessionist

68 'Visoki Dečani: Monaštvo strahuje od novih napada' ['Visoki Dečani: Monks Fear New Attacks'] (*Večernje Novosti*, 9 February 2013) <www.novosti.rs/vesti/naslovna/aktuelno.290.html:419014-Visoki-Decani-Monastvo-strahuje-od-novih-napada> accessed 15 March 2013.

Kosovo authorities made themselves accomplices in the crimes of the communist regime by failing to undertake systemic restitution of religious property.

Support to the Serbian Orthodox Church in restoration and conservation of damaged and destroyed edifices in holy places has been provided so far mostly by the EU and the Council of Europe, as well as by individual countries. Notable is the so-called RIC mechanism, under which the EU provided funds for the reconstruction of 34 Serbian Orthodox religious sites in Kosovo and Metohia that had been damaged in the 2004 Pogrom. The restoration of frescoes in the Bogorodica Ljeviška Church in Prizren is funded by donations from Bulgaria, the Czech Republic, Greece, Italy and the Russian Federation. The Russian Federation has also funded restoration works at the three other UNESCO cultural heritage sites: the Visoki Dečani Monastery, the Gračanica Monastery and the Bogorodica Ljeviška Monastery. The reconstruction was planned and monitored by the Council of Europe (RIC).[69]

Nationalization During the Communist Regime

On the grounds of the *Law on agrarian reform and colonization No. 64* of 27 August 1945, the state took away land and forests from the Serbian Orthodox Church and religious endowments (Clause 3, line 1, under 'v' and Clause 26). 'The surplus above 10 ha of the total area of fields, gardens, vineyards, orchards, commons and forests' was taken away from the churches, religious legacies, monasteries and religious institutions (Clause 8, line 1), with an exception that those of greater importance or historical value were left with up to 30 ha. According to Clause 7, line 1 of the *General law on managing expropriated and confiscated forest properties*, the owners were not given any compensation. Even in legal forms of appropriation in which compensation was provided for it amounted, without exception, to a symbolic sum.

Assets of endowments, both religious and secular, were also appropriated pursuant to the *Law on nationalization of leased buildings and building land*. All buildings passed to state ownership together with the land they had been built upon. Agrarian reform also consisted of large-scale confiscations, without any compensation for the owners.

Analysis of the available documentation has shown that the land of an area of at least 5,600 ha was confiscated in Kosovo and Metohia from the Serbian Orthodox Church, Diocese of Raška and Prizren.

The Republic of Serbia enacted the *Law on Restitution of Religious Property* in 2006 [Zakon o vraćanju imovine crkvama i verskim zajednicama],[70] but

69 Reconstruction Implementation Commission for Serbian Orthodox Religious Sites in Kosovo <www.coe.int/t/DG4/CULTUREHERITAGE/COOPERATION/RIC/inc/eng/mechanism.html> accessed 15 March 2013.

70 *Zakon o vraćanju (restituciji) imovine crkvama i verskim zajednicama [The Law on Restitution of Property to Churches and Religious Communities]*, Službeni glasnik R. Srbije [Official Gazette of the Republic of Serbia] 46/2006.

the application of this statute on the territory of Kosovo and Metohia remains subject to the solution of the status of the territory, as well as to coordination with the representatives of the international community. The nature of the matter, however, requires the urgent implementation of a provisional ban on the disposal of nationalized religious property in Kosovo and Metohia.

In contrast to the restitutions all over Eastern and Central Europe that ensued after the fall of the Berlin Wall, in Kosovo and Metohia restitution on a systemic level has not taken place to the present day, which represents the most significant limitation of ownership of religious institutions and the greatest impediment for the sustainability of their survival and continuation of service. Paradoxically, Western democracies, the United States in particular, who had the greatest influence on the international administration of Kosovo and Metohia from 1999 until 2008, have not enabled restitution of property appropriated during communism, although they had fully supported the same process after the fall of the Berlin Wall throughout Central and Eastern Europe.

Property Rights Violations Related to the Absence of Public Records and Planning/Zoning Misuses

A particular difficulty in protecting Serbian Orthodox religious and historical monuments, as well as property rights, arises from the fact that many municipalities in Kosovo and Metohia possess neither detailed zoning/regulation plans nor public real property records. Therefore individuals use the existing legal vacuum to occupy as much land as possible, most commonly with the full knowledge and support of municipal councils. Quite often third persons build facilities for various functions in the immediate vicinity of the holy places, endangering property rights and use for religious purposes. Reportedly, monks and nuns at some monasteries from time to time are not able to access parts of their institution's estate – particularly land outside monastery walls – due to safety concerns.[71]

According to the International Civilian Mission for Kosovo, during the period between 2007 and 2011, 'the threat (in respect of the special protective zones) is gradually shifting from the monument to the site and landscape surrounding the monuments, largely due to uncontrolled and illegal development, even within the perimeters of the protected CSP monuments' (ICO Progress Report 2011, 4).

71 US Department of State: Under Secretary for Democracy and Global Affairs: Bureau of Democracy, Human Rights, and Labor, *Report on International Religious Freedom 2009: Kosovo,* <www.state.gov/documents/organization/134432.pdf> accessed 15 March 2013.

Figure 12.6 Church of Mother of God Hodegetria at Mušutište (14th century) before it was demolished in 1999

Source: Serbian Orthodox Diocese of Raska and Prizren.

Figure 12.7 Remains of the Church of Mother of God Hodegetria at Mušutište (14th century), after it was set on fire and destroyed by explosives in 1999

Source: Serbian Orthodox Diocese of Raska and Prizren.

The Case of the Visoki Dečani Monastery

Limitations on property rights pertain to properties in the immediate vicinity of sacred/holy places that are protected as cultural assets.[72] For example, Executive decision No. 2005/5 on the Special Zone Area Dečani (UNMIK/IO/2005/5) defined the following limitations:

- There should be no building, reconstruction, industrial or commercial activity, including the exploitation of forests, water or mineral resources, without a proper authorization by UNMIK;
- The existing road, which remains under the supervision of KFOR, may not be widened without a proper authorization by UNMIK. Heavy commercial transport is not allowed on this road without authorization by KFOR and UNMIK;
- The municipal government must undertake proper measures considering any structure built without a properly issued building permit;
- The activities in and around the monastery must completely match the conventions and directives by UNESCO.

In spite of Executive decision No. 2005/5, a restaurant that had been built without any building permit in the immediate vicinity of the monastery in 2005 was additionally expanded in late November 2006. The owner of the illegal building commenced building a new tourist facility (more than 30m long) as well as wooden cabins that spoil the landscape around the monastery. To make the matter worse, the Municipality of Dečani proclaimed the area around the monastery to be an urban development zone, which amounted to an *ex post facto* approval of the illegal building, directly contravening the cited UNMIK decision.

A diplomatic and legal struggle to have the illegally built edifices in the vicinity of the Visoki Dečani Monastery removed was quite difficult due to the obstruction by the municipal government of Dečani. The solution was finally reached under strong international pressure, so that in January 2007 Kosovo Protection Corps members removed the illegal structures.

The Visoki Dečani Monastery has been involved in another high-profile dispute – a long-standing court case against two local socially owned enterprises over more than 20 ha of land located in the vicinity of the monastery. The land had been appropriated from the monastery by the communist regime after World War II, and returned to the monastery in 1997. The dispute was finally decided by the Kosovo Supreme Court in December 2012, which ruled in favour of the monastery. The ruling provoked a harsh response by the local (Albanian) municipal leadership, which severed relations with the monastery.

72 Branislav Todić and Milka Čanak-Medić, *Monastery of Dečani* (Museum in Priština, Mnemosyne Center, Monastery of Visoki Dečani 2005).

These cases highlight the importance of securing that both the local authorities and the international community comply with the provisions on institutional protection of Serbian Orthodox holy places in Kosovo and Metohia. Informal centres of influence are working at a local level, so that proper implementation of laws and regulations in this area requires constant pressure by international diplomatic and military circles. This need is best illustrated by the fact that the US Ambassador to Kosovo, HE Ms Jacobson, felt obliged to publicly state support for the enforcement of the Kosovo Supreme Court ruling regarding the claim of Dečani Monastery to 20 ha of land.[73]

Other Examples of Threats to Holy Places Related to Zoning, Development and Public Records

Regarding the illegal buildings near Gazimestan, Gorioč and Velika Hoča, the Special Envoy for Kosovo Martti Ahtisaari sent a letter to the head of UNMIK Joachim Rücker on 5 October 2006, suggesting that Rücker 'consider the measures that would include, if possible, a freeze on building other structures around the [*three above-mentioned*] objects until the decisions on protective zones are not finalized in the negotiation process ...' According to Ahtisaari's opinion, 'there are reasons to believe that building activities (around these objects) may have a goal to create facts in the area, which would complicate the negotiations and the later implementation of agreements'. In the Albanian-language press the representatives of temporary Kosovo institutions have denied that they were given any direction on this topic, so it remains unclear if Ahtisaari's proposal was accepted by UNMIK and if these measures have already, or will be implemented at all.

Simultaneously with the continuation of building near Gazimestan, terrain was cleared near the Gorioč Monastery, in the area which, according to the proposal by the 'Office of the Special Envoy of the Secretary-General of the United Nations for the future status process for Kosovo' (UNOSEK), should be within the protective zone of the monastery. The nuns noticed a bulldozer clearing the bushes and digging a trench. There was a serious possibility that an edifice was about to be built without the approval of the municipality government, which is a tried and trusted method for creating the situation of *fait accompli*, as Ahtisaari wrote to Rücker. Two swimming pools were also recently built in the immediate vicinity of the Gorioč Monastery, and music was played loudly all summer, disturbing the prayer rituals at the monastery.

73 'Američka ambasadorka u Prištini gđa. Trejsi Džekobson pozvala na poštovanje zakona i odluke Vrhovnog suda o imovinskim pravima manastira Dečani' ['American Ambassador to Prishtina Ms Tracy Jacobson Called for Respect of the Law and the Decision of the Supreme Court on Property Rights of Dečani Monastery'] (*Eparhija-prizren.com*, 31 January 2013) <www.eparhija-prizren.com/sr/vesti/americka-ambasadorka-u-pristini-gdja-trejsi-dzekobson-pozvala-na-postovanje-zakona-i-odluke-vr> accessed 15 March 2013.

Two years before (in 2004) a restaurant had been illegally built near the Visoki Dečani Monastery in a similar fashion, without any approval but with the knowledge of the municipal government, and that was one of the direct reasons why the protective zone of UNMIK was formed around the monastery.

There have been similar problems in the settlement Velika Hoča, the only one in the province with a heritage of 13 medieval churches and monasteries from the 12th to the 14th centuries and the only remaining examples of traditional secular architecture. Activities on building a new factory of cardboard packages had continued without any pause. The inhabitants of Hoča are particularly worried as the factory was close to their centuries-old famous vineyards. In addition, one businessman managed to lease a small factory of plastic mass, '18. Novembar', in a very controversial way from UNMIK's Privatization Agency. A court trial started at the municipality court in Orahovac regarding the title to the factory land, as a family from Velika Hoča produced documentation showing that the factory had been built on their land. It seems probable that the two factories will close the entrance into this only remaining Serbian village in the Orahovac municipality, with places of worship appearing in the endowments of Serbian kings since the 12th century (Church of St John, Church of St Nicholas, Church of St Stefan from the later period and so on).

Even though the Monastery of St Healers Cosmas and Damian in Zočište near Prizren had been razed to the ground in 1999 by an explosion and rebuilt in 2004 after the Pogrom, in 2011 the Orahovac municipal government commenced works for the construction of a road along the very edge of the special protective zone of that monastery, in violation of the Law on Special Protective Zones. The work resulted in damage to the monastery's walls.[74]

'Virtual' Special Protective Zones

On 20 February 2008, the so-called Assembly of Kosovo adopted the *Law on Special Protective Zones*.[75] Pursuant to this law, 45 sites listed in Annex V of the Comprehensive Proposal for the Kosovo Status Settlement have been granted the status of 'special protective zones'. These sites encompass Serbian Orthodox churches and monasteries, as well as the medieval town of Novo Brdo, the Vojnovic medieval bridge in Vucitrn, the medieval fortress in Zvečan and the Gazimestan memorial. Most of these zones are located in southern and western Kosovo. A special protective zone is defined in the law as follows:

74 US Department of State: Under Secretary for Democracy and Global Affairs: Bureau of Democracy, Human Rights, and Labor, *Report on International Religious Freedom 2011: Kosovo* <www.state.gov/j/drl/rls/irf/religiousfreedom/index.htm?dlid=192825> accessed 15 March 2013.

75 SPZ Law (Law Nr. 03/L-039 on Special Protective Zones) <www.assembly-kosova.org/common/docs/ligjet/2008_03-L039_en.pdf> accessed 15 March 2013.

> A 'Special Protective Zone' shall be an area defined by a map, or by a defined area surrounding a monument, building, group of buildings, ensemble, village, or historic town center that is safeguarded from any development or activity which could damage its historical, cultural, architectural or archeological context, natural environment or aesthetic visual setting. (SPZ Law, Article 2)

The Law on Special Protective Zones contains references to similar mechanisms in the Law on Cultural Heritage of 2006 and in the Law on Spatial Planning of 2003. A major objection of the International Civilian Office for Kosovo in a 2011 report alleged the lack of any mechanism for implementing and enforcing the Law on Cultural Heritage, that is, for protecting cultural heritage in a practical way (ICO Progress Report 2011, 11,12).

The objectives of the protective zones, according to the Comprehensive Proposal for the Kosovo Status Settlement, are: 'to provide for the peaceful existence and functioning of the sites to be protected; preserve their historical, cultural and natural environment, including the monastic way of life of the clergy; and prevent adverse development around them, while ensuring the best possible conditions for harmonious and sustainable development of the communities inhabiting the areas surrounding such sites' (Article 4.1, UNSC 2007b).

As of the beginning of 2013, KFOR was providing full-time protection on site of only two holy places: the Visoki Dečani Monastery and the Peć Patriarhate, after KFOR transferred responsibility for the protection of the Devič Monastery to the Kosovo police in 2012. Responsibility for the protection of a number of other special protection zones has been transferred to the Kosovo police. According to an ICO Report of September 2011, the Kosovo police at the time provided full-time protection for monasteries Gorioč, Budisavci, Gračanica, Holy Archangels and Zočište, while a greater number of sites were only monitored by regular patrols of Kosovo police (ICO Progress Report 2011, 18).

The International Civilian Office for Kosovo stressed that two of the UNESCO World Heritage sites, the Patriarchate of Peć and the Visoki Dečani Monastery, 'have been exposed to a number of construction activities which were not properly regulated, while there are many more planned activities which are restricted or even prohibited by SPZ provisions', as well as that 'the Church of the Holy Virgin Ljeviška, in the historic centre of Prizren ... is exposed to rapid and uncontrolled urban development all around it ... This is actually the case for many more CSP-listed monuments and their respective SPZs' (ICO Progress Report 2011, 17).

The main deficiency of the institutional set-up that the International Civilian Office for Kosovo perceived was the lack of requisite municipal spatial plans, as well as the lack of coordination of these plans with the regulation of the special protective zones (ICO Progress Report 2011, 25). However, it perceived that in the case of the Visoki Dečani Monastery a municipal spatial plan was being used contrary to the applicable regulations and with a clear agenda for grossly violating the Visoki Dečani Special Protective Zone – by the construction of a road right through it, leading to a planned border crossing with Montenegro (ICO Progress Report 2011, 21).

Property Rights Violations by Way of Denial of Ethnic-cultural Identity

A peculiar method of violating property rights, as well as of the denial of the Serb ethnic-cultural identity, manifests itself in claiming the Albanian provenance of local Serbian Orthodox religious and cultural heritage, particularly by way of changing toponyms. Although such attempts may seem naïve and ignorant when viewed separately, they can also be perceived as forming a carefully planned propaganda effort, designed to give birth to palpable results after a longer period of time, in synergy with the destruction of assets and bullying of the remaining population. The result of the effort is creation of the appearance of an academic polemic over the identity of the local religious and cultural heritage between two sides possessing roughly approximate seriousness and argumentation. In fact, historical facts on the Serbian Orthodox origin of local religious and cultural sites are faced with a plain political and nationalist program of instrumentalization of historical science.

The challenges of the Serbian Orthodox identity of holy places in Kosovo and Metohia are particularly clearly described by Clause 57 in the Report by the UN Special Envoy Kai Eide: 'The Serbian Orthodox Church is experiencing pressure against its identity. In addition to intimidation and threats, there are attempts to rewrite the history and origin of Serbian Orthodox heritage. They see uncontroversial and neutral names of streets in the vicinity of their sites being changed and "Albanized". The Kosovo Albanian leaders should react and bring a halt to these activities'.

Holy sites reflect profound religious identities of individuals and religious groups, where religion, history and politics converge.[76] In the case of Serbian Orthodoxy they also mark an important part of national identity. Any form of contesting, changing, suppressing or violating such identity may have grave consequences. At the same time, attempts at creating a new cultural identity of the holy sites violate fundamental property rights.

Freedom of Access to Holy Places

As the continuity of purpose of a holy place is one of its most important traits, and as the exercise of *sabornost* and religious services represent principal purposes of the holy places, freedom of access is the crucial precondition for maintaining the relationship between the holy place and the believers. Freedom of access

76 Oslo Center 2008, *Statement of Intention on a Code for Holy Sites. The Oslo Center for Peace and Human Rights* <www.oslocenter.no/index.php?option=com_content&task=view&id=122〈=en> accessed 15 March 2013.

represents the basic foundation of free and undisrupted expression of individual and collective religious freedom.

The Serbian Orthodox Church does not limit or condition access in any way to any of the holy places. Fees for entry are not charged, and the only condition is that bare skin on the body, arms and legs is covered before entering certain churches.

However, in many cases the owner does not have any power to guarantee free access to the Serbs. For example, the clerics and monks of the Church of Mother of God Hodegetria at Mušutište, the Church of St George at Rečani and the Monastery of the Presentation of the Mother of God at Dolac were forced out of their properties and since 1999 have remained unable to enter the holy places themselves. In most other cases, clerics and monks maintain the holy places in a hostile environment so that, due to the high security risk, every visit has to be arranged in advance and an armed escort obtained from KFOR. The very complexity of these procedures amounts to restriction of access. As a result, the devotees visit these places less often, only during the most important religious holidays. Even on the Day of the Dead, when the internally displaced Serbs feel the need to visit their ancestral graveyards, the visitors are threatened by bullying, and by physical and death threats.[77]

Examples of Disruption and/or Prevention of Access to Holy Places

Holiday Zadušnice (All Souls' Day) is the occasion on which members of the Serbian Orthodox Church pay respect to the souls of their ancestors and deceased family members. The atmosphere on that day is sad and solemn. However, on 4 November 2006, several dozens of Albanians used vehicles and chopped trees to block the road in the immediate vicinity of the graveyard in the village Lešane near Suva Reka, thus preventing refugees and internally displaced Serbs from visiting the graves of their relatives.[78] Assaults, insults and humiliating treatment of the Serbian Orthodox population intending to visit their family members' graves on this holiday have become a regular practice.

According to the US Department of State *Annual International Religious Freedom Report for Kosovo* for 2008,[79] Serbian pilgrims travelling by bus from Serbia to attend services at the Visoki Dečani Monastery often had rocks thrown at

---

77 US Department of State, *Report on International Religious Freedom 2009: Kosovo*, op. cit.

78 'Mitrovdanske Zadušnice na Kosovu i Metohiji: Albanci blokadama puta zaustavili autobus Srba kod Suve Reke' ['Mitrovdan All Souls' Day at Kosovo and Metohia: Albanians blocked the road in order to stop a bus full of Serbs near Suva Reka'] (*KIM Info-bilten*, 4 November 2006) <www.kosovo.net/news/archive/2006/November_04/1.html> accessed 15 March 2013.

79 US Department of State: Under Secretary for Democracy and Global Affairs: Bureau of Democracy, Human Rights, and Labor, *Report on International Religious*

their vehicles. In the western municipalities of Peć, Dečani, Djakovica, Istok, Klina and Srbica, as well as in south Mitrovica (areas that include the monasteries of the Peć Patriarchate, Dečani, Gorioč, Budisavci, and Devič), clergy requested and received KFOR escorts. Clergy stated that they could not visit Church members in the west (where the most important SOC holy sites are located) without an escort, and members cited threats to their security as impediments to their ability to visit holy sites.

The UN Secretary-General noted that the number of pilgrims attending Christmas services (according to the Julian calendar adhered to by the Serbian Orthodox Church) throughout Kosovo on 7 January 2013 was far lower than usual as a result of threats by local Albanian activist groups to hold protests directed at such services.

Security Responsibilities with Respect to Holy Places

Security of access to Serbian Orthodox holy places and public order at and around the holy places form part of the freedom of access. The main obstacle to freedom of access in the case of Serbian Orthodox holy places in Kosovo and Metohia is the lack of security.

The severity of the problems related to protection and safety is clearly described in the report by the UN Special Envoy Kai Eide. Clause 55 states:

> The Serbian Orthodox religious sites and institutions represent a critical element of the spiritual fabric of Kosovo Serb society. The sustainability of the Serb community in Kosovo and Metohia is related to the preservation of its cultural and religious heritage. However, the Serbian Orthodox sites also represent more than an important part of Serb identity. They are a part of the world cultural heritage. Many of these sites have been seriously damaged or destroyed since 1999. Finally, the reconstruction is now about to start. However, they will continue to need protection. While the readiness of KFOR to maintain its protection of religious sites is essential, a durable solution cannot be built on military forces.

According to the US Department of State *Annual International Religious Freedom Report for Kosovo* for 2009, numerous incidents directed against the Serbian Orthodox community and property continued to take place, including threats, thefts and vandalism.

The destruction of religious objects results not only from the ethnic antagonisms but also from the traditionally different attitudes towards heritage between the

---

Freedom 2008: Kosovo http://www.state.gov/g/drl/rls/irf/2008/109483.htm> accessed 15 March 2013.

natives protecting their ancestral holy places and the newcomers who tend to clear the space for new development.

Until 2010, KFOR was primarily entrusted with the security of key holy Serbian Orthodox places in Kosovo and Metohia, so that between 2004 and 2010 a total of eight holy places were under full-time on-site KFOR protection (ICO Progress Report 2011, 24). A gradual transfer of security responsibilities from KFOR to the Kosovo police began in 2010, when a total of six sites were transferred officially, while unofficially Kosovo police began guarding, in the course of 2010 and 2011, another 17 sites (US Report on Intl. Relig. Freedom 2011). As of February 2013, as mentioned above, only two sites remain under full-time KFOR protection – the Patriarchate of Peć and the Visoki Dečani Monastery.

The Secretary-General assessed in April 2012 that 'crimes affecting minority communities, including intimidation, assault, theft, arson, vandalism and damage to Serbian Orthodox churches and household property, appeared to be on the increase from the same period one year ago'.[80]

For example, at the Devič Monastery near Srbica, the Kosovo police have taken over from KFOR the responsibility for securing the monastery complex. Without the permanent supervision by international military forces (KFOR) in the first decade after 1999, the survival of the monastic order would not have been possible due to the high level of hostility of the local community (Albanian majority). In the spring of 1999 the monastery was looted, the plate on the shrine of St Joannicius was broken, and the icons were desecrated. In the years that followed, the problem was aggravated by the attitude of certain members of the international forces in Kosovo and Metohia, which was more one of passive bystanders than of active guarantors of safety. The drastic proof were the events in March 2004, when the French forces of KFOR, after the announcement of a new attack, evacuated the sisterhood from the monastery without the consent of their monastic order, which was then followed by the infliction of severe damage on the church and other buildings. The monastery was looted, burned and devastated, and the graveyard was desecrated. At the Church of the Presentation of the Mother of God, the grave of St Joannicius was broken and desecrated, the iconostasis and movables were burnt and the wall paintings were heavily damaged with a layer of soot and carved graffiti. The whole complex was set on fire and completely demolished (Figures 12.4 and 12.8). The infrastructure was also destroyed: the systems of water supply and removal of waste water, as well as electric installations.

80 UN Security Council, *Report of the Secretary-General on the United Nations Interim Administration Mission in Kosovo* (S/2012/275, 27 April 2012) <www.un.org/ga/search/view_doc.asp?symbol=S/2012/275> accessed 15 March 2013.

Figure 12.8 Remains of the Devič Monastery, after it was burned and demolished in March 2004

Source: The Information Service of the Serbian Orthodox Church.

The Case of Prizren

The lack of power and/or of decisive willingness on the part of the forces in charge of security is particularly visible in the case of a consecutive series of destructive acts against Serbian Orthodox holy places in the old town of Prizren.

I

The medieval Church of St Nicolas, from the 14th century, was destroyed, and the Church of Sveta Tri Jerarha [St Three Wise Men] (built in the 19th century on the foundations of a church from the 14th century) was damaged. All this happened after the arrival of KFOR in June 1999.

II

During the March pogrom in 2004, the following churches and buildings of the Serbian Orthodox Church in or near Prizren were heavily damaged, looted or destroyed:

1. Temple of the Mother of God Ljeviška was burnt from the inside, 12th–14th century frescoes were heavily damaged, the altar area was desecrated, the top of the altar was broken (Figure 12.9), parts of the structure and exterior, especially the ornaments around the windows and openings, were heavily damaged;
2. The Temple of Christ the Savior (14th century) was burned and the frescoes were damaged;
3. Saborni Hram Sv Đorđa [The Cathedral Temple of St George] (1856) was set on fire and demolished by explosives (Figure 12.10);
4. The Church of St Nicolas (Tutić, 14th century) was burned inside and desecrated;
5. The Church of St George (Runović, 16th century) was burned inside, while frescoes from the 16th century were heavily damaged;
6. The Church of Holy Sunday at Potkaljaja (14th century, later reconstructed) was burned;
7. The Church of St Pantelejmon at Potkaljaja (16th century, later reconstructed) was burned;
8. The Church of St Cosmas and Damian at Potkaljaja (14th century, later reconstructed) was damaged;
9. The School of Theology of St Cyril and Methodius was burnt and heavily damaged; and
10. The Bishop's Palace was burnt.

III

Since the process of renewal of churches in Prizren since 2005, numerous instances of stealing the roof topping which is made of lead and tin have occurred. For example, 50 kg of lead roofing was stolen from the Church of the Holy Virgin Ljeviška in October 2007, and 30 kg were stolen from the Church of Saint Kyriake, with a monetary value of €10,400 (US Report on Intl. Relig. Freedom 2008).

In September 2011, the School of Theology (seminary) in Prizren was reopened after 12 years, after it had been rebuilt by the European Agency for Reconstruction (US Report on Intl. Relig. Freedom 2011).

Devastated Holy Places

Destroyed and deserted holy places are left without any protection. One example is the deserted Church of the Mother of God Hodegetria at Mušutište near Suva Reka, from the early 14th century, which was set on fire and demolished by explosives in 1999 (Figures 12.6 and 12.7). Since then, there have been no priests at the church and religious services have not been performed. All the buildings around the church were burnt down, as well as the centennial pine tree forest in the churchyard. All this happened after the deployment of KFOR. This holy place has remained vacant. Looting and further devastation are highly probable.

Figure 12.9 The broken altar and violated altar space of the Church of the Holy Mother of God Ljeviška in Prizren

Source: The Information Service of the Serbian Orthodox Church.

Figure 12.10 Charred front wall of the Cathedral Temple of the Holy Great-Martyr George after the temple was burned and mined in March 2004

Source: The Information Service of the Serbian Orthodox Church.

The Church of St George at Rečani near Suva Reka, from the second half of the 14th century, was mined, destroyed and deserted in 1999, after the arrival of KFOR (Figure 12.11). Since then, this sacred place has remained completely vacant as well.

Exceptionally, the Monastery of the Presentation of the Mother of God at Dolac near Klina was still guarded by the Kosovo police in 2008, although it was deserted. The church was built in the late 14th century, and is commonly known as Sveta Prečista (the Holy Most Pure): the bell tower and the lodges were destroyed with explosives and by mechanical means after the arrival of Italian forces of KFOR in 1999. By 2011, Kosovo police stopped securing the site (ICO Progress Report 2011, 18).

Persistent Attacks

Due to a very high degree of intolerance shown by the local majority Albanian population, the Monastery of Saints Healers Cosmas and Damian at Zočište is guarded by Kosovo police. On 17 June 1999 the church was burnt and the monastic brotherhood was forced out of the monastery. In September of the same year the church was completely destroyed with explosives and the monastery buildings were burnt (Figure 12.12). The monastery graveyard was also heavily damaged. The monastery was later restored (Figure 12.13), but physical access to it remains extremely difficult for Orthodox believers.

The Church of Presentation of the Mother of God at Lipljan (with the church of St Flora and St Lavra) is guarded by Kosovo police as well. There is constant tension due to the open hostility of a majority Albanian community toward the Serbs and Serbian Orthodox priests. Although KFOR units prevented both churches from being burned during the March pogrom in 2004, provocations by local people are still common.

The attitude of the majority Albanian community toward the Serb devotees and Serbian Orthodox priests of the Church of St Nicolas at Gnjilane is hostile. The front wall and the southern facade of the church were damaged with a hand grenade in 2000. On 19 October 2007 a flammable device (assumed to be a Molotov cocktail) was thrown at the church, but failed to cause significant damage.

The Visoki Dečani Monastery is guarded by KFOR (monastery complex) and Kosovo police (monastery land and forests in the immediate surroundings). Without the permanent protection by KFOR, the survival of the monks would not be possible. From 1999 until March 2007, grenades were thrown at the monastery on four occasions, encompassing a total of 23 grenades.

Visoki Dečani assumes the highest profile among Serbian holy places, along with the Patriarchate of Peć. Only these two have remained under KFOR protection as of the beginning of 2013, while responsibility for protecting other holy sites has been transferred to the Kosovo police. In spite of this high profile, throughout the first two months of 2013 the Visoki Dečani Monastery has been faced with a prolonged pressure of violent protesters threatening to break into

Figure 12.11 UNESCO experts observe the remnants of the Church of St. George in Rečani near Suva Reka, which was completely levelled to the ground in the summer of 1999

Source: The Information Service of the Serbian Orthodox Church

Figure 12.12 The Church of Saint Healers Cosmas and Damian in Zočište was levelled to the ground in September 1999 with explosives

Figure 12.13 The first service on the day of Saint Healers Cosmas and Damian in the restored church devoted to these saints in Zočište, in November 2006

Source: Serbian Orthodox Diocese of Raška and Prizren, KIM Info Service

the monastery complex as a result of the local Albanian community's discontent with the decision of the Kosovo Supreme Court that some 20 ha of land belong to monastery.[81]

The most recent series of attacks on Serbian cultural and religious heritage in Kosovo and Metohia took place in the night between 20 and 21 January 2013, when several dozens of Serbian graves were desecrated throughout Kosovo and Metohia, including the desecration of 27 tombstones in the village of Klokot, the burning of a cemetery chapel and destruction of several graves in the village of Miloševo, destruction with explosives of a tombstone in Prilužje and desecration of 50 Serbian graves in the cemetery of Prizren. A group of Albanians in the town of Djakovica headed for the nearby Serb Orthodox monastery, but was prevented from reaching it by KFOR and the Kosovo police.

The cited cases were mentioned only as the most drastic examples of security threats and violations, while attacks of lesser intensity on priests, devotees and holy objects have been much more numerous. Adequate protection of holy places and devotees has thus not been provided, and the feeling of insecurity is very pronounced.

The diocese of the Serbian Orthodox Church that encompasses most of Kosovo and Metohia is the Diocese of Raška and Prizren. The Bishop of Raška and Prizren H.G. Teodosije stated in January 2013 that 'the security situation in Kosovo was at the lowest level since March 2004 Pogrom'.[82] Such an assessment is supported by the shift of the Threat Intensity Coefficient, a tool within the UNESCO World Heritage in Danger List. This coefficient has steadily risen from the value of 0 in 2006 to 60 (out of a maximum 100) in 2011 for the 'Medieval Monuments in Kosovo', that is, a group of four Serbian Orthodox monasteries included in the abovementioned list.It is obvious that the primary task in protecting holy places is to guarantee their basic security. Various aspects of security provision must be adequately regulated and implemented vigorously. As presently the feeling of insecurity among priests and monks of the Serbian Orthodox holy places, as well as among the believers, is very pronounced, the issue of security should involve the serious involvement of local and international institutions.

---

81 'Situacija u manastiru Dečani mirna, ali neizvesna – organizatori demonstracija najavljuju upad u manastirsko imanje' ['Situation in Dečani Monastery calm but unpredictable – organizers of demonstrations announce incursion into Monastery complex'] (Eparhija-prizren.com, 9 February 2013) <www.eparhija-prizren.com/sr/vesti/situacija-u-manastiru-decani-mirna-ali-neizvesna-organizatori-demonstracija-najavljuju-upad-u-> accessed 15 March 2013.

82 'Bishop Teodosije: Security situation in Kosovo at the lowest level since March pogrom 2004' (*Eparhija-prizren.com*, 24 January 2013) <www.eparhija-prizren.com/en/news/bishop-teodosije-security-situation-kosovo-lowest-level-march-pogrom-2004> accessed 15 March 2013.

Proposals for the New Legal Framework for Holy Places

Present International Legal Framework for Cultural Heritage Protection

The UNESCO Declaration concerning the Intentional Destruction of Cultural Heritage listed principal international law provisions serving the purpose of protection of cultural heritage.[83] The rules applicable to armed conflicts encompass the 1954 Hague Convention for the Protection of Cultural Property in the Event of Armed Conflict and its two – 1954 and 1999 – Protocols.[84] Certain prominent members of the international community, that is the USA, have not signed the Convention and its Protocols, but recognize that certain provision of the Convention form part of the international customary law.[85] In addition, Article 53 of Protocol I, as well as Article 16 of Protocol II to the 1949 Geneva Conventions, forbid directing hostilities at, as well as military use of, 'historic monuments, works of art and places of worship which constitute the spiritual and cultural heritage of peoples'.[86]

Peace-time protection should be directed by the principles and objectives of the 1972 UNESCO Convention for the Protection of the World Cultural and Natural Heritage, as well as by the 1956 Recommendation on International Principles Applicable to Archaeological Excavations, the 1968 Recommendation concerning the Preservation of Cultural Property Endangered by Public or Private Works, the 1972 Recommendation concerning the Protection, at National Level, of the Cultural and Natural Heritage and the 1976 Recommendation concerning the Safeguarding and Contemporary Role of Historic Areas. The oversight of the implementation of the 1972 UNESCO Convention was confided to the World Heritage Committee, which in turn from time to time issues operational guidelines for the Implementation of the World Heritage Convention. Besides detailed provisions on listing properties as world heritage and maintaining them on the list,

---

83 Declaration concerning the Intentional Destruction of Cultural Heritage, Adopted by the 32nd session of the UNESCO General Conference, Paris, 17 October 2003 <http://portal.unesco.org/en/ev.php-URL_ID=17718&URL_DO=DO_TOPIC&URL_SECTION=201.html> accessed 15 March 2013.

84 Convention for the Protection of Cultural Property in the Event of Armed Conflict with Regulations for the Execution of the Convention 1954, First Protocol of 1954, Second Protocol, of 1999 <http://portal.unesco.org/en/ev.php-URL_ID=13637&URL_DO=DO_TOPIC&URL_SECTION=201.html> accessed 15 March 2013.

85 Patty Gerstenblith, 'Protecting Cultural Heritage in Armed Conflict: Looking Back, Looking Forward' (2009) *Cardozo Public Law, Policy & Ethics Journal* 677.

86 Protocol Additional to the Geneva Conventions of 12 August 1949, and relating to the Protection of Victims of International Armed Conflicts (Protocol I), 8 June 1977, and Protocol Additional to the Geneva Conventions of 12 August 1949, and relating to the Protection of Victims of Non-International Armed Conflicts (Protocol II), 8 June 1977 <www.icrc.org/Web/Eng/siteeng0.nsf/html/genevaconventions#a4> accessed 15 March 2013.

the guidelines in greater detail define the criteria of authenticity and/or integrity that properties proposed for listing need to fulfil, as well as the requirements on protection and management of the protected properties.[87]

In addition, intentional destruction of cultural heritage is punishable under Articles 8(2)(b)(ix) and 8(2)(e)(iv) of the Rome Statute of the International Criminal Court, as well as under Article 3(d) of the Statute of the International Criminal Tribunal for the former Yugoslavia, within the chronological and geographical limitations applicable.

An indispensable supplement to binding treaties are the principles, recommendations and standards promulgated by ICOMOS – International Council on Monuments and Sites – an international non-governmental organization of professionals dedicated to the conservation of the world's historic monuments and sites. The Venice Charter of 1964 is important, for it clearly defined the concepts of a historic monument, as well as its conservation and restoration.[88] The Charter for the Protection and Management of the Archaeological Heritage provided principles of recommended protection for a much wider target of 'archaeological heritage', defining it as all material heritage subject to archaeological methods.[89] Besides protection, all remedial measures in connection with a monument can fall into two other categories: reconstruction and restoration. A number of declarations by ICOMOS or other similar international expert bodies have been issued, setting forth principles that should govern the application of reconstruction and restoration. Among other documents, of particular importance for Kosovo and Metohia issues may be Recommendations for the Analysis, Conservation and Structural Restoration of Architectural Heritage.[90]

The Need for Additional Protection

Several reasons for the immediate and decisive protection of sacred/holy places in Kosovo and Metohia are of equal importance: the holy places belong to the common cultural heritage of humanity; they are indivisible from the protection of both the religious freedom and minority rights, if applicable, of the community

87 UNESCO World Heritage Centre, *Operational Guidelines for the Implementation of the World Heritage Convention* (January 2008 WHC 08/01) <http://whc.unesco.org/en/guidelines> accessed 15 March 2013.

88 International Council on Monuments and Sites, *The Venice Charter – International Charter for the Conservation and Restoration of Monuments and Sites* <http://www.icomos.org/venice_charter.html> accessed 15 March 2013.

89 International Council on Monuments and Sites, *Charter for the Protection and Management of the Archaeological Heritage* <www.international.icomos.org/e_archae.htm> accessed 15 March 2013.

90 ICOMOS – International Scientific Committee, Recommendations for the Analysis, Conservation and Structural Restoration of Architectural Heritage for Analysis and Restoration of Structures of Architectural Heritage <www.civil.uminho.pt/masonry/Publications/Recommendations_ICOMOS.pdf> accessed 15 March 2013.

they belong to; the lack of regulation of their status is conducive to conflicts between different religious groups and so on. A balanced approach to each of the cited (and other) reasons would lead to the development and implementation of a new legal framework that would be elastic enough to be applicable to a great number of vastly different cases. In contrast to holy places situated in safe environments, such as Mount Athos, the Vatican or Mecca, the holy places in Kosovo and Metohia should be put under a special regime of protection, as most of them are located within in an insufficiently tolerant religious, political and social environment. Their owners and believers represent a religious minority in the present circumstances, so that additional mechanisms of special protection should be provided.

Protection and Politics

Some of the risks are highly idiosyncratic for the Orthodox holy places in Kosovo and Metohia, although probably in some other theatres of centennial historical conflicts there are probably analogous cases and similar circumstances under which holy places are more than cultural monuments and represent the cornerstones of religious and ethnic identity, giving them a particularly wide political importance. In an environment of political conflict, traditional legal concepts and existing mechanisms of protection turn out to be tragically useless. This brings into focus propositions for developing and establishing a new, internationally acceptable legal framework, which would preserve the common global and local heritage even in situations when all other means prove inefficient. This particularly includes holy places in foreign or hostile surroundings.

Most of the Serbian Orthodox holy places had legal protection as cultural assets, with a substantial number belonging to the highest category of conservation. However, that has not saved them from violence. As already mentioned, all four holy places that had been included in the UNESCO List of Cultural Heritage were also included in the List of World Heritage in Danger.[91] The Serbian Law on Cultural Assets, the listing by UNESCO and the regulations of the Kosovo secessionist authorities have all proved to be insufficient for securing protection of these holy places.

The existing laws and regulations have effectively failed not because of their incompleteness or poor wording, or because they lacked the capacity for their implementation, but primarily because there were political and other interests that obstructed their implementation. However, from a legislative perspective, the disadvantage of these laws (when applied to holy places) was the fact that

91 UNESCO World Heritage Centre, World Heritage Committee puts Medieval Monuments in Kosovo on Danger List and extends site in Andorra, ending this year's inscriptions <http://whc.unesco.org/en/news/268> accessed 15 March 2013; UNESCO World Heritage Centre, *Medieval Monuments in Kosovo* <http://whc.unesco.org/en/list/724/indicators/> accessed 15 March 2013.

they dealt primarily with the protection of the materialization of artistic-historical values included under the term 'heritage', while they remained inept to capture the unique interrelatedness of religious freedom, and the national, cultural and spiritual identity with the physical protection of holy places. To this end a new approach to the legal protection of holy places is needed.

Proposed Objects of the New Model of Protection

The study of the situation in which Serbian Orthodox holy places in Kosovo and Metohia presently find themselves has shown that they are being subjected to continuous and systematic isolation from their religious community, mostly through:

- Emigration of the Serbian Orthodox population, caused by the well-founded perception of insecurity;
- Changes of the ethnic structure in the area surrounding holy places;
- Illegal development in the immediate vicinity of holy places.

By the same token, had the holy places been properly protected, it would have in turn substantially improved the chances of survival and/or return of refugees to Serbian Orthodox communities in the region. Preserving holy places means at the same time protecting the most basic human rights of the Serbian Orthodox believers.

The fact that Serbs consider the monuments of sacred heritage in Kosovo and Metohia to be their ethnic holy places, and the territory of Kosovo and Metohia to be their spiritual cradle and a sacred place of suffering cannot be ignored, nor can it be ignored that holy sites in Kosovo and Metohia have been exposed to intentional destruction precisely due to their significance to the Serbian Orthodox population. This type of significance for national and ethnic identity should not be regarded as an anachronism and obsession with the past, but should instead be treated in accordance with relevant international human rights treaties and standards.

Therefore the object of protection should be the entire complex of rights, which includes property rights to buildings and land, preservation of the architectural/cultural environment of surrounding areas, safety of the holy places, as such, and of the monks and clerics who maintain their religious use, as well as of the believers whose religious freedom substantially consists of the right to access the holy places.

Along the proposed lines, the object of protection could be defined as

- the undeniable right of the (Serbian Orthodox) religious community to undisrupted, limitless and safe access to Orthodox holy places,
- guaranteeing protection of religious and cultural-historic values of the holy places,
- as well as the safety, self-governance and economic functionality

(sustainability) of the religious entities that use and maintain the holy places,
- particularly including protection of pertinent property rights and preservation of the architectural and cultural identity of the areas surrounding the holy places.

Such an approach would shift the focus of the protection of the holy places from the domain of heritage into the domain of human rights. International pressure in favour of the respect of human rights seems to be much stronger and more efficient than consequences for breaking conventions and laws on heritage conservation, and, more importantly, the predicament of the Serbian Orthodox holy places in Kosovo and Metohia, as has been shown throughout this chapter, judging by its motives and direct consequences, deserves by all means to be treated within the framework of human rights and minorities protection.

Survival and Sustainable Preservation of Holy Places – Possible Paths

Three concepts, which can easily be referred to as the 3Rs, stand out as being crucial for enabling the survival and sustainable preservation of the sacred places in Kosovo and Metohia. At the same time, these concepts are directly related to internationally recognized rights, along with those that directly fall within the basic human rights framework, such as security, free access and so on:

Restitution is indispensible if the property rights of the Serbian Orthodox community are to be respected. As His Eminence Cardinal Cottier said at the Conference on Holy Places and Religious Institutions, on 10–11 December 2008 in Rome, '(the subject of ownership is a fundamental issue of religious freedom)'. Respect for private property would be an important pillar of survival of the holy/sacred places (areas, zones). The fear of sanctions for violations of private property and of compensation for damages should join the set of instruments for preventing violation against holy places. Of course, it is also important to develop, at the same time, proper mechanisms for preventing the misuse of property rights related to sacred places. However, bearing in mind the immense appropriations conducted under communist rule, the first and most important step towards the affirmation of property rights related to sacred places would be the restitution of religious property.

Reconstruction (and preservation) is connected to the right to protection of cultural heritage. This issue is particularly important in cases in which the intentional violent destruction of sacred sites took place. The issues that should be considered are: liability for reconstruction costs (the public authorities, the wrongdoer, or the religious community as the owner), who should decide on who is contracted for the works and who the contractors can be (what kind of qualifications the experts should have – only technical and professional, or proper insight into the religious, cultural and artistic features of the tradition to which the destroyed sacred object had belonged), what kind of influence the religious institution as the owner should have on reconstruction and so on. Reconstruction and preservation should be performed in accordance with the religious and overall identity of its owner and under his supervision, in order to secure that changes are not made to the character and features of the destroyed or damaged holy site.

Revitalization depends on the respect of the right of worship and right to access. It would be meaningless to reconstruct a sacred site as a tourist attraction and historical monument, so that it cannot any more serve the religious function of the believers, particularly as a place of active pilgrimage and of living religion and community life. The goal should not be to merely recreate the subject monument in the physical sense, but to preserve the religious dynamics related to the holy site. Revitalization is a security issue too, and may contribute to political stability in the society. In the case of Kosovo and Metohia, the first precondition for revitalization is the fourth R – the *repatriation* of refugees and displaced persons who had originally inhabited such sacred areas. Unfortunately, instead of returning, the 'internally displaced persons (IDPs)' continue to flee their 'Holy Land' of Kosovo and Metohia.

The idiosyncratic feature of the holy places in Kosovo and Metohia is that their protection is not merely a matter of cultural heritage protection, nor it is only a question of religious freedom, but it has also become a matter of minority protection, for the Serbian population has for the most part been expelled from the area by violent means, during the period that started with the outbreak of World War II, and this expulsion has still not ended. In the course of promoting both freedom of religion and minority rights as fundamental human rights and a source of stability in all societies, it is particularly necessary to secure respect and protection for the sacred places and areas of all religions. The holy/sacred places should be protected from desecration and other forms of violation, as well as from any kind of intimidation of, and threats to, devotees. The most important issue is freedom of access of the devotees to places sacred to them, so that holy sites can be preserved as venues of living religious experience by enabling individuals and groups to exercise their faith at holy places.

Toward a New Legal Framework

The new model of protection of holy places needs to be implemented in phases. A multilateral treaty, preferably under the auspices of the United Nations, would be ideal for securing grounds for regional and bilateral treaties, as well as national statutes and other legal instruments. Since the issues involved are quite complex, it is probable that the statutes would leave excessive room to the wording of bylaws and technical regulations, so great care should be invested in ensuring that such acts be appropriately drafted. Finally, the specific synthesis of human rights and cultural heritage protection frameworks would demand that mechanisms for ensuring the reliable, efficient and appropriate implementation of such legal frameworks be put in place.

In parallel, the predicament that is currently affecting the holy sites in Kosovo and Metohia – and consequently the Serbian Orthodox community whose identity is intrinsically related to these holy sites – requires new tools to exert influence over public authorities. The public authorities should be obliged to stringently abide by and apply the existing international legal standards and obligations, as well as the existing laws and regulations on human rights, minority and cultural heritage protection in respect of holy sites and communities whose identities are tied to such sites. Experience so far in the case of Kosovo and Metohia suggests that such implementation cannot be expected from the provisional and secessionist local authorities without substantial involvement and supervision by the international community.

The protection of holy places represents a focal point at which the responsibilities and rights of religious organizations, local authorities, national government and the international community intersect. The suggested approach, if applied by all stakeholders, may provide room for the hope that the status of holy sites can be appropriately regulated, so that the holy sites cease to be the subject of conflicts and become venues of mutual understanding and landmarks of common religious heritage.

In cases in which holy places are located in an extremely hostile environment, so that the threat of their complete destruction exists, terms for establishing permanent international military missions should be envisaged.

Elements for Applying the New Legal Framework to the Case of Kosovo and Metohia

Fourteen years after the war in which the Federal Republic of Yugoslavia was forced to abandon most of its prerogatives of sovereignty over Kosovo and Metohia, the process of the return of refugees from Serbia to Kosovo and Metohia has not as yet commenced. The passage of time makes commencement of that process at this or at an even later point in time highly improbable.

Most of the Serb Orthodox holy places are located in the part of Kosovo and Metohia inhabited by ethnic Albanians. These holy places are of key importance for the religious, cultural and traditional identity of the Serbian nation. In spite of such importance, with the gradual departure of KFOR and the decrease in the size of the International Civilian Mission, Serb Orthodox holy places remain vulnerable to a possible new series of destructive attacks, similar to those that transpired in the summer of 1999, or in March 2004.

Any claim that the police protection provided by the secessionist authorities of Kosovo may serve as assurance against the possibility of such widespread destruction of Serb Orthodox holy places may be rebutted by a two facts: the Kosovo secessionist authorities have been unable, or unwilling, to secure the sustainability of free access to Serb Orthodox holy places, as well as to protect these holy places from the encroachment of adjacent illegal construction and the resulting gradual degradation.

Notwithstanding the future course and outcome of the ongoing dispute over the statehood of Kosovo, and having in mind that the threat of the complete destruction of Serb Orthodox holy places in Kosovo and Metohia is real, serious and has been increasing since the unilateral declaration of independence in 2008, as long as Serbia is effectively deprived of sovereignty over Kosovo, the only possible legal grounds that may warrant security for the holy places is some form of extraterritorial status for the holy places. Such status would entail partial or complete loss of sovereignty over the holy places by the political community from which the threat of destruction originates which, in the case at hand, are the secessionist authorities of Kosovo.

Even if the threat of complete destruction in a massive series of attacks is set aside, trends of all aspects necessary for sustainability of holy places in the medium term – freedom of access, zoning protection, security of pilgrims and clerics, property rights – fail to show any material improvement during the period from 1999 until 2012. It is therefore evident that, *rebus sic stantibus*, the Serbian Orthodox holy places are faced with gradual and imminent disappearance.

UNSC Resolution 1244(1999) expressly provided for the return of Serbian security forces to Kosovo and Metohia, with the limited aim of securing holy places. This provision may only be interpreted as allowing Serbia to preserve sovereignty over the holy places notwithstanding what the 'political settlement' turns out to be.

The essential purpose of granting extraterritorial status to holy places would be the protection of religious freedom and other basic human rights.

The extraterritorial status, and/or security of the holy places located in a hostile environment should be effectively warranted by an international military mission. While the UN Security Council must approve any such mission, a broader framework for establishing and conducting such missions should be set forth by virtue of a specific multilateral treaty executed under the auspices of the UN. In the case of Kosovo and Metohia, the EU, as the global power with the greatest interest for peace and security in the subject region, as well as a global leader in the domain of protection of human rights, would be the most suitable power for conducting the mission. The participation of Serbian security forces in such a mission would be in accordance with UNSC 1244(1999).

Chapter 13
Sacred Places and Religious Institutions in Kosova

Comparative Legal and Religious Approach

Baki Svirca

Introduction

> ... it can never be said too often that questions of chronological priority in ancient history – who got there first – are simply irrelevant to deciding the rights and wrongs of any present-day political situation.[1]

With a surface of 10,887 km² (4,203 square miles), Kosova is located in south-eastern Europe, in the central region of the Balkan Peninsula. It borders on Albania to the south-west, Montenegro to the north-west, Serbia to the north and Macedonia to the east and south-west. Its territory lies between 41° 50' 58" and 43° 15' 42" of longitude and between 20° 01' 30" and 21° 48' 02" of latitude.

The State of Kosova is the youngest State in Europe, with a population of 1,739,825 inhabitants (in addition to 600,000 in the Diaspora). The ethnic structure is composed of 1,616,869 Albanians (92 per cent), 25,532 Serbs, 18,738 Turks, 27,533 Bosnians, 8,824 Roma, 15,436 Ashkali, 11,524 Egyptians, 10,265 Gorani, and 2,352 others.[2]

Religious freedom is a basic human right. Therefore every citizen of Kosova has the right to choose his/her affiliation (one can choose whether or not to have any religious affiliation, to maintain or change it or to manifest it publicly or privately). This is guaranteed by State laws.

Kosova's population is divided into three main religions:

- Muslim
- Catholic
- Orthodox

The religious affiliation of the majority of Kosova's population is Muslim (1,663,412), while the rest are Catholic (38,438), Orthodox (25,837) and non-religious (1,242).[3]

1 Noel Malcolm, *Kosovo: A Short History* (New York University Press 2001) 22.
2 <http://esk.rks-gov.net/rekos2011/> accessed 30 April 2013.
3 <http://esk.rks-gov.net/rekos2011/> accessed 30 April 2013.

In Kosova there is a large number of mosques, but the number of churches is not low either, for both Catholic and Orthodox. Many of these mosques and churches in Kosova are monuments with great historical and cultural value, being protected by law. Religious communities, in accordance with the laws in force, have their own educational institutions.[4]

The religious communities have the following number of buildings in use:

- Islamic religious buildings – around 750, and 600 are active
- Orthodox religious buildings – around 114, and 80 are active
- Catholic religious buildings – around 50, and 40 are active.

The best definition for religious coexistence in Kosova has been given by the Bishop of Prague, Vaclav Mali. After his visit to Kosova, in a press conference held in Prague, Monsignor Mali said: 'Kosova currently is a model of coexistence between Christians and Muslims for other parts of Europe. There is mutual understanding in the religious scene of Kosovo, especially between Muslims and Catholics, who are united because they are Albanian. The coexistence with the Serbian Orthodox Church was not easy, because unfortunately its leaders have tried the nationalist card'.[5]

With such diversity in ethnic and religious composition, it is natural for Kosova to have this reflected in the richness of its cultural heritage. This diversity is a result of the creativeness of the people of Kosova over centuries. Events in our past have not always respected this creative spirit. Knowing this and trying to prevent the same mistakes from being made again, the government of Kosova and the international community are engaged in creating a legal framework which promotes the cultural and spiritual richness of all communities.

The current legal framework of Kosova is made up of documents produced as a result of international conferences on the country, proposals for the definition of its political and legal status and of local legislation.

In the frame of international documents the cultural and religious heritage is dealt with in a variety of legal instruments:

1. Documents produced through discussion and negotiations on the political status of Kosova, known as the Ahtisaari package',
   - Annex V[6]
2. Kosova's Declaration of Independence[7]
   - Points 2, 3, 4, 5, 8 and 9
   - Constitution of the Republic of Kosovo (Articles 8; 19, §§ 1 and 2; 22;

4 <www.rks-gov.net/sq-AL/Qytetaret/KulturaDheKohaLire/Pages/Religjioni.aspx> accessed 30 April 2013.

5 <http://www.rtklive.com/arhive> accessed 30 April 2013.

6 From the name of the Former Finnish President Martti Ahtisaari, UN Special Envoy at the status process negotiations.

7 Declaration of Independence of Kosova made on 17th February 2008.

38; 39)
   - Article 145 point 1 and 2
3. Law on Cultural Heritage
4. Law on Special Protective Zones
5. Law on Freedom of Religion
6. Anti-Discrimination Law
   - Article 2 under a, c,
   - Article 6
   - Article 10
7. Law on Official Holidays
   - Article 2
8. Penal Code[8] (Chapters II, XIII, XIV,XVI, XXIII, XXIV)

History of Religion and Religious Heritage in Kosova

In Kosova religion has been an integral part of the history and life of society throughout the ages. The territory of today's Kosova was inhabited by an Illyrian tribe called the Dardanians.[9] According to the majority of experts of Illyrology (Fanulla Papazoglu, Aleksandër Stipçeviç, Neritan Ceka, Kristo Frashëri, Noel Malcolm and so on), this tribe was the largest Illyrian tribe living in the central part of the Balkan Peninsula.

The region where both Illyrians and Dardanians lived was among the first territories where Christianity spread. Dioceses in this territory have a 16-centuries-old tradition.[10] According to Monsignor Dr Don Gasper Gjini, Dardania was an ecclesiastical and administrative province with its Metropolia in Skupi (Skopje).[11] In sacred literature, this region was mentioned by Saint Paul: '… so that from Jerusalem and round about, even to Illyricum, I have fulfilled the Gospel of Christ …'[12] St Paul said: 'Today you preached the Word of the Lord not only in Macedonia and Achaia, and your faith in the Lord has spread in every place'[13] The spreading of the belief in one God in Dardania also had martyrs. Let us just mention here the case of two Dardanian martyrs, Florus and Laurus, who witnessed Christ in the ancient Ulpiana,[14] *sub Licinio Praeside*.[15] Both were martyrs at the time of

---

8 <www.assembly-kosova.org> accessed 30 April 2013.

9 Malcolm, op. cit.

10 Gasper Gjini, *Bishopric Shkup-Prizren in Centuries* (Drita 2002) 5.

11 Ibid., 5.

12 Ibid., 23.

13 Ibid., 23.

14 Archaeological locality in Kosova. It is located 11 kilometres south-east of Prishtina. According to ancient authors, it was established as a municipium in the year 168 and the name was given to honour the Roman Emperor Trajan (Marcus Ulpius Trainaus) who ruled from 98 to 117. So far only the Paleochristian basilica, a Roman Military Castrum, Necropolises and the northern gate of the city have been discovered.

15 Gjini, op. cit. 25.

the Roman Emperor Hadrian (117–38). In his writings, Farlati[16] says: '… Then he addressed them to Licinius, who gave them money to build a temple to idols. They distributed this money to the poor and then they built a temple. When they finished the temple they destroyed idols and dedicated it to Christ. When Licinius had heard this, he put both of them in a deep well, where they gave their souls to God'.[17] Knowing that – according to old writings – the two were martyrized in Ulpiana, we think that the temple built by them is the first Christian temple in Kosova. The foundations of this temple lie within the walls of the ancient city of Ulpiana. We also have other writings confirming the spreading of Christianity in Kosova. In his book *Illyricum Sacrum*, Farlati says that apostle Matthaeus was chosen instead of Judas to convert the Macedonians, Dardanians, Tribals and Bastarns to Christianity.[18] According to these references and resources on Christian missionaries, the Christian religion in Dardania was only established after the First General Council. As far as the ecclesiastical organization is concerned, we find the first records in the Council convened by the Roman Emperor Constantine in Nicaea in AD 325 where the name of the Bishop is also mentioned, that is, the Metropolitan of Dardania.[19] In the documents drawn up during this Council we also find the signature of the bishop of Dardania *Dacus Dadanieae*.[20] From the information of the time, which proves the participation of local bishops in the early Councils, we know that in Dardania there was a quite consolidated Church, with its religious buildings where religious ceremonies were held. Vestiges of these buildings can be seen in Kosova and are known as Paleochristian churches (that is, from Early Christianity). These churches date back to the 4th–6th centuries and in some places to the 8th century. Scholars who study such buildings consider them as examples of Paleochristian art.[21] Religious sites from this period are mainly chapels, churches and basilicas.[22] Here we can mention the remains of the Church of Saint Peter in the Korishe village of Prizren,[23] the Basilica in Ulpiana, another Basilica in Rahovec, the Ruins of the Monastery in Banja of Mitrovica and so on.[24]

Divisions within the Church in Dardania started very early. They began some six centuries before the split known as the Great Schism of the year 1054. The administrative division of the Roman Empiret had a great impact on this split. This impact was reflected in Illyricum itself as it was divided into two parts.[25]

16 Quoted in Gjini, op. cit. 5.

17 Ibid., 59.

18 Ibid., 25.

19 Ibid., 27.

20 Ibid., 30.

21 Fejaz Drançolli, *Ruining the Albanian Kulla* (Biblioteka Kombëtare dhe Universitare e Kosovës, 2004) 34.

22 Ibid., 33.

23 Ibid., 34.

24 Ibid., 35.

25 Illyricum was the land of Illyrians. This denomination in ancient times referred to the western part of the Balkan Peninsula.

The western region was put under the administration of the *praefectus pr. Italiae, Africae et Illyrici* and the eastern one under the *praefectus pr. Illyrici*. In eastern Illyricum there were the two dioceses of Dacia (Dardania and Macedonia) but later, in approximately 424–7, western Illyricum was also put under the jurisdiction of the Eastern Roman Empire.[26] The territorial manoeuvres of the emperor came as a result of disagreement between the Bishop of Rome and the Patriarch of Constantinople. Along this line, when this part of Illyricum was put under the eastern emperor, the patriarchs of Constantinople considered themselves entitled to put all the churches of this area under their own jurisdiction.[27]

There are numerous records about the Dardanian Church. These records can be found in some letters of the Pope, documents of councils and other correspondence of the time. Here we can mention a letter of Pope Innocent I of 3 August 494 ('*universis episcopis per Dardaniam sive per Illyricum constitutis*') entitled *Audientes orthodoxam*.[28] Indeed this was the time when some bishops were abandoning the rituals and the authority of the Roman Apostolic Church.

Another papal letter, which is important to prove the direction that the Church in Dardania took is *Suscepti regiminis* of the year 599 by Pope St Gregory the Great where he informs the metropolitans of Illyricum about the frictions within the Church of Constantinople because of the Synod, which was considered as 'ecumenical'. This letter was sent to the metropolitan of Justiniana Prima (Dardania), John.[29]

In addition to these papal letters, there is further evidence of correspondence between the bishops of Dardania, proving the organizational continuity of the Dardanian Church, despite disagreement and problems between the two churches.

Let us just mention the order of the Emperor Leo III who, in the year 733, separated western Illyricum from the Church of Rome and put it under the jurisdiction of the Patriarch of Constantinople.

Slavs penetrated the Balkans in the 7th century. These tribes were mainly pagan but according to Konstantin Porfirogenet,[30] they subsequently began to convert to Christianity thanks to Latin missionaries. However, although these records mention only missionaries, the largest wave of conversions among the Slavs took place at the time of the Bulgarian Empire. 'We can realize that the Slavic population, which settled Kosova, was under the influence of the Bulgarian Empire, which means that it was included in the dioceses of the Orthodox Church ...'[31]

The territory of Kosova was under Bulgarian domination from 850 until the 11th century; then the Byzantine rule was re-established. The latter continued until

26 Gjini, op. cit. 37.
27 Ibid., 37.
28 Ibid., 65.
29 Ibid., 66.
30 Malcolm, op. cit. 42.
31 Ibid., 42.

Kosova was occupied by the State of Rasi (Rashka) which was the embryo of the Serbian State.[32] According to historical sources, Kosova was occupied by the State of Rashka in 1216.[33] During the reign of Samuel, most churches in Kosova as well as the bishops of Shkupi, Lypjan and Prizren come under the jurisdiction of the archbishop of Ohri.

Although Constantinople enjoyed jurisdiction over churches in Dardania (hereinafter we refer to it as Kosova), there is evidence of the continuous presence of Catholic churches and believers. There were many reasons for that but we will refer here only to some of them. The main one is that the definitive split took place only in 1054. Another reason is that some of the kings in the region swung between the east and the west, depending on their need to keep in power. We refer especially to the rulers of Rashka (Serbia), who swung between loyalty to the Western Church and that to the Eastern Church. Economic relations also played a central role. In the 13th and the 14th centuries Kosova was known for its rich mines. Next to these mines colonies of Saxons and Ragusians – who were Catholic – were established. According to historical records, the local population preserved its Catholic faith: '… this can be seen from two references made to the Bishopric of the Roman Church of Shkupi …'[34] More proof of the existence of Catholic churches in Kosova can be found in the letter sent by Pope Benedict XI to the Archbishop of Tivar, where rectors of the parishes of Bërskova, Runiku, Rogozna, Trepça and Graçanica[35] are mentioned. In the same document a reference is also made to the Church of Saint Kolla in Janjeva whereas in a letter by Pope Clement VIII of the year 1346 it is written that the Bishop of Kotorri had under his care also the Church of Saint Mary, the Church of St Peter in Prizren and 'Prisren, Nouaberda, Trepte, Janeua …'[36]

It is quite obvious that the fact that Kosova remained under the jurisdiction of the Eastern Church had an influence on the reconstruction, adaptation as well as construction of churches in the Byzantine style. This was true not only during the domination of the Bulgarian Empire but also during that of the State of Rashka (Serbia). During the first three generations of the rulers of Rashka (Serbia) the See of the Church was located outside the current territory of Kosova. Only later, after the foundation of the Patriarchates of Peja and the establishment of Graçanica, Deçan and of the Monastery of Archangels in Prizeren was the See of this Church placed in Kosova.

The first period (we refer to it as the first period because the second one started after the withdrawal of the Ottomans in 1912) of Slavic rule ended following the arrival of the Ottomans, who occupied Kosova. According to the records of the

32 Ibid., 44.
33 Ibid., 45.
34 Ibid., 43.
35 Gjini, op. cit. 84.
36 Ibid., 85.

time, Kosova was definitively conquered with the occupation of its main cities – Novobërda, Vushtrri, Lipjan, Prizren and so on – in the period 1455–62.

As we have already pointed out, the Ottoman rule in Kosova was consolidated by the end of 15th century, although there is broad evidence of previous Ottoman campaigns. We can mention here the battle of Kosova in 1389. Not only did the Ottomans diffuse Islam among the people of Kosova but they also built the first mosques in the country. At the beginning, these mosques were built to meet the religious needs of the military, and then they were built systematically for the local population itself. This happened because the locals accepted Islam. There is a document, in the form of an order, dating back to 1537 and stating that 'in every settlement a mosque should be built …'[37]

Many religious Islamic sites, which are still very important in Kosova, were built at the end of the 15th and during the 16th centuries. Obviously, these constructions continued until the termination of Ottoman rule. The first sites were built in rich cities with an economic potential. These cities were generally big ecclesiastical centres.

Among the Islamic religious buildings from the 15th century which still exist are: Gazi Beg Mosque in Vushtrri, Çarshi Mosque, Fatih Mosque and Llapi Mosque in Prishtinë and Bajrakli Mosque in Pejë.[38] The Mosques of Mehmet Pasha and of Sinan Pasha in Prizren, that of Koxha Sinan Pasha in Kaçanik and the Hadum Mosque in Gjakovë[39] were built in the 16th century.

It is known and documented that not only during the Byzantine, Bulgarian or Rashka period, but also during the Ottoman domination, religious sites were reconstructed and even converted, as will be explained in the following paragraphs.

Although Islam was heavily promoted, Orthodox and Catholic churches in Kosovo remained active. The Orthodox Church was allowed to lead its own believers.[40] But also the Latin Church was still present in the country with its own religious sites. In a Vatican report from the year 1584 (in this period the Ottoman regime was firmly established), among other things, churches are also mentioned: one in Prizren, two in Novobërda, Trepça, Prishtina[41] and so on. Another report worth considering was the one prepared by Marin Bici, Archbishop of Tivari, in the year 1610 where he mentions local Catholics and religious buildings.[42]

By comparing the reports from the Vatican, where the cities of Kosova are mentioned, variations in the number of believers can be noticed, depending on the year the report was drawn up. Year after year, the number of believers decreased, as a result of conversions to Islam. But it is interesting to mention that the number of churches remained the same. Only after the rebellion of the year 1689, which was

37 Ibid., 131.
38 Fejaz Drançolli, op. cit. 48.
39 Ibid., 48.
40 Malcolm, op. cit. 97.
41 Gjini, op. cit. 134.
42 Ibid., 134–5.

led by the Austrian General Piccolomini (the Ottoman Empire won this war), did the conversion of churches to mosques take place. The reason lies in the fact that the rebellion was organized and led by the Catholic clergy. Among these priests, the most distinguished was the Albanian bishop and philosopher Pjetër Bogdani.

Among many elements that caused the decrease in the number of Catholics, we should mention here the fact that the Catholic Church was under double pressure. On the one hand there were the taxes Catholics had to pay to the emperor, while on the other hand there was the Orthodox Church, which managed to get a *ferman*[43] from the Sultan, through which Catholics were obliged to pay the ecclesiastical tax to the Orthodox Church. Therefore, until the end of the Ottoman period, the majority of the population converted to Islam. The current percentage of believers of all the three main religions is a result of such phenomena. So history is reflected in Kosova's religious background.

At the conclusion of this chapter on the history of religion and religious heritage, a historic detail should be mentioned which makes the Kosovar people special. The reference is to the so-called '*piebald*'. This term designated those believers who were only 'formally' converted to Islam as a way to escape taxes. The so-called '*piebald*' process continued until the end of the Ottoman rule. As a result, in some villages in Kosova there are still families with both Islamic and Catholic members. This can be noticed from their Muslim names and Catholic surnames or vice versa.

Religious Institutions

As far as religious affiliation is concerned, as stated above Kosova's population belongs to three main religions: Muslim, Orthodox and Catholic. But there are also some Protestants, who have their own churches and other ecclesiastical institutions.

All these denominations have their own religious sites and the Constitution guarantees their autonomy. Therefore Muslims are organized in the Islamic Community of Kosova, Orthodox in the Serbian Orthodox Church (Rashka-Prizren Diocese) and Catholics in the Kosova Bishopric, which was previously known as the Shkup-Prizren Bishopric. Protestants belong to the Kosova Protestant Evangelical Church with its See in Prishtina. Through the Law on Freedom of Religion in Kosova also Judaism enjoys the status of recognized religion.[44]

Internal management of these religious denominations is regulated according to their own laws. For instance the Islamic Community of Kosova has its

43 Malcolm, op. cit. 131.

44 This is somehow odd since there is no Jewish community in Kosova. The Jewish community left for Israel after the establishment of the State. There are references that until the 1990s there were still some Jewish families in Kosova but even those few families have left the country.

Constitution, called the Constitution of the Islamic Community of the Republic of Kosova, adopted in 2003. On the basis of this document, the Islamic Community has its Assembly, Presidency and President. It also has 25 local councils, divided into 8 administrative regions. This document regulates relations between believers, the administration, rights and obligations of members as well as the management of all assets owned by this community. These properties include mosques, masjeeds (Islamic places of worship which do not have to look like a mosque, being more similar to common public buildings), mektebs (religious secondary schools), educational institutions, administrative and business centres, tekkes (dervish shrines), turbets (monumental dervish graves), hammams (public baths from the Ottoman period),[45] gasullhanets (places where Muslims' corpses are cleaned) and graveyards.[46]

As stated at the beginning of this chapter, there are 750 Islamic sites in Kosova. Due to historic circumstances – but also political ones – a large number of them were destroyed or nationalized over different periods during the 20th century.

Since it is to this community that around 90 per cent of the total population in Kosova belongs, it is obvious that it possesses the highest number of religious buildings. According to the list provided by this community (but also to experts in cultural heritage) the most important of them[47] are:

- Gazi Ali Beg Mosque in Vushtrri;Çarshia Mosque in Prishtinë; Fatih Mosque in Prishtinë; Llapi Mosque in Prishtinë; Bajrakli Mosque in Pejë; Lead Mosque in Pejë; Mehmet Pasha Mosque in Prizeren; Sinan Pasha Mosque in Prizeren; Koxha Sinan Pasha Mosque in Kaçanik; Hadum Mosque in Gjakovë.

The Serbian Orthodox Church in Kosova is represented by the Diocese of Rashka and Prizren. The See of this diocese is in Prizren. According to Orthodox canon law, dioceses are led by a bishop appointed by the Serbian Orthodox Church. This diocese has its churches and monasteries. There are both monasteries in use and others which are disused and also nunneries. The Orthodox Seminary is located in Prizren. The Orthodox community is the second biggest community in Kosova. Since it took part in all political developments (directly or indirectly) of the country, this community enjoys the most advanced protection within the legal framework of the State of Kosova, both for its clergy and its various properties.

---

45 In the early Ottoman period mosques were built within a group of buildings. It usually included a mosque, as the central religious building, mektebs where the Coran was taught, public baths (Hammam) and the place where corpses were cleaned in accordance with Islamic rituals (gasulname), popular kitchens and so on.

46 Constitution of the Islamic Community of Kosova.

47 We tried to classify these sites according to their importance for cultural / religious heritage. But since the subject of this study is the legal status of Serbian Orthodox sacred places, the list is not complete.

The Catholic Church in Kosova is represented by the Kosova Bishopric. This diocese includes 24 parishes. Twenty-two parishes out of the total are served by diocesan priests while the two remaining (Gjakovë and Prishtinë) are served by Franciscans and Salesians respectively. The diocese has also its Diocesan Seminary Monsignor Lazër Mjeda in Prizren. The most notable Catholic sites are:[48]

- Basilica in the archaeological area in Ulpiana; Basilica in Trepçë – ruins; Cathedral of St Kolli in Novobërdë – ruins; Co-cathedral of Helping Lady in Prizeren; Church of St Ndou, Prishtinë; Church of the Lady, Letnicë; Church of St Kolli, Janjevë; Church of St Andou, Binçë.

The Kosovar Protestant Evangelical Church is among those communities which have only recently started their religious activity. This community was set up in 1985, but it was not recognized by law until the creation of the Republic of Kosova. The seat of the Protestant community is in Prishtina. According to canon law, this Church has its institutions, that is, presbytery, synod and bishop. Its religious activity takes place in 30 sites; six of them are registered as churches, two are private houses and the remainder are rented buildings.

As already stated, the Jewish community has also been recognized but does not have any active site or institution in Kosova. At present the building of a synagogue is planned. According to the documents available, until 1955–56 there were five small synagogues in use in Kosova but they were ruined by the regime of the time.

Religion in the Legislation of the Republic of Kosova

Kosova's legal framework is quite complete as far as religion is concerned. The political process Kosova went through, until its declaration of independence, has had an influence on this part of the legal framework. In my opinion many legal and constitutional norms on religious matters were particularly influenced by the political process itself. This is also due to the fact that Kosova went through this long transition that ended up with its declaration of independence after almost 100 years of Serbian rule.

For some time Kosova has enjoyed an autonomous status within the Former Federal Republic of Yugoslavia. During this period religious communities were administered according to the laws in force. Thus there was both a Presidency of

48 We faced great difficulties in determining what the most important sites are. One of the problems was the fact that a certain number of Latin religious buildings were transformed into Churches of the Eastern rite in different periods. According the sources we have at our disposal such cases are numerous. I tried to be as accurate as possible in defining the importance of them. For instance, in this study, I have not mentioned the Church of St Florus and Laurus in Lypjan as well as other churches.

the Islamic Community of Yugoslavia and Islamic Communities in each republic or province where Muslims lived. The Catholics of Kosova were organized in the Bishopric of Shkupi-Prizren, while the Orthodox were represented by the Rashka-Prizren Diocese. After the break-up of this State, administrative changes occurred only with respect to the Islamic Community, since Albanian Muslims did not want to remain part of the Islamic Community of Serbia. Therefore the Islamic Community of Kosova was set up. Other religious communities maintained the same organization. During these years, the Protestant Church was established.

Repression under Milosevic's regime[49] obviously had a strong impact on interreligious relations. In particular, the role of the Orthodox Church had a strong impact on the deterioration of relations between religious communities.[50]

After the war Kosova was put under UN administration, whose mission created the first legal framework for war-stricken Kosova. It consisted of three legal sub-frames: legal framework of Kosova-Yugoslavia until the year 1990, legal framework of Serbia after 1990 (this was conditioned to make it not discriminatory and it was to be replaced by UNMIK laws) and finally the legislation drafted by UNMIK, which includes the Constitutional Framework, Regulations and Administrative Instructions.[51] The latter remained in force until the proclamation of Kosova as a sovereign and independent State on 17 February 2008 (or, more precisely, until the approval and entry into force of the Constitution on 15 June 2008).

Due to the political circumstances (both local and international) under which Kosova's independence was declared, the whole legal framework of Kosova, starting from the Constitution, was based on the document produced as a result of the negotiations known as 'Ahtisaari package'. Actually, independence was declared on the basis of it.

The Ahtisaari package is a legally binding document for Kosova. Therefore, starting from the Constitution, all laws have been drawn up in accordance with this package. In the following paragraph I will try to describe the religion-related issues it deals with.

The Ahtisaari package[52] has an annex where the protection and rights of religious communities and their own properties are regulated. Because of the long Albanian-Serbian frictions and the conditions in which the independence of Kosova was declared, this document entirely refers to the protection of religious

49 Slobodan Milosevic had been president of what remained of Tito's Yugoslavia for some time. He was also president of Serbia. The International Criminal Tribunal for the Former Yugoslavia charged him with crimes against humanity, war crimes and genocide for his role during the wars in Croatia, Bosnia and Kosova. He was found dead in his cell before his sentence.

50 See Monsignor Mali's statement cited in the *Introduction* to this chapter.

51 Some parts of the UNMIK legal framework are still in force, and will remain so until they are replaced by laws of the Republic of Kosova. For this, see <www.rks-gov.net> accessed 30 April 2013.

52 This document was voted and adopted by the Parliament of Kosova.

rights and properties of Serbs in Kosova. It requires the State authorities to recognize the Serbian Orthodox Church in Kosova. This is explicitly stated in Chapter V of the package. Not only does the document recognize the authority of the Serbian Orthodox Church but it also requires Kosovar institutions to guarantee denomination, objects, property, monastic life, autonomy and freedom of movement and many other aspects of religious autonomy. The implementation is to be accompanied by special measures and mechanisms, that is, the creation of special protective zones around churches and monasteries as well as the establishment of the Implementation and Monitoring Commission – IMC. The International Civilian Officer is provided for by this document to guarantee the implementation of the plan. The adoption of additional laws is envisaged in Annex XII of this document.

On the basis of this document the Assembly of Kosova declared the country's independence. The reason why we mention it at this moment is because in several parts even the declaration of independence refers to the Ahtisaari package, especially when it deals with the rights and freedoms of communities as well as respect of cultural, ethnic and religious diversity. This declaration also confirms all international obligations binding upon the State of Kosova.

Article 8 of the Constitution of the Republic of Kosova states that, 'The Republic of Kosova is a secular State and is neutral in matters of religious belief'. Article 19, §§ 1 and 2 deals with obligations arising from international law: it defines the status of ratified international agreements within Kosova's internal legal framework. Article 22 refers to the direct applicability of international agreements and other instruments. Eight documents are mentioned as directly applicable, that is, among others: the Universal Declaration of Human Rights; the European Convention for the Protection of Human Rights and Fundamental Freedoms and its Protocols; the International Covenant on Civil and Political Rights and its Protocols; the Council of Europe Framework Convention for the Protection of National Minorities. Articles 38 and 39 deal with freedom of religion and religious denominations.

Article 39 states:

1. The Republic of Kosovo ensures and protects religious autonomy and religious monuments within its territory.
2. Religious denominations are free to independently regulate their internal organization, religious activities and religious ceremonies.
3. Religious denominations have the right to establish religious schools and charity institutions in accordance with this Constitution and the law.

The Constitution also deals with the aspect of the equality of minorities, or, in other words, it regulates their status on the basis of obligations arising from international law. A particular aspect worth mentioning is the fact that minorities are defined as 'Communities', and it is also envisaged to treat them in accordance with the so-called process of 'Positive Discrimination for Communities'.

Since the subject of this study is religious communities, we will focus on laws covering this matter.

Issues related to freedom of religion within our legal system are complex and inextricably linked to socio-political circumstances. By taking these laws into consideration we can see that religious communities in Kosova and religions in general are treated on the basis of the processes Kosova went through in the 20th century.

From the numerous interviews I had with leaders of different religious communities in Kosova[53] I noticed that even if they are not entirely satisfied with this legislation, they accept it as such because of the political circumstances, with the exception of the Serbian Orthodox Church which is enjoying all the rights deriving from this legal framework without recognizing the laws of the Republic of Kosova. Religious communities complain about the fact that they are not all equally treated. As examples of this they take the Special Protective Zones, since they are created around Orthodox churches and monasteries, and the law on customs, according to which the Serbian Orthodox Church enjoys a special mention and is exempted from any customs duty, while all the other communities are only mentioned as 'other religious denominations'. This was explicitly mentioned in the Ahtisaari package on the status resolution. Article 2.2 of Annex V specifies fiscal incentives for the Serbian Orthodox Church:

> Kosovo shall grant customs duty and tax privileges to the Serbian Orthodox Church, in addition to those enjoyed by all religions in Kosovo, for economic activities of the Church specific to its financial self-sustainability, such as the production of embroidery and clerical vestments, candles, icon painting, woodcarving and carpentry, and traditional agricultural products. These privileges shall cover import and purchase of relevant products, materials, machinery, tools and livestock; and export of products resulting from the said activities.[54]

The special treatment for the Serbian Orthodox Church made other religious communities, that is, the Islamic Community and the Catholic Church, feel unsatisfied for the fact that not all religious communities enjoy the same fiscal incentives.

They also recall the Cultural Heritage Law, as well as the drafts of two special laws[55] – one on Prizren and the other on Hoça e Madhe – which have been drawn up explicitly to advance the protection and preservation of the Orthodox cultural and religious heritage.

53 We had interviews with representatives of the Islamic Community, Catholic Bishopric, Evangelist Protestant Church and with some senior Orthodox priests.

54 Ahtisaari package on the status resolution, Article 2.2.

55 The Law on the Historical Zone of Prizren and the Law on Hoça e Madhe have not been completed yet and according to the legislative agenda these laws should have been adopted by the end of 2009.

The basic law on religious matters is the Law on Freedom of Religion. This law is quite liberal and represents the main framework for religious freedom in Kosova. Freedom of organization, autonomy and freedom in using religious assets, with no intervention from the State, are thereby regulated. Clearly, subjects of protection in this law include places of worship and access of believers and pilgrims to them as well as ecclesiastical legal entities (religious institutions of different denominations) established by the competent church authority, according to their own rights.

Treatment of religious heritage in the frame of cultural heritage is regulated through Article 9 of the Constitution ('The Republic of Kosovo ensures the preservation and protection of its cultural and religious heritage') and the Cultural Heritage Law. This law presents a set of responsibilities which are spread throughout all its provisions on public bodies acting in the field of cultural heritage, providing for concrete obligations and measures aiming at:

- Scientific identification and adequate legal protection, as defined in international acts, that is, the Granada and Valetta Conventions;
- Development of a dynamic conservation strategy, mobilizing economic potential for urban regeneration and rural development;
- Contribution to a responsible service, controlling the conservation and restoration work on cultural heritage, in all forms of its occurrence;
- Contribution to the decrease in risks and threats on cultural heritage. When an owner is not taking care of his property, which has a cultural value, then the authorities should intervene by taking the necessary measures for preserving it, up to expropriation;
- Hiring qualified staff for registration and preservation;
- Cooperation for compiling a protection strategy, by implementing activities to protect registration and other immediate measures;
- Support through assistance and educational-technical guidance, preparing restoration projects and their continuous application.

According to this Law all the competent institutions, from the Kosovo Council for Cultural Heritage to local level institutions, are clearly instructed to bear in mind the unity of the cultural heritage of Kosova as a whole, regardless of cultural diversity.

Along this line, the Kosovo Council for Cultural Heritage as the highest body – which in its composition represents the ethnic composition of Kosova (another way to show the diversity of cultural heritage) – '... will identify necessary financial support measures for the Cultural Heritage for each year' (Article 4.9).

Kosovar legislation grants an extraordinarily high level of legal protection to sacred sites. This practice is unique in my opinion, owing to the fact that, along with basic laws like the Law on Spatial Planning and the Cultural Heritage Law, there are also special laws dealing with this matter, that is, the Law on Special Protective Zones (adopted and currently in force), which also mentions the need for two other laws, the Law on the Special Protective Zone of Prizren and the Law for Hoça e Madhe. We consider our practice as unique as it concerns the process and the criteria through which these special protective zones were established.

Equality of rights among citizens in Kosova is also guaranteed by the definition of official holidays and equality of languages. Our Law on Official Holidays includes both traditional profane holidays and religious holidays with an equal approach. The following are recognized official religious holidays: Eid Al-Fitr (Muslim); Eid Al Addha (Muslim); Christmas Day (Catholic) – 25 December; Christmas Day (Orthodox) – 7 January; Easter Monday, (Catholic); Easter Monday (Orthodox). The basic concept is equal treatment for all religions and believers, irrespective of their number or distribution. The Law foresees the establishment of a holidays committee whose composition reflects the religious diversity of Kosovar society.

Equality of languages is another important element in Kosovar legislation. According to the Constitution, the official languages in Kosova are Albanian and Serbian. Their use is regulated through the Law on the use of languages, which allows 'the use of official languages, as well as languages of communities whose mother tongue is not an official language, in Kosovar institutions and other organizations and enterprises who carry out public functions and services' and guarantees 'the right of all communities in Kosovo to preserve, maintain and promote their linguistic identity'.

Definition of Sacred Places in Kosova

First of all, I will try to provide definition, as clear as possible, of a sacred place. I do not want to refer to practices or definitions from different countries, but I will try to refer only to the case of Kosova. As a consequence of historic and socio-political developments, buildings and premises belonging to religious communities, recognized by the State, dedicated to performance of religious ceremonies are considered as sacred objects. The definition includes premises when these are active. It has not always been so and the legal status of such sites has always depended on circumstances and on who defined them in each particular period during the 20th century.

After Kosova's war, due perhaps to our particular context, not all places of religious nature were treated as such. This was maybe due to the fact that during the 1990s or even after 1945 the sacred places of different communities were discriminated as to legal status and definition. As far as the treatment of religious sites is concerned, you will probably notice that Kosova's experience is quite unique. Although religion was not a strong element among the population, most of these religious buildings are usually treated as common heritage and property. This is due to the facts we presented about the historical development of religion in Kosova.

Knowing that Kosova was administered by Resolution 1244 of the UNSC, religious objects were treated as religious and cultural sites. Also the documents produced later treated these objects in the same way. For instance the Ahtisaari package treats them as religious sites, without taking into consideration whether they consist of only one object or more. Along this line the new legislation of the State of Kosova treats them according to two categories, as objects and as sites.

But while analysing definitions in the law, we have to take some other elements into consideration, such as, architectural importance, landscape, cultural forms, spiritual heritage, forms of social and religious organization, historical/cultural context, natural environment and visual aesthetical frame. One of the objectives mentioned in the Law on Special Protective Zones is 'to provide for the peaceful existence and functioning of the sites to be protected and to preserve the monastic way of life of the clergy'.

According to the Ahtisaari package the aims of Protective Zones are

> … to provide for the peaceful existence and functioning of the sites to be protected; preserve their historical, cultural and natural environment, including the monastic way of life of the clergy; and prevent adverse development around them, while ensuring the best possible conditions for harmonious and sustainable development of the communities inhabiting the areas surrounding such sites.

By reading these provisions we can get a clear idea of the aspects characterizing sacred or religious value. Therefore, bearing in mind the historical, political and social features of the people and the State of Kosova, I will give the following definition of sacred place:

> … buildings or sites where historical events, spiritual tradition, character, use and where religious and spiritual life are combined, making them the object of veneration for a particular religious or ethnic community (or wider) can be considered as sacred place in Kosova's context.

- Protective zones for specific categories of monuments

The definition of protective zones will depend on, among other issues, the category of the protected monument, since the first category monuments of international significance will be protected by larger protective zones than monuments of the second category (regional significance) and third category (local significance). The Council for Cultural Heritage will take into account the categorization of each monument in defining an appropriate protective zone for it. There will be a possibility that a protected monument does not need a protective zone, especially in the case of third category monuments.

- Site visits

The purpose of site visits should not be to define the boundaries of protected zones but to gather information that will assist the institutions in charge of defining these boundaries subsequently.

- Management system

To protect, integrate and present the whole of Kosova's cultural heritage without special privileges or discrimination, exclusiveness or favouritism is a very complex, costly and challengeable issue – but at the same time it is a key for making protection, integration and presentation a long-lasting commitment to proper appreciation, understanding and safeguarding by individuals and communities in Kosovo.

We will welcome any bilateral or multilateral form of cooperation in the field of protection, integration and preservation of heritage. The Kosovar Authorities commit themselves and are willing to undertake strong efforts to get proper preservation and an appropriate use of Kosova's cultural heritage. The Kosovar Authorities are trying to provide all the legal, administrative as well as technical preconditions necessary in order to implement a future agreement based on these principles.

- Regulatory body: Council for Cultural Heritage

Composition

a. The Council for Cultural Heritage will be designated and authorized by the Kosovar Parliament. It will be composed of seven leading experts: one historian, two conservation architects, two art historians, one archaeologist, one ethnologist (or anthropologist, or cultural heritage manager, or musicologist, or similar).

At least one member of the Council has to be: i) a leading expert of Byzantine architecture and arts; ii) a leading expert of Ottoman architecture and arts; iii) a Kosovar Serb (iv) an expert representing UNESCO or the Council of Europe.

At least three members of the Council have to be Kosovar Albanians.

- Terms of References of the Council for Cultural heritage – or TOR

b. The Council is Responsible for the (i) designation of cultural heritage from the Tentative List – Registering; (ii) definition of the area and the scope of protection; (iii) provision of the description of all measures that have to be undertaken; (iv) conditions for integration and the way of presentation of the cultural heritage depending on each case; (v) definition of responsible stakeholders and those in charge of implementing decisions; (vi) monitoring of the implementation of its decisions including the approval of the organization of public hearings concerning the projects; (vii) establishment of a documentation centre and a database for heritage; (viii) planning of priorities; and (ix) budget planning.
c. All decisions of the Council will be based upon a detailed analysis of all the facts relevant for cultural property and discussion with owners and other interested parties. Decisions of the Council are binding and definitive.

d. The Council will have its technical secretariat composed of legal experts, historians, conservation architects and area conservation experts, archaeologists, art historians and technical staff (the technical Secretariat of the Council can be an already existing institution). At least four members of the Council are fully employed by the Council. The Council defines its criteria for the designation of heritage.
e. Automatic protective zones for the heritage on the Tentative List. There will be no construction, mining or other works that might change the present condition of the city, landscape or environment within a 50 metre (in cities) or 100 metre protection zone (outside the settlements) around the site that is on the Tentative List.
f. The final protection regime and the protective zone for heritage on the Tentative List is the subject of the decision of the Council for heritage. The 'automatic tentative protective zone' and the protection regime for heritage on the Tentative List can be changed only through a decision of the Council. If there is an intention to start any kind of works in the vicinity of the protection zone, the owner or the developer or the local authorities may request that Council urgently puts on its agenda the designation procedure of the monument in question, so that the protection regime is defined. Each decision of the Council defines precisely the area that is protected and the protective zone, with the possibility to have several levels of restrictions in the protective zone (that is, for example – prohibition of any construction and agricultural activities; prohibition of activities that have stronger environmental impact; restriction of construction of certain buildings; restrictions concerning the height, use of material or similar). Each case is different and decisions are based upon the full knowledge of all conditions relevant for a certain property.
g. Permits for any work in the protected or protective area are issued by the Ministry responsible for civil works and spatial planning with the consent of the Council for Cultural Heritage. The Ministry of Culture, Youth and Sports can transfer its responsibility to the local authorities in special cases that will be defined.
h. Movable heritage that is either an integral part of designated immovable heritage or an independent cultural property that is designated or included in the Tentative List is the subject of full protection in accordance with the legal provisions of UNESCO and the Council of Europe. The Council for heritage keeps a database on this heritage. The Council defines conditions, protection and security measures and other usual measures to be undertaken if movable heritage is exhibited in Kosova or out of Kosova. The owners have the right to exhibit movable properties and authorities are obliged to undertake all necessary security measures to protect the exhibits. If the exhibition takes place out of Kosova the owner informs the Council of Heritage about the place and time of exhibition as well as about the time of return of the exhibits. The owner may request police escort and

other security measures to be undertaken by the Kosova authorities for the transfer of the movable goods. Kosova authorities may request the owner to use the movable properties for exhibitions on Kosova heritage or for publications. In these cases the agreement is signed between the owner, the Kosovar authority and the Council for Heritage in which all conditions of the exhibition or presentation of the property as well as of its returning are defined, including the right of the owner to be present during packing, transport and unpacking of the property, as well as during the exhibition if it is needed.

Serbian Orthodox Church in Kosova – Special Protective Zones

Defining the importance of religious sites is a very difficult, if not impossible, task. This is particularly true in the case of Kosova, if we bear in mind information presented in various official websites or even by diplomatic chancelleries. In our case, we also have difficulties in giving their exact number. This became clear during the status negotiations on Kosova. It should be stressed that the issues of the name, ownership, originality and other social elements have always been hot topics in Kosova. For instance, there are cases where Serbian political institutions, in various public statements, allege the existence of more than 1,000 Serbian Orthodox sites in Kosova, a figure which has never been proven with any official list. The debate on the number of religious objects/sites was very long and absurd, especially in view of the fact that this issue is irrelevant to the political and social processes in Kosova. We say this because through the artificial and often mythical census of the number of churches, the Serbian state and politicians are trying to argue 'the right' to keep Kosova.

Along this line, the institution which administered Kosova after the war – UNMIK, in cooperation with OSCE – made an inventory of Serbian Orthodox churches in Kosova. According to this list their number is 114, including chapels and half-ruined buildings.

The definition of the importance of religious sites was also the topic of numerous debates during Serbian rule in Kosova. In this research, I will mostly refer to the documents which were produced as a result of two-year negotiations on the status of Kosova, and which are entirely accepted by Kosovar institutions and the international community – under whose auspices these negotiations were indeed conducted. Furthermore, these data for religious and cultural heritage were presented by the Serbian representatives in these negotiations. In other words, these are objects presented by the Serbian Orthodox Church itself. On the ground of these records, the Ahtisaari package and the Law on Special Protective Zones were drawn up. Buildings and sites listed in these documents are also considered for their importance.

Orthodox Religious Sites

In the Law on Special Protective Zones there is a list of sites surrounded by such zones which is presented here. These sites are divided according to the size of the protective zone created thereby. The following list contains all these buildings and is drawn from the map attached to this document:

- Monastery of Deçani, Deçan: (this protective zone is identical to the previously established 'Special Zoning Area'); Peja Patriarchate, Pejë; Graçanica Monastery, Prishtinë; Church of the Presentation of the Virgin, Lipjan; Deviç Monastery, Skënderaj; Gorioç Monastery, Istog; Budisavci Monastery, Klinë; Sokolica Monastery, Zveçan; Draganac Monastery, Gjilan; Holy Archangels Monastery, Prizren; Banjska Monastery, Zveçan; Zoqishte Monastery, Zoqishtë, Rahovec; Hoqë e Madhe Village, Hoqë e Madhe, Rahovec; Duboki Potok Monastery, Zubin Potok; Church of St George,Gornjasellë, Prizren; Soçanica Monastery, Leposaviq; Hermitage with Church, Uljaricë Klinë; and Hermitage of St Peter of Korishe, Korishë, Prizren.

Churches with a special zone within a 100-metre perimeter:

- Monastery of St Friday, Leposaviq; Monastery of Holy Healers, Leposaviq; Monastery of the Holy Virgin of Hvosno, Istog; Monastery of St Marco, Korishë, Prizren; Trinity Monastery, Mushtisht, Suharekë; Church of the Holy Virgin, Sredskë, Prizren; Monastery of St Urosh, Nerodime, Ferizaj; and Monastery of Binaçi, Buzovik, Viti.

Churches with a special zone within a 50-metre perimeter:

- Monastery of Dollc, Klinë; Church of St Nicholas, Gjurakoc, Istog; Church of Holy Virgin Hodegetri, Mushtisht, Suharekë; Church of St Nicholas, Shtërpcë; Church of St Theodore, Biti e Poshtme, Shtërpcë; Church of St Nicholas, Gotovushë, Shtërpcë; Church of the Holy Virgin, Gotovushë, Shtërpcë; Church of St George, Biti e Epërme, Shtërpcë; Church of St Nicholas, Mushnikovë, Prizren; Church of St Nicholas, Bogoshevc, Prizren; Church of St Nicholas, Drajçiq, Prizren; Church of St Nicholas, Sredskë, Prizren; Church of the Holy Apostles (or Holy Friday), Mushnikovë, Prizren; Church of St George Serdskë, Prizren.

The protection of the following buildings is guaranteed through two special laws, that is, the Law on the Historical Zone of Prizren and the Law on the Special Protective Zone of Hoça e Madhe:

- Church of the Holy Virgin Levishka; Church of St Savior; Cathedral of

St George, with Chapel of St George (Runovic); Church of St Nicholas (Tutic); Church in the village Hoça e Madhe.

Out of these churches, which are included in the above-mentioned law as the most important ones, four sites are included in the list of cultural heritage at risk. For these sites I will give a short description on construction and development, as well as on their importance for cultural heritage of Kosova.

- Monastery of Deçani, Deçan; Peja Patriarchy, Pejë; Monastery of Graçanica, Prishtinë; Church of Holly Virgin, Levishka -Xhuma Mosque.[56]

As we know, Kosova went through a process of negotiations to determine its political status. One of the most important topics in these negotiations – led by the chief negotiator President Ahtisaari and his team – was the cultural and religious heritage of Serbs in Kosova. Several documents were proposed by the negotiating parties. An agreement was subsequently reached for the protection of what is called Serbian cultural and religious heritage in Kosova. It is also worth mentioning that on this issue the Kosovar team was well disposed towards all possible protection for the cultural and religious heritage of Serbs. At the beginning the Serbian representatives had a passive attitude in presenting their proposals. Later, when no doubts remained about the status of Kosova, which was definitively going to split from Serbia, the first obstacles to the process appeared. Initially, the Serbian Orthodox Church was quite cooperative and in the first two meetings even supported the Kosovar team's proposal on the level of protection of churches and other religious objects.

The debate was focused on criteria for determining special protective zones (whether to use criteria mentioned in international documents or some practical and more easily applicable examples). Many international criteria were considered, but in the end the international negotiators dictated their status proposal. This was widely accepted in Kosova and was reflected in the legislation, directly stemming from the Ahtisaari package. The Serbian representatives have never accepted this document and, in the meantime, they started to put pressure on the Serbian Orthodox Church in Kosova to refuse its cooperation in implementing this document, even unofficially. Currently, the consequences of such an attitude are still perceivable when the need occurs for cooperation from the Serbian Church in the implementation of these legal acts.

How did we come to the definition of special protective zones around Serbian churches? In my opinion, the process started when the international community realized that the country was moving towards its political and legal independence. Of course, the damages of the war in 1998–99 in Kosova and the events that occurred in March 2004 had their impact. Along this line, the UNMIK administration adopted Executive Decision N 205/5 definition of the special zone

56 <http://whc.unesco.org/en/list/724> accessed 30 April 2013.

for the Monastery of Deçan. This decision aimed to declare a space around the Monastery of Deçan as a special zone, in order to avert, or at least to put under control, spatial and urban development therein, for the sole purpose of protecting the Monastery. This decision, which enjoyed a legislative status, stated that:

1. There should be established a special zone, which includes the Deçan canyon, including the Orthodox cemetery near the Monastery, the bridge over the Bistrica river and the crest around the canyon, as described on the map.
2. Inside the special zone:
   - no construction, industrial or commercial activity, or natural resource exploitation will be allowed in the canyon without a duly issued authorization approved by UNMIK.
   - the existing road, which will be controlled by KFOR, cannot be widened without prior approval from UNMIK. Heavy commercial traffic should not be allowed without prior approval by UNMIK and KFOR.
   - municipal authorities should undertake all necessary measures to respect the existing objects, and those concerning structures built without any construction permit.
   - activities in and around the Monastery must be conducted strictly in accordance with UNESCO conventions and guidelines.
3. The creation of the special zone should not have any impact either on the commercial and construction activities of the Monastery carried out for its own benefit, or on the approved activities of the hydro-central of Kozhner, which is outside the special zone.
4. Relevant activities should take into consideration a better system of municipal and regional roads, to meet the requirements of the special status of this region.
5. A local council led by the municipal representative of UNMIK and by representatives nominated by UNMIK, the Municipality of Deçan, the Monastery, KFOR and the UNMIK Police Commissioner has to be established in order to make recommendations to SRSG for any issue related to implementation of this decision.
6. The creation of this special zone, according to the decision, should not have an impact of any kind on the underlying titles of the properties in this region.[57]
7. This decision enters into force on 25 April 2005 with a six-month validity and possibility of renewal.

As a result of the status negotiations process the document on status was approved. This document has an annex (Annex V) which regulates the rights and privileges of the Serbian Orthodox Church. According to this annex, Kosova is obliged to recognize

57 This means that the zoning does not have any impact on the ownership of the land within special protective zones.

the Church and its privileges and to respect its autonomy in religious matters but, on the other hand, the Church is obliged to recognize the new reality in Kosova, that is, its independence. Although the Church has not recognized this fact yet, Kosova's legal framework has been further developed, along with the adoption of the Law on Special Protective Zones. According to this, a 'Special Protective Zone' is an area – identified through a map or otherwise – which surrounds a monument, building, group of buildings, ensemble, village or historic town centre that is safeguarded from any development or activity which might damage its historical, cultural, architectural or archeological context, natural environment or aesthetic visual setting.

The objectives of the Special Protective Zones are:

a. to provide for the peaceful existence and functioning of the sites to be protected, and to preserve the monastic way of life of the clergy;
b. to preserve the character and appearance of the sites to be protected, in particular the historical, cultural, architectural or archeological context, natural environment or aesthetic visual setting; and
c. to avert adverse development around the sites to be protected, while ensuring the best possible conditions for harmonious and sustainable development of the communities inhabiting the areas surrounding such sites by regulating development and other activities.

Through this law, those activities which are considered to violate the monastic life of clergy, values of sites and in general their originality are limited or prohibited.

Activities Prohibited within Special Protective Zones

Any new activity in the following areas shall be prohibited:

a. Industrial construction or development, such as the exploration and exploitation of mineral resources and the building of dams, power plants or power lines, kilns and factories, and transit roads in rural areas; and
b. Construction or development leading to deforestation or pollution of the environment.

Activities Restricted within Special Protective Zones

Any new activity from the following list of activities may be restricted as circumstances warrant. Prior to any such activities being conducted in the following areas, the municipality concerned shall seek the agreement of the Serbian Orthodox Church. If no agreement is reached, the parties shall refer the matter to the IMC for review, in accordance with point c of Article 4 of this Law:

a. Commercial constructions or development such as structures or edifices taller than the monastery/church/cultural monument to be protected;

road/street construction; construction of warehouses, workshops, shops, restaurants, bars, cafes, hotels/motels, food stalls and kiosks, petrol and automobile repair stations, supermarkets, night clubs, any other large scale construction in rural areas;

b. Public gatherings, recreation and entertainment; and
c. Urbanization of agricultural land.

With regard to these definitions, public debates have developed and are still going on. There are people who consider that these definitions for such zones violate property rights, since there are some private properties within these zones. Others consider these proposals as made for the preservation and promotion of the cultural and religious value of these sites, as a heritage of all Kosovars.

International Legal Approach

Terminology

Perimeter of a Monument
'Perimeter of a monument' means an area of land directly associated with a protected monument.

Protected Zone
'Protected zone' means an area of land surrounding the perimeter of a protected monument. This area should be safeguarded from any development or activity which could damage the visual setting or otherwise damage the cultural heritage. The definition of the special protected zone should be determined by the Council for Cultural Heritage (Kosovo Cultural Heritage Law).

Protected Area
'Protected area' means an area of land which may include protected cultural heritage, protected natural and environmental resources, or both of the above (Kosovo Cultural Heritage Law).

Special Protective Zone
'Special protective zone' means a protective area around a declared World Heritage Site. The definition of the special protective zone should be determined by the Council for Cultural Heritage.

Setting
'Setting' means the natural and built environment that modulates the aesthetic perception of the heritage or that is linked to the heritage in an immediate spatial manner or through social, economic or cultural ties (ICOMOS Recommendation of Nairobi).

Conventions and Recommendations

Enforcement of international legal documents is an issue which remains a topic for discussion and debate in Kosova. Kosova is still a State without the possibility of ratifying these documents; therefore until its final recognition by the international community, as an interim solution, documents signed by the Former Socialist Federal Republic of Yugoslavia and by the international bodies which administered Kosova after the war apply. This matter was regulated in two documents; in the Declaration of Independence, point 9, and in the Constitution of the Republic of Kosova, Article 145, points 1 and 2. Based on these documents written treaties are legally binding in Kosova:

> 9. We hereby undertake the international obligations of Kosovo, including those concluded on our behalf by the United Nations Interim Administration Mission in Kosovo (UNMIK) and treaty and other obligations of the former Socialist Federal Republic of Yugoslavia to which we are bound as a former constituent part, including the Vienna Conventions on diplomatic and consular relations. We shall cooperate fully with the International Criminal Tribunal for the Former Yugoslavia. We intend to seek membership in international organizations, in which Kosovo shall seek to contribute to the pursuit of international peace and stability.

Article 145 [Continuity of International Agreements and Applicable Legislation]:

1. International agreements and other acts relating to international cooperation that are in effect on the day this Constitution enters into force will continue to be respected until such agreements or acts are renegotiated or withdrawn from in accordance with their terms or until they are superseded by new international agreements or acts covering the same subject areas and adopted pursuant to this Constitution.
2. Legislation applicable on the date of the entry into force of this Constitution shall continue to apply to the extent it is in conformity with this Constitution until repealed, superseded or amended in accordance with this Constitution.

Among international legal texts we can mention the following:

> <u>Council of Europe's Amsterdam Declaration (1975)</u>:An inventory of buildings, architectural complexes and sites demarcating *protected zones* around them is required.
>
> <u>Council of Europe's Resolution concerning the Adaptation of Laws and Regulations to the Requirements of Integrated Conservation of the Architectural Heritage (1976) Article 3, Section B3</u>:Around protected monuments, there should be a protection zone in order to ensure the harmonious evolution of the man-made environment.

International Charter for the Conservation and Restoration of Monuments and Sites (Charter of Venice, 1964):
Article 6

> The conservation of a monument implies preserving a setting *which is not out of scale.* Wherever the traditional setting exists, it must be kept. No new construction, demolition or modification which would alter the relation of mass and color (….)

Convention for the Protection of the Architectural Heritage of Europe (Granada Convention, 1985):
Article 7

> In the surroundings of monuments, within groups of buildings, and within sites, each Party undertakes to promote measures for the general enhancement of the environment.

Council of Europe's Recommendation 1484 on the Management of Cathedrals and Other Major Religious Buildings in Use (2000):
Article 10

> Governments of Member States should draw up conservation plans for each major religious monument or site in consultation with the religious authorities involved.

UNESCO Convention Concerning the Protection of World Cultural and Natural Heritage (1972):
Article 4

> Each State Party to this Convention recognizes that the duty of ensuring the identification, protection, conservation, presentation and transmission to future generations of the cultural and natural heritage referred to in Articles 1 and 2 and situated on its territory, belongs primarily to that State. It will do all it can to this end, to the utmost of its own resources and, where appropriate, with any international assistance and co-operation, in particular, financial, artistic, scientific and technical, which it may be able to obtain.

UNESCO Operational Guidelines for the Implementation of the World Heritage Convention (2005):
Paragraph 104

> For the purposes of effective protection of the nominated property, a buffer zone is an area surrounding the nominated property which has complementary legal and/or customary restrictions placed on its use and development to give an added layer of protection of the property. This should include the immediate setting of

the property, important views, and other areas that are functionally important to the property and its protection. The area constituting the buffer zone should be determined in each case through appropriate mechanisms.

Recommendations of Nairobi Concerning the Safeguard of Historic Ensembles and Their Function in Contemporary Life (1976):The setting of immovable cultural heritage is the natural and built environment that modulates the aesthetic perception of the heritage or that is linked to the heritage in an immediate spatial manner or through social, economic or cultural ties.

Criteria for Protection Zones

According to relevant European and international heritage conventions and recommendations, three criteria should determine the definition of protection zones: immediate spatial setting; visual context; functional context and traditional setting:

1. Immediate spatial setting is the area of land immediately around the protected monument;
2. Visual context is the area of land that is aesthetically tied to the protected monument, for example by sharing particular architectural features or by an associated landscape;
3. Functional context is the area of land that is socially, economically or culturally tied to the protected monument; and
4. 'Traditional setting': according to relevant European and international heritage conventions, the size of the protection zone should be proportional to the protected monument (see Charter of Venice, Article 6).

Miscellaneous Points about Sovereignty

Sarah Eagen contends that 'Perhaps the largest weakness in the World Heritage Convention is the power it gives source nations to determine the fate of cultural objects within their national territories. Under the Convention, non-source nations have no authority to ensure that cultural objects are being protected … Although the concept of territorial sovereignty is firmly established throughout the world as a method of establishing power, political independence and maintaining order, its use does not make sense in the context of cultural property preservation. Mrs Catherine Vernon states that "current national boundaries often have no connection or alignment with the peoples that inhabited the land in past centuries and left cultural clutter as evidence of their existence. Culture is defined by linguistic, religious, or other criteria, not by an artificially placed boundary line"'. Sarah Eagen, 'Preserving Cultural Property: Our Public Duty: A Look at How and Why We Must Create International Laws that Support International Action' (2001) 13 *Pace Int'l L Rev* 407, 430–43.

According to the UNESCO Convention Concerning the Protection of World Cultural and Natural Heritage:

> Whilst fully recognizing the sovereignty of the states on whose territory the cultural and natural heritage … is situated, and without prejudice to property rights provided by national legislation, the States Parties to this Convention recognise that such heritage constitutes a world heritage for whose protection it is the duty of the international community as a whole to co-operate.

The nature of the obligations that the Convention places on individual States Parties is established by Article 4, which states 'each State Party to this Convention recognises that the duty … belongs primarily to that State'. When a State becomes party to the Convention, it acknowledges its duty to ensure 'the identification (etc) … of … heritage … situated on its Territory'. The Convention respects the sovereignty of a Member State upon whose territory properties of outstanding universal cultural and natural value are located.

Conclusion

As a conclusion for this chapter I will present just one part of Kosova's position paper which was proposed during the negotiation process. All the proposals were refused by the Serbians.

> The above-mentioned instruments are to be developed within one year after the final decision on the status of Kosovo.
>
> Until these instruments are not completely developed a Temporary Legal Body will be in charge of the implementation of the DECLARATION in the parts that have not been properly implemented or implemented at all through Kosovar law – providing the authorities of Kosovo with all definitions, guidelines, ordinances and directives that are to be implemented.
>
> The Temporary Legal Body for the Implementation of the Declaration will be composed of 5 members – legal experts (2 representatives of the Orthodox Church, and 2 representatives of Kosovo's Authorities and 1 international expert).
>
> If all legal, administrative and technical instruments for the implementation of the Declaration are not passed in a year, the Orthodox Church may ask to prolong the work of the Temporary Legal Body for the Special Issues of SPC.
>
> Any violation of this statement should be the subject of consideration by Kosovar Courts as well as of the European Court for Human Rights.

This Declaration reflects the best and most open position of the Kosovar delegation to implement the best practices about human rights standards in Europe. All provisions in this Declaration concerning the responsibility of the Kosovar Authorities are unconditional.

However, we are offering this Declaration in order for it to be signed by the Serbian Orthodox Church as well and to be witnessed and monitored by the international community.

Chapter 14
The Regime of Mount Athos

Charalambos K. Papastathis

Introduction

The peninsula of Athos in Chalkidiki, in Central Macedonia, had been for several centuries a centre of Christian hermits. In 963 the first cenobite monastery of the Great Lavra was founded by the monk Athanasius the Athonite, with the financial support of the Byzantine Emperor Nicephorus Phocas. Ever since then, Byzantine emperors have granted to the whole monastic community, to various particular monasteries and establishments, as well as to individual monks, privileges of self-administration (as regards the exercise of administrative, legislative and judicial powers), in addition to other religious, personal and financial privileges: they have also provided generous financial aid. Sovereign princes of Eastern and South-Eastern Europe made large donations to the monasteries of Mount Athos and ensured privileged protection to their dependencies (*metochia*) in the territories they ruled. At the same time, the Ecumenical Patriarchs in Constantinople granted to Mount Athos special protection in the form of ecclesiastical self-administration, as well as direct spiritual obedience to the Patriarchal See of Constantinople, the Ecumenical Patriarch being the bishop of Mount Athos. The privileged status of the peninsula continued to be respected even after it was conquered by the Ottomans in 1430.

Soon after the foundation of the Great Lavra, many other monasteries were established and gradually Mount Athos came to be called *Hagion Oros*, the Holy Mountain. It became the most significant centre of Orthodox faith, with monks coming from almost all parts of the Orthodox world, and it exerted a tremendous influence upon the secular and religious culture of the peoples of Eastern and South-Eastern Europe during the Byzantine and Post-Byzantine periods.[1] All the

1 For a bibliography on Mount Athos published before 1963, see P. Irénée Doens, 'Bibliographie de la Sainte Montagne de l'Athos', in *Le Millénaire du Mont Athos, 963–1963* (Éditions de Chevetogne 1964, 337–495, 2nd ed., Bibliothèque Athonite, 2001, preface by Ch. Papastathis, 182); for Russian works concerning chiefly the relations between Russia and Mount Athos, see Ananatolij Prosvirnin, 'Afon i Russkaja Cerkov. Bibliografija' [1976] *Bogoslovskie Trudy* 185. Basic works on the history and art of Mount Athos: Manuel Gedeon, *Ὁ Ἄθως. Ἀναμνήσεις, ἔγγραφα, σημειώσεις* [*Mount Athos. Memoirs, Documents, Notes*] (Constantinople 1885, repr. Athens 1990); Episkop Porfirij Uspenskij, *Istorija Afona* (č. I, Kiev 1877), Id., *Vostok christianskij-Afona. Istorija Afona*

foundations and monks in Mount Athos, regardless of ethnic origin, enjoyed the benefits of the Athonite status.[2]

Legislative Sources of the Athonite Regime

Internal Sources

Mount Athos has never been a sovereign State or region: at first it was part of the *territorium* of the Byzantine Empire, then of the Ottoman Empire. The agents of its self-administration were invested with *potestas delegata*, while State sovereignty was confined, as a rule, to maintaining order and to ensuring the implementation chiefly of financial regulations.

During the First Balkan War, in November 1912, the Greek Navy liberated the Athos Peninsula from the Ottomans. The Hellenic State made strenuous efforts in order to:

(č. II–III, 1–2, Sankt Peterburg 1892); Deacon Cosmas Vlachos, *Ἡ χερσόνησος τοῦ Ἁγίου Ὄρους Ἄθω καὶ αἱ ἐν αὐτῇ μοναὶ καὶ οἱ μοναχοὶ πάλαι τε καὶ νῦν* [*The Peninsula of the Holy Mountain Athos and its Monasteries and Monks in Past and Present Times*] (Volos 1903); Archimandrite Gerasimos Smyrnakis, *Τὸ Ἅγιον Ὄρος* [*The Holy Mountain*] (Athens 1903, repr. Karyae 1988); Frederick William Hasluck, *Athos and its Monasteries* (Kegan Paul 1924); Archimandrite Christophoros Ktenas, *Ἅπαντα τὰ ἐν Ἁγίῳ Ὄρει ἱερὰ καθιδρύματα* [*All the holy Foundations in Mount Athos*] (Athens 1935); Emmanuel Amand de Mendieta, *La presqu'île des Caloyers. Le Mont Athos* (Desclée de Brouwer 1955); Ioannis Mamalakis, *Τὸ Ἅγιον Ὄρος (Ἄθως) διὰ μέσου τῶν αἰώνων* [*The Holy Mountain (Athos) through the centuries*] (Society of Macedonian Studies 1971).

2 For a selective legal bibliography on Mount Athos, see: P. Irénée Doens and Charalambos Papastathis, 'Νομική βιβλιογραφία Αγίου Όρους (1912–1969)' [Legal Bibliography on Mount Athos (1912–17)] [1970] Makedonika 121; P. Irénée Doens, Charalambos Papastathis, Konstatinos Papageorgiou and Dimitrios Nikolakakis, *Νομοκανονική βιβλιογραφία Αγίου Όρους Άθω (1912–2000)* [*Nomocanonical Bibliography on Mount Athos (1912–2000)*], (Mount Athos 2007; Philipp Meyer, *Die Haupturkunden für die Geschichte der Athosklöster* (J.C. Hinrichs 1894, repr. 1965); Dimitrios Petrakakos, *Τὸ μοναχικὸν πολίτευμα τοῦ Ἁγίου Ὄρους Ἄθω* [*The Monachal Regime of Mount Athos*] (Athens 1925; Panayos Panayotakos, 'Ἡ ὀργάνωσις τοῦ μοναχικοῦ πολιτεύματος ἐν Ἁγίῳ Ὄρει' ['The Organization of the Monachal Regime in Mount Athos'] [1949] *Archeion Ecclesiastikou kai Canonikou Dikaiou* 79; Charalambos Papastathis, 'The Status of Mount Athos in Hellenic Public Law', in Anthony-Emil N. Tachiaos (ed.), *Mount Athos and the European Community* (Institute for Balkan Studies 1993) 55–75; Eyaggelos Doris, *Το δίκαιον του Αγίου Όρους Άθω* [*The Law of Mount Athos*] (1994–2004) vols I–II; Nikolaos Antonopoulos, *Η συνταγματική προστασία του αγιορειτικού καθεστώτος* [*The Constitutional Protection of the Athonite Regime*] (Trokalia 1997); P. Grigorios Papathomas, *Le Patriarcat Œcuménique de Constantinople (y compris la politeia monastique du Mont Athos) dans l'Europe Unie* (Epektasis 1998) 169–491, 754–82.

1. safeguard the centuries-old existing regime through constitutional provisions. Articles 109–112 of the 1927 Constitution of the Hellenic Republic did indeed contain provisions recognizing the general privileged status of Mount Athos, as did later Articles 103 and 105 of the 1952 and 1975 Constitutions respectively.[3]
2. draw up a new Regulation for Mount Athos, to replace the Athonite General Regulations of 1911–12. The relevant work resulted in 1924 in the Mount Athos Charter (henceforth MAC), drawn by a commission of Athonite monks and voted by the competent authorities of the Holy Mountain. It was subsequently ratified by the Hellenic State in the Legislative Decree (henceforth LD) of 10/16 September 1926. Both the MAC and the LD came into force one day after the Constitution of 1927, that is, on 4th June 1927.

The Hellenic State has always recognized and protected the existing status of Mount Athos. It has added, from time to time, regulations for both religious and ideological reasons, and also out of a sense of responsibility arising from its international law obligations towards Athos. This special treatment, however, is

---

3 Article 105 (C. 1975):

'§ 1. The Athos peninsula extending beyond Megali Vigla and constituting the region of the Holy Mountain of Athos in accordance with its ancient privileged status, is a self-governed part of the Hellenic State, whose sovereignty thereon remains intact. Spiritually, Mount Athos is under the jurisdiction of the Ecumenical Patriarchate. All persons leading a monastic life thereon acquire Hellenic citizenship without further formalities, upon admission as novices or monks.

§ 2. Mount Athos is governed in accordance with its regime by its twenty Holy Monasteries among which the entire Athos peninsula is divided; the territory of the peninsula is exempt from expropriation.

Administration of the Mount Athos region is exercised by representatives of the Holy Monasteries, which constitute the Holy Community. No change whatsoever is permitted in the administrative system or in the number of Monasteries of Mount Athos, or in their order of preeminence, or in their position with regard to their subordinate dependencies. Heterodox or schismatic persons are prohibited from dwelling thereon.

§ 3. The determination in detail of the regimes of Mount Athos and the manner of operation thereof is effected by the Charter of Mount Athos which, with the cooperation of the State representative, is drawn up and voted by the twenty Holy Monasteries and ratified by the Ecumenical Patriarchate and the Parliament of the Hellenes.

§ 4. Faithful observance of the regimes of Mount Athos in the spiritual field is under the supreme supervision of the Ecumenical Patriarchate, and, in the administrative field, under the supervision of the State, which also is exclusively responsible for safeguarding public order and security.

§ 5. The afore-mentioned powers of the State are exercised through a governor, whose rights and duties are determined by law.

The law likewise determines the judicial power exercised by the monastic authorities and the Holy Community, as well as the customs and taxation privileges of Mount Athos'.

compatible with the constitutional principle of equality (Article 4), for the latter in fact requires equal or same treatment for all persons in the same or similar circumstances.

As far as the nature of the MAC is concerned, the Constitution declares that the MAC is the law determining in detail the Athonite regimes and the manner of their operation. The MAC is a law of superior formal force in comparison with the other laws of the Hellenic Republic: none of its provisions may be modified or repealed by common laws. Such a change has to be drawn up and voted by the representatives of all the Athonite monasteries and ratified by the Ecumenical Patriarchate and the Hellenic Parliament. Furthermore, the Council of State (the supreme administrative court) has ruled (Rulings 869/1967 and 2140/1975) that any modification of the MAC should be explicitly mentioned in subsequent law. In other words, it is not sufficient, as is usually the case in law, to simply include a clause to the effect that any previous general or special provision is henceforth repealed.

International Sources

In 1878 Mount Athos first received international protection.[4] The Treaty of San Stefano (1878) recognized and protected it, but only as regards its Russian monks.[5] The Treaty of Berlin (1878), which superseded that of San Stefano, also recognized the status of Mount Athos in its existing form and extended protection to all the monks, regardless of their national origin.[6]

When Ottoman rule ended in 1912 there followed a veritable tug-of-war over who should have State sovereignty over Mount Athos. Owing to Russian interests, the Ambassadors' Conference in London (1913) called for Mount Athos' autonomy.[7] However, the Peace Treaties of Bucharest (July–August 1913), Athens

4 Nicolas Antonopoulos, 'La condition internationale du Mont Athos', in *Le Millénaire du Mont Athos, 963–1963* (Éditions de Chevetogne 1963) 381–405.

5 Article 22 of the San Stefano Treaty refers to Mount Athos as follows: '… Les moines du Mont Athos d'origine russe seront maintenus dans leurs possessions et avantages antérieurs et continueront à jouir, dans les trois couvents qui leur appartiennent et dans les dépendances de ces derniers, des mêmes droits et prérogatives que ceux qui sont assurés aux autres établissements religieux et couvents du Mont Athos', see Gabriel Noradounghian, *Recueil d'actes internationaux de l'Empire Ottoman* (vol. III, F. Pichon 1902) 519.

6 Article 62 § 8: 'Les moines du Mont Athos quel que soit leur pays d'origine, seront maintenus dans leurs possessions et avantages antérieurs et jouiront, sans aucune exception d'une entière égalité de droits et prérogatives', see Gabriel Noradounghian, op. cit., vol. IV, 191–2.

7 'Le Mont Athos aura une autonomie indépendante et neutre …', Nicolas Antonopoulos, op. cit., 398; see also, Charalambos Papastathis 'Το καθεστώς του Αγίου Όρους και της Εκκλησίας στην Μακεδονία μετά την Συνθήκη του Βουκουρεστίου' ['The Regime of Mount Athos and the Church in Macedonia after the Treaty of Bucharest'], in *Η Συνθήκη του Βουκουρεστίου και η Ελλάδα* [*The Treaty of Bucharest and Greece*], IMXA,

(November 1913) and Neuilly-sur-Seine (1919) included Mount Athos within Hellenic territory and said nothing about an autonomous status. Finally, the Treaties of Sèvres (1920) and Lausanne (1923) recognized Greece's sovereignty over the territory of Mount Athos and the persons therein. Article 13 of the special Treaty of Sèvres concerning the protection of minorities in Greece (which was included in the Sixteenth Protocol of the Treaty of Lausanne), safeguarded the rights and liberties of the non-Greek monastic communities,[8] repeating in principle the provisions of Article 62 § 8 of the Treaty of Berlin.

This international protection of the Athonite regime is still in force and has been furthermore corroborated by the European Union. The Final Act (1979) of the Agreement concerning the accession of the Hellenic Republic to the European Economic Community includes Joint Declaration no. 4 concerning Mount Athos, which specifies that:

> Recognizing that the special status granted to Mount Athos, as guaranteed by article 105 of the Hellenic Constitution, is justified exclusively on grounds of a spiritual and religious nature, the Community will ensure that this status is taken into account in the application and subsequent preparation of provisions of Community law, in particular in relation to customs franchise privileges, tax exemptions, and the right of establishment'[9]

The Constitutional Protection

The Constitution recognizes and protects the centuries-old status of Mount Athos. This protection takes three forms: 1. specific provisions of a special nature; 2. specific provisions of a general nature; 3. authorization of the common legislator (that is, Parliament) to regulate certain specific issues.

1. The first category includes self-administration, with a wide range of directly related issues, such as the delimitation of the territory of Mount Athos and its subordination to Hellenic sovereignty; the inalienability of the peninsula's

---

1990, 197–8; Id., 'The Incorporation of Macedonia into the Greek State. Ecclesiastical incorporation', in Ioannis Koliopoulos and Ioannis Hassiotis (eds), *Modern and Contemporary Macedonia* (vol. II, Papazizzis – Paratiritis 1992) 34–7.

8 'La Grèce s'engage à reconnaître et maintenir les droits traditionnels et les libertés, dont jouissent les communautés monastiques non grecques du Mont Athos d'après les dispositions de l'article 62 du Traité de Berlin du 13 juillet 1878', see Georg F. de Martens, *Nouveau recueil général de traités et autres actes relatifs aux rapports de droit international* (3e série, par H. Triepel, vol. 12) 806. This Treaty was sanctioned by the Decree of 29.9/30.10.1923 'On the protection of Minorities in Greece', Official Gazette of Greece A.311/30.10.1923.

9 Official Journal of the European Communities 291/19.11.1979, 186; N. Skandamis, 'Το Άγιο Όρος και οι Ευρωπαϊκές Κοινότητες' ['Mount Athos and the European Communities'] [1983] *Helleniki Epitheorissi Europaikou Dikaiou* 271.

territory, which is distributed exclusively amongst the ruling monasteries; the direct spiritual jurisdiction of the Ecumenical Patriarchate of Constantinople; the prohibition of any change in the administrative system, the number of ruling monasteries (20), their hierarchical order and their position in relation to their dependencies; the process of drawing up, adopting and ratifying the MAC; and the allocation of supreme supervision over spiritual matters to the Ecumenical Patriarchate and administrative matters to the State, which is also in charge of public order and security (Article 105, §§ 1–4).

2. The specific provisions of a general nature are included in §§ 3 and 4 of Article 105 and refer, obviously, to any kind of privilege which has ever been recognized or granted, regardless of whether or not it has anything to do with self-administration. The Council of State has asserted that constitutional protection covers only those provisions for Athonite status relating to self-administration.[10] I hesitate to accept this opinion. It is quite clear that the provisions of §§ 1 and 2 of Article 105, which concern the καθεστώς (status) of Mount Athos, are limited to the context of its self-administration ('... [it] in accordance with its ancient privileged status, is a self-governed part ...'); but in §§ 3 and 4 the Constitution uses the term καθεστώτα (regimes) and stipulates that their determination in detail and the manner of their operation is effected by the MAC. Furthermore, it also states clearly which authorities are to exercise supreme supervision over their faithful observance. In other words, I believe that §§1 and 2 introduce special provisions, which safeguard self-administration to its fullest extent (both in scope and in content), whereas §§3 and 4 introduce a general provision, which safeguards the scope both of self-administration (together with the provisions of §§ 1 and 2) and of any other kind of regulation which has ever been enacted in relation to Mount Athos. At the same time, this provision also safeguards the content of these regulations, but only partially, since the Constitution assigns their detailed determination to the MAC, which is a law of superior formal force. These regulations arise from various old legal sources, such as Byzantine *chrysobulls* (imperial decrees), charters (*Τυπικά*), *sigils* (patriarchal decrees), *firmans* of various Ottoman sultans and general regulations issued at various times, as also from age-old monastic institutions and regimes, as stated in Article 188 of the MAC. I therefore believe that the privileged regulations of the MAC (regardless of whether they are wholly or partially favourable or unfavourable to Mount Athos and its inhabitants): i) may not be abolished or modified by a unilateral legislative act of the Hellenic State; ii) may not be repealed by any revision of the MAC without being replaced; and iii) may be modified, as to their content, by revision of the MAC, insofar as the constitutionally safeguarded Athonite legal tradition allows, but by constitutional order the extent and the type of the various privileged regulations cannot be ignored in this case.

It seems to me that Joint Declaration No. 4 of the Agreement concerning the accession of the Hellenic Republic to the European Economic Community points

10 Council of State 869/1967; 2140/1975.

in this direction. The Joint Declaration interprets Article 105 of the Hellenic Constitution as recognizing the whole scope of the special status of Mount Athos – not merely with regard to self-administration – and it goes on to consider as manifestations of that status the issues of tax and customs exemption and right of establishment. The special and general regulations for Mount Athos are described in the sources of Athonite law as "καθεστώτα" (regimes), "προνόμια" (privileges), "ασυδοσίαι" (immunities), and πλεονεκτήματα (benefits).

Most of these Athonite institutions have not been included in the MAC and the LD. The Arios Pagos (Greece's supreme civil court) and modern legal theory agree that provisions and institutions which were laid down in the distant past and are not included in the MAC and the LD remain valid if, at the time when Mount Athos was first granted constitutional protection (by the 1927 Constitution), they were not specifically repealed.[11] The provisions and institutions relating to these regimes may be written or unwritten, as I believe is understated in MAC 188 §2. It is only if such legal sources were not instituted, or if they were instituted but were repealed or not implemented because they had lost *opinio juris* when the 1927 Constitution came into force, that general Orthodox canon law and common Hellenic ecclesiastical law apply.

Thus, even regulations which have at various times been instituted for the monastic community, the establishments and the monks of Mount Athos, but have not been included in the MAC and the LD, continue to be valid, as long as: i) they were not repealed explicitly or implicitly when Mount Athos was first granted constitutional protection; and ii) they do not contravene the provisions of Article 105 of the Constitution, the MAC, or the LD. The protection granted to Mount Athos by explicit constitutional provisions (both specific protection relating to the scope and content of its self-administration and general protection relating to the extent of its general regimes) binds the common legislator and applies even if it happens to contravene other provisions of the Constitution.

3. Constitutional protection also extends to other areas, which are enumerated in § 5 of Article 105. They are the rights and duties of the Governor (the Hellenic State's representative on Mount Athos), the judicial power of the monastic authorities and the customs and taxation privileges of Mount Athos. The Constitution stipulates that all this shall be determined by common law. Constitutional protection is confined here to: i) the safeguarding of the existence of the Governor's rights and duties; ii) the exercise of judicial power by the monastic authorities; and iii) the granting of financial exemption by the State. The scope of these regulations, however, lies with common laws by constitutional authorization.

---

11 Arios Pagos 170/1964.

Self-administration of Mount Athos

The administrative power of Mount Athos lies in self-administration in the first and second degree.

First-degree self-administration is exercised by the 20 sovereign monasteries.[12] This number may not be changed, nor may the order of preeminence, or even their position towards their dependencies (*sketes*, *kellia* and hermitages). According to the MAC, the monasteries are either cœnobitic or *idiorrhythmic*, depending on the way in which their members conduct their lives. In a cœnobitic monastery everything is communal; the monks share a common way of life and have no private property. The monks in an idiorrhythmic monastery are allowed to support themselves through private resources, to have their own property and to dispose of it as they wish (though not by an act *mortis causa*). The *idiorrhythmic* system came into being in the early 15th century. The monasteries can change from idiorrhythmic to cœnobitic, but not vice versa. Today all the monasteries in Mount Athos are cœnobitic. The cœnobitic monasteries are administered by the Abbot (Hegumen/Ηγούμενος) and the Elders' Assembly (Gherontia/Γεροντία), while *idiorrhythmic* monasteries were administered by the Leaders' Assembly (Σύναξις των Προϊσταμένων).

Each monastery draws up and votes its own Internal Regulation, on which is based its self-administration. The Regulation covers all matters concerning the internal life of the monastery, its administration, the election of its representatives, and the management of its property. Each monastery submits its Regulation to the Holy Community for approval and it must to accord with the Constitution, the MAC and the various institutions of the privileged status. Each monastery elects its administrators and property managers with no intervention from other Athonite, State or ecclesiastical authorities. The elected officials administer the monastery, manage the property and they constitute a court of first instance, without any external intervention or interference.

Second-degree self-administration is exercised territorially throughout the peninsula and personally over all individuals upon it, whether monks, clergy or laymen. The members of the agencies of second-degree self-administration: i) are elected by the monasteries without State or patriarchal intervention; and ii) are the only bodies competent to deal with every issue relating exclusively to Mount Athos.

The Holy Community (Ιερά Κοινότης) is the main agent of second-degree self-administration. It sits in the capital of Mount Athos, Karyes, and comprises 20 members, each of whom represents one sovereign monastery. They serve for one year, but can be re-elected an indefinite number of times. The Governor,

12 The 20 monasteries, in the order of preeminence, are: Megisti Lavra, Vatopedi, Iviron, Chilandari, Dionyssiou, Koutloumoussi, Pantocrator, Xeropotamou, Zographou, Docheiariou, Karakallou, Philotheou, Simonos Petra, Hagiou Pavlou, Stavronikita, Xenophontos, Grigoriou, Esphigmenou, Rossikon (Hagios Panteleimon) and Kastamonitou (MAC 1).

representing the Hellenic State, may attend the sessions in a consultative capacity, if called upon. The administrative power of the monastic community rests with the Holy Community, as the supreme permanent agency which also functions as a court of law (sect. VI).

The Holy Community's executive organ is the Holy Superintendence (Ιερά Επιστασία), which comprises four monks drawn annually from four different monasteries in rotation. Thus, each monastery is represented at the Holy Superintendence every five years.[13] The leader of the four is known as the Πρωτεπιστάτης or Πρώτος (Protos = First), and is also in charge of the administration and management of the Holy Community. Apart from being the Holy Community's executive organ, the Holy Superintendence also performs specific duties of certain State authorities, namely the police force and police court. It also has municipal competence: it is responsible for keeping Karyes clean and repairing roads; it maintains public lighting; it carries out hygiene inspections; it fixes the prices of foodstuffs in the shops and restaurants of Karyes; it ensures that both monks and laymen conduct themselves with decency and decorum, prohibiting disorderly behaviour, secular songs, gambling, horse-riding and smoking in the main streets; it forbids shops to open during Vespers, on Sundays and on official holidays; it forbids the sale of meat and the preparation or public consumption of non-Lenten food on Wednesdays, Fridays and other fast-days; it expels laymen and non-Athonite clerics and monks who engage in misconduct. It has the Athonite police force under its command and may, if necessary, also call upon the State police force (MAC 37). Under common penal law, it tries the minor offenses committed in Karyes by monks and laymen (MAC article 40), imposing (LD 7; MAC 71) upon monks the penalties laid down by canon law or a fine, which consists in giving the Church of the Protaton in Karyes an amount of wax or oil, and upon laymen detention of between one and 30 days or a fine and/or expulsion from the peninsula. Prison sentences are served on the premises of the State police force. The Holy Superintendency also processes and stamps the Holy Community's correspondence (MAC 37). It issues pilgrims with the permit (*diamonitirion*) necessary for their visit, which will be discussed further on. It also administers the Common Fund, which consists of contributions by the monasteries. With this fund, the Church of the Protaton and the motor road between Karyes and Daphne (Karyes harbour) are maintained and the Holy Community's employees as well as the Athonite police force are remunerated. Every expense must be supported by a decision of the Holy Community (MAC 35 and 36).

---

13 1. Megisti Lavra, Docheiariou, Xenophontos, Esphigmenou; 2. Vatopedi, Koutloumoussi, Karakallou, Stavronikita; 3. Iviron, Pantocrator, Philotheou, Simonos Petra; 4. Chilandari, Xeropotamou, Hagiou Pavlou, Grigoriou; and 5. Dionyssiou, Zographou, Rossikon, Kastamonitou (MAC 28). The Regulations of all the monasteries, as well as those of the agencies of second-degree self-administration, have been published by Ch. Papastathis, *Εσωτερικοί Κανονισμοί Αγίου Όρους* [*Regulations of Mount Athos*], Athens-Komotini 2004.

There are two further organs of self-administration, which, unlike the preceding ones, are not permanent. The Extraordinary Biannual Twenty-Member Assembly (Έκτακτος Δισενιαυσία Εικοσαμελής Σύναξις) comprises the abbots of all the monasteries. It sits twice a year in order to vote the Regulative Provisions of Mount Athos and to act as a special court (sect. VI). The other non-permanent organ of self-administration is the Extraordinary Double Assembly (Έκτακτος Διπλή Σύναξις), which consists of all the members of the Holy Community plus a representative from each monastery, therefore it has 40 members. This organ is not provided for in the MAC or the LD, and that is why its authority has been called into question.[14] Personally, I do not agree with this view which, anyway, has not prevailed in practice. The Extraordinary Double Assembly has convened repeatedly in the past and continues to function today. It was this body, indeed, that voted the MAC in 1924. It has on occasion been summoned by the Holy Community to deal with serious matters. In other words, it was operating when the constitutional provision for Mount Athos came into force in 1927. Consequently, regardless of the fact that it is not stipulated *expressis verbis* in the Constitution, the MAC and the LD, its basis cannot be challenged, precisely because it is one of the customary regimes of Mount Athos. In any case, the MAC and the LD do not include or regulate all the institutions of Mount Athos.

The question which now arises is: how can the *status quo* be maintained and safeguarded? Is there any authority empowered to intervene if or when the organs of self-administration exceed the bounds of their competence, and, if so, which is it? There are two controlling agents: the Governor of Mount Athos and the Ecumenical Patriarchate.

The Governor is a government official, answerable to the Ministry of Foreign Affairs and residing in Karyes. He is invested with public authority, but is not an agent of Athonite self-administration. For this reason, I consider the use of the term 'Governor' (*dioiketes*) in the Constitution to be inexact. Should the Constitution be revised, this term really ought to be replaced.

L. 2594/1998, which deals with the internal organization of the Ministry for Foreign Affairs, in Article 21 regulates matters relating to the personnel of the (civil) administration of Mount Athos. It provides that a Presidential Decree determine the section, the rank and specialty of each staff member. The personnel consists of the (civil) Governor, the Deputy (civil) Governor and a number of clerks who occupy permanent posts under private law contracts. The qualifications formally required for the Governor are limited to '… (having) a personality of great prestige, with experience in administration and knowledge of the affairs of Mount Athos' (sic). Fortunately, the Deputy Governor is required to hold a university degree.[15]

14 Ioannis Iliakis, *Οἱ αγιορειτικοὶ θεσμοί* [*The Athonite Institutions*] (Athens 1938) 16; Panayos Panayotakos, op. cit. 130–132. Contra: Dimitri Th. Tsatsos, 'Άγιον Όρος. Προνομιακόν καθεστώς' ['Mount Athos. Privileged status'] [1953] *Themis* 428.

15 Charalambos Papastathis, 'Church and State in Greece in 1997' [1998] *Journal of Church and State Research* 48.

The Constitution entrusts the Governor with the task of ensuring that the Athonite regime is strictly observed, from an administrative point of view. He fulfills this duty: 1. at the decision-making stage, by attending the sessions of the Holy Community, if and when called upon to do so; and 2. after decisions have been made, when he has to check the legality of the actions proposed by the organs of self-administration. If he finds that any of their decisions contravene the regimes, the MAC or other provisions, the Governor draws the Holy Community's attention to the fact. If the Holy Community disagrees with his appraisal of the situation, then the Governor seeks the guidance of the Minister for Foreign Affairs. The Governor's actions are subject to the control of the Council of State,[16] as also are the administrative actions of the Athonite agencies, with the exception of those which relate to the internal administration of Mount Athos. The jurisprudence of the Council of State accepts that internal issues include all the relations between the monastic establishments and the monks themselves, both between each other, the monastic authorities and the Holy Community.[17]

The other controlling agent is the Ecumenical Patriarchate of Constantinople, whose jurisdiction covers matters of a spiritual nature. The Patriarchate also ratifies the Extraordinary Biannual Twenty-Member Assembly's regulative provisions relating to spiritual matters and – in the past – any decision aimed at converting an *idiorrhythmic* monastery to the cœnobitic system; it issues permits to clerics to go to Mount Athos and officiate there and provides letters of recommendation to scholars wishing to study in the archives and libraries. The Patriarchate must be informed of the election, resignation and deposing of abbots, as well as of the chair-persons and members of the monastic assemblies. The Patriarch with the Patriarchal Synod, convened together, form the Athonite court of justice (sect. VI).

The Legislative Power

Legislative power on Mount Athos is regulated by the provisions of: 1. the MAC; 2. the laws referred to in § 5 of Article 105 of the Constitution; and 3. the Regulative Provisions of the Extraordinary Biannual Twenty-Member Assembly of Mount Athos.

The MAC is drawn up and voted by the 20 ruling monasteries of Mount Athos, that is to say by the Holy Community (Constitution, Article 105, § 2, sect. b). The Governor also may get involved in drawing up the MAC, but does not have the right to vote. After being voted, the MAC is submitted to the Ecumenical Patriarchate and the Hellenic Parliament for ratification. I believe that the Patriarchate's ratification is confined to the spiritual provisions and the Parliament's to the administrative provisions, since § 4 of Article 105 of the Constitution stipulates that the strict observance of the regimes of Mount Athos in the spiritual field shall be under the

16 Council of State 339/1976; 2421-2424/1980.

17 Council of State 1093/1936; 1267/1966.

supreme supervision of the Ecumenical Patriarchate and in the administrative field under that of the Hellenic State.

As has already been pointed out, sect. IV, Article 105, § 5 of the Constitution stipulates and safeguards: i) the rights and duties of the Governor; ii) the judicial power exercised by the Athonite authorities; and iii) the customs and taxation privileges granted by the Hellenic State to Mount Athos. The scope of all these rights, however, is not determined by the Constitution or the MAC, but by common laws passed by the Hellenic Parliament.

The Regulative Provisions are drawn up and voted by the Extraordinary Biannual Twenty-Member Assembly, which is the 'supreme legislative and judicial body of Mount Athos' (MAC 43 and 45). The Regulative Provisions are issued in order to regulate various specific points in the MAC and the LD, as also others for which these texts make no provision. They are communicated to the Governor and the competent minister, while those related to spiritual matters are submitted to the Ecumenical Patriarchate for approval. Both the minister and the Patriarchate may grant or withhold ratification of the Regulative Provisions, but they may not amend them.

The Judicial Power

Matters relating to judicial power are regulated by the provisions of the MAC and the LD. The Athonite courts exercise civil, penal and ecclesiastical jurisdiction.

The Athonite courts are: 1. the monastic courts (the Elders' Assembly and the Abbot in each cœnobite monastery); 2. the Holy Community; 3. the Holy Superintendence; and 4. the Ecumenical Patriarch with the Patriarchal Synod, who, however, have the right to delegate their powers in this sphere to a special tribunal, comprising a three-member exarchate of patriarchal metropolitans dispatched on Mount Athos and the Extraordinary Biannual Twenty-Member Assembly.

Private law disputes which may be resolved by the Athonite courts are those which arise in connection with: 1. the boundaries of the various monasteries' property; and 2. the *homologa* (bonds), that is, written agreements drawn up between monasteries and their dependencies concerning the use of land on the peninsula.

It is the monastic court which deals with boundary disputes between two or more of its dependencies. The Holy Community is a court of both first and second instance. As a court of first instance, it deals with: 1. boundary disputes between monasteries; 2. disputes over 'bonds' between a monastery and its dependency; and 3. disputes between dependencies of two or more monasteries. As a court of second instance, it handles appeals against the decisions of the monastic courts. The Ecumenical Patriarchate (or the Special Tribunal) acts as a court of second instance for appeals against decisions by the Holy Community. All other disputes arising in private law between the Athonite establishments are brought before the ordinary civil courts: the Court of First Instance in Halkidiki, initially, and, subsequently, the Court of Appeal in Thessaloniki.

Offences and felonies committed under common penal law are tried by the penal courts in Thessaloniki. Mount Athos enjoys a special privilege in this respect: the relevant inquiries are carried out on Mount Athos and a member of the Holy Superintendence is present throughout the proceedings.

Misdemeanors under common penal law, and market and police offenses committed on Mount Athos by monks, clerics and laymen are tried by Athonite courts: the monastic court, when the offense is committed within the monastery premises, and the Holy Superintendence, when it is committed in Karyes.

Canonical offenses (ecclesiastical and disciplinary) committed by Athonite monks are dealt with by the court of the monastery concerned, with the exception of those offenses which entail unfrocking, whether simple monks or monks who are also ordained priests (*hieromonks*). The Holy Community acts as a court of appeal against the decisions of the monastic courts. Applications for review of the Holy Community's decisions are examined by the Patriarch and Synod (or by the Special Tribunal). If the accused is a hieromonk and his offense is punishable by unfrocking, he is tried in the first and last instances by the Patriarch and Synod, in which case the Holy Community is restricted to an investigatory role. Furthermore, if a non-Athonite monk or cleric commits a canonical offense on the Athos Peninsula, the investigation is carried out by the Holy Community, which remits the brief to the ecclesiastical authority of the accused.

Further Treatment of Mount Athos

In addition to self-administration in the broadest sense, the Hellenic State has also recognized (in the Constitution, the MAC, the LD and other laws) various other privileges for Mount Athos. Some of them are mentioned in the Joint Declaration No. 4 of the Final Act of the Agreement concerning the accession of the Hellenic Republic to the European Economic Community (1980). The privileges that are not mentioned in the Joint Declaration areas are the following:

1. The territory of the whole peninsula (including the littoral) is the inalienable and exclusive property of the 20 sovereign monasteries, as divided among them (Constitution, article 5, § 2; MAC 2).
2. The protection of the heirlooms of each monastery lies with the monastery itself (LD 2).
3. Only the Holy Community, the monasteries and the sketes may have and use a seal (MAC 25, 31, 172).
4. It is forbidden to form any associations on the peninsula (MAC 183).
5. Athonite monks and novices are exempt from military service (MAC 93; LD 38; Law 1763/1988, article 6, § 1, sect. Iii).
6. The documents of the Holy Community, as well as those sent by the monasteries and their dependencies to the Holy Community, must be written

in Greek (MAC 26); other documents may be written in any language the monasteries and dependencies wish.

7. Only the Holy Community may establish a printing-press on the peninsula (MAC 180).
8. When a layman dies on Mount Athos intestate and without heirs, his belongings and money are inherited by the Holy Community or by the monastery in which he passed away, in lieu of the State (MAC 179).
9. Collections of money may be made with the permission of the Holy Community and only for religious, educational or charitable purposes (MAC 185).
10. 'Proselytism and propaganda – moral, religious, ecclesiastical, social, national or of any other nature – are prohibited, on pain of expulsion from the peninsula' (MAC 184).
11. The peninsula's forests do not come under the forestry laws of the Hellenic State (MAC 169).
12. On Mount Athos it is forbidden to sell icons or handicrafts not made on the peninsula itself; the production of icons and handicrafts on the peninsula by laymen is also prohibited (MAC 174).
13. Land on the peninsula may not be sold, but only exchanged between monasteries (MAC 100).
14. The Holy Community and the monasteries do not pay the employer's quota to the various social security funds for their lay employees and workers (Law 1759/1989, article 4, § 1).
15. Usucaption by third parties of the monasteries' property off the peninsula is not possible (LD of 22 April 1926); this in fact applies in Greece to all monasteries, whether Athonite or not, Orthodox or not.
16. Athonite monks (like all monks in Greece) are insured by the Agrarian Insurance Organization, from which they receive medical care and pensions (Law 4169/1961).
17. The Hellenic Republic offers an annual subvention to the monasteries: in 1924, some 200,000 acres of land outside the peninsula, belonging to monasteries of Mount Athos, were expropriated for the benefit of refugees from Asia Minor, and as the Hellenic State was unable to indemnify the monasteries at that time, an annual subvention was agreed upon. Law 1166/1981 provides that this subvention should not amount to less than 30,000,000 drachmas per year (= € 88.000).
18. Law 1198/1981 established the State-run Centre for the Preservation of the Heritage of Mount Athos, which is based in Thessaloniki (Ministry of Macedonia and Thrace) and carries out various construction works on the peninsula, financed by the Hellenic State and the European Community.

Special Treatment According to Joint Declaration No. 4 between the European Union and Greece

Let us now come to the customs franchise privileges, tax exemption[18] and the right of establishment which are explicitly mentioned in the Joint Declaration of the Agreement concerning Greece's accession to the European Economic Community.

Article 105, § 5 of the Constitution safeguards Mount Athos' financial privileges and empowers the law to determine their extent. This does not violate the principle of equality of taxation (Constitution 4, § 5) because the same principle recognizes certain exceptions which serve the general interest. The customs and most of the tax privileges of Mount Athos directly concern the monks: the total extent of some privileges is determined on the basis of the number of inhabitants of the peninsula, while others are instituted for their direct benefit.

Customs Franchise Privileges

1. Exemption from duties on any goods imported to Mount Athos for the monasteries and other foundations, up to a total value of 1,000 official judicial monetary units (*metalliki drachmi*) per monk per year (MAC 167; LD 2, i). The goods must be imported by the agents of Athonite self-administration (not by merchants or visitors). At the moment the official judicial monetary unit for Mount Athos' customs exemptions is equivalent in value to € 1.50, according to a Decision of the Ministry of Finance[19] (that is, € 1,500 per monk per year).
2. Exemption from duties on both forestry and other products exported from Mount Athos (MAC 168, § 1). The said products must have been produced on the peninsula and be exported by the foundations.

Tax Privileges

Mount Athos' tax privileges consist in the exemption of the foundations or of the monks, or of both, from the obligation to pay various taxes. These are:

1. Tax on income from real property (Law 2238/1994, Article 103 § 1, sect. b).
2. Tax on large real property (L 2459/1997, Article 23).
3. Tax on donations of movables, money and real property, as well as on inheritances (L. 2961/2001, Article 25 § 1, a; Article 43 § 1).

---

18 Konstantinos Papageorgiou, 'Το προνομιακό φορολογικό και τελωνειακό καθεστώς του Αγίου Όρους' ['The privileged tax and customs regime of Mount Athos'] [2003] *Nomocanonica* 31.

19 Law 4055/1960, Article 2 § 5.

4. Tax on real property transfer transactions (purchase and sale, L. 1882/1990, Article 14 §7).
5. Municipality and community rates on real property (L.2130/1993, Article 24 § 7, b).
6. Value added tax and other excise duties (L. 1642/1986, Article 2 § 2 a; L. 2127/1993, Article 16; L. 2187/1994, Article 16).
7. Fishing off the coast of Mount Athos is exempt from all tax, as long as it is carried out for the purpose of the monks' own sustenance (MAC 170).
8. Purchase tax on those products which are produced and consumed by the monks on the peninsula (LD 2, sect. b, 3).
9. Donations to the monasteries of Mount Athos are subtracted from the donor's taxable income (LD 3223/1955, Article 4, 7, iv).
10. Transfer of property on the peninsula is exempt from property transfer tax. This privilege applies to the exchange of real property between monasteries and the transfer of movables by the foundations and the monks (LD 2, sect, b, 2).
11. Income from property on the peninsula is exempt from taxation (LD 2, sect. b, 2). This privilege is particularly useful to the *kellia* (cells off the main facility of the monastery), the residents of which subsist on their own agricultural produce and handicrafts. However, laymen engaged in commerce on the peninsula are not exempt from this tax.
12. Contracts drawn up on Mount Athos by the Holy Community and the monasteries relating to the transfer of rights over real property on the peninsula are exempt from stamp duty (LD 2, sect, b, 4). This privilege has been extended to cover 'contracts of all kinds' made between the Holy Community or the monasteries and any third party, as are also all documents issued by or submitted to the Holy Community or the various establishments of Mount Athos (LD 2561/1953, Article 13, § 4).
13. The Athonite monks are exempt from the tax and general state levies on the alcohol produced and consumed on the peninsula. They are also exempt from certain formalities governing the production of alcohol (Forced Law of 14/14.10.1935) and tax on the purchase of cars for the needs of the monastery.

The abovementioned exemptions are extended to the dependencies of each monastery, which are situated outside the peninsula (*metochia*).

Restrictions On the Right of Establishment

1. Any male, irrespective of ethnic origin or nationality, may settle on Mount Athos as a monk or novice. He must, however, be an Orthodox Christian and a member of a regular Orthodox Church. Schismatic and non-Orthodox persons and members of most other religions are excluded (Constitution 105, § 2, sect, ii; MAC 5). Like any other Greek citizen, the monk and

the novice have the right to abandon the Orthodox faith and adopt another Christian doctrine or become atheists. In this case, however, they cease to be Athonites and may no longer dwell on Mount Athos.

2. The MAC imposes special restrictions on the monks' right of free movement, owing to their monastic status and the observance of monastic obedience. Thus the monks may not leave the peninsula without written permission from their monastery, which must be informed of the reason for the absence and its duration. However, the monastery may not refuse leave of absence to monks who are following a course of study (MAC 96).
3. Monks who do not belong to Athonite monasteries or dependencies and are found wandering about on Mount Athos are expelled by the Holy Superintendence (MAC 177). The Holy Superintendence also has the right to expel laymen who cause a disturbance (MAC 37).
4. Until 1998 everyone (non-Athonite monk, clergyman, or layman) who visited Mount Athos (for any purpose other than that of settling there) was obliged to previously obtain a permit (*diamonitirion*) in Karyes, which gave him the right to travel on the peninsula and seek hospitality from the monasteries. The *diamonitirion* was issued by the Holy Superintendence, which also determined its duration (MAC 176). Clergymen, whether Orthodox or not, also had to obtain a permit from the Ecumenical Patriarchate (MAC 173). In addition, both clergymen and laymen who were not Greek citizens had to obtain a permit from the Ministry of Foreign Affairs in Athens or the Ministry of Macedonia and Thrace in Thessaloniki. If the visitor did not leave when the permit expired, he was expelled by the Holy Superintendence.

All these procedures, however, were not stipulated in the Constitution, the MAC or in any other legal source of Mount Athos. They contravened the MAC as well as the international protection of Mount Athos, as has been mentioned above. The Athos monks expressed their opposition to these practices, especially after 1974 when the political climate in Greece changed. There were threatening tensions between Mount Athos on the one hand, the Greek State and the Ecumenical Patriarchate on the other.

These tensions ended favourably for the foreign visitors. On 28 July 1998 Presidential Decree No. 227/1998 'On the Organization of the [Civil] Governance of Mount Athos' was published in the *Official Gazette of the Hellenic Republic* (A, No. 176). According to Article 3 § 2, '… the entry to Mount Athos and the visit to the Monasteries and their dependencies is unrestricted to any male individual that resides, stays, or has legitimately entered the territory of the Greek state'. This measure was followed by Circular No. P20a-18949/AS8706 issued by the Secretary General on Administration and Organization of the Ministry for Foreign Affairs. The Circular makes clear that

> ... it is explicitly stipulated [in the Presidential Decree], in congruence with the constitutionally guaranteed principles of individual and religious freedom (articles 5 and 13 of the Constitution) and the international agreement of the country that ... the entry into Mount Athos and the visit of the Holy Monasteries and of their dependencies is unrestricted to every male individual ... Regardless of national origin or religion ... From the aforementioned provisions it becomes evident that the entry to Mount Athos and the pilgrimage to its Holy Monasteries and their Dependencies can in no way be dependent on the license of any state authority or agency. This also applies to foreigners, regardless of their country of origin, on the self-explanatory condition that they have legitimately entered into Greek territory, the region of Mount Athos being a part of this territory.

From then on, anyone wishing to visit Athos needs only a *diamonitirion*, which he can obtain from the offices of the Holy Superintendence in Thessaloniki or in Ouranoupolis (a village at the 'border' of Mount Athos). For Orthodox worshipers – regardless of their citizenship – according to the customary institutions of Mount Athos, there is no waiting list, as is the case for followers of other cults and religions. This practice is not provided for in the Presidential Decree but is followed by the Holy Superintendence. The civil Governor of Mount Athos is allowed to intervene only in case he has strong indications that a visitor will commit punishable acts upon his entry. He may then petition the Holy Superintendence requesting that no *diamonitiorion* be granted him. If the Holy Superintendence agrees, the Governor may order the police to forbid the entrance of the specific visitor or to deport him if he has already entered the peninsula (Article 3 § 1, c). On the other hand, the procedure by which the Governor granted a license to those wishing to indwell is no longer in effect.

5. Anyone wishing to study in the monasteries' libraries and archives must present at the Holy Community with a letter of recommendation from the Ecumenical Patriarchate or the Hellenic Ministry of Foreign Affairs (MAC 185 § 2).
6. The presence of all females, whether women or animals, on Mount Athos has always been prohibited (MAC 186). Violation of this rule is an offence under Canon law, which means that sanctions may be applied only to Orthodox Christians. The Hellenic State has therefore issued LD 2623/1953, which was included as Artcle 43 b in the LD that ratified the MAC. It imposes a prison sentence of between two and 12 months, with no alternative fine, on any woman who sets foot on the peninsula. In 1956, the Extraordinary Biannual Twenty-Member Assembly passed a Regulative Provision punishing anyone who introduces female animals onto Mount Athos with a fine and detention of up to five days. A more recent Regulative Provision of the same Assembly decrees that any ship with women onboard must sail at least 500m off shore. In 1975, which was declared International Women's Year, a member proposed to the Hellenic Parliament that the

prohibition on women entering Mount Athos be lifted by law. Parliament rejected the proposal because: i) the prohibition has always existed, and therefore comes under the constitutional and international protection of Mount Athos; ii) the prohibition is included in the MAC, any amendment of which lies exclusively in the hands of the Athonite monks.[20]

7. Laymen may exercise their profession on Mount Athos only with the permission of the Athonite authorities. Further, the practice of trade is restricted to Karyes and its harbour of Daphne, since it is 'absolutely' forbidden to set up commercial establishments in the monasteries and their dependencies, as well as to trade anywhere on the peninsula in goods which are not essential there (MAC 175).
8. Foreigners who come to live on Mount Athos as monks or novices acquire Hellenic citizenship *ipso jure* upon their enrollment in the relevant monastery's register (Constitution 105, § 1; MAC 6). Loss of Hellenic citizenship is not expressly mentioned in any legislative text concerning Mount Athos; in this case the provisions of the Code on Hellenic Citizenship (LD 3370/1955, Law 1438/1984) should apply.[21]

Epilogue

The acquisition of Hellenic citizenship is a privilege, because thus it is not possible for a foreign-born monk or novice to be expelled. Foreigners who wish to settle on Athos may do so in whichever monastery they wish. Russians, Serbs, Bulgarians and Romanians traditionally choose St Panteleimon, Chilandari and Zographou Monasteries, and the Skete of St John the Baptist respectively. Like the other 17, these three monasteries are under the ecclesiastical jurisdiction of the Ecumenical Patriarchate, as well as legal persons under Hellenic public law.[22] At the same time, however, they are also sanctuaries of the Russian, Serbian and Bulgarian people, as the Skete of the Baptist is a sanctuary of the Romanian people.[23] They enjoy self-administration and all the other privileges given by the Constitution and the laws of the Hellenic Republic. They also receive international protection, in accordance with the provision of the Treaty of Sèvres concerning the protection of minorities in Greece, which was carried on by the Treaty of Lausanne. Despite the intervening wars and the national and political differences which have crept into

20 See Charalambos Papastathis, 'The Enclosure of Mount Athos in the Framework of Gender Discrimination' [2000] *Kanon* 265.

21 Charalambos Papastathis, 'The Nationality of the Mount Athos Monks of non-Greek Origin' [1967] *Balkan Studies* 84.

22 Council of State 1093/1936; Court of the first Instance of Athens 7922/1954.

23 See Charalambos Papastathis, 'The legal Status of the Monks of non-Greek Origin in Mount Athos' in *Medžunarodni Naučen Skup Osam Vekova Hilandara* (SANU 2000) 179–85.

its relations with other Orthodox countries, it is a fact that Greece has respected the rights and liberties of these establishments. They were the cradles of their respective countries' national and cultural rebirth and to this day continue to offer them spiritual sustenance. The existence of these monastic communities may be considered as an indisputable token of the ecumenical nature of Mount Athos, where Orthodox, regardless of ethnic origin, live together as monks and novices. In the 1,000-year Amphictyony of Mount Athos, this peculiar society has much to teach our world. From this point of view Joint Declaration No. 4 of the Final Act (1979) of the Agreement for the accession of Greece into the European Economic Community concerning Mount Athos was not only a starting point for the study of Athonite issues in the age of the United Europe, but also an occasion for the European Union to discover its 1,000-year-old spiritual expression.
In conclusion:

1. The Character of Mount Athos as Holy Place is justified on spiritual and religious grounds, on the common cultural heritage of the whole Orthodox world and on the survival of the traditions of the united Church before the Schism of 1054.
2. The present legal regime functions smoothly and whenever new necessities appeared a legislative initiative took place (for example accession of Greece to the EU).
3. Object of the protection is the multinational religious community indwelling in the peninsula.
4. The protection is based upon: a) international law; b) the Constitution of the Hellenic Republic; c) the Charter of Mount Athos, which is drawn up by the Holy Community itself; d) laws of the Republic; e) regulations of the first- and second-degree Athonite administrative organs; and f) the written and customary Athonite institutions existing *ab antiquo* (953).

Chapter 15

Sacred Heritage in Cyprus: Bolstering Protection Through the Implementation of International Law Standards and the Adoption of an Object-Oriented Approach

Alessandro Chechi

Introduction

Cyprus possesses a rich archaeological and artistic heritage reflecting its turbulent history. Different civilizations conquered the island over the centuries, such as the Romans, the Arabs, the Byzantines, the Venetians and the Ottomans. Each civilization contributed towards shaping the heritage of Cyprus and the identity of its people. Nevertheless, the cultural tradition of the island has remained in the orbit of Greek civilization and Christianity, especially as a result of the influence of the Byzantine culture. The marks of this influence can be traced in the Byzantine Orthodox Christian art, such as monastery wall paintings, churches, icons and wood carvings.

Regrettably, Cyprus' rich cultural patrimony is in large part lost or crumbling. Archaeological sites have suffered theft and spoliation. Religious monuments have been demolished, vandalized or abandoned. In addition, the content of religious buildings, including icons and mosaics, have been stolen and illegally exported abroad. Only a few items have been repatriated. An example is the litigation over four Byzantine mosaics removed from the Church of the Panagia Kanakaria, in the village of Lythrankomi.[1] In this case, a United States court ruled that art dealer Peg Goldberg had to surrender possession of the mosaics to the plaintiffs, the Autocephalous Greek-Orthodox Church of Cyprus and the Republic of Cyprus (RoC). Another telling example is the restitution of two 13th-century Byzantine frescoes by the Menil Foundation in Houston.[2]

---

1 *Autocephalous Greek Orthodox Church of Cyprus v. Goldberg*, 717 F. Supp. 1374 (S.D. Ind. 1989), *aff'd*, 917 F.2d 278 (7th Cir. 1990).

2 The frescoes were acquired by Dominique de Menil in 1983. After a thorough investigation, Mrs de Menil learned that the artworks had been looted. She alerted the Church of Cyprus and together agreed on a rescue plan. Under its terms, the Foundation

These cases are important in that they depict the efforts made by the Cyprus authorities to fight against the impoverishment of the unique cultural heritage of the island. Moreover, they are noteworthy as they bring to light two fundamental problems. The first concerns the cause of the losses. The heritage of the island has been attacked mostly as a consequence of the fights between Greek and Turkish Cypriots. The second problem relates to the nature of the property that has been 'victimized'. The rival groups have mostly destroyed or looted the religious heritage sacred to the enemy. This chapter focuses on this type of property.

This is not a marginal issue. Today the protection of cultural heritage from the vicissitudes of war is, at the same time, one of the goals on the agenda of the international community and one of the components of the so-called 'Cyprus problem'. This chapter attempts to identify some principles for enhancing the legal protection of the heritage sacred to the peoples of Cyprus with a view to contributing to the scholarly debate relevant to the eventual settlement of the Cyprus problem. For these purposes, this chapter provides some historical background and examines three key legal questions: (i) whether the assets of religious importance located in Cyprus qualify as 'cultural property' entitled to international protection; (ii) whether the northern part of Cyprus meets the legal definition of 'occupied territory'; and (iii) whether the 'victimization' of religious property in northern Cyprus could give rise to international responsibility on the part of the occupying power.

The 'Cyprus Problem' – an Overview

In order to examine the Cyprus problem it is essential first to provide a brief overview of the recent history of the island to illustrate the events that have led to the current impasse. However, the present inquiry cannot be carried out without formulating two preliminary caveats: (i) in Cyprus almost every action is related to the politics of the Cyprus problem; (ii) historical narrative and the media constitute powerful means through which the parties involved seek to foster their respective interests and objectives.[3] But academic detachment is crucial, while selective perceptions of the Cyprus problem actually fuel its persistence.[4] Therefore, the

bought the works on behalf of the Church; in exchange, the Menil Foundation was granted a long-term loan of the frescoes. See Menil Foundation, Letter from the Director, 23 September 2011, available at <www.menil.org/ByzantineFrescoChapelNews.php> accessed 23 January 2014.

3 See Nicholas Augustinos, 'The Protection of Cultural Heritage in the Event of Armed Conflict: The Cyprus Experience', in Norman Palmer (ed.), *The Recovery of Stolen Art* (Kluwer Law International, 1998) 217–9. See also Christophoros Christophorou, Synthia Pavlou and Sanem Sahin, *Media Narratives, Politics and the Cyprus Issue* (Peace Research Institute Oslo [PRIO], Report I 2010).

4 Brendan O'Malley, 'Victims and Villains: The Influence of Foreign Military Interests and Ethnic Fighting on the Division of Cyprus', in Fouskas K. Vassilis and Richter A. Heinz (eds), *Cyprus & Europe. The Long Way Back* (Bibliopolis, 2003) 51.

guiding spirit behind this chapter is to focus on the problem of the protection of the sacred heritage of Cyprus judiciously and impartially.

Historical Background

Cyprus fell under the rule of the Ottoman Empire in 1571. This is an important date in Cyprus history because the Ottoman victory affected the pre-existing composition of the population. In effect, after 1571 around 20,000 Muslims settled on the island. However, the Ottomans sought neither to establish a Turkish majority nor to set up a dominant Turkish economic class. On the contrary, they followed a lenient policy toward the autochthonous population. The Ottomans emancipated the Greek Orthodox Cypriots from the oppression of the Catholic Venetians, abolished the feudal system,[5] and established a system of 'ethnarchy' (the *millet* system).[6] Under this system the population was divided by religious affiliation, which allowed Cypriots of Greek descent and Greek-Orthodox faith to coexist with Cypriots of Turkish descent and Muslim faith.[7] Yet the two communities were not concentrated in any one specific geographical area. Greek Cypriot villages were intermingled with Turkish Cypriot towns throughout the island, and in these towns and villages Christian Orthodox churches frequently stood next to Muslim mosques. The two communities coexisted for the most part in peace and mutual respect, tolerant of religious differences, and they often joined together in commercial transactions and social functions; however, they rarely intermarried due to religion-based restrictions. In spite of this, the Greek Cypriots became the dominant economic and political power and regarded themselves as the rightful rulers.[8]

The relationship between Turkish and Greek communities began to deteriorate in 1878, following the occupation of the island by the United Kingdom.[9] The Greek Cypriots believed that the British would allow them to realize their ambition to unite the island with Greece (*Enosis*). But Britain made it clear that it had no intention of relinquishing control of Cyprus. This was confirmed in 1925, when Britain formally declared Cyprus a Crown Colony following the dissolution of the Ottoman Empire in 1923.[10] In contrast, the Turkish Cypriot minority (approximately 20 per cent of the population) resisted the idea of *Enosis* for fear of discrimination and supported the partition of the island and its annexation to Turkey (*Taksim*). Tensions between Greek and Turkish Cypriots intensified at the beginning of the 1950s, when violent attacks by extremist groups resulted in the death of many

5 Clement Dodd, *The History and Politics of the Cyprus Conflict* (Palgrave Macmillan, 2010) 1–2.

6 Brendan O'Malley, 'Victims and Villains', op. cit., 52.

7 Ibid.

8 Clement Dodd, *The History and Politics of the Cyprus Conflict*, op. cit., 2.

9 In return for the island, the United Kingdom undertook to give diplomatic and material aid to the Ottoman government against the Tsarist Kingdom of Russia. Ibid., 3.

10 Ibid., 3 ff.

innocent civilians – Turks, Greeks and British – and the wanton destruction of much property.[11] The prospect of a civil war between the two communities on the one hand, and of a conflict between Greece and Turkey on the other, paved the way for the conference between representatives of the Greek and Turkish governments in Zurich in February 1959. At the conference, Greece and Turkey agreed on the independence of Cyprus from the United Kingdom (which was proclaimed on 16 August 1960), on a Constitution,[12] and on three treaties that aimed to preserve the political order established by the Constitution: the Treaty of Guarantee, the Treaty of Establishment and the Treaty of Alliance.[13]

Although the Constitution safeguarded the basic rights and freedoms of all its citizens, it contained a number of unworkable provisions. In 1963, the president of the Republic proposed constitutional amendments, which however were rejected by the Turkish Cypriot community and Turkey. As a result, Greek Cypriots became increasingly estranged from Turkish Cypriots and a violent inter-ethnic conflict broke out in 1963–67. This conflict brought to an end the bi-communal power-sharing system envisaged by the Constitution and provoked the displacement of both Greek and Turkish Cypriots from their homes. In particular, Turkish Cypriots moved into armed enclaves in the north.[14] The United Nations Security Council (hereinafter 'UNSC') defined the situation in Cyprus as a potential threat to international peace and security, and requested the government of Cyprus to take all 'measures necessary to stop violence and bloodshed'.[15] Yet war broke out on 20 July 1974, when Turkish troops landed on the north coast of Cyprus and advanced to Nicosia. On 22 July a cease-fire was negotiated between the two sides under UN auspices. This paved the way for the start of formal peace talks in Geneva between the three Guarantor Powers and the representatives of the island's two

11 Ibid., 20 ff.

12 The Constitution aimed to reconcile Greek and Turkish Cypriot political ambitions by providing, *inter alia*: (i) a non-territorial power-sharing system; (ii) the allocation of government posts and public offices along a 70:30 per cent ratio; and (iii) autonomy in cultural and religious matters through the institution of communal chambers. Ibid., pp. 42–8.

13 The Treaty of Guarantee gave recognition to the basic articles of the Constitution, required the RoC to maintain the state of affairs established by the treaties and acknowledged the entitlement of the three named Guarantor Powers, the United Kingdom, Greece and Turkey, jointly or separately, to maintain the state of affairs being established. The Treaty of Establishment included the right of the United Kingdom to retain military bases on the island. The Treaty of Alliance obliged the signatories (Greece, Turkey and Cyprus) to cooperate in their common defence. Dodd, ibid., pp. 38–9, 41. The treaties are reproduced in Nathalie Tocci, *The 'Cyprus Question': Reshaping Community Identities and Elite Interests within a Wider European Framework* (*CEPS Working Document No. 154,* 2000) 48 ff.

14 Clement Dodd, *The History and Politics of the Cyprus Conflict*, op. cit., 53–5.

15 Resolution 186 (1964). With this Resolution the UNSC established the United Nations Peacekeeping Force in Cyprus (UNFICYP) with the task of preventing 'a recurrence of fighting and, as necessary, to contribute to the maintenance and restoration of law and order and a return to normal conditions'.

main communities. After the negotiations broke down on the morning of 14 August, Turkish forces began the second phase of their military operations. As a result, by late August Turkish military forces had extended their control over the northern 37 per cent of the island.[16] The Turkish invasion caused the displacement of one-third of the population: an estimated 170,000 to 200,000 Greek Cypriots fled to the south, whereas over 65,000 Turkish Cypriots were forced to move northward. Moreover, it was estimated that around 6,000 Greek Cypriots died during the conflict, with an additional 3,000 missing. Turkish Cypriots estimated 1,500 dead, with an additional 2,000 wounded.[17] To this one must add that during the invasion and the first weeks after the cessation of the hostilities Turkish troops committed large-scale looting and destroyed or occupied immovable property abandoned by Greek Cypriots.

Different narratives concerning the causes of the invasion are found on both sides. Be that as it may, it is certain that the Turkish intervention followed a Greek-sponsored military coup (planned with the assistance of the Cypriot armed forces and aimed at achieving *Enosis* through the overthrowing of Makarios, the President of Cyprus),[18] as well as intense, self-interested Cold War-style manoeuvring orchestrated by the British, Russian and United States governments.

After the termination of hostilities the authorities in the Turkish held area of Cyprus declared the establishment of the 'Turkish Federated State of Cyprus', which became the 'Turkish Republic of Northern Cyprus' (TRNC) in 1983. However, no country except Turkey has recognized the TRNC. Instead the RoC government is recognized internationally as the government of the island in the context of diplomatic and treaty relations and the working of international organizations[19] – with *de jure* but not *de facto* sovereignty over the north.

Since 1974 attempts to resolve the Cyprus problem have failed dismally and the division of the Greek and Turkish communities has deepened, further with the migration of Turkish nationals to northern Cyprus.[20] As a result, today Cyprus is divided ethnically, politically and geographically by a tract of barbed wire (the 'Green Line') that is under the control of UN troops. The TRNC relaxed boundary restrictions in 2003, allowing free movement of people on both sides of the divide. In 2007, the boundary between the RoC and the UN buffer zone was demolished in Ledra Street, in the heart of Nicosia, and was reopened in the

16 Clement Dodd, *The History and Politics of the Cyprus Conflict*, op. cit., 110–128.

17 Brendan O'Malley, 'Victims and Villains', op. cit., 59.

18 Ibid., 57–9.

19 See UNSC Resolution 541 (1983). See also Resolution (83) 13 of the Committee of Ministers of the Council of Europe of 24 November 1983.

20 Richter A. Heinz, 'The Policy of Ankara towards Cyprus and the EU', in Fouskas K. Vassilis and Richter A. Heinz (eds), *Cyprus & Europe. The Long Way Back*, op. cit., 159–71. Despite the lack of consensus on the exact figures, both parties concurred that Turkish nationals arrived in northern Cyprus. According to reliable estimates, the number of post-1974 Turkish settlers was more than 100,000. Council of Europe, Parliamentary Assembly, Recommendation 1608 (2003), *Colonisation by Turkish Settlers of the Occupied Part of Cyprus*.

presence of Greek and Turkish Cypriot officials in April 2008.[21] Nevertheless, the peace process is still a work in progress and is further complicated by a bizarre aberration: Turkey occupies illegally the territory of a member of the European Union (EU), the very Union that Turkey is trying to join.[22]

The Cultural Losses Sustained by Cyprus

When the Turkish Cypriot government opened the checkpoints in 2003, countless Cypriots crossed over to visit their homes and villages. For many of them it was a time of disillusionment. They found that everything had disappeared or irreversibly changed. At the same time, the country's chief cultural institutions as well as international and regional organizations witnessed the degradation of the cultural heritage in the Turkish-held area.

One of the appraisals[23] was carried out in 1989 by Senator Ymenus Van Der Werff, General Rapporteur to the Council of Europe's Sub-Committee on Architectural and Artistic Heritage.[24] Van Der Werff visited both parts of the island and produced a detailed report providing examples of the considerable and irretrievable damage to the island's immovable heritage. The 1989 Report pointed out that most of the damage was sustained by Greek Orthodox sacred sites in the Turkish-held area. Furthermore, the Report described the disappearance of religious property, namely icons originally displayed in churches and monasteries. In 2002, a second report was submitted to the Committee on Culture, Science and Education of the Council of Europe by General Rapporteur Vlasta Stepová.[25] The 2002 Report confirmed that the heritage of the whole island was still threatened and stated that the reasons were 'diametrically different in the north and the south. The north lack[ed] resources for the maintenance of a number of monuments and to prevent the outflow of movable cultural goods due to thefts and illegal export. In the south, the integrity of the historic settlements and the beautiful Cypriot cultural landscape [were] threatened by excessive urbanization [...]'[26]

21 Paul Hamilos, 'Hundreds Gather for Reopening of Divided Cyprus Street', *The Guardian* (3 April 2008).

22 Cyprus joined the EU in 2004.

23 The first official investigation was conducted on behalf of UNESCO by Jacques Dalibard, but his report (*Cyprus: Status of the Conservation of Cultural Property*, UNESCO, 1976) was classified confidential and never made public in its entirety. Subsequently, UNESCO was precluded from visiting and providing expert advice to the TRNC; to do otherwise would have implied recognition.

24 Council of Europe, Parliamentary Assembly, Report *Cultural Heritage of Cyprus*, Doc. No. 6079, 6 July 1989 (hereinafter '1989 Report'). The report of art historian Dr Robin Cormack was annexed to the 1989 Report.

25 Council of Europe, Parliamentary Assembly, Report *Cultural Heritage of Cyprus*, Doc. No. 9460, 7 May 2002 (hereinafter '2002 Report'). The report of Dr Josef Štulc was annexed to the 2002 Report.

26 Ibid.

Besides the monitoring by international organizations, various journalists visited northern Cyprus after 1974. These substantiated the accounts of refugees about desecrated graves, damaged monasteries, churches demolished or littered with excrement, rubbish and the remains of ecclesiastical furniture.[27] Later on, other journalistic accounts described the desecration of frescoes, the theft of icons, mosaics and other ecclesiastical items and the transformation of religious buildings into mosques, military camps, stables, latrines, shops, gyms, hotels and so forth.[28] Regrettably, not all reports have acknowledged the relationship between the losses sustained by the Greek Cypriot heritage that occurred after 1974 and the gratuitous destruction of mosques, graves and other Ottoman and Islamic religious sites since the early 1960s and after 1974.[29] For instance, in 1964 in Paphos the main mosque was burned down and the nearby cemetery was heavily damaged.[30]

Finally, the loss of Cypriot heritage in the occupied part of the island is demonstrated by the numerous restitution claims brought against museums and private collectors. In effect, Greek Cypriot authorities and the Church of Cyprus have been very diligent in their search to recover wrongfully removed materials. For instance, the *Goldberg* case brought to light the existence of a sophisticated, worldwide smuggling ring that operated with impunity in the Turkish-held area and involved local looters, Turkish Cypriot officials and art traders.[31]

The Sacred Dimension of Cultural Heritage

Against this background it seems appropriate to provide a definition of 'sacred heritage'. This will help to clarify why cultural heritage is intertwined with the settlement of the Cyprus problem.

The international instruments that have been adopted by the United Nations Educational, Scientific, and Cultural Organization (UNESCO) in order to protect

27 See John Fielding, 'The Rape of Northern Cyprus', *The Guardian* (6 May 1976), cited in Patroklos Stavrou, 'The Destruction of the Cultural Heritage of Cyprus following the Turkish Invasion of the Island', in *Cyprus: The Plundering of a 9000 Year-Old Civilization* (Cultural Centre of the Municipality, 1994) 39–43.

28 See Yasin Mehmet, 'The Cyprus which Is Vanishing', *Olay* (26 April 1982), and Heinz Gstrein, 'Painful Loss', *Hannover Anzeiger* (1 June 1982), cited in Patroklos Stavrou, 'The Destruction of the Cultural Heritage of Cyprus', op. cit. See also Dan Hofstadter, 'Annals of the Antiquity Trade – The Angel on Her Shoulder', *The New Yorker* (13 June 1992 [Part I] and 20 July 1992 [Part II]), cited in Nicholas Augustinos, 'The Protection of Cultural Heritage', op. cit., 222.

29 A notable exception is John Fielding, 'The Rape of Northern Cyprus', op. cit.

30 1989 Report, supra note 24.

31 Further evidence was gathered in October 1998, when German police arrested Aydin Dikman, the 'mastermind' of the pillaging in northern Cyprus. See Mark Rose, 'From Cyprus to Munich' (1998) *Archaeology* <http://archive.archaeology.org/online/features/cyprus/> accessed 23 January 2014.

the tangible and intangible cultural heritage do not provide a definition of the term 'sacred heritage'. Nevertheless, these instruments apply to assets and sites that are important to communities belonging to different faiths or beliefs.

The treaties concerning the protection of the *tangible* heritage from the vicissitudes of war and illicit trafficking merely establish that they apply to 'monuments', 'buildings', 'centres' and movable 'cultural property' as long as these are important, *inter alia*, on 'religious' grounds.[32] It is also worth noting that the Statute of the UNESCO Intergovernmental Committee for Promoting the Return of Cultural Property to its Countries of Origin or its Restitution in Case of Illicit Appropriation[33] establishes that a 'request for the restitution or return [...] may be made concerning any cultural property which has a fundamental significance from the point of view of the spiritual values [...] of the people of a [...] State [...] and which has been lost as a result of [...] foreign occupation [....]' (Article 3(2)).

The instruments regarding the *intangible* cultural heritage are also noteworthy. These emphasise two important aspects. The first is that the tangible and intangible heritage are inherently interdependent: any cultural manifestation – either material or immaterial, irrespective of its aesthetic significance or monetary value – embodies distinctive spiritual, historical and intellectual values that are collectively created, valued, shared and handed down from generation to generation. This aspect is evidenced by Article 2 of the 2003 UNESCO Convention for the Safeguarding

32 The Convention for the Protection of Cultural Property in the Event of Armed Conflict (14 May 1954, 249 UNTS 240 – hereinafter '1954 UNESCO Convention') establishes that only 'movable or immovable property of great importance to the cultural heritage of every people' falls within its scope of application (Article 1). *The Convention on the Means of Prohibiting and Preventing the Illicit Import, Export and Transfer of Ownership of Cultural Property* (17 November 1970, 823 UNTS 231 – hereinafter '1970 UNESCO Convention') includes in the definition of 'cultural property' to be protected the 'property which [...] is specifically designated by each State as being of importance for archaeology, prehistory, history, literature, art or science' and which belongs to one of the categories list therein (Article 1). The Convention on Stolen or Illegally Exported of Cultural Objects (24 June 1995, 34 ILM 1322), which was adopted by UNIDROIT (International Institute for the Unification of Private Law) upon request of UNESCO, covers the same categories identified by the 1970 UNESCO Convention, but does not include the requirement of State designation. The UNESCO Convention Concerning the Protection of the World Cultural and Natural Heritage (16 November 1972, 1037 UNTS 151) does not define the notion of 'cultural heritage' on the basis of religious or spiritual meaning. However, the Operational Guidelines for the Implementation of the World Heritage Convention clarify that the inscription of certain places on the List set under the Convention is justifiable by virtue of their religious meanings or purposes.

33 Established with Resolution 20 C4/7.6/5 of 24 October–28 November 1978. The Committee was entrusted with the mandate to assist UNESCO Member States in dealing with cases falling outside the framework of the 1970 UNESCO Convention, such as the disputes concerning historical cases of cultural objects lost as a result of colonial or foreign occupation, or as a result of illicit appropriation that occurred prior to 1970.

of the Intangible Cultural Heritage.[34] This includes in the definition of 'intangible cultural heritage' to be protected 'the practices, representations, expressions, knowledge, skills – as well as the instruments, objects, artefacts and cultural spaces associated therewith – that communities, groups and, in some cases, individuals recognize as part of their cultural heritage' and which provide such communities, groups and individuals 'with a sense of identity and continuity [...]'. The second aspect relates to the fact that, 'in so far as cultural heritage represents the sum of practices, knowledge and representations that a community or group recognize as part of their history and identity, it is axiomatic that members of the group, individually and collectively, must be entitled to access, perform and enjoy such cultural heritage as a matter of right'.[35] Indeed, cultural heritage cannot be treated in isolation from human rights. In this respect it is useful to recall Article 5 of the Universal Declaration on Cultural Diversity: 'The flourishing of creative diversity requires the full implementation of cultural rights as defined in Article [...] 15 of the International Covenant on Economic, Social and Cultural Rights [ICESCR]'.[36] The rights set forth in Article 15 of the ICESCR include the freedom of thought, conscience and religion and entail the State's obligation to: (i) recognize the existence of different cultures within its jurisdiction; (ii) protect the freedom of individuals to choose, express and develop their own culture; and (iii) maintain and preserve the artistic, historic and archaeological property located on the territory as an integral aspect of advancing the cultural life of the inhabitants and for the benefit of all humankind.[37]

In light of the analysis set out above, it results that 'sacred heritage' is composed of three layers. The first is the 'artistic' (or 'cultural') layer. This refers to the fact that buildings, places and artefacts are the tangible creation of artists, architects or craftsmen. The second is the 'symbolic' layer. This relates to the relationship between a space or an item, the rituals, memories, traditions and legends that surround it, and the identity of individuals or of a given community. For instance, many sanctuaries have played an important role in the history of a religion and hence have a profound spiritual connection with peoples, be they religious or not. As such, sacred assets are important for the cultural heritage of the whole human community as witnesses of cultural diversity. The third is the 'religious' (or 'spiritual') layer. This entails that certain buildings, places and objects are essential to a specific living religious group to manifest, practise, develop and teach its religious customs and ceremonies. This is often the consequence of the fact that divine manifestations or supernatural events occurred in such spaces or are associated with certain objects. As a result, these spaces or objects have a special

34 17 October 2003, UNESCO Doc. 32C/Resolution 32.

35 Francesco Francioni, 'Culture, Heritage and Human Rights: An Introduction', in Francesco Francioni and Martin Scheinin (eds), *Cultural Human Rights* (Brill, 2008) 1–15, 6.

36 2 November 2001, 41 ILM 57.

37 Roger O'Keefe, 'The "Right to Take Part in Cultural Life" under Article 15 of the ICESCR' (1998) *International and Comparative Law Quarterly* 904–923, 909.

value in people's existence beyond their value as art or as historical or education objects, as intermediaries with a power beyond the people or used in ceremonies which attempt to connect the people with that power.[38] Clearly, the religious layer is closely linked to certain fundamental human rights, such as the right to freedom of religion, the right to own, maintain, protect and have access to religious sites and the right to manifest one's religion or belief in teaching, practice, worship and observance, alone or in community with others, in public or private.[39]

On the basis of this conceptualization, it appears that sacred heritage is as varied as the human perception of the sacred and as various as the world's faiths. As such, it constitutes a fundamental expression of the identity of the people to which such heritage is ascribed. This is why the destruction and desecration of monuments and artefacts that followed the 1974 Turkish invasion constitute issues of paramount importance for the people of Cyprus. Many monuments and artefacts used for religious rituals and purposes signify Greek Cypriots' deep links to their faith. This is underlined by the statement by Costas Katsaros, head of the Autocephalous Greek-Orthodox Church of Cyprus' legal department, in relation to the restitution of the Lysi frescoes by the Menil Foundation: '[the Lysi frescoes] are living monuments and symbols of our faith. [...] Those treasures of our religion and cultural heritage are of invaluable merit for Cypriot people, who were long waiting for their return in their homeland'.[40]

Analysis of the Principles of International Law Applicable to Situations of Armed Conflict and Occupation

The definition provided above makes it possible to argue that the *ratio* for the safeguarding of the sacred heritage resides in the protection of the rights and identity of individuals and groups. It logically follows that subjects in search of their identity should be enabled to protect and recover their heritage. In turn, States should remove any obstacle inhibiting or limiting access to a person's heritage. These are the challenges at stake in Cyprus, where a protracted ethnic conflict involving political turmoil and humanitarian needs is accompanied by claims concerning sacred sites and heritage practices.[41]

The sections that follow examine these challenges through the prism of international law. Yet space permits but the briefest of overviews of the relevant international practice. The objective of this analysis is threefold: to emphasise that

38 Patrick J. O'Keefe, 'Repatriation of Sacred Objects' (2008) *Art Antiquity and Law* 225–243.

39 See Article 18 UDHR and Article 9 ECHR.

40 Douglas Britt, 'Houston's Menil Is Returning Holy Artworks to Cyprus', *Houston Chronicle* (26 September 2011).

41 Costas M. Constantinou and Mete Hatay, 'Cyprus, Ethnic Conflict and Conflicted Heritage' (2010) *Ethnic and Racial Studies* 1600.

the assets of religious importance located in Cyprus qualify as 'cultural property' entitled to international protection; to examine the acts by which the international community has reacted to the crimes committed against cultural heritage; and to demonstrate that the protection of sacred heritage in times of war and occupation is guaranteed by a number of principles. These principles are the obligation to protect cultural heritage from the vicissitudes of armed conflict, the prohibition of acts of violence against cultural heritage, the prohibition of plundering artworks and the ensuing obligation of restitution. These principles have achieved the status of customary international law, thus they are binding on all States, irrespective of whether or not the State concerned has ratified the treaties regulating these issues. These general principles can be considered the corollaries of the prohibition to use force set forth in Article 2(4) of the Charter of the United Nations (hereinafter 'UN Charter').

The Obligation to Protect Cultural Heritage and the Prohibition of Acts of Violence Against it

The destruction of cultural materials during armed conflicts is nothing new. Any armed conflict is characterized by the loss of cultural property having no military value. Yet in recent times the international community has been called upon to react to acts of barbarism whereby damage was inflicted on properties with religious significance in order to hurt the enemy through the elimination of the tangible symbols of their existence and identity. Although the effects of such destruction are emotional rather than physical, they are no less painful. As emphasised above, a people's sense of heritage and identity is often linked to objects and their elimination may produce feelings of loss and annihilation.[42] The response provided by international law has been resolute: it sanctions the inviolability of cultural heritage and confirms that the practice of destroying the symbols of the defeated is no longer permitted.

The earliest codification of the rules on the protection of cultural heritage from the direct and indirect effects of armed conflict took place in 1863 when the Lieber Code was drafted at President Lincoln's orders.[43] This was designed to regulate the conduct of the Union forces in the American Civil War and it prohibited acts of violence against movable and immovable cultural assets. The influence of the Lieber Code can be traced through the Hague Conventions of 1899 and 1907 and their annexed Regulations.[44] Article 23(g) of the Regulations annexed to the 1907

42 Wayne Sandholtz, *Prohibiting Plunder. How Norms Change* (Oxford University Press, 2007) 196.

43 Instructions for the Government of Armies in the Field as Authorized by the Laws and Usages of War on Land, General Orders No. 100 of 24 April 1863, Articles 34–6.

44 Convention (II) with respect to the Laws and Customs of War on Land, 29 July 1899, AJIL, 1907, 66; and Convention (IV) respecting the Laws and Customs of War on Land (18 October 1907, AJIL, 1908, 165 – hereinafter '1907 Convention').

Convention establishes that, during hostilities, monuments and buildings dedicated to art and science ought not to be attacked or bombarded, unless necessary for military reasons. Moreover, Article 47 formally prohibits pillage, whereas Article 56 provides that 'destruction or wilful damage done to institutions [dedicated to religion, charity and education, the arts and sciences], historic monuments, works of art and science, is forbidden [...]'.

The Hague Regulations did not succeed in preventing widespread and systematic destruction during the two World Wars. UNESCO reacted to the devastation that took place during World War II with the adoption of the 1954 UNESCO Convention.[45] This treaty, whose obligations are widely regarded as reflecting customary international law,[46] obliges the High Contracting Parties to take special care to avoid damage to 'movable or immovable property of great importance to the cultural heritage of every people' (Article 1(a)), because 'damage to cultural property belonging to any people whatsoever means damage to the cultural heritage of all mankind' (Preamble). The 1954 UNESCO Convention distinguishes between the 'safeguarding of' and 'respect for' cultural property. The former concept refers to the obligation of each State to adopt (preventive and) protective measures in time of peace (Article 3). Moreover, Article 7 underlines that States are required to take measures before the outbreak of hostilities by introducing specific provisions into their military regulations or instructions and by fostering a spirit of respect in the members of their armed forces for the culture and cultural property of all peoples. The concept of 'respect' applies to situations of war and military occupation and regards the property situated within the territory of the occupying power as well as within the territory of other States (Article 4). Article 5 of the 1954 UNESCO Convention regards the case of military occupation. This article establishes that the occupying State 'shall [...] support the competent national authorities of the occupied country in safeguarding and preserving its cultural property' (paragraph 1). On the other hand, '[s]hould it prove necessary to take measures to preserve cultural property situated in occupied territory and damaged by military operations, and should the competent national authorities be unable to take such measures', the occupying State 'shall [...] in close co-operation with such authorities [...] take the most necessary measures of preservation' (paragraph 2). In the intention of the drafters, this provision was essential to deal with the problem of the preservation of the original features and functions of properties. It has been contended that Article 5 does not place a heavy burden on the occupying State because, on the one hand, that State is not prevented from engaging in archaeological excavations and, on the other, it is required to provide its assistance for the preservation of the properties situated in the occupied territory only 'as far as possible'. However,

45 Turkey has ratified the 1954 UNESCO Convention (15 December 1965) and the First Protocol (15 December 1965) but it has not ratified the Second Protocol; the RoC has ratified the 1954 UNESCO Convention (9 September 1964), the First and the Second Protocol (9 September 1964 and 16 May 2001, respectively).

46 UNESCO General Conference, Resolution 3.5, 13 November 1993, Preamble.

the prevailing view is that a prohibition is implied by the language and spirit of Article 5.[47] Furthermore, Article 28 of the 1954 UNESCO Convention obliges the States Parties to 'prosecute and impose penal or disciplinary sanctions upon those persons, of whatever nationality', accused of violations of the Convention.

Since 1954 other relevant treaties have been introduced, most notably the Additional Protocols to the 1949 Geneva Conventions.[48] Protocol I relates to international wars, Protocol II to internal conflicts. Both Protocols forbid military actions directed at, or any military use of, 'historic monuments, works of art or places of worship which constitute the cultural or spiritual heritage of peoples'.[49] Moreover, Article 85(4)(d) of Protocol I establishes that 'making the clearly-recognised historic monuments, works of art or places of worship [...] the object of an attack [...]' is a serious breach. These Protocols therefore confirmed one of the fundamental principles of warfare, that attacks shall be limited strictly to military objectives.

The looting and destruction that characterized the First Gulf War and the Yugoslav War triggered further developments in international law. For the purposes of this chapter it is sufficient to focus on the Second Protocol to the 1954 UNESCO Convention.[50] This significantly improved the legal regime for the protection of cultural heritage in time of war by: (i) defining clearly and restrictively the limits of 'military necessity' (Article 6); (ii) introducing the new system of 'enhanced protection' (Articles 10–14); (iii) setting up a permanent Committee (the Intergovernmental Committee for the Protection of Cultural Property in the Event of Armed Conflict) to supervise the operation of the Protocol (Articles 24 ff.); and (iv) framing in clear terms the duty of protection, thereby improving the protection regime provided for by the 1954 UNESCO Convention. With respect to the latter innovation, Article 9(1) of the Second Protocol affirms that occupying States 'shall prohibit and prevent in relation to the occupied territory [...] (c) any alteration to, or change of use of, cultural property which is intended to conceal or destroy cultural, historical or scientific evidence'. Moreover, Article 9(2) provides

47 Theresa Papademetriou, 'Destruction of Cultural Property in the Northern Part of Cyprus and Violations of International Law' (The Law Library of Congress, Directorate of Legal Research LL File No. 2008-01356, April 2009), 33.

48 Protocol Additional to the Geneva Conventions of 12 August 1949 Relating to the Protection of Victims of International Armed Conflict (8 June 1977, 1125 UNTS 3 – hereinafter 'Protocol I') and Protocol Additional to the Geneva Conventions of 12 August 1949 Relating to the Protection of Victims of Non-International Armed Conflicts (8 June 1977, 1125 UNTS 609 – hereinafter 'Protocol II').

49 Article 53 of Protocol I, ibid., and Article 16 of Protocol II, ibid.

50 26 March 1999, 38 ILM (1999) 769. It is worth mentioning that, at the judicial level, the International Criminal Tribunal for the former Yugoslavia has repeatedly confirmed that the prohibition of acts of destruction and willful damage to sites of educational, religious and cultural relevance has achieved the status of customary international law. See for example *Prosecutor v. Strugar*, IT-01-42-PT, Judgment, 31 January 2005; and *Prosecutor v. Jokić*, IT-01-42/1-S, Judgment, 18 March 2004.

that any 'alteration to, or change of use of, cultural property in occupied territory shall, unless circumstances do not permit, be carried out in close co-operation with the competent national authorities of the occupied territory'. Evidently these provisions single out the alteration and change of use as a specific threat.

The last instrument that it is worth mentioning in order to demonstrate that the prohibition to attack works of art or places of worship belongs to customary international law is the UNESCO Declaration Concerning the Intentional Destruction of Cultural Heritage of 2003. This act was adopted by the UNESCO General Conference to condemn the gratuitous demolition of the Buddhas of Bamiyan committed by the Taliban in 2001.[51] By adopting the Declaration, the UNESCO General Conference confirmed: (i) that the deliberate destruction of cultural heritage constitutes a breach of customary international law; and (ii) that State responsibility and individual criminal responsibility derive from the intentional destruction or the failure to take appropriate protective measures. Accordingly, the Declaration invalidates the shield of territorial sovereignty.[52] In other words, the importance of cultural heritage for the identity of nations, communities and individuals justifies the limitation of the territorial State's absolute discretion and the corresponding attribution of State responsibility for the wanton destruction or failure to protect the autochthonous heritage.

The Obligation to Halt or Prevent the Looting of Cultural Objects and the Corresponding Obligation of Restitution

The plundering of religious articles, military symbols, works of art and archives was the symbolic dimension of war by which the victors demonstrated their superiority over the vanquished.[53] The 1907 Convention provided the first codification of the rule that the plundering of cultural property is unlawful and that all loot should be returned. Article 56 of the Regulations annexed to the 1907 Convention stated that all cultural objects, including State property, were to be treated as private property, and hence could neither be confiscated (Article 46) nor plundered (Article 47) by occupying forces. The same principles were reaffirmed in the peace treaties concluded in the aftermaths of the two World Wars.[54]

---

51 Francesco Francioni and Federico Lenzerini, 'The Destruction of the Buddhas of Bamiyan and International Law' (2003) *European Journal of International Law* 619.

52 Ana F. Vrdoljak, 'Intentional Destruction of Cultural Heritage and International Law', *Thesaurus Acroasium* (vol. XXXV, Institouton Diethnous Dēmosiou Dikaiou kai Diethnōn Scheseōn Thessalonikēs 2007) 377–96; Joseph Fishman, 'Locating the International Interest in Intranational Cultural Property Disputes' (2010) *Yale Journal of International Law* 347.

53 Wayne Sandholtz, *Prohibiting Plunder*, op. cit., 32–3.

54 See for example Treaty of Saint-Germain between the Allied Powers and Austria (1919), Treaty of Trianon between the Allies and Hungary (1920), and the Treaty of Peace with Italy (1947).

State practice developed primarily as a reaction to Nazi spoliation of cultural objects. Before the end of World War II, the Allies took steps against the systematic looting carried out by the Nazi regime by adopting the 'London Declaration'.[55] This warned the enemy States and neutral countries that the Allies intended 'to do their utmost to defeat the methods of dispossession practiced by the [Nazis]' and reserved the right to annul transfers or dealings taking the form of open looting or plundering as well as seemingly good faith transactions. In this way the Allies made it clear that restitution was a means of reversing the genocidal and discriminatory Nazi practices.[56] Following the end of World War II, the prohibition of looting and the restitution principle became treaty standards as they were transplanted into the 1954 UNESCO Convention and the 1970 UNESCO Convention. The 1954 UNESCO Convention calls upon the States Parties 'to prohibit, prevent and, if necessary, put a stop to any form of theft, pillage or misappropriation of, and any acts of vandalism directed against, cultural property' as well as the 'requisitioning [of] movable cultural property […]' situated in occupied territory (Article 4(3)). Binding regulations in matters of restitution are contained in the First Protocol to the 1954 UNESCO Convention.[57] According to Article I(1) of the First Protocol, States Parties are required to prevent the exportation of cultural property from territories they have occupied during armed conflict. If the occupying State fails to comply with this obligation, it 'shall pay an indemnity to the holders in good faith of any cultural property which has to be returned' (Article I(4)). The First Protocol requires the cooperation of all the High Contracting Parties in the fight against trafficking in looted art objects. All States Parties – including the occupying State – must take into custody the cultural property imported into their territory from any occupied territory (Article I(2)) and return it to the competent authorities of the territory previously occupied at the close of hostilities (Article I(3)).[58] The latter provision also emphasises that the cultural property that has been illicitly exported from an occupied territory 'shall never be retained as war reparations'. It can be asserted that the obligation to return illicitly taken cultural objects belongs to customary international law because it is inherent in the obligation to respect cultural property and in the prohibition on seizing cultural property: if such objects should not be seized by the occupying State and if they have been wrongfully exported, *a fortiori*, they should be returned.[59] Article 11 of the 1970 UNESCO Convention regards as illicit

55 Declaration of the Allied Nations against Acts of Dispossession Committed in Territories under Enemy Occupation or Control, 5 January 1943 (8, Department of State Bulletin 21).

56 Ana F. Vrdoljak, *International Law, Museums and the Return of Cultural Objects* (Cambridge University Press, 2006) 141.

57 14 May 1954, 249 UNTS 358.

58 Article II(5) imposes an obligation of restitution upon the State where cultural property has been deposited by another State for the purpose of safekeeping.

59 Jean-Marie Henckaerts and Louise Doswald-Beck (eds), *Customary International Humanitarian Law* (vol. I, *Rules*, The International Committee of the Red Cross, 2005) 137.

the export and transfer of ownership of cultural materials under compulsion arising from the occupation of a country by a foreign power. This provision reinforces the First Protocol. However, Article 11 goes further than the First Protocol in that it not only outlaws the export of property but also transfer of ownership. Article 7 of the 1970 UNESCO Convention is also relevant to the present analysis in that it applies both in peacetime and in situations of armed conflict.[60] It requires Contracting States to ensure that their museums do not acquire illegally exported cultural objects, to prohibit the import of property that has been stolen from museums, religious or secular monuments and to assist other Contracting States to obtain the return of such property, provided the property is on the inventory of the institution concerned. Therefore, Article 7 applies to property that has been looted from museums, religious or secular monuments and subsequently exported abroad contrary to the provisions of the 1954 UNESCO Convention.

The Second Protocol strengthened the prohibitions contained in the UNESCO Conventions of 1954 and 1970. Article 9(1), which deals with the protection of cultural property in occupied territory, requires an occupying party to prohibit and prevent certain activities in the territory concerned, such as 'any illicit export, other removal or transfer of ownership of cultural property [and] any archaeological excavation [...]'. Furthermore, Article 21 of the Second Protocol explicitly obliges the States Parties to adopt legislative, administrative or disciplinary measures to suppress 'any use of cultural property in violation of the Convention or this Protocol' as well as 'any illicit export, other removal or transfer of ownership of cultural property from occupied territory in violation of the Convention or this Protocol'. This clause implies a positive obligation to prevent or put a stop to the prohibited acts regardless of who is responsible. Commanders of military forces therefore have the obligation to prevent the looting of cultural assets and to adopt punitive measures against individuals who have violated or have ordered a violation to be committed, be they soldiers or civilians.

Judgments of national and international courts as well as the practice of States and international organizations have shown that the prohibition of looting and trafficking and the obligation of restitution mirror rules of customary law. In this respect it is essential to emphasise the importance of UNSC Resolution 1483 (2003).[61] This addressed the losses sustained by the Iraqi heritage in the aftermath of the entry of United States forces into Baghdad in April 2003 and provided that: '[...] all Member States shall take appropriate steps to facilitate the safe return to Iraqi institutions of Iraqi cultural property and other items of archaeological, historical, cultural, rare scientific, and religious importance illegally removed from the Iraq National Museum, the National Library, and other locations in Iraq [...], including by establishing a prohibition on trade in or transfer of such items and items with respect to which reasonable suspicion exists that they have been illegally removed [...]' (para. 7).

---

60 Kevin Chamberlain, *War and Cultural Heritage* (Institute of Art & Law, 2004) 17.

61 UN Doc S/RES/1483, 22 May 2003, ILM, 2003, Vol. 42, 1016 ff.

The Turkish Invasion and the Sacred Heritage in Cyprus

On the International Response to the Turkish Invasion

A lot of ink has been poured about the history and politics of the Cyprus problem. In particular, attention has been dedicated to the question of the legality of the war of 1974. As said above, Greek and Turkish Cypriots have very different views on this issue. For the Greek Cypriots the invasion was an illegal act of aggression under the pretext of the restoration of the constitutional order. Turkey and the Turkish Cypriots regard the intervention as a legitimate peace operation aimed at protecting the Turkish Cypriot minority and ensuring an end to their persecution by the Greek Cypriot majority.

In coming to any conclusion about the question of the legality of the Turkish action in northern Cyprus, it is necessary to consider the events of 1974 and their aftermath in the light of the international rules outlined above. With this in mind, it is convenient to analyse separately the two phases of the war. As for the operation staged in the first phase, which took place on 20–22 July 1974, Turkey contended that it was legal under the terms of Article IV of the Treaty of Guarantee of 1960. This provided for Greece, Turkey and the United Kingdom 'to consult together with respect to the representations or measures necessary to ensure observance' of the provisions of the Treaty. It further established that in the absence of agreement on concerted action, 'each of the three [Guarantor powers] reserves the right to take action with the sole aim of re-establishing the state of affairs created by the present Treaty'. In effect, Turkey consulted with Britain when the Greek military junta staged the military coup aimed at overthrowing President Makarios. Instead, Archbishop Makarios refused to meet the then Turkish Prime Minister.[62] Therefore, at first sight, it would appear that Turkey was within its powers. However, on closer examination it appears that the military intervention was illegal: first, because Article IV did not explicitly grant a right to wage war; second, because if Article IV had granted such a right, it would have violated Articles 2(4) and 103 of the UN Charter;[63] third, because Articles I and II of the Treaty of Guarantee prohibited any activity to promote union with any other State or partition of the island.[64] As for the second phase of the Turkish intervention, which began on 14 August 1974, following the failure of peace talks in Geneva, it appears that it was not aimed at re-establishing the state of affairs agreed by the parties in 1960 – which is one of the conditions contained in the Treaty of Guarantee – but at creating a radically different situation. This is demonstrated by the eviction of Greek Cypriots from the northern part of the island, the Turkey-sponsored immigration of settlers after 1974 and the enduring occupation. It can

62 Clement Dodd, *The History and Politics of the Cyprus Conflict*, op. cit., 110.

63 Article 103 establishes that States' obligations under the UN Charter override States' obligations under any other treaty.

64 See supra note 13.

therefore be suggested that the second military operation was also contrary to the Treaty of Guarantee and to the UN Charter.

For these reasons the 1974 Turkish action prompted strong and unanimous international condemnation. The United Nations General Assembly (hereinafter 'UNGA') adopted a number of resolutions deploring the Turkish invasion and all unilateral actions aimed at changing the demographic structure of Cyprus. These resolutions also demanded an immediate withdrawal of Turkish armed forces and affirmed the right of the RoC and its people to full and effective sovereignty and control over the entire territory of Cyprus. The UNGA also called for the return of refugees to their homes.[65] Similarly, the UNSC passed resolutions demanding the immediate end of military occupation through the withdrawal of Turkish armed forces other than those allowed by the treaties of 1960.[66] Furthermore, the UNSC declared the 1983 Declaration of Independence of the TRNC 'legally invalid' and called upon 'all States not to recognize any Cypriot State other than the Republic of Cyprus'.[67] Moreover, in 1999 the UNSC rejected the TRNC government's demand for the recognition of the existence of two peoples in Cyprus and their respective rights to self-determination.[68] However, no concrete international action has been taken to put an end to the unlawful occupation of Cyprus. Arguably, the configuration of the geopolitical interests in the region is such that the States sitting in the UNSC do not want to pressure Turkey over the Cyprus problem.[69]

Other condemnations of the Turkish invasion have come from the Council of Europe[70] and the European Court of Human Rights (hereinafter 'ECtHR'). The ECtHR has issued various pronouncements on the problem of the Greek Cypriot properties in the Turkish-held area.[71] Since 1996, when it delivered its landmark

---

65 See Resolutions 3212 (XXIX) of 1 November 1974, 3395 (XXX) of 20 November 1975, 33/15 of 9 November 1978, 34/30 of 20 November 1979, 37/253 of 13 May 1983.

66 See for example Resolutions 353 (1974), 357 (1974), 360 (1974), 361 (1974), 364 (1974), 365 (1974), 367 (1975), 391 (1976), 410 (1977), 422 (1977) and 430 (1978).

67 See Resolutions 541 (1983) and 550 (1984).

68 Resolution 1251 (1999).

69 Nicholas Augustinos, 'The Protection of Cultural Heritage', op. cit., 236. See also United States Commission on International Religious Freedom, Annual Report, May 2011, 333 ff. <www.uscirf.gov/images/book%20with%20cover%20for%20web.pdf> accessed 23 January 2014.

70 See Resolution (83) 13 of 24 November 1983 of the Committee of Ministers of the Council of Europe <www.mfa.gov.cy/mfa/mfa2006.nsf/All/C1E21396890CA83CC22571D2001E8A47/$file/Res%2083.pdf?OpenElement> accessed 23 January 2014. See also Resolution 1628 (2008) of the Parliamentary Assembly of the Council of Europe <http://assembly.coe.int/Mainf.asp?link=/Documents/AdoptedText/ta08/ERES1628.htm> accessed 23 January 2014.

71 This problem relates to the properties (houses and agricultural, commercial and industrial enterprises) that Greek Cypriots left behind in 1974 and that the TRNC government has expropriated and assigned to Turkish soldiers, Turkish Cypriots or to the

decision in the *Loizidou* case,[72] the ECtHR has rendered numerous judgments in favour of the applicants, namely Greek Cypriots claiming that they were prevented from having access to and from using their property by the Turkish army. With these judgments the ECtHR has established that: (i) Greek Cypriots displaced from northern Cyprus are the legal owners of properties abandoned and expropriated; (ii) Greek Cypriots applicants are entitled to financial compensation for the loss of use of their property;[73] (iii) Turkey is responsible for the continuing violation of the right to property (Article 1 of Protocol No. 1 of the European Convention for the Protection of Human Rights and Fundamental Freedoms[74] – hereinafter 'ECHR') as well as the right to respect for private and family life, home and correspondence (Articles 8 ECHR). By attributing international responsibility for ECHR violations to Turkey,[75] the ECtHR recognized that the RoC is the only legitimate government and that Cyprus is under Turkish military occupation as Turkey exercises 'effective overall control' over northern Cyprus.[76]

---

settlers that arrived from Turkey after 1974. See also the case law of the Court of Justice of the European Union, in particular cases C-432/92, *Anastasiou I* [1994] ECR-3087, Judgment of 5 July 1994, on the introduction of trade restriction on TRNC products for the lack of certificates of origin issued by RoC institutions; and C-420/07, *Meletis Apostolides v. Linda and David Orams* [2009] ECR I-3571, Judgment of 28 April 2009, establishing that the decisions of the courts of the RoC against anyone occupying Greek Cypriots properties in the north can be enforced in any other EU Member State, even though the RoC does not exercise *de facto* control in northern Cyprus.

72 *Loizidou v. Turkey* (Application No. 1518/89, ECtHR Judgment of 18 December 1996).

73 The ECtHR established a new pattern with its decisions in the cases *Xenides-Arestis v. Turkey* (Application No. 46347/99, Judgment of 22 December 2005) and *Demopoulos and Others v. Turkey* (Applications Nos 46113/99, 3843/02, 13751/02, 13466/03, 10200/04, 14163/04, 19993/04, 21819/04, Decision of 1 March 2010) as a result of the compensation mechanism instituted by the TRNC Government in 2005 in order to provide effective remedies to dispossessed Greek Cypriot property owners.

74 4 November 1950, ETS No. 005.

75 The Constitutional Court of the TRNC has implicitly admitted that Northern Cyprus was under Turkish military control in *National Unity Party v. TRNC Assembly of the Republic* (Judgment D 3/2006 of 21 June 2006). In this case the Court recognized that the international law on occupation prohibiting the confiscation of private property by the invading belligerent (Article 46 of the 1907 Convention) applied in the TRNC.

76 The ECtHR based its reasoning on the presence of a large number of Turkish troops engaged in active duty in northern Cyprus and on the fact that the TRNC is not regarded as an independent State but as a satellite of Turkey. Notably, the conclusion that Turkey exercises an 'effective overall control' over northern Cyprus does not contradict the view adopted by the international community that the RoC government is the sole legitimate government of Cyprus: territorial conquest does not imply the transfer of sovereignty from the occupied State to the occupying State.

Finally, it is interesting to mention the 2006 Declaration of the Parliament of the European Union.[77] The Parliament reaffirmed the responsibility of the Turkish State by acknowledging that 'more than 133 churches, chapels and monasteries that are located in the northern part of Cyprus and have been controlled by the Turkish army since 1974 have been desecrated, 78 churches have been converted into mosques, 28 are used as military depots and hospitals and 13 are used as stockyards [...] whereas their ecclesiastical items, including more than 15,000 icons, have been illegally removed and their location remains unknown'.[78]

On the Responsibility of the Turkish State Regarding the Sacred Heritage in Northern Cyprus

In the light of the foregoing discussion, it can be asserted that the continuing occupation of northern Cyprus by Turkey meets the criteria of military occupation. Under international humanitarian law, that is, the law of armed conflict, a territory is considered occupied when it is placed under the authority of a hostile army as a result of an armed conflict between two or more States – regardless of the reasons that led to the occupation. This is so even if the said occupation meets with no armed resistance and even if there is no declaration of war or occupation or recognition of the state of war by one of the States.[79] Furthermore, it can be argued that the failure to protect the cultural and religious heritage situated in northern Cyprus, and the toleration of – or failure to – prevent the destruction, desecration, seizure and illicit exportation of artworks belonging to the heritage of the island amount to violations of the laws and customs of war. As such, they constitute war crimes that could give rise to Turkey's responsibility under international law as well as individual criminal responsibility. As for the issue of State responsibility, it is a recognized principle of international law that '[e]very internationally wrongful act of a State entails the international responsibility of that State'.[80] An internationally wrongful act, which may consist of either an action or omission, constitutes a violation of an international obligation of the State and can be considered to have a continuing character if it extends for the entire period during which the causal conduct of a

77 Declaration on the Protection and Preservation of the Religious Heritage in the Northern Part of Cyprus, OJ EU C 305 E/92, 14 December 2006 <http://eur-lex.europa.eu/LexUriServ/LexUriServ.do?uri=OJ:C:2006:305E:0092:0093:EN:PDF> accessed 23 January 2014.

78 Ibid. See also the information made available by the Ministry of Foreign Affairs of Cyprus on its website <www.mfa.gov.cy/mfa/mfa2006.nsf/cyprus07_en/cyprus07_en?OpenDocument> accessed 18 November 2012.

79 See Article 42 of the 1907 Convention, Article 2 of the Fourth Geneva Convention, and Article 18 of the 1954 UNESCO Convention.

80 See Article 1 of the Articles on Responsibility of States for Internationally Wrongful Acts, International Law Commission, Report on the Work of Its Fifty-third Session, UN GAOR, 56th Sess., Supp. No. 10, 43, UN Doc. A/56/10 (2001).

State continues and remains contrary to an international obligation.[81] The Articles of the International Law Commission further establish that when a State breaches an international legal obligation there are three key principles that come into play. First, the responsible State has a duty to perform the obligation breached (Article 29). Second, if the violation is ongoing, the responsible State has the obligation to cease the act (Article 30(a)) and to guarantee non-repetition (Article 30(b)). Third, the responsible State has to make full reparation (Article 31). There are three main forms of reparations: restitution, compensation and satisfaction (Articles 34–7). With respect to restitution, material restitution should be distinguished from juridical restitution. Examples of material restitution include the return of wrongly seized property. Juridical restitution requires the modification of a legal situation either within the legal system of the responsible State or in its legal relations with the injured State. Such cases include the revocation, annulment or amendment of legislative provisions enacted in violation of international law or the reconsideration of judicial measures unlawfully adopted in respect of property of foreigners.[82]

As far as northern Cyprus is concerned, it can be suggested that Turkey, as the occupying power exercising 'effective overall control' over northern Cyprus, bears responsibility for acts against cultural property committed in contravention of the obligations contained in the treaties to which it was party at the time of the invasion[83] and the relevant principles of customary international law. Specifically, the actions and omissions committed by the Turkish government, Turkish commanders and Turkish Cypriot authorities since the military invasion of July 1974 constitute interferences of the sort contemplated by the legal instruments analysed above in that they failed to: (i) refrain from using properties of cultural and religious importance and their immediate surroundings for purposes that were likely to expose them to destruction or damage; (ii) avoid and prevent acts of hostility against such property not only by their own soldiers but also by the civilian population; (iii) prohibit, prevent and (if necessary) stop any form of theft, pillage, misappropriation, import and export of cultural property; (iv) return any illegally exported property and pay damages to any good-faith holder of such property; (v) refrain from any act against cultural property as a reprisal; (vi) allow religious communities living in the RoC and religious minority communities living in northern Cyprus access as well as the right to restore, maintain and utilize places of worship and cemeteries that are located within the borders of Turkish military zones in northern Cyprus; (vii) establish criminal jurisdiction to prosecute individuals who have engaged in acts of destruction, desecration and pillage; and (viii) respect the norms regulating the alteration and change of use of the property located in the occupied territory.

81 See Article 14 of the Articles on Responsibility of States for Internationally Wrongful Acts, ibid.

82 Ibid., 97–8.

83 See supra note 45.

With respect to the obligation to prevent the exportation of cultural assets, various reports – also by Turkish and Turkish Cypriot newspapers – have demonstrated that the Turkish and TRNC government and military officials colluded or were bribed and that antiquities have not only disappeared from archaeological sites and religious buildings situated within or nearby military zones but also from the places where they were taken for safekeeping.[84] As regards the inability of Orthodox Christians, other religious communities (including Armenians, Maronites and Jews) and religious clergy to access and hold services at their places of worship and cemeteries in the north, particularly those that exist within the borders of Turkish military zones, it must be stressed that the obstacles faced by believers and clerics hamper the religious freedom of the remaining members of these communities.[85]

A Reappraisal of Responsibilities and Solutions

The analysis set out above provides an oversimplified version of the Cyprus problem whereby only one party is held responsible for the damage sustained by Cyprus' sacred heritage. In reality, barbaric attacks against the religious heritage of the enemy and human rights violations were committed by both sides.[86] It is therefore it is essential to reconsider the roles of Greek and Turkish Cypriots as regards the impoverishment of the island's heritage. With this in mind, it is necessary to identify the periods in which the attacks against the cultural heritage took place.

The first period, which goes from 1960 to 1974, witnessed various actions of Greek Cypriot paramilitary groups against the Turkish Cypriot minority. The worst incident took place in 1963, when Greek Cypriot extremists attacked and destroyed 103 Turkish villages.[87] As a result, half of the Turkish Cypriot community was driven into enclaves and several Turkish religious sites were destroyed across the island. The second period coincides with the military operations that started on 20 July 1974. In this phase, the attacks against cultural heritage in northern Cyprus were the – intentional or unintentional – outcomes of the armed conflict.

84 Nicholas Augustinos, 'The Protection of Cultural Heritage', op. cit., 221, 223.

85 In connection to this, in 2010 the Church of Cyprus lodged an application with the ECtHR against Turkey complaining of a violation of Article 1 Protocol 1 ECHR – for the alleged lack of access and enjoyment of the religious property belonging to the Church in the Turkish held area – and Articles 9 and 11 ECHR – as Turkish Cypriot authorities have continuously prevented the Orthodox Church and its parishioners from holding religious services in buildings located in northern Cyprus. *Chrysostomos v. Turkey* (Application No. 66611/2009, Decision of 4 January 2011). The application was rejected for non-exhaustion of domestic remedies pursuant to Article 35 ECHR.

86 Clement Dodd, *The History and Politics of the Cyprus Conflict*, op. cit., 132.

87 John Fielding, 'The Rape of Northern Cyprus', op. cit.

The third period began shortly after the end of military operations and continues until today. It is possible to identify at least three causes for the looting and neglect that characterize this phase. First, the sites sacred to Greek Cypriots were attacked as retaliation by the Turkish Cypriots who had been ousted from their homes.[88] The spontaneous violence of Turkish Cypriot villagers against Christian Orthodox buildings was rooted in the memories of massacre and plundering committed by the Greek Cypriots in the 1960s. Christian Orthodox churches were perceived as symbols of oppression that invited revenge.[89] Second, the cultural heritage of Cyprus was (and still is) exploited as a money-making enterprise. As explained above, if they were not damaged, the artworks contained in churches, monasteries, museums, collections or libraries were removed and sold on the international art market. Antiquities excavated from archaeological sites suffered the same fate.[90] Unfortunately, this is not surprising: whenever there is an inter-State or inter-ethnic war or some kind of unrest, cultural objects invariably get destroyed or looted. Third, cultural heritage was 'targeted' for political reasons. In the Greek Cypriot view, the sacred sites located in the northern part of the island fell prey to Turkish and Turkish Cypriot nationalist extremists who aimed to 'Turkify' the area. In other words, Greek Cypriots contend that the destruction and desecration of religious sites was (and still is) aimed at eradicating the Hellenic cultural character of the area after the eviction of Greek Cypriot people.[91] This argument is opposed by the Turkish Cypriots. They contend that this claim is part of the propaganda employed by Greek Cypriots to discredit Turkish Cypriots and the TRNC. They deny that there was widespread plundering or looting after 1974.[92] On the contrary, the TRNC government has repeatedly argued that its competent authorities are engaged in actions designed to preserve and protect religious sites, regardless of their origin.

These are the dominant arguments in Cyprus: each party points to the (ongoing) ethnic conflict as the reason for the destruction of heritage, complains that it is the victim of attempts at ethno-cultural cleansing and blames the other for the deliberate targeting or neglect of its own heritage.[93] However, the allegations of ethnic cleansing were rejected in the 1989 Report by Van Der Werff. This categorized both the Greek and Turkish Cypriot claims as 'propaganda'[94] and attributed most of the damage to the organized looting carried out by the art thieves that raided the island after 1974.[95] Equally, the 2002 Report by Vlasta Stepová

88 2002 Report, supra note 25.

89 John Fielding, 'The Rape of Northern Cyprus', op. cit.

90 2002 Report, supra note 25.

91 Nicholas Augustinos, 'The Protection of Cultural Heritage', op. cit., 221.

92 Ibid., 222.

93 Costas M. Constantinou and Hatay Mete, 'Cyprus, Ethnic Conflict and Conflicted Heritage', op. cit., 1600–1601.

94 1989 Report, supra note 24, paras 4, 4.2.3. and 4.3.

95 Ibid., para 5.1.

did not validate the argument that the TRNC administration 'intentionally and systematically' supported a process aimed at 'destroying historical memory by the gradual annihilation of all evidence of the continuity over more than 3000 years of Greek settlement and Greek culture in Cyprus'.[96] On the contrary, it pointed out that 'the effective prevention of the illegal export of cultural goods is [...] not within the power of local northern administration [...] given the relative poverty of the country and, therefore, its other more urgent needs'.[97]

In the light of these findings, it can be concluded that – regardless of whether the 1974 armed conflict in Cyprus was lawful or unlawful – the Greek and Turkish Cypriots share responsibility for the damage sustained by the sacred heritage of the island since 1960. The destruction and looting of Christian Orthodox heritage as well as the obliteration of Ottoman and Turkish monuments and Islamic antiquities are deeply rooted in the inter-ethnic conflict between Greek and Turkish Cypriots. Therefore, the recognition and condemnation of the desecration of the Greek Cypriot heritage call for the recognition and condemnation of the destruction of the Turkish Cypriot heritage. Indeed, the loss of Islamic heritage sites at the hands of the Greek Cypriot extremists before and after 1974 should not be downplayed or denied. Likewise, the responsibility of the Greek Cypriot authorities for having permitted or tolerated such events should not be condoned.

Furthermore, the argument for joint responsibility can be reinforced by considering that the issue of heritage preservation has been (and still is) exploited by both sides of the Green Line to promote political objectives unrelated to purely cultural heritage concerns.[98] On the one hand, Greek Cypriots deplore the loss of the Christian Orthodox heritage in the north and emphasise the necessity to recover or rebuild it in order to pursue the reunification of the island. For the same reason, the concern of successive RoC governments has been the identification and protection of monumental sites and places which are associated with the ethnic communities on the island, including the 'Turkish' ethno-religious heritage. Accordingly, mosques, castles, hamams and archaeological ruins have been brought under the jurisdiction of the RoC department of antiquities.[99] On the other hand, the official argument of Turkish Cypriot authorities is based on the idea that the Ottoman and Islamic heritage in the south is best redeemed through its reconstruction in the north, which in turn legitimates the partition.[100] Instead, only a few ancient Greek

96 2002 Report, supra note 25.

97 Ibid.

98 See Nicholas Augustinos, 'The Protection of Cultural Heritage', op. cit., 221, and Costas M. Constantinou and Hatay Mete, 'Cyprus, Ethnic Conflict and Conflicted Heritage', op. cit., 1614.

99 This was acknowledged in the 1989 Report, supra note 24. However, Van Der Werff criticized from a strictly cultural heritage point of view the rebuilding of mosques which had 'no architectural importance'.

100 Costas M. Constantinou and Hatay Mete, 'Cyprus, Ethnic Conflict and Conflicted Heritage', op. cit., 1614.

sites and historically valuable Byzantine churches have been preserved in northern Cyprus because of the presence of some Greek Cypriot villagers, whereas more recent or less valuable buildings have been either neglected or transformed.[101]

These *selective* perceptions and policies signify that the RoC and TRNC exploit the island's treasures to advance their claims and strengthen their bargaining power in European and international fora. This is both dangerous and at odds with the basic tenets of international cultural heritage law.

In the light of these circumstances and of the current diplomatic impasse, it appears that the best alternative for the protection of the sacred heritage situated in Cyprus and for the proper implementation of the applicable international law standards is the adoption of an *object-oriented* approach. According to this approach, concern for the protection and preservation of sacred objects and places should be separated from concern for their enjoyment. In other words, the island's treasures should be protected and preserved by the RoC and TRNC governments as examples of Byzantine or Ottoman art and architecture regardless of whether Christian Orthodox and Islamic worshippers are prevented from having access to and from using them. In practical terms, international organizations and non-governmental organizations should persuade the RoC and TRNC governments, through suitable incentives, to abide by the existing legal standards in order to obtain the protection of the heritage located within their – *de facto* – jurisdiction for the purpose of international appreciation and study. The RoC in the south and the TRNC in the north should thus agree to become the custodians of the heritage under their control. Evidently, the adoption of this object-oriented approach entails that international organizations and non-governmental organizations should cooperate with the TRNC government, regardless of the legality of its existence.

Clearly, this option is a palliative that is suggested only because an agreement between the parties involved in the conflict is not expected in the near future and irrespective of the flaws of this object-oriented approach. Admittedly, it is pointless to pursue preservation for the sake of the objects and not for the sake of the people for whom they have a meaning. As explained above, sacred places are not supposed to be merely appreciated, but should be accessible and used for rituals and ceremonies. Moreover, only the use of sacred heritage by the people whose religious identity that heritage expresses affords an adequate context in which it can be protected and preserved.

As said, the object-oriented approach makes practical sense for Cyprus only because of the enduring demographic and ethnic partition and the current diplomatic impasse. However, there are other reasons favouring the adoption of such an approach. One is that it does not jeopardize the 'cultural' and 'symbolic' layers identified above. On the contrary, the approach under consideration makes it possible to 'freeze' such dimensions. These could then be revived when a

101 The Hellenic heritage has not been duly preserved also because of the lack of expertise and financial resources given the poverty and the relative isolation of the TRNC and the lack of use. See 2002 Report, supra note 25.

political decision on the overall conflict will allow people access to the spaces and artefacts sacred to them. Another reason is that an object-oriented approach can act as a catalyst for enhancing the relations between Greek and Turkish Cypriots. As proved by the cooperative endeavours initiated by the two communities in the field of cultural heritage protection in the last decade,[102] this alternative approach can make it possible to bridge divisions, reduce misconceptions and fears and erode the causes of the inter-communal conflict.[103] In short, Cypriots could set aside the multiple issues related to the conflict if they are encouraged to focus on the island's heritage as the subject of international obligations and as a resource for economic and social development only. This can happen if, for instance, cultural heritage preservation is associated with development policies as a resource for providing suitable responses to the existing economic challenges in the TRNC.[104]

Concluding Remarks

The Cyprus conflict, which is rooted in the events that took place during the Ottoman and British domination, erupted after 1960 also as a result of complex Cold War geopolitical strategies. As explained in this chapter, Cyprus' sacred heritage is a hostage of this conflict. The legal framework necessary for directing a change is already in place: the destruction of Cyprus' heritage can be diminished or prevented through the application of the rules codified in the treaties adopted since the end of the 19th century for situations of armed conflict and military occupation. These rules, which are widely regarded as reflecting customary international law, are the prohibition of acts of violence against cultural heritage, the obligation to protect cultural heritage from the vicissitudes of armed conflict, the prohibition against plundering artworks and the ensuing obligation of restitution. The binding nature of these rules is further reinforced by the international legal regime of State responsibility, which identifies the obligations ensuing from the violations of international legal precepts. Finally, this chapter advocates the adoption of an object-oriented approach as a modest palliative for overcoming the ethno-religious dichotomies that conceal the common responsibility for the cultural losses sustained in Cyprus. Thus, it is only through solidarity and joint action against art theft and destruction that the island's sacred heritage can be handed down to future generations.

102 For an overview see Alessandro Chechi, 'Beyond Protection: Cooperation as a Tool to Cope with Unresolved Cultural Heritage Issues in Post-Conflict Cyprus' (2011) *Cultural Heritage and Arts Review* 22.

103 Nathalie Tocci, *The 'Cyprus Question'*, op. cit., 18.

104 For an overview of various examples of cooperative endeavours in the field of cultural heritage protection initiated by the two communities in the last decade see Alessandro Chechi, 'Beyond Protection', op. cit., 31.

Chapter 16
Mecca: The 'Blessed Heart' of Islam

Simon Page

Mecca in History, Tradition and Revelation

Around the early 6th century AD the Arab tribe of Quraysh began their rule over a small area in the Hejaz of Arabia at about 70 km inland from the Red Sea. Over time they adapted from their centuries-old nomadic life and settled in a torrid valley there by a well that went by the name of Zamzam. Beside the well was a little sanctuary known as the Ka'bah ('cube', in virtue of its shape). The Ka'bah had been a sacred site from very ancient times. According to Muslim tradition, the city of Mecca (latitude of approximately 21 degrees to the north and longitude of 39 degrees east, about 300 metres above sea level) was established by the Jurhumite tribe at the time of the Prophet Abraham.[1]

Abraham took his second wife, Hagar, and their son, Ishmael, into exile to the valley known as 'Bakka'[2] in Western Arabia. According to tradition, Abraham left Hagar and Ishmael alone. Eventually they were overcome by thirst. There were two hills in the valley, named Safa and Marwa. Hagar climbed first one, then the other, looking in all directions to find water. She passed seven times between the two hills, until at the end of the seventh passage she sat down for a rest and an angel came to their aid, showing Hagar a spring of water.[3] A very similar story is narrated in Genesis, 21 (17–19):

---

1 It is not a matter here of judging the historical grounds of such an account, as in the Islamic world it is not always easy to differentiate a clear boundary between history and tradition. Moreover, in this same Muslim world context economic, political, legal, social, religious or spiritual spheres are considered as coexisting and interacting with each other, and they are dealt with accordingly. The methodological challenge of this paper is not to refute such ambiguity a priori.

2 'The first House (of worship) appointed for men was that at Bakka: full of blessing and of guidance for all the worlds'. The Qur'an, 3: 96, from *The Holy Qur'an, English translation of the meanings and commentary* (The Presidency of Islamic Researches, IFTA, Call and guidance, King Fahad Holy Quran printing complex 1990). The valley is mentioned in the Psalms too, verses 84:4–6: 'Blessed are those who dwell in Your house; They will still be praising You. Selah. Blessed is the man whose strength is in You, whose heart is set on pilgrimage. As they pass through the Valley of Baca, they make it a spring; the rain also covers it with pools'. Psalm 84:4–6 (New King James version).

3 Martin Lings, *Muhammad. His life based on the earliest sources* (Inner Traditions 2006).

> And God heard the voice of the lad. Then the angel of God called to Hagar out of heaven, and said to her, 'What ails you, Hagar? Fear not, for God has heard the voice of the lad where he is. Arise, lift up the lad and hold him with your hand, for I will make him a great nation'. Then God opened her eyes, and she saw a well of water. And she went and filled the skin with water, and gave the lad a drink.[4]

The well of Zamzam was situated in an extremely dry valley and the environment was not suitable for a large-scale settlement. However, it was favourable for trade as it was at the crossroads of important routes leading northwards to Syria, north-eastwards to Iraq, southwards to Yemen and westwards to the Red Sea (to Abyssinia and elsewhere). At the end of the 6th century the Quraysh formed the ruling class of Mecca. Other tribes had also poured into Mecca from different parts of the Arabian Peninsula. However, since the times of Abraham the local tribes had abandoned the monotheistic belief and had embraced pagan practices.

The holy sanctuary of the Ka'bah was already a destination for pilgrimage even during pagan times, attracting thousands of people from all over the region and thus bringing wealth to the inhabitants of Mecca. The sanctuary was also known as the House of God (*Baitullah*). Although it has been destroyed and rebuilt several times since its foundation, it has always remained a very simple building made of stone, with a cuboid structure,[5] originally devoted to receiving donations from pilgrims.

At the eastern corner of the Ka'bah was 'the Black Stone' (*Al-Hajar al-Aswad*). It is a dark basaltic stone, believed to be a meteorite found on the nearby hill of Abu Qubays, preserved there until it was brought to Mecca.[6] The stone is still visible today,[7] while the ancient ritual of circumambulation around the Ka'bah (*tawaf*) is practiced in our times by millions of pilgrims from all over the world, and the sanctuary indicates the direction (*kibla*) that all Muslims should face when praying.[8]

---

4 Genesis 21:17–19 (New King James Version).

5 Its dimensions are approximately 10m by 12m (horizontally) by 16m (vertically). Titus Burckhardt, *Art of Islam. Language and Meaning* (commemorative edition, World Wisdom, 2009).

6 Martin Lings, *Muhammad*, op. cit., 2006.

7 'It is raised from the ground at about one and a half meters. Its length is half a cubit and its width is one third a cubit'. Mohammed H. Al Mojan, *The Honorable Kabah. Architecture and Kiswa* (Al Kawn Center, 2010).

8 'We see the turning of thy face (for guidance) to the heavens: now shall we turn thee to a Qibla that shall please thee. Turn then thy face in the direction of the Sacred Mosque: wherever ye are, turn your faces in that direction', *The Holy Qur'an*; op. cit.; 2, 144. It is worth noting that until about the 2nd year from the Hijra (the migration to Medina), the direction of prayer had been to the holy temple mount in Jerusalem. After the Quranic revelation Mohammed commanded the Muslims to pray facing Mecca.

As concerns the spiritual meaning of the Ka'bah, it corresponds to myth or to revelation, depending on the point of view. Its role as liturgical centre of the Islamic world is directly related to the fact that it constitutes a crucial bond with the Prophet Abraham, and therefore with the origins of all monotheistic religions.[9] Indeed according to the Qur'an the Ka'bah was built by Abraham and his son Ishmael, and Abraham himself instituted the ritual of the pilgrimage to the holy sanctuary.

In the words of the Qur'an:

> And remember Abraham and Ismail raised the foundations of the House (with this prayer): 'Our Lord! Accept (this service) from us: for Thou art the All-Hearing, the All-Knowing'.[10]
>
> Allah made the Ka'ba, the Sacred House, a means of support for men, as also the Sacred months, the animals for offerings, and the garlands to mark them: that ye may know that Allah hath knowledge of what is in the heavens and on earth and that Allah is well acquainted with all things.[11]
>
> Behold! We pointed the site, to Abraham, of the (Sacred) House, (saying): 'Associate not anything (in worship) with Me; and sanctify my House for those who compass it round, or stand up, or bow, or prostrate themselves (therein prayer).[12]

The building is traditionally covered with a garment (*kiswa)*, replaced every year, made of black cloth embroidered with gold lettering.

The custom of 'clothing' the sanctuary was apparently introduced by an ancient Himyarite king, and seems to be part of an extremely venerable Semitic tradition which is, in any case, alien in style to the Greco-Roman world: to 'clothe' a house is, in a way, to treat it as a living body or as an ark bearing a spiritual influence, and that is how the Arabs understood it.[13]

At the time when the Prophet Mohammed was born in Mecca, about 570 AD, the city was the most important religious and commercial centre of the Hejaz. But because agriculture was impossible in the city, the Quraysh relied solely on commerce and on the income from pilgrims. In other words, they needed peace in order to prosper, and therefore 'they established the Haram, a zone with a twenty-mile radius, with the Kabah at its center, where all violence was forbidden'.[14]

---

9 Titus Burckhardt, *Art of Islam*, op. cit.

10 *The Holy Qur'an*; op. cit.; 2,127.

11 Ibid.; 5, 97.

12 Ibid.; 22, 26.

13 Titus Burckhardt, *Art of Islam*, op. cit. Moreover, this author establishes a parallel between the Ka'ba and the Holy of Holies, containing the Ark of the Covenant, in the Temple of Jerusalem (because of their cubic shape).

14 Karen Armstrong, *Mohammad. Prophet for our time* (Harper Perennial, 2007).

Since the time of the Quraysh the landmarks that indicate the borders of the *Haram* (sanctified area) have been renovated by all the rulers that subsequently controlled Mecca. The sacred precincts include the area around Mecca and are marked by special landmarks, on all roads leading to and from Mecca. The most well known are the ones on the roads towards Medina (3 miles from the Ka'bah), Yemen (7 miles), Iraq (7 miles), Taif (11 miles), Jaa'ranah (9 miles), Jeddah (10 miles).[15]

What happens within these borders is governed by special rulings according to traditional Islamic sources. Therefore, non-Muslims are prevented from entering the Haram area (in Mecca as well as in Medina). No blood should be spilled within the sacred precincts, and hunting is prohibited as well as uprooting trees and carrying any weapon.

Ibn Abbas reported that on the day of the conquest of Makkah (Mecca), the Prophet (peace be upon him) said, 'Verily this is a Sacred City, its thorns and its plants must not be cut, its wild game must not be frightened, and none is allowed to pick up lost articles unless one knows its owner (in order to return it to him)'.[16]

Many other ahadith[17] contain clear references to the inviolability of Mecca. For example, it was related that Abd Allah ibn Zaid Assem (may God be pleased with him) said that the Messenger of God (prayers and peace upon him) said: 'Abraham avowed Makkah to be inviolable and invoked blessings upon those who dwell in it. I avow Makkah to be inviolable as Abraham avowed it to be inviolable, and I invoke twofold measure of blessings upon those who dwell in it'.[18]

At the time of the Prophet, 360 idols were surrounding the Ka'bah, while the most revered deity was probably the Moabite idol Hubal, which had been set up within the Ka'bah itself. But there were other temples throughout the region, the most important being those of the so-called 'daughters of God' (*banat Allah*): al-Lat in the town of Taif, al-Uzzah in the valley of Nakhla and Manat at Qudayd, on the Red Sea. 'Even though they had no shrine in Mecca, the Quraysh loved those goddesses and begged them to mediate on their behalf with the inaccessible Allah'.[19]

It is only with the conquest of Mecca by Mohammad and the Muslim forces in 630 AD that all the idols in and around the Ka'bah were destroyed. The Prophet himself contributed to the destruction of the idols, while reciting the Quranic verse: 'Truth has come; vanity has vanished; in truth vanity is evanescent'.[20] The Prophet, in other words, had succeeded in restoring 'the position of the Ka'ba and the haram around it to its original Abrahamic role as centre of a monotheistic cult'.[21]

15 Mohammed H. Al Mojan, *The Honorable Kabah*, op. cit.

16 Cit. in As-Sayyid Sabiq, *Fiqh us-Sunna* (American Trust Publications 1991).

17 Sing.: hadith, maxim or saying attributed to the Prophet.

18 *Mokhtaser Sahih Muslim* (collection of sayings of the Prophet), revised and translated by A. & D. Zidan, Islamic Inc.

19 Karen Armstrong, *Muhammad*, op. cit.

20 *The Holy Qur-an*, 17,81, cit. in T. Burckhardt, *Art of Islam*, op. cit.

21 Hugh Kennedy, 'Journey to Mecca, A History', in Venetia Porter (ed.), *Hajj, journey to the heart of Islam* (The British Museum Press, 2012).

The Grand Mosque

In the last few decades the number of visitors to the Grand Mosque of Mecca and the Mosque of the Prophet in Medina has been growing rapidly, reaching several million every year. This constant flow of pilgrims brought about the decision of the authorities to extend considerably the two Holy Mosques. This was done at the cost of destroying several historical neighbourhoods and ancient buildings around them.[22] As concerns the Grand Mosque in Mecca, the main extensions, since the Quraysh time, have been the ones under Umar ibn al-Khattab (638 AD), Uthman ibn Affan (646 AD), Abdullah ibn al-Zubayr (684 AD), al-Walid al-Malik (709 AD), Abu Jafar al-Mansur (754 AD), Mohammed al-Mehdi (777–80 AD), Mutadid al-Abbasi (897 AD), Muqtadir al-Abbasi (918 AD), Farj ibn Barqouq (1399–1400 AD), Ottoman Sultans Salim II and Murad III (1571–86 AD), Ottoman Sultan Murad IV (1629 AD), Saudi King Abdulaziz Al Saud (1955–76 AD), Saudi King Fahd bin Abdulaziz (1988–95), Saudi King Abdullah bin Abdulaziz (2011–onwards).

The renovation decided by Sultan Salim II was commissioned from the great Turkish architect Sinan who carried out large-scale renewal of the entire Mosque. The colonnade surrounding the Ka'bah was extended with new columns in marble and stone in order to support the arches and domes. About 500 Ottoman-style domes, decorated with calligraphic designs, replaced the roof that had previously been flat. The courtyard was extended to 164 by 168 metres. During the reign of Murad IV three more minarets were added, to reach the number of seven. The Ka'bah itself underwent extensive renovations.

The general conditions of both the Grand Mosque and the Ka'bah were unchanged for about 400 years until the renovation work carried out by the Saudi dynasty began in 1955. The work continued for about 20 years. The pathway between the two hills of Safa and Marwa, 420 metres long, was fully paved and covered by a passageway that allows the flow of pilgrims on two separate levels. Once the outer structure of the new complex was completed, the area for the circumambulation of the Ka'bah (*mataf*) was expanded and the staircase leading to the well of Zamzam was constructed. The works were also aimed at integrating part of the Ottoman structure into the new complex, although several of the architectural features of Ottoman times were demolished.

Under King Fahd a new impressive wing and outdoor prayer area were built, two minarets added, a King's residence overlooking the Mosque was erected and many other adjustments were made, including the adoption of new technologies (climatic floors, air conditioning, automatic escalators and drainage infrastructure).

In 2011 King Abdullah laid the first stone of the new expansion of the Mecca Haram. It is expected to enlarge the area of the site by an additional 400,000 sq. metres in order to accommodate approximately 1.2 million additional worshippers

22 Seyyed H. Nasr and Ali K. Nomachi, *Mecca the Blessed, Medina the Radiant. The Holiest Cities of Islam* (Aperture 2004).

(increasing the total capacity of the Grand Mosque to more than 2.5 million). The project expects to add two minarets, bringing the total number to 11, and to increase the area of the *mataf.*

These extensions were made necessary in order to accommodate the ever-increasing numbers of pilgrims, especially during the Hajj[23] season. The authorities try to contain the numbers of pilgrims by imposing quotas. However, disapprobation has been growing at the apparent unwillingness to conserve and protect the historical and archaeological heritage of Islam's two holy cities. It is estimated by the Washington-based 'Gulf Institute' that 95 per cent of the 1,000-year-old buildings in the two cities have been destroyed in the past 20 years:[24]

In Mecca, the Masjid al-Haram (Grand Mosque), the holiest site in Islam and a place where all Muslims are supposed to be equal, is now overshadowed by the Jabal Omar complex, a development of skyscraper apartments, hotels and an enormous clock tower. To build it, the Saudi authorities destroyed the Ottoman era Ajyad Fortress and the hill it stood on.[25]
Other historic sites destroyed included the houses of the Prophet Mohammed, his first wife Khadija, Caliph Abu Bakr and several mosques built on the graveyards of companions and relatives of the Prophet.[26] This can be explained also by considering the Wahabi interpretation of Islam that opposes anything which may embolden the faithful towards idol worship. People are strongly discouraged from visiting locations connected to the birth of Islam and powerful clerics encourage their destruction.[27]

Anything that departs from the oneness of God as defined by the Wahhabis is considered as 'shirk' (idolatry), and implies 'kufr' (disbelief). From its earliest appearance, Wahhabism has thus viewed many Hijazi customs and rituals – especially those that involve honouring the Prophet Mohammed or his companions, particularly celebrations of the Prophet's birthday, visiting of shrines, reverence of the dead, dreams and visions, the sanctity of sites or shrines and especially Sufi practices – as superstitious, if not heretical.[28]

---

23 The annual pilgrimage to Mecca that is incumbent on every Muslim at least once in his lifetime, if he has the means to carry it out. It is one of the five pillars of Islam (arkan al Islam).

24 Jerome Taylor, 'Medina: Saudis take a bulldozer to Islam's history', *The Independent* (London 26 October 2012) <www.independent.co.uk/news/world/middle-east/medina-saudis-take-a-bulldozer-to-islams-history-8228795.html?printService=print> accessed 27 October 2012.

25 Ibid.

26 Ahmed Irfan, 'The destruction of Holy Sites in Mecca and Medina' [2010] *Islamica Magazine*.

27 J. Taylor, *Medina*, op. cit.

28 Mai Yamani, *Cradle of Islam. The Hijaz and the quest for identity in Saudi Arabia* (I. B. Taurus 2009).

Madawi Al Rasheed, Professor of Anthropology of Religion in London, has also tackled this subject, commenting on the religious literature aimed at preventing visits to the holy cities of Islam and thereby committing 'blasphemous acts'.[29]

But the personality who has been more adamant about the fate of Islamic historic sites in Mecca and Medina is no doubt Architect Sami Angawi.[30] Dr Angawi, a well renowned expert of Islamic architecture and art and founder in 1975 of the Hajj Research Center, believes that 'we are witnessing now the last few moments of the history of Mecca' and that 'we are destroying physical links to our past and turning our religion and history into a legend'.[31]

It is not our intention to judge or condemn such a policy or habit, especially in a highly controversial field like religious belief. What can be stated is that such an approach by the official religious establishment of the Kingdom of Saudi Arabia can easily be traced in publications related to the matter. For example, the Standing Committee for Scholarly Research and Issuing Fatwas issued a series of fatwas on this subject[32] such as:

> Building on graves is an abominable 'bid'ah' (innovation in religion) that involves excessive veneration of those who are buried there. It is also a means that can lead to 'shirk' (associating others with Allah in His Divinity or worship). It is therefore obligatory for a Muslim ruler or his representative to order the removal of these buildings on graves and that they be levelled to the ground, to end this 'bid'ah' and to block the means to 'shirk'.[33]

> In case that the land on which the Masjid (mosque) was built is free of graves, performing Salah (prayer) there is permissible otherwise the Masjid should be destroyed.[34]

> It is impermissible to construct buildings over graves or to plaster or marble them, as the Prophet (peace be upon him) forbade all of this. Islam does not allow any form of Ibadah to be offered at graves whether it is Salah, recitation of the Qur'an, slaughtering animals, distributing food or Tawaf (circumambulation)

---

29 Madawi Al Rasheed, *Contesting the Saudi State. Islamic voices from a new generation* (Cambridge University Press 2007).

30 Laith Abou-Ragheb, 'Dr Sami Angawi on Wahhabi Desecration of Makkah. Developers and Purists Erase Mecca's History' (Reuters 12 July 2005) <www.islamicpluralism.org/467/dr-sami-angawi-on-wahhabi-desecration-of-makkah> accessed 30 April 2013.

31 Ibid.

32 Published on the website of the Saudi General Presidency of Scholarly Research and Ifta, <www.alifta.com>.

33 Fatwas of the Permanent Committee, Group 1, Volume 1: Aqidah (1), Creeds, Exaggeration regarding graves and building Masjids (mosques) over them, Ruling on building over graves (fatwa n. 7210).

34 Ibid., fatwa n. 10422.

> (…) There is a Hadith which proves that seeking blessings from graves and those who dwell therein is prohibited and is regarded as major Shirk.[35]

Sheikh Abdulaziz ibn Baz, Grand Mufti – the highest religious figure of the Kingdom –also issued many fatwas on the subject from 1993 until his death in 1999.[36] Some Hejazi scholars commented that this disregard towards the conservation of the heritage of Mecca and Medina by the religious scholars of Wahhabi inspiration can also be explained considering that their origin is mostly the region of Qassim, in central Arabia (in the wider region known as Najd), almost 1,000 kilometres from Mecca and the Hejaz.

This phenomenon reflects also a general attitude towards the sacred which is very different from the one we find in the West or in other parts of the world, where there is a direct and natural connection between antiquities, ancient art, cultural heritage and religious practices and ceremonies. This has to be emphasized, because it would otherwise be difficult to understand the completely different standards of preservation of historic heritage in the holy cities of Islam compared to similar places of worship elsewhere. Similarly, it has been written that 'the Great Mosque, which for centuries held the role of a university, became solely a place for pilgrimage and prayer under Saudi adherence to Wahhabism's exclusionary tenets'.[37] It is therefore important to draw our attention now to the significance of the pilgrimage to the holiest city of Islam.

The Pilgrimage

The pilgrimage to Mecca (Hajj) is the so-called fifth pillar of Islam,[38] and its obligatory character – for every member of the faithful who can afford it and who is mentally and physically fit – derives directly from the Qur'an (3:97). It comprises a set of rituals taking place in Mecca and in other locations in its

---

35 Ibid., fatwa n. 5339.

36 For example: 'The Prophet (peace be upon him) explains that the people who build Masjids (mosques) and domes over graves as well as those who make idols in them are the worst people in the sight of Allah. He cursed them in the Hadith of 'Aishah and did not differentiate between those who built them for worship and those who took them as memorials. Therefore building (domes and Masjids over graves) is not permissible, because they are a big means to Shirk. It is also a tradition of the Jews and the Christians which we were prohibited to follow'. Fatwas of Ibn Baz, Volume 1, Refuting Mustafa Amin www.alifta.net.

37 Mai Yamani, *Cradle of Islam*, op. cit.

38 The other four being 1) the Shahadah, that is 'to acknowledge verbally that one accepts the reality of God and the prophecy of Muhammad'; 2) the Salat or ritual prayer; 3) Zakat, commonly translated as 'alms tax'; and 4) fasting during the month of Ramadan. Cf. Sachiko Murata and William C. Chittick, *The Vision of Islam* (Paragon House, 1994).

surroundings (Mina, Arafat and Muzdalifah),[39] from the 8th to the 13th day of the month of Dhu'l-Hijja (the last month of the Islamic calendar). Hajj is also called the 'major pilgrimage' to distinguish it from the 'minor pilgrimage' (*Umrah*) that can be undertaken at any time of the year, and takes place only in the area of the Grand Mosque in Mecca, performing circumambulation around the Ka'bah and walking back and forth between the hills of Safa and Marwa (a ritual called *Sa'i*).

As Sachiko Murata and William C. Chittik point out, today it is possible to reach Mecca to perform Hajj in a matter of few hours, from any location on the planet. But in the past the journey was made on foot or at best on horseback or on camels. The journey could take months or even years, as in the case of the famous Arab traveller Ibn Battuta whose journey to Mecca from his hometown Tangier (Morocco), in the early 14th century, took about 16 months:

> In the past, most Muslims had to fulfil strict conditions in order to make the journey. In effect, they had to be prepared for death. They had to assume that they would never return, and make all the necessary preparations for that eventuality. One of the conditions for making the hajj is that people have to pay off all their debts (…) Traditionally, the hajj was looked upon as a great rite of passage, a move from involvement with this world to occupation with God. In order to make the hajj, people had to finish with everything that kept them occupied on a day-to-day basis.[40]

Nowadays, Hajj is possibly the greatest gathering of people on the planet. Unlike most of the pilgrimages of the other main religions, it has to be performed in a single location, at a specific time and in a prescribed manner. Now more than 3 million men and women from all over the world come to Mecca every year to perform Hajj. It is not only the peak of the spiritual life for millions of pilgrims, but also an event that has important political implications for governments and communities of the Islamic nation (*Ummah*).[41]

It is estimated that in the last three decades almost 3,000 people lost their lives during Hajj, primarily because of overcrowding, stampedes and fires in the pilgrims' camps. This has led the Saudi authorities to adopt new measures to protect the pilgrims, first of all improving Hajj infrastructure and services, and particularly inaugurating in 2005 a massive new structure in Mina for the

39 'The highpoints of the hajj are not in Mecca but on the outskirts in 'Arafat and Mina. On the ninth day of the month of Dhu al'Hijja (…) all two million pilgrims assemble at the Plain of 'Arafat for the Day of Standing – a time of prayer and meditation from about noon until sunset. The congregation at 'Arafat replicates the gathering Muhammad addressed during his "Farewell Pilgrimage", when he revealed the final verses of the Qur'an just months before his death'. Robert R. Bianchi, *Guests of God* (Oxford University Press, 2004).

40 Sachiko Murata and William C. Chittick, *The Vision of Islam*, op. cit.

41 For these aspects, my main reference is: Robert R. Bianchi, *Guests of God*, op. cit.

ritual of the *Jamarat* or 'stoning of the devil'. Moreover, a quota system that controls *per capita* Hajj participation and pegs national quotas to population size was adopted, essentially freezing such participation at 1990 levels (no more than 1,000 pilgrims for every million people, in the case of Islamic countries; exceptions are made for Muslim minorities in non-Islamic Countries), so that the total number of *Hajjis* (pilgrims performing Hajj) from overseas would not exceed, originally, 1.3 million annually (currently the number allowed is 1.8 million). At the same time the number of internal pilgrims resident in Saudi Arabia was also limited.[42]

According to Robert Bianchi,

> … the hajj has transformed international relations as much as domestic politics (…) The need for a global pilgrimage policy and a permanent international authority to implement it is a driving force behind the Organization of the Islamic Conference (OIC). Debates over hajj policy frame the struggle for power in international Islamic organizations and affect relations between Muslim states and their world diplomacy.[43]

Robert Bianchi highlights Muslims' expectations that their rulers make every effort to guarantee their right to visit Mecca in order to fulfil their religious duties. Eventually a compromise was reached between different and conflicting approaches to sovereignty and free access to the Holy Cities. Moreover, Bianchi establishes a pertinent comparison between Hajj management and maritime law:

> … like the law of the sea, the hajj is a field where customary law rules that governed for centuries broke down rapidly and where the formation of new rules exposed sharp disagreement over the role of international law. Just as the maritime powers of the West used their navies to enforce a universal code for the high seas, the great land empires of the Islamic world used their armies to provide safe passage for Muslims visiting the Holy Cities. In each instance, a few hegemonic powers laid down the law, but trade and travel everywhere benefited.[44]

However, he probably overestimates the reconciliation between 'seemingly incompatible principles of universal access and exclusive jurisdiction' and the role of the OIC in determining the Hajj policies and monitoring their implementation.

Indeed it is difficult to acknowledge the existence of a Hajj regime based on customary international law as Bianchi does. And if anything like an Islamic international law exists, an issue that cannot be discussed here, it certainly does not have much influence on the administration of the Hajj and of the Holy Cities. On the contrary, Saudi Arabia appears to be keeping a firm grip on the sovereign

---

42 Ibid.

43 Ibid. In 2011 the name of the organization was changed to Organization for Islamic Cooperation.

44 Ibid.

rule over Mecca and Medina. And above all there seems to be nothing like a Hajj regime ensuring a common heritage preservation of the Islamic holiest sites, as we have seen in this chapter.

The End of Mecca?

It is sad to think that we are maybe witnessing, as Dr Angawi has said, the last few moments of the history of Mecca. The image of this sacred city as the 'heart' of the Islamic world is well known. According to this metaphor, Hajj therefore represents the circulation of the 'blood' – that is, the faithful – of Islam moving across the Islamic world, with Mecca and the Ka'bah being the heart.[45] The end of Mecca, or of its history, could have severe consequences for Islam as a whole, and particularly for it as a world civilization. In this regard, and in conclusion, it is worth mentioning the words of a renowned British Sufi writer and scholar Martin Lings, who is also known as Sheikh Abu Bakr Siraj Al Din, an author that we have already quoted here. In a beautiful documentary[46] using some extraordinary archive material Dr Lings recollects the experiences of the two Hajj pilgrimages that he performed in 1948 and in 1976. At the end of the interview he cannot refrain from observing that Mecca changed immensely in the almost three decades between his two Hajj experiences. He expresses his regret that even Safa and Marwa, that are among the 'monuments' (or 'symbols') of God,[47] in the meantime have been more or less destroyed. Nonetheless, he adds that after the first Hajj he made a certain spiritual progress, and thus became more sensitive to certain things, and especially to the *Baraka* (blessing, spiritual presence). The Qur'an often mentions this term, whose source is always and only Allah. God's blessing pervades many things, humans and places. It pervades Mecca, as stated in the Qur'an (3,96). Being more spiritually sensitive during the 1976 Hajj, in a certain sense Martin Lings appreciated more his second pilgrimage. Despite all the changes that had occurred in Mecca over the decades, what remains totally unchanged, he concludes, is the *Baraka*.

---

45 'According to a Sufi interpretation, the Ka'ba corresponds to the heart, as the seat of the Divine "Presence", and the encircling movement of the pilgrims around the Ka'ba recalls the movement of thoughts or meditations turning perpetually around the soul's ungraspable center'. Titus Burckhardt, *Art of Islam*, op. cit.

46 *Circling the House of God: Reflections on Hajj with Martin Lings* (documentary film, Matmedia productions, 2009).

47 'Behold! Safa and Marwa are among the symbols of Allah. So if those who visit the House in the season or at other times, should compass them round, it is no sin in them'. *The Holy Qur-an*; op. cit.; 2, 158.

Chapter 17
Conclusion: A Soft-law Approach to the Protection of Sacred Places?

Silvio Ferrari

The third part of this book was an illustration of how different the sacred places of the Mediterranean are. Although they are grounded on a theological conception of sacred space that is shared by Judaism, Christianity and Islam, sacred places include different physical entities (buildings, open spaces, towns, geographical areas and so on) that are subjected to legal regimes ranging from extraterritoriality to systems of international guarantees, from full subordination to State control and to a large degree of autonomy and self-determination.[1] A single legal instrument containing a uniform and analytical regulation of all the sacred places of the Mediterranean would be of little help to provide effective protection to such diverse realities. A more sophisticated and diversified approach is required, based on a number of distinctions that take advantage of all the multiple functions that law can perform. As stated in Peter Petkoff's chapter, developing a new category of protection of sacred places under international or national law is not the priority at this stage. Such an endeavour requires a previous reflection on 'the ways in which different, and sometimes overlapping, legal tools are applied in the protection of different, and sometimes overlapping, objects, which could be broadly described as sacred places'. This book aims to offer this type of food for thought, following a bottom-up methodology clearly illustrated by the pages devoted to the study of the single sacred places of the Mediterranean. They show that whatever the discussion of a protection framework for the sacred places may be, it has to be based on an analytical examination of their legal discipline: in this way the elements of commonalities that support the framework emerge from the investigation of the diversities that characterize each sacred place.

The contributions collected in this book suggest that such a goal is best attained by striking the correct balance among the tensions that exist between general/specific and hard/soft legal provisions.

First of all it is helpful to identify two different levels of legal intervention. This distinction reflects the two dimensions which are a recurrent theme when dealing with the sacred places of the Mediterranean: on the one hand there are

1 For these differences see the chapter by Umberto Leanza in this book.

the commonalities which characterize them and suggest the need to identify some shared principles that set the stage for further activity; on the other, there is the specificity of each sacred place which makes it impossible to adopt the same uniform legal discipline for them all. At the first level, a few guidelines which serve as a general framework of protection and promotion can be identified, at the second these common principles must be translated into more detailed provisions that apply to single sacred places. While this last task is primarily the responsibility of local actors, the building of the general framework can involve subjects that have a broader scope of action, like international organizations, NGOs and obviously religious communities. The Declaration that is published at the end of this book is an example of the form that such a framework could take, but it needs to be complemented by provisions that fit the specific requirements of each sacred place.

Second, taking into consideration the suspicion with which States and religious communities look at a legal discipline of sacred places that could limit their power to rule over them, the first step towards a protecting system should take the form of soft law – that is, non-binding provisions that are accepted by all the involved parties. A few guidelines contained in a declaration that is open to the signature of States, international organizations, religious communities and other stakeholders is a good way to introduce a 'gentle' regulation of sacred places that is not perceived as threatening by the powers that have their control. Once these provisions are implemented and have proved their capacity to provide a sound legal status for the sacred places without encroaching upon the States' and religious organizations' prerogatives, a discussion about the opportunity to move towards more binding rules could be started without raising the suspicions and encountering the obstacles that it would face today.

The combination of general and specific provisions and of soft and hard law outlines a multi-layered system, where different rules taken from different legal fields and covering different profiles of sacred places may interconnect in the area of their legal protection. The nature itself of sacred places – that is, places where religion, culture and history meet – suggests the need for multiple legal tools that 'approach sacred places through their multiple identities and serve as a model for legal reasoning which would see these identities in conjunction and not in isolation'.[2] In this context provisions safeguarding freedom of religion and belief, conventions protecting cultural heritage and laws regarding minority and property rights could converge in a protection system of the sacred places.[3] A soft-law text like the one mentioned above is the place where such convergence takes shape. It does not want to be a legal tool for a detailed regulation of sacred places. Rather, it is the place where their different facets that require to be legally regulated are identified and the legal principles guiding their discipline are outlined.

2 Peter Petkoff, in this book.

3 See on this point the intervention of Cesare Mirabelli in Andrea Benzo (ed.), *Proceedings of the Seminar 'Protecting the Sacred places of the Mediterranean'* (Brussels, 6 March 2012, Sovereign Order of Malta 2012) 30.

Five guiding principles for the protection of the sacred places of the Mediterranean are singled out in the text of the Declaration. They are:

1. *the religious nature of sacred places and their link with religious freedom.* As explained in the introduction to this book, sacred places are primarily to be regarded as living heritage that answers the religious needs of people. The right to establish, maintain and use a sacred place is an integral part of the fundamental human right of religious freedom and should be protected as such, as well as for the fact that it is a part of the world cultural heritage (when this is the case).[4]
2. *the significance of the sacred places for the development of a plural society.* This principle stresses the need to promote the awareness that sacred places play an irreplaceable role in safeguarding the diversity of religious and cultural traditions, without which no fruitful dialogue is possible between the different civilizations coexisting in the Mediterranean area. For this reason the protection and promotion of the sacred places is not a concern of the religious communities only. It is of central importance for the development of a vital civil society and, as such, it requires the attention and participation of all the individuals and organizations that are interested in building the Mediterranean as a space of exchange and dialogue, independently from their religious or non-religious affiliation.
3. *the protection of sacred places*, understood both as preservation of their physical integrity and as respect for their sacred and cultural significance. Frequently, sacred places are places of outstanding religious and cultural importance at the same time: this concomitance gives rise to the problem of finding a balance between interests that may be in competition – the physical preservation of buildings, sites and objects on the one hand and their continuing use as indispensable components of the religious practice of a community on the other. The dialogue between the representatives of the organizations that are in charge of these interests and the involvement of the religious communities in the conservation work aimed at preserving the religious and cultural heritage is the most promising path to follow.[5]
4. *the relationship between sacred places and communities of the faithful*, which is manifested by the latter's interest in living in the vicinity of their sacred places and in managing them without outside interference. The presence of a religious community is essential to maintain the character of *living* heritage of a sacred place. Its permanence frequently depends

4 See Declaration, Article 1, annexed to this book.

5 The need for this dialogue has been stressed by Mounir Bouchenaki in his intervention in Andrea Benzo (ed.), *Proceedings*, op. cit. 73–4. A number of good practices are described in Herb Stovel, Nicholas Stanley-Price and Robert Killic (eds), *Conservation of Living Religious Heritage. Papers from the ICCROM 2003 Forum on Living Religious Heritage: conserving the sacred* (ICCROM 2005).

on social and economic processes on which law has little impact. Within these limits, facilitating the continuing life of the religious community that formed around a sacred place should be understood as part of the protection framework as the religious community itself is part of the heritage that has to be protected.[6]

5. *access to sacred places*, recognized to all without distinction of nationality or religion but subject to compliance with the rules – established by the religious authority in charge of the sacred place – that are necessary for the preservation of the nature and purpose of a sacred place and of the activities taking place in it.[7] The right to exclude entire categories of people – women, members of a different religion, people who do not profess any religion – from access to some sacred places is one of the most delicate topics currently debated. While limitations based on the respect of rules aimed at safeguarding the dignity and sacred character of the place or the performing of religious rites (which may be reserved to the members of the religious community) are acceptable, a general exclusion that is not functional to these goals may raise some questions, in particular because it prevents people from having access to places that have not only a religious but also a cultural significance.

These five principles are developed in the 'Declaration on the Protection of the Sacred Places in the Mediterranean Area' that follows these conclusions. The declaration aims to be a tool available to all stakeholders who, by adhering to it, manifest their willingness to respect its principles in the government and management of sacred places. It merely contains some fundamental principles, without going into the details of the protection of sacred places nor indicating the legal forms through which it can be guaranteed (international or national instruments, agreements, codes of good practice and so on): this task is left to the parties that are involved in the management and conservation of particular sacred places, as they are best placed to assess the protection system that is most appropriate for the identity, history and characteristics of each of them. Moreover, the declaration wants to complement (and not to replace) the existing provisions that protect sacred places as a common heritage of the whole of humankind.[8] In

6 See on this point Jørgen Bøytler, 'Christiansfeld: a religious heritage alive and well', in Herb Stovel, Nicholas Stanley-Price, Robert Killick (eds), *Conservation of Living Religious Heritage*, op. cit., in particular 25–9. The author writes that 'the religious body' (that is the Christian congregation) that created the settlement 'is part of the heritage', so that its disappearance affects the heritage itself: 'once the religious dimension, on which certain religious cultural heritage is founded, is overruled or even overrun by new economic, political and cultural interests, the next generation will inherit something different; what was there is gone forever' (25–6). See also Declaration, Articles 4.3 and 6.5.

7 See Declaration, Article 3.

8 See Declaration, Article 8.

doing so, it underlines the religious significance of sacred places, a profile that has not yet been fully developed in the legal instruments aimed at their protection.

In her opening address at a conference on sacred places, the EU Commissioner Androulla Vassiliou said that there is 'a sacred geography of the Mediterranean' that makes it possible to draw 'a map that would show the region as a network of regional and international places of pilgrimage, of monumental temples, synagogues, churches and mosques'. This map, she concluded, 'is part of our common history' but 'sadly, it coincides with the map of scars and conflicts'.[9] It is difficult to disagree with her remark: historically, sacred places have been places of conflict as well as of peace. However, this outcome is not the unavoidable fate of sacred places; rather, it is the result of human actions. Recalling Maimonides, Kellner writes that 'holiness [...] is a challenge, not a given; normative, not descriptive [...]. This sort of holiness does not reflect objective reality; it helps constitute social reality'.[10] Building a sound system of protection and promotion of sacred places goes towards constituting a social reality where the elements of peace prevail over the elements of conflict. If this book can be a little step in this direction, this will be the best reward for the work its authors put into it.

9 Androulla Vassiliou, 'Opening Remarks', in Andrea Benzo (ed.), *Proceedings*, op. cit. 8.

10 Menachem Kellner, *Maimonides' Confrontation with Mysticism* (The Littman Library of Jewish Civilization, 2006).

Appendix
Declaration on the Protection and Enhancement of Sacred Places in the Mediterranean Area

Explanatory Note

The present Declaration constitutes the main outcome of a research project commissioned in 2008 by the Sovereign Order of Malta aimed at contributing to the establishment of some core principles on access to and the legal protection and enhancement of sacred sites of universal significance.

A group of well-known academics chaired by Professor Silvio Ferrari of the University of Milan was appointed to study the situation of several prominent sacred sites in the Mediterranean area. Their studies, which now feature in this book, have provided a clearer assessment of the differences in typology, size, history and current legal discipline that exist among these places. The variety these studies have shed light on has provided a wide spectrum of patterns and experiences, thus enabling the authors to identify those features that are common to all sacred places: these have therefore been put at the core of this new and comprehensive legal framework.

Within the general framework set by the following Declaration, each sacred place may then be the subject of a more specific legal discipline allowing it to fulfill its own religious, cultural and civilizational role stemming from history and tradition.

Declaration on the Protection and Enhancement of Sacred Places in the Mediterranean area

The Signatories,

Reaffirming the fundamental right to religious freedom as enshrined notably in Article 18 of the Universal Declaration of Human Rights, in Article 18 of the International Covenant on Civil and Political Rights, and in other international instruments,

Stressing that the right to religious freedom includes, inter alia, both the availability of a place of worship, as affirmed in Article 6(a) of the Declaration on the Elimination of All Forms of Intolerance and of Discrimination Based on

Religion or Belief, and the enjoyment of the places that are sacred to each religious community;

Recognizing that sacred places are part of the religious experience and the cultural heritage of humankind and are a fundamental component of the memory and identity of individuals and communities;

Keeping in mind the central role that sacred places have played in religion, culture and international relations throughout history, and appreciating their value for promoting dialogue, mutual respect, peace and reconciliation;

Aware that sacred places have too frequently become an issue of conflict and sometimes the target of destruction and desecration;

Believing that a clear comprehension of the universal dimension of sacred places and of the specific characteristics of each of them is a pre-condition for safeguarding their religious significance, fostering respect for them and avoiding any improper exploitation thereof;

Convinced that every sacred place and its immediate surroundings should be regarded as a balanced whole where physical space and human presence and activities are inextricably linked;

Acknowledging the need for a comprehensive and shared set of guidelines on the protection of the sacred places of the Mediterranean area, their preservation and appropriate use, that provide a framework where, if necessary, specific rules governing each of them could be inserted, and concerned that prompt and effective measures should be taken in this field in the interest of the whole humankind,

Have agreed as follows:

Article 1. Freedom of religion and sacred places.

1. Freedom of religion and belief includes the right of the faithful of a religious community to establish, maintain, administer and use the places sacred to them.
2. The signatories recognize that they have a common interest in providing the sacred places with legal protections that safeguard their outstanding cultural, historical, spiritual and religious value and their distinctive character both for the communities to which they are associated and for humankind.

Article 2. Definition of sacred place.

1. For the purposes of the present Declaration, a sacred place is a place actually reserved to purposes and activities of religion that for foundational, historical, ideal or other reasons has a unique and irreplaceable significance to the faithful of particular religious communities, whether universally or in the region where the place is located. For the avoidance of any doubt, the notion of sacred place does not apply only to buildings but can include

other definite areas, for example cemeteries or shrines, that meet the requirements indicated above.

Article 3. Access to sacred places.

1. Public authorities shall guarantee the right to have free and unhindered access to any sacred place. The exercise of this right can be limited only in the presence of compelling reasons of public order and security.
2. The access to a sacred place is subject to the restrictions established by the respective religious authorities and to the regulations aimed at granting respect for the religious nature of the place and of the activities taking place in it.
3. States will facilitate the permanent presence in their territory of religious personnel serving the sacred places and entry into the country of visitors and pilgrims to the sacred places coming from abroad.

Article 4. Religious communities.

1. The signatories shall respect the distinctive relationship of the followers of a religious community with their own sacred places and shall safeguard the religious and cultural role of the latter in the life of the communities concerned.
2. Religious communities shall enjoy full freedom in the administration of their own sacred places. Public authorities shall cooperate with the respective religious communities with reference to the maintenance of safety, security and public order at sacred places.
3. States shall do whatever possible to ensure that the followers of a religious community, in particular when they constitute a minority, can continue to live in the neighbourhood of and in vital contact with their sacred places as a means of preserving and fostering both the community identity and the full significance of the sacred place. Such measures should be undertaken with the greatest possible participation of the communities and groups of people concerned.

Article 5. Preservation of sacred places.

1. The integrity of sacred places shall be safeguarded. They shall not be destroyed, damaged or disfigured for any reason or purpose.
2. Religious communities shall not be deprived of their sacred places through expropriation, nationalization, confiscation or other similar measures.
3. In the case of transfer of the ownership of a sacred place from one owner to another, its nature, destination and use will be safeguarded.

4. In compliance with public regulations, religious authorities shall be free to undertake works aimed at the maintenance and preservation of the sacred places and at the enhancement of their use.

Article 6. Protection of sacred places

1. Public authorities shall protect sacred places from any act or conduct that desecrates or in any way harms or impairs their religious character and functioning or that can reasonably be perceived as deliberately offensive to the religious sensibilities of the faithful.
2. Public authorities shall not subject any sacred place to adverse discrimination in matters of taxation or in the application of any laws.
3. The designation of a given sacred place as a humankind heritage site or as a national, historic, cultural site, however defined, shall be without prejudice to its character and functioning as a sacred place.
4. Public authorities shall ensure that the area surrounding a sacred site is made and kept proper and is appropriately safe and decorous.
5. When necessary for the preservation and functioning of a sacred place, the area surrounding it may need to be safeguarded by special measures aimed at (a) avoiding any development or activity that could damage the historical, cultural, architectural or archeological context in which the sacred place is located and (b) fostering the harmonious and sustainable development of the communities inhabiting that area.

Article 7. Education

The Signatories shall take effective measures, in consultation and cooperation with the religious communities concerned, to reinforce mutual respect for the sacred places and for the individuals and communities who manifest their faith there.

Article 8. Final article

1. The articles of this declaration add to and do not detract from any rights or protections recognized or accorded by any instrument or custom or under any law.
2. The articles of this declaration shall not be so construed as to exclude conferring or according a more favourable treatment in relation to all or some sacred places.
3. The application of the articles of this declaration to any sacred place can only take place at the request or with the free consent of the competent authority of the religion concerned.

Index

For Product Safety Concerns and Information please contact our EU representative GPSR@taylorandfrancis.com
Taylor & Francis Verlag GmbH, Kaufingerstraße 24, 80331 München, Germany

www.ingramcontent.com/pod-product-compliance
Ingram Content Group UK Ltd.
Pitfield, Milton Keynes, MK11 3LW, UK
UKHW020021200926
475702UK00014B/1995
* 9 7 8 0 3 6 7 6 0 0 5 5 6 *